AGAINST THE DEPORTATION TERROR

In the series *Insubordinate Spaces*,

EDITED BY GEORGE LIPSITZ

RACHEL IDA BUFF

AGAINST THE DEPORTATION TERROR

Organizing for Immigrant Rights
in the Twentieth Century

TEMPLE UNIVERSITY PRESS
Philadelphia • Rome • Tokyo

TEMPLE UNIVERSITY PRESS
Philadelphia, Pennsylvania 19122
www.temple.edu/tempress

Library of Congress Cataloging-in-Publication Data

Names: Buff, Rachel, 1961– author.
Title: Against the deportation terror : organizing for immigrant rights in
   the twentieth century / Rachel Ida Buff.
Description: Philadelphia : Temple University Press, 2017. | Series:
   Insubordinate spaces | Includes bibliographical references and index.
Identifiers: LCCN 2017012956 (print) | LCCN 2017022024 (ebook) |
   ISBN 9781439915356 (e-book) | ISBN 9781439915332 (hardback : alk. paper) |
   ISBN 9781439915349 (paper : alk. paper)
Subjects: LCSH: Immigrants—Civil Rights—United States—History—20th
   century. | Immigrants—Government policy—United States—History—20th
   century. | Deportation—United States—History—20th century. | BISAC:
   HISTORY / United States / 20th Century. | SOCIAL SCIENCE / Emigration
   & Immigration.
Classification: LCC JV6455 (ebook) | LCC JV6455 .B84 2017 (print) | DDC
   325.73—dc23
LC record available at https://lccn.loc.gov/2017012956

♾The paper used in this publication meets the requirements of the American
National Standard for Information Sciences—Permanence of Paper for Printed
Library Materials, ANSI Z39.48-1992

Printed in the United States of America

9 8 7 6 5 4 3 2

For Joe, Ruby Lou, and Ellie Rae

CONTENTS

AGAINST THE DEPORTATION TERROR

INTRODUCTION

The Subaltern Past of
Immigrant Rights

Thus the writing of history must implicitly assume a
plurality of times existing together, a disjuncture of the
present with itself. Making visible this disjuncture
is what subaltern pasts allow us to do.
—DIPESH CHAKRABARTY, *Provincializing Europe*

You have made me indestructible because with you
I do not end in myself.
—PABLO NERUDA, "To My Party"

Struggles for immigrant rights have a long history in the United States. Most people, including those deeply involved in contemporary immigrant rights organizing, are unaware of the existence of this subaltern past. It has been obscured by a more familiar "Nation of Immigrants" narrative, in which immigrants arrive and face minor obstacles before assimilating to become part of a nation that is, in turn, enriched by the diversity conveyed by their presence. Yet the other past of immigrant rights—in which migrants contend with protracted animosity to their presence by collectively creating alternative political and cultural formations—has been there all along.[1]

By tracing the subaltern past of immigrant rights organizing during the twentieth century, this book aims to render this elusive history visible. It does so in large part by pursuing the history of the American Committee for the Protection of the Foreign Born (ACPFB), a multiracial organization with a broad national network among foreign-born communities. Emanating from the liberal-left coalitions of the Popular Front era, the ACPFB started operations in New York City in 1932; the organization's central office closed its doors there in 1982, which was a moment of ascendance for other immigrant rights organizations.

The multiracial, networked nature of the ACPFB makes its archives rich in the subaltern pasts of twentieth-century immigrant rights organizing. Founded in response to crises of what the organization referred to as "the deportation terror," the ACPFB was shaped by broad, transnational mobilizations around labor and civil rights throughout the twentieth century. The mobilizations of the 1930s drew on different aspects of the left, including, as Benjamin Balthaser describes, Communists as well as "liberal antifascists, socialists and black nationalists, often linking questions of racial oppression in the United States to colonialism abroad." Immigrant rights formations in this era connected the transnational experiences of migrants to the internationalist, antiracist analysis and political channels of the Communist Party and the Popular Front.[2]

The ACPFB advocated for the foreign born against the increasing repression of immigration enforcement over the course of the twentieth century. The central office in New York organized supporters and engaged in media and political advocacy. The office also functioned as a hub connecting networks of foreign-born communities throughout the nation: northern Minnesota, southern Texas, and the Lackawanna Valley in Pennsylvania, to name only a few. Sometimes these connections resulted in the lasting formation of a local Committee for the Protection of the Foreign Born. As often, they did not. The history of the ACPFB, therefore, embeds myriad subaltern pasts. Some of them are traceable through the archives left in the correspondence of short-lived organizations, such as the Klamath Valley Committee for the Protection of the Foreign Born. Many others left little in the way of a paper trail. But the short-term connections between the central office and migrant crises reflected flashpoints in ongoing struggles. The history of this one organization, then, contains the traces of a much broader story.[3]

Struggles for immigrant rights exist in a dialectical relationship with technologies of immigration enforcement that imbue the status of being "foreign born" with distinct juridical meaning. Evidenced by the migration of the immigration service from its inception as part of the Treasury Department in 1891 to the Department of Labor (1903), the Department of Justice (1940), and, most recently, the Department of Homeland Security (2011), immigration enforcement became a central aspect of domestic as well as international governance over the course of the twentieth and twenty-first centuries. Migrants contested the enhanced regulation of their daily lives. Immigration enforcement affected their access to work, housing, relief, and education, and, as deportation became a key technology of the immigration service, their right to remain in the country. Being foreign born meant being vulnerable to deportation and constant subjection to inspection, surveillance, and policing by the federal immigration forces. Very often, these forces collaborated with local law enforcement to repress labor and civil rights organizing among the foreign born and their allies.[4]

The access of the foreign born to assimilation was regulated by laws regarding race and national origin. Many migrants were legally or culturally prohibited from becoming citizens by exclusionary immigration laws and labor policies, and by a racial common sense that equated eligibility for citizenship with whiteness. And, because ideological loyalties could impede their progress toward Americanization, migrants were particularly vulnerable to deportation or denaturalization on grounds of their politics, actual or suspected. Migrants racialized by the infrastructure of U.S. immigration laws and those with radical political beliefs and/or associations felt the brunt of immigration enforcement. As a result, these migrants often became engaged in immigrant rights organizing.

Resisting immigration enforcement, migrants forged alternative identities. They summoned transnational histories and drew on alliances formed after their arrival, creating "migrant imaginaries" that, in the words of Alicia Schmidt Camacho, "define[d] justice in terms that surpass[ed] the sovereignty of nations or the logic of capital accumulation, just as their struggles revive[d] the repudiated body of the migrant as the agent for ethical survival." These migrant imaginaries deployed identities created by immigration enforcement: immigrant, foreign born, racialized, and/or un-American other. Through the networks that connected them to the ACPFB, migrants drew on the language of the transnational left to describe their experiences of repression as part of a larger system of global racial capitalism. Political theorist Chantal Mouffe describes the political necessity of creating a "chain of equivalence" that allows for a "convergence . . . that recognizes the specificities of different struggles but also fiercely recogniz[es] the commonalities and solidarities among the various struggles." Over the course of its fifty years of existence, the ACPFB provided such a space of convergence for a broad array of migrants facing deportation and repression.[5]

As a juridical category, the identity of being "foreign born" took on increased meaning over the course of the twentieth century, locating migrants in an alien category, distinct from the native born. The term circulated in legal as well as in mass-media discourse, conjuring a sense of alienness. Being "foreign born" placed migrants into a queer relationship with the state, which, by the logic of the "Nation of Immigrants" paradigm, functioned as police and parent. In this paradigm, immigration enforcement regulated the process of harmonious assimilation into national life, which was to culminate in naturalization into citizenship and full membership in the nation. The Americanization process had an implicit developmental teleology, in which assimilation represented individual and collective uplift. The naturalization of immigrants also functioned to affirm the legitimacy of claims to land confiscated by prior generations of Euro-American migrants from indigenous people, who themselves were able to naturalize broadly only as a result of the Indian Citizenship Act of 1924.

Their collective queer natality located migrants outside the linear time frame, or temporality, of assimilation and eventual naturalization into a narrowly defined national identity, conveying, as Mark Rivkin explains in another context, "a sense of being out-of-sync with Euroamerican narratives of development."[6] The "Nation of Immigrants" narrative, with its assumptions of common progress toward an American identity modeled on the experience of European immigrants, failed to describe the experiences of many twentieth-century migrants, including contract laborers, transnational activists, and itinerant workers.

Many of these foreign-born Americans inhabited what Jack Halberstam calls "nonnormative logics and organization of community, sexual identity, embodiment and activity in space and time." Eric Tang describes the alternative sense of time prevalent among contemporary Cambodian refugees as a "refugee temporality" linking their struggles in Cambodia with those of refugee transit and their new homes in the United States. This alternative temporality resists the "Nation of Immigrants" narrative, in this case, what Tang calls a "refugee exceptionalism" equating their resettlement with salvation. "Out-of-sync" formations like refugee temporality have long been a wellspring for migrant imagination and organizing. Often in concert with native-born allies, migrants participated in creating rich American identities defined outside a developmentalist trajectory, innovating new interpretations of citizenship and rights.[7]

Literary scholar Elizabeth Freeman points to conflicts over "not only the shrapnel of failed revolutions but also one or more moments when an established temporal order gets interrupted and new encounters consequently take place." The disruption of established temporal orders, Freeman explains, can lead to new relationships. Many migrants inhabited temporalities that looked to other horizons besides assimilation and citizenship: they did not recognize the necessity of their slow transformation into Americans. Instead, they claimed membership in a nation of workers linked by "transnationalism from below." Their Americanism was constituted through internationalism. As Guatemalan American labor organizer Luisa Moreno proclaimed in 1949, prior to her eventual deportation: "This Latin American alien came here to assist you in building and extending American democracy." Moreno parodied the logic of assimilation by asserting that her encounter as an "alien" with the nation enabled her contribution to American democracy.[8]

While their experience took place in nonnormative temporalities, the foreign born also inhabited alternative spatial imaginaries that inspired their resistance to immigration enforcement. Transnational migrants carried with them cognitive maps of the world that differed radically from those dictated by national diplomatic and security priorities, often recognizing parallels between immigration enforcement and military policies abroad. These alternate spatial imaginaries drew them into international- ist alliances with migrants from other national origins. For example, the multiracial Los Angeles Committee for the Protection of the Foreign Born (LACPFB) came into being in 1950, when foreign-born Euro-Americans, diasporic Koreans, and Mexican Americans recognized the parallels be- tween the repressive, U.S.-backed regime in South Korea, McCarthyist attacks on foreign-born organizers, and the immigration dragnets of Op- eration Wetback. The historical memories and alternate geographies of these foreign-born communities shaped the LACPFB.

The subaltern past of immigrant rights coexists with the liberal multi- culturalism of the "Nation of Immigrants" narrative, in which even po- litical struggles for rights lead gradually to broad acceptance. The "Nation of Immigrants" story is progressive and uplifting, claiming that the forces of tolerance and inclusion prevail over racism and nativism, to the broad benefit of the nation. In contrast, the subaltern past of immigrant rights is not a triumphant narrative. Immigrant rights advocates created multira- cial alliances that advanced the causes of equal access to citizenship and rights; they publicized their positions, at times gaining traction in the mass media as well as in national political and human rights advocacy dis- courses. But although advocates succeeded in defending some individuals against deportation, the ACPFB was unable to prevent federal immigra- tion enforcement from waging repeated campaigns of deportation terror, which wrought havoc on well-ensconced migrant communities. These campaigns have continued into the twenty-first century. Barack Hussein Obama, whose American birth was frequently contested by his political enemies, left office after having presided over record-high deportation numbers. His successor, Donald Trump, brandishes the deportation terror against supposed "criminal aliens" in the name of "national security and public safety," making such public spaces as schools and courthouses in- creasingly dangerous for the approximately twelve million undocumented immigrants currently residing in the United States.[9]

What is the legacy of this subaltern past? As Robin D. G. Kelley argues in his analysis of contemporary Black university student organizing, "win- ning is not always the point." Resistance is a long, creative, collaborative process of struggling to understand and build institutions counter to the powers that be. Nadia Ellis draws on Jose Esteban Muñoz to describe fail- ure as a "territory of the soul," noting that failure always contains a "uto- pian reach." What appears to be failure in the short term, then, seeds al- ternate futures.[10]

The achievements of the subaltern past can be difficult to discern. Because the history of immigrant rights is dialectically entwined with that of immigration enforcement, limited successes often resulted in enhanced repression. For example, ACPFB general counsel Carol Weiss King's successful defense of Australian-born labor organizer Harry Bridges against accusations of Bridges's "past membership" in the Communist Party in 1940 was followed almost immediately by new federal legislation authorizing deportation on grounds of prior activities. Lightning-fast responses like these function to obscure accomplishments taking place in the subaltern past.[11]

Over the course of the twentieth century, immigrant rights advocates mustered substantial resistance to escalating surveillance, enforcement, and deportation, creating alliances and coalitions among foreign- and native-born communities. They forged connections that often spilled over into other struggles, defining their own terms of belonging. They aspired to alternative horizons for democracy and justice throughout the twentieth century and beyond; they created networks that persisted despite repression, generating other spaces and times for resistance. Ellis describes the alternative horizon of queer Black diasporic temporality: "This, to recapitulate, is a future-oriented belonging, a feeling for place that relies on the belief in a surely finer place to come."[12]

The history of immigrant rights is entwined with the emergence of what some scholars have called "neoliberalism." As a distinct phase of global racial capitalism, neoliberalism is characterized by "free trade," or increasing economic collaboration across national borders; by the deregulation of industrial, agricultural, and resource extraction; and by declining investments in the social wage through the defunding of public institutions. Economic deregulation means fewer workplace protections and lower wages for workers, while lowered investment in public infrastructure leads to increased economic inequality and declining civil rights protections. Neoliberal doctrine prescribes austerity for workers and for the public sector as a means to prosperity for transnational corporations and their executives; it undermines labor rights in the name of "free trade."[13]

The contradictions of neoliberalism have particularly severe implications for the foreign born. Many migrants leave homelands wracked by the effects of enforced austerity and free trade, finding work on their arrival in the industries with the lowest wages and the fewest workplace protections. An enhanced security regime distances Latinx and Asian migrants, in particular, from the protections of citizenship. It posits them, instead, as potential lawbreakers and/or terrorists. At the same time, neoliberal political discourse emphasizes "personal responsibility" to explain social inequalities. Chandan Reddy explains that "the state has effectively managed to increase the numbers of immigrants, as the economy continues to demand low-wage noncitizen labor, and at the same time use immigration as a vehicle to dismantle its welfare responsibilities." While Reddy describes contemporary, twenty-first-century formations, the demand for low-wage, low-rights labor has been consistent over the course of U.S. history.[14]

Sociologist Loïc Wacquant argues that the emergence of neoliberalism is paralleled by the formation of what he calls the "centaur state": human at the top, with strong, equine legs for trampling the working classes beneath. Enforcing austerity within the nation and maintaining the infrared technology that secures its borders require constant monitoring by an expensively militarized state force; the poor are forced into what Wacquant describes as racialized "hyperghettos." Tang describes the ways Cambodian refugees navigate the hyperghettos into which they are resettled by drawing on their experiences surviving the genocidal regime in Cambodia. Of necessity, racialized migrant communities resist the austerity and enhanced policing of neoliberalism.[15]

The ACPFB and its allies paid careful attention to the developing brutality of this "centaur state." Having fled the depredations of capital accumulation in their home countries, only to find themselves struggling for basic labor and social protections, many migrants were familiar with the ongoing processes of "accumulation by dispossession," as David Harvey describes it. Their migration linked regions undergoing different phases of capitalist economic development; therefore, their analysis of immigrant rights connected struggles against imperialist expropriation in their home nations to the ways in which hierarchies of race and class limited protections in the United States. ACPFB advocates criticized immigration policy as an arm of global racial capitalism. The organization is an important junction of the internationalist analysis of the mid-twentieth century and the transnational critique of neoliberalism in the twenty-first.[16]

Most accounts of neoliberalism place it as emerging in the 1970s. But careful attention to the subaltern past of immigrant rights indicates that many of the characteristics of neoliberal developments, including transnational industrial collaboration, the forced "flexibility" of labor, and the diminution of workplace protections, began much earlier. Agriculture and shipping, in particular, depended on international capitalist political and economic collaboration. These industries employed a transnational labor force whose flexibility derived partially from their racialized deportability. As workers in these industries organized during the 1930s and 1940s, they contended with resistance from agricultural and shipping interests allied strongly with local police departments and federal immigration enforcement. This alliance worked to keep migrant laborers deportable and at the same time to increase the transnational flexibility of these industries.

The ACPFB advocated for the rights of Filipinx and Latinx agricultural workers and Greek and Indonesian sailors, defending them in the inevitable deportation cases that ensued from their union activity. Precisely because they were "out of sync" with dominant formations of space and time, migrants were able to resist the depredations of transnational capital and immigration enforcement. Through the networks of the ACPFB, the internationalist, anti-imperialist analysis of the Popular Front converged with transnational migrant imaginaries; activists recognized the roots of emergent neoliberalism in ongoing practices of global racial capitalism. Sociologist Jordan Camp points out that the ensuing struggles "sustained and naturalized unprecedented prison expansion during the emergence of neoliberal capitalism"; to this important formation, I would add the acceleration of migrant detention and deportation in the same period.[17]

Drawing on the work of French theorists Gilles Deleuze and Félix Guattari, Peter Funke describes the "rhizomatic logic" informing "contemporary movement-based counter-power." Like many theorists of neoliberalism, Funke assumes that the decentered nature of protests articulated by Zapatistas or the Coalition of Immokalee Workers are recent responses to the ascent of neoliberal capitalism, and that such "New Social Movements" differ in character from labor and civil rights movements. He argues that these movements bridge the class-based emphasis of the "Old Left" with the identitarian multiplicity of the "New Left." While the ACPFB differed in many ways from the groups that Funke describes, its reliance on a network of resistance, or what Mouffe calls a "chain of equivalence," anticipated these movements and created a precedent for them. Because the ACPFB survived to span the periods considered "Old" and "New" Lefts, the organization provides a link between them.[18]

A defining characteristic of subaltern pasts is that they are hidden. The history of immigrant rights organizing in the twentieth century has been occluded by the dominance of the "Nation of Immigrants" narrative, a liberal multiculturalism that sees the conflicts of the past as necessarily being resolved by the national progress. Dipesh Chakrabarty describes a "minority history" that grants the presence of subaltern groups like the foreign born while recruiting them into a broader story of national progress. Of necessity, this minority history eclipses the gorgeous imaginings and limited victories, the rough roadmap of the subaltern past. In the next section, I examine the consequences of this eclipse and what revisiting this subaltern past might mean.

A Gap in the Record

By tracing the work of the ACPFB and its allies over half a century, this book provides much in the way of historical precedent for contemporary immigrant rights organizing. The chapters that follow illuminate the history of a multifaceted, multiracial, ongoing, and geographically dispersed immigrant rights organization originating in the mid-twentieth century and lasting until the 1980s, at which time other organizations took precedence. Small but definitely continuous, the ACPFB brought immigrant rights advocates of different national origins together to fight against the increasingly widespread threat of deportation; it united them in opposing policies targeting progressive activists and communities of color. The ACPFB continually asserted an antiracist critique of federal immigration policy and advocated for the labor rights of noncitizen workers, who often had the least power.

Why has this story not been told before? As I discuss presently, pieces of the story of the ACPFB, most notably the Los Angeles chapter, have begun to be recounted through creative and diligent historical labor. Still, with the exception of these important works, the story of the ACPFB—nothing less than the story of a national, multiracial movement for immigrant rights over much of the course of the twentieth century—has largely remained untold.

There are a few reasons for this gap in the record. One is the lingering legacy of ethnic particularism in the writing of immigration history. Although new approaches move away from this trend, the tendency has been to tell the story of immigration based on the experiences of individual, usually European, nationality groups. Historians have explored the encounters of such groups with deportation and restrictive immigration policy. Some have even referred to the ACPFB in the context of its work in defense of particular individuals or groups. But by and large, the story of immigration has tended to unfold with one group's journey from Europe to America and its subsequent assimilation into a "Nation of Immigrants."

In response to this overemphasis on one-way migration from Europe to the United States, many scholars have labored to describe migration from Latin America, Asia, the Middle East, and Africa, arguing that many of the frameworks designed to explain immigration from Europe do not work as well for the experiences of migrants perceived as nonwhite in the United States. This important work has often focused on particular groups of migrants. But overall, this tendency to narrate immigration history one ethnoracial group at a time may have limited our ability to recognize trends and movements taking place among many different groups, across geography and time.

In recent years, many historical accounts have begun to consider migration as a social process and to analyze experiences across different ethnic and racial groups. Because it emphasizes experiences across migrant cohorts, this important scholarship gives us a basis for comparison. A key development has been scholarship that analyzes the ways in which migrant identities are created by immigration law and policy. Such scholarship recognizes the ways in which the experience of migration is structured by what historian Erika Lee calls "gatekeeping" policies. Much of this scholarship has tended to focus on the interactions of migrants with the state, at the border and after entry. As a result, this important scholarship has been somewhat less inclined to look at migrants as actors, particularly as actors in a unified social movement, such as the immigrant rights movement.[19]

Perhaps the very word "immigrant," used in a scholarly context, tends to stress the processes of migration and adjustment rather than the possibilities for immigrant political engagement. This language is the legacy of the pioneering scholarship of the Chicago School of Sociology of the early twentieth century. These scholars focused on what seemed at the time to be pressing questions about the possibilities of Americanizing then-"new" immigrants. Therefore, these scholars tended to prioritize who and what these migrants were becoming, paying less attention to who they were and where they were born. In contrast, the work of the American Committee for the Protection of [the] *Foreign Born* assumed that to be foreign born, regardless of national origin or ethnic identity, meant sharing common political problems. The term "foreign born" emphasized the accident of birth rather than legal status and suggested possibilities for political coalition with the "native born"; it also suggested a legible and legitimate subjectivity outside the citizenship imagined by the "Nation of Immigrants" narrative as a reward for assimilation. The popular media picked up and used the term "foreign born" when describing the travails of immigrants with deportation. "Foreign born" was a common term until it was eclipsed in the mid-1950s by much harsher, more racialized language describing those struggling with deportation as "illegal aliens." As I discuss in Chapter 6, the consequences of this change in language for popular understandings of immigrant rights have been immeasurable.

The experiences of different migrant cohorts with deportation and repression varied widely. Because of its internationalism and explicit commitment to antiracism, the ACPFB connected, for example, the struggles of Mexican Americans against the mass deportations of Operation Wetback to those of Greek sailors fighting certain imprisonment and possible death on being forced to return to their homeland. Because scholars have tended to think about migration according to racial-ethnic cohort and have generally perceived the identity of being an immigrant or "foreign born" to be a product of interaction with the state, immigration historians have missed the ongoing existence and significance of connections like this one, and of such organizations as the ACPFB, which advocated for the rights of the foreign born collectively.

The scholarly tendencies explored above partially explain the disappearance of the story of the ACPFB from historical accounts of twentieth-century immigration and social movements. But there is a larger reason for this absence. The ACPFB was an offshoot of the liberal American Civil Liberties Union (ACLU) and the International Labor Defense (ILD), which was closely allied with the Communist Party USA (CPUSA). The organization represented a coalition between Communist and non-Communist organizations. The ILD was founded by the Communist Workers Party of America in 1924 to handle legal defenses of labor and civil rights activists. It played a central role in celebrated cases, like those of Nicola Sacco and Bartolomeo Vanzetti and the Scottsboro defendants; it also coordinated legal work on behalf of strikers. During the long New Bedford textile strike of 1928, the ILD provided key relief and legal defense efforts. Young Portuguese migrant Eulália Mendes, who was later defended by the ACPFB against deportation, became involved in labor organizing during this strike.

As Michael Denning explains, Popular Front organizations brought workers, artists, and intellectuals together, shaping new, grassroots approaches to politics. Denning and Kelley, among many others, emphasize the ways in which grassroots organizations were able to make use of the Communist Party's organizing resources during the era of the Popular Front, which began in the 1930s and persisted into the early Cold War period. For these historians, the presence of Communists in progressive organizations was less important than what these groups were able to achieve in advancing social justice. The Popular Front framed local struggles, such as those of migrants against deportation, in a broad and international context. This internationalism was particularly valuable to the development of a multiracial, multiethnic immigrant rights movement.[20]

Particularly in context of the post–World War II Red Scare, the Communist background of the ACPFB and the leftist leanings of many of those involved with the organization made it a target for suspicion. Many of the foreign-born individuals it represented had been party members at one point in their lives; many of the lawyers and advocates involved faced accusations of Communist associations as well. According to historian Robert Justin Goldstein, U.S. attorneys general had long kept informal lists of subversive organizations. Official publication of these lists commenced in 1947 as the Attorney General's List of Subversive Organizations. The ACPFB was designated as a subversive organization in 1948. In 1952, the organization was compelled to register with the Subversive Activities Control Board (SACB); it was required to continue doing so until a 1965 Supreme Court case absolved it of being a subversive organization, because the evidence used against it was "stale." In its publications, the ACPFB linked enhanced surveillance of the organization with increasing attacks against the foreign born.[21]

In contrast to the Popular Front described above, the idea of a "Communist front" emerged from the language of the Red Scare. Such organizations were considered to be controlled not by domestic organizers and priorities but by the much-feared international network of the Union of Soviet Socialist Republics (Soviet Union [USSR]). The McCarran Internal Security Act of 1950, which also targeted many foreign-born residents for deportation, created the SACB to police the infiltration of the United States by anti-American, Communist agents. These agents were thought to work by founding dummy, "Communist front" organizations to dupe Americans into supporting causes that, in fact, syphoned funds and sympathies to Moscow.

At almost the same time of the SACB investigation, New York State attorney general Jacob Javits ordered leaders of the ACPFB to appear before the New York State Joint Legislative Committee on Charitable and Philanthropic Organizations, charging that it had violated the New York State social welfare law governing charitable organizations by using monies for "political" purposes. Javits sought "the liquidation of the American Committee for the Protection of the Foreign Born on the charge that it is operating in violation of the State Law relative to philanthropic and charitable organizations."[22]

Because it was accused of fraud in the solicitation of public funds, the organization could not accept dues or sponsorships after 1955; instead, it was reduced to petitioning its remaining supporters for "voluntary contributions." The organization speculated that Javits's accusation originated with his political mentor, federal attorney general Herbert Brownell. By 1958, the situation had been rectified by the ACPFB's registration under a different section of the New York State social welfare law. Goldstein points out that state laws were often used to discredit and destroy "Communist front organizations."[23]

Abner Green, who led the organization from 1940 until his death in 1959, quipped: "Somebody must be wrong—either Mr. Brownell [U.S. attorney general] in Washington or Mr. Javits in New York. We obviously cannot be doing both—taking money from the Communist Party and giving money to the Communist Party, since that would be a completely fruitless procedure."[24]

Despite Green's levity, charges of being a "Communist front" affected the organization's work, making certain key allies and funders leery of being associated with it and consuming valuable time and resources in defending itself against these charges rather than doing legal defense or policy advocacy work. Further, suspicion that the organization was Communist may well have led to the charges emanating from Attorney General Javits's office. Green himself spent six months in jail for refusing to submit a list of contributors to the New York chapter of the Civil Rights Congress (CRC), of which he was a board member.[25]

As historian Gerald Horne points out in his work on the CRC, an organization that was in some ways quite similar to the ACPFB and was closely allied with it, the notion of the "Communist front" itself—an organization set up to dupe the general public and many of its members into collusion with Moscow—was very likely a product of the active imagination and excellent spin machine of J. Edgar Hoover. Horne describes the character of charges of "subversion" against the CRC: that its members were just "using" the cause of African American civil rights to cover their real purpose, which was to cause dissent and chaos in American civil society, ultimately laying the groundwork for a Communist takeover of the country. Refuting these charges, Horne argues that the CRC was genuinely committed to the legal defense of primarily Black defendants in the politically and racially charged early Cold War period. While he confirms that there were active Communists involved, he also points out the effectiveness and dedication of the short-lived organization, questioning the motives of the Federal Bureau of Investigation's (FBI's) allegations against it. In other words, Horne comes down on the side of Denning's and Kelley's arguments about the Popular Front. He concludes that such organizations as the CRC included Communist members, some of whom were active in the party and some of whom were not, but that these organizations advanced goals directed and controlled by key local imperatives, such as the struggle for racial justice.[26]

Most important to explaining the absence of such organizations as the ACPFB and the CRC from the historical record, Horne points out that "Communist front" allegations outlived the organizations they targeted, tainting the mention of them by even progressive historians. The red-baiting of such organizations as the CRC and the ACPFB during the Cold War had powerful consequences for these organizations. Importantly, the idea of the "Communist front" has created a gap in the historical record. It is as though, once branded as potential "Communist fronts," these organizations disappeared entirely as legitimate historical actors. The historical record has been whitewashed to cover any trace of red, even if the red was skillfully tinted by false accusations and paranoia. Balthaser writes, "What has not been taken into account is the extent to which the Cold War has shaped our cultural memory of the Popular Front, beyond anti-communism to the erasure of a whole fabric of political and cultural anti-imperialism." The history of immigrant rights is among those that have been erased by anti-Communist whitewashing.[27]

Such whitewashing emanates from deep misunderstandings about the nature of Popular Front organizations, including the ACPFB. These organizations included and defended current and former members of the Communist Party. At the same time, they worked during the Cold War to defend a democratic vision of the United States that was the creation of a broad coalition that included many foreign-born activists. Many of these migrants linked repression in their home countries to the emerging depredations of the Cold War regime. Describing the deportation campaign against diasporic Korean intellectuals Diamond Kimm and David Hyun, Cindy I-Fen Cheng notes the ways in which the government's case twisted the advocacy of the two men on behalf of democracy for Korea, accusing them of "Communism" because of their criticism of the U.S.-backed regime of Syngman Rhee. The "Communist" slur was a Cold War shorthand for "un-American." This taint has had a lasting impact.[28]

The only recent, full-length study of the ACPFB is John W. Sherman's *A Communist Front at Mid-Century: The American Committee for Protection of Foreign Born, 1933–1959* (2001). As its title proclaims, this book falls into the pattern Horne describes, in which prior accusations of being a "Communist front" continue to determine the ways historians represent an organization. Throughout the book, Sherman works to discredit the other book-length account of the organization: *Torch of Liberty: Twenty-Five Years in the Life of the Foreign Born in the U.S.A.* (1959), which was written by active ACPFB member and Wellesley College professor Louise Pettibone Smith and is currently out of print. While most historians would treat a contemporary account like Smith's with the kind of critical perspective that accrues with the benefit of time, Sherman assumes that Smith's purpose in writing it was to provide cover for the covert agenda of the organization. Citing an unnamed government informant along with arch-conservative anti-Communist Archibald Roosevelt, Sherman asserts that Smith's claim that the ACPFB was founded by the ACLU in concert with the ILD is false and that the organization was merely a spin-off of the "Communist" defense organization.[29]

Because Smith was deeply involved with the work of the ACPFB, *Torch of Liberty* is an unapologetically partial account. In it, she advocates quite clearly for the significance of the ACPFB and the importance of its work in defense of the foreign born. But Sherman's account is also limited, burdened by its tremendous ideological impetus. Sherman hunts relentlessly for evidence to support his conviction that the organization was nothing more than a "front." To Sherman, their membership in the National Lawyers Guild is enough to indicate that ACPFB lawyers Carol Weiss King and Ira Gollobin were Communists. In the case of Abner Green, Sherman's evidence is composed of a single reference to Green in the *Daily Worker* in

1938, a tribute to the man in a 1979 "official history" of the CPUSA, and the assertion that, because Green was Jewish and from New York City, he "certainly matches up with [the party's] primary demographic composition." It is questionable scholarly practice to substitute assumptions about an ethnic group for historical research; moreover, even if Green had been a member of the Communist Party at one time in his life, this would prove little about his later work for immigrant rights. Further, this anti-Communist lens predisposes Sherman to dismiss the accomplishments of the ACPFB—such feats as winning stays of deportation and forging coalitions against coercive legislation at the height of the Cold War—as mere skullduggery.[30]

Against the Deportation Terror: Organizing for Immigrant Rights in the Twentieth Century places the ACPFB in its broader context. A key ambition of this book is to fill in the gap left in the record by recounting the subaltern past of immigrant rights organizing in the twentieth and twenty-first centuries. This book adds to other considerations of Cold War and migrant activism, such as Horne's study of the CRC, which provides a portrait of Cold War civil rights activism among African Americans and their allies, and recent studies of migrant anarchism by Jennifer Guglielmo and Kenyon Zimmer, which have revealed similar multiethnic, transnational subaltern pasts. Because the ACPFB has disappeared into the gap in the record that has consumed so many of the accomplishments of Communist-allied organizations in the twentieth century, its story reveals an almost completely obscured history of geographically diffuse, multiracial advocacy by and for the foreign born. The following section outlines how the history of the ACPFB contributes to our understanding of the history of social movements, immigration, and labor in the twentieth and twenty-first centuries.[31]

The Persistence of Subaltern Pasts

A program from the ACPFB's 1959 Memorial Tribute to Abner Green features messages and tributes from a long list of individuals and organizations, including W. E. B. Du Bois, David Hyun, Diamond Kimm, Paul Kochi, Edo Mita, and Japanese Friends in Los Angeles; the Coordinating Committee of Greater Miami, "representing all Progressive Jewish Organizations"; the Michigan Committee for the Protection of the Foreign Born; the Polish American Committee for the Protection of the Foreign Born–Detroit; the Council to Regain Citizenship of Gus Polites; the Midwest Committee for the Protection of the Foreign Born; the Philadelphia Committee to Defend the Foreign Born; the Russian American Women's Society; A Pioneer of the Red River Valley; Oscar A. Christensen; the Yugoslav Seamen's Club, New York; the Finnish American Harlem Committee; the Rumanian American Committee for the Protection of the Foreign Born; Grupo Mexicano del Comité para la Protección de los Nacidos en el Extranjero; the New Haven Neighbor Women's Group; Local #347 United Packing House Workers Association, AFL-CIO, Chicago; the Los Angeles Harbor Committee for the Protection of the Foreign Born; the East Side Committee for the Protection of the Foreign Born, Los Angeles; the Needle Trades Committee for the Protection of the Foreign Born, Los Angeles; the Washington State Committee for the Protection of the Foreign Born; the Committee for Protection of Oregon's Foreign Born; the Committee for Defense of Morning Freiheit Writers; Greek Friends in New York; and A Group of Bronx Women.[32]

I recount this broad array deliberately, because it imparts a sense of the vitality and expanse of the ACPFB. Many of the organizations advertising in this program were small and ephemeral, organized around a single defense case or a particular crisis precipitated by changing immigration policy or local enforcement. Many of these tiny organizations have left little trace in the historic record. Their presence at the memorial gathering for Green represents such a trace and allows us to imagine what stake, for example, "A Group of Bronx Women" and a Danish Minnesotan living in the Red River Valley might have shared in efforts on behalf of the foreign born. What mobilized the women of New Haven? How did "progressive Jewish" organizations in Miami view immigration issues? Like fossils, such records bear imprints of entities that are otherwise tough to trace and, therefore, to imagine. If we begin to imagine them, how does our understanding of the past change?

By 1959, according to most historians, "not yet white ethnics"—foreign-born Americans and their children—had figured out that dissent in general, and solidarity with communities of color in particular, could impede their process of assimilation and upward mobility. This behavior is what historians have explained as the trajectory of these immigrant communities in "becoming white": assimilating and gaining access to work and residential opportunities reserved for white Americans. Perplexingly, then, the Memorial Tribute list includes members of foreign-born communities on their way to being considered white along with African Americans, Latinx, and Asian Americans excluded from the benefits of whiteness. Some Finnish, Jewish, Rumanian, Greek, and other "not yet white ethnics" clearly saw fit to continue to work for better treatment of the foreign born alongside migrant cohorts considered nonwhite. Some of these groups persisted in their support for immigrant rights well into the 1970s, working in coalitions with newly arrived migrants from the Caribbean and Latin America. The power of race and the allure of white privilege for those who had access to it often limited such alliances, but the presence of these European-origin migrants in immigrant rights organizations indicates the ongoing existence of multiracial coalitions advocating for fair immigration policies. These alliances mark lingering points of solidarity among communities separated by racial divides.[33]

Also listed in the Memorial Tribute Program, such labor organizations as the United Packinghouse Workers of America and needle trades unions were key to immigrant rights organizing. Throughout its history, the ACPFB allied itself with labor, defending individuals whose political affiliations were deemed suspect because of their work with labor unions. Historically, foreign-born workers have been among the most vulnerable members of the labor force. Their exclusion from full citizenship rights has often meant a lack of workplace protections, including the right to organize.

Legal histories of deportation have tended to focus on high-profile cases of progressive activists and labor leaders, such as Russian Jewish anarchist Emma Goldman and Australian longshoremen's union leader Harry Bridges. In contrast, social and labor historians have examined the mass deportations of workers, such as the Bisbee Deportation of 1916, the campaign to repatriate Mexican Americans during the Great Depression, or Operation Wetback in the early 1950s. Looking at the records of the ACPFB, it becomes clear that mass deportations often targeted workers and labor activists, and that high-profile cases like those of Bridges or Goldman are only the most visible of these. Responding to "the deportation terror" in immigrant communities meant working closely with labor unions to defend union members from deportation and to advocate for labor and immigration policies more favorable to foreign-born workers. As migration patterns changed over time, the collaboration of labor and immigrant rights advocates allowed them to define shifting strategies. In the 1970s, for example, longtime immigrant rights and labor organizer Bert Corona was instrumental in persuading farmworker leader Cesar Chavez to include undocumented workers in his organizing efforts rather than exclude them as a threat to the wages of citizens and legal residents. Corona also worked closely with longtime ACPFB lawyer Ira Gollobin to define what they called "A Bill of Rights for the Foreign Born."[34]

Support from diverse national communities and from the labor movement indicates the pressing need for immigrant rights organizing throughout much of the course of the twentieth century, and into the twenty-first. Tracing this support also reframes our understanding of the period's history. In an era of political repression and pressure to assimilate, some "not yet white ethnics" made common cause with communities of color. Some labor unions, facing political pressure from restrictive legislation aimed at limiting organizing and making leadership less responsive to grassroots participation, struggled to expand workplace protections to noncitizens. Examples of such unions include the National Maritime Union of America, which acted on behalf of foreign-born sailors during the 1940s and 1950s; the Fur, Leather and Machine Workers Union, whose Joint Board advocated for newly arrived Caribbean and Latin American workers in New York during the 1970s; and garment workers' unions across the twentieth and twenty-first centuries. Such ongoing advocacy contradicts much of what we think we know about the United States at mid-century, yielding a much deeper and more complex view of the period.

The organizational life of the ACPFB spanned what are often considered decisive eras in immigration history. Focusing on shifts in national policy, historians of migration have generally thought of the period from 1875 to 1965 as the "exclusion period," because the development of immigration law led from the exclusion of Chinese immigrants to that of Asians more broadly, to the 1924 Johnson Reed Act, which limited migration from southern and Eastern Europe. Immigration quotas based on race or national origins were reinforced by the McCarran-Walter Act of 1952, which the ACPFB strongly opposed, and were finally ended by the Immigration Act of 1965. Throughout its existence, the ACPFB worked to make immigration law more inclusive by removing the hated national origins provisions of 1924 and 1952 and by limiting the incursions on civil liberties that invariably accompanied expanding the Immigration and Nationalization Service's (INS's) police and deportation powers.

Further, the institutional life of the ACPFB spans eras usually considered by historians to be distinct periods of the "Old Left" and "New Social Movements," or "New Left." Like the ACPFB, many "Old Left" organizations took a beating during the Red Scares that followed both world wars. The historical consensus tends to see McCarthyism as dealing a mortal blow to the "Old Left." Subsequent social justice movements were at pains to distance themselves from any taint of Communism. As discussed above, this red-baiting has found its way into the historical record, and "New Social Movements" have tended to be seen as distinct from the "Old Left," despite evidence to the contrary. Because the organization was networked across migrant communities, the ACPFB survived the Red Scare, outliving many other "Old Left" organizations.

The distinctions I have drawn here convey a general, historical division and the overwhelming power of McCarthyist repression in shaping the way we think about the past. But many subaltern pasts bridge this divide. Civil rights activists struggling for racial justice in the 1940s and 1950s made common cause with Popular Front organizers who had long considered white supremacy the central obstacle to working-class unity. Labor unions, particularly the maritime, cannery, agricultural, longshoremen's, and garment workers' unions most likely to be involved in defending migrant rights, recognized the significance of struggles for civil rights by Latinx, African Americans, and Asian Americans in the 1960s and 1970s. Many veterans of Popular Front organizations, such as the CRC, later became active in organizations characterized as "New Social Movements," bringing along experiences and priorities shaped by the "Old Left." The anticolonialism prevalent in the "New Left" was preceded by a fierce antiimperialism on the part of the "Old Left."[35]

As historian Donna Gabaccia argues, immigrants have historically maintained a particular stake in conditions in their home nations. Gabaccia dubs the process of creating and maintaining such transnational connections "foreign relations."[36] A vital part of the ongoing work of the ACPFB involved advocating for those who were forced to leave the country through deportation or its alternative: "voluntary departure." The organization monitored questions of civil liberties internationally to advance arguments against deporting progressive activists to right-wing regimes, such as those in Greece, Portugal, Haiti, the Dominican Republic, and South Korea. With the active advocacy of the ACPFB, for example, Eulália Mendes opted for voluntary departure to Poland instead of her native Portugal; Diamond Kimm and Alice Hyun, who did not recognize the legitimacy of the U.S.-backed regime in South Korea, obtained visas for North Korea through the Czechoslovakian consul. "Foreign relations" constituted an ongoing part of the work of the ACPFB throughout its existence. George Lipsitz points out that the Popular Front's deployment of American exceptionalism and virtue allowed the privileging of whiteness to be unchallenged immediately after World War II. The ACPFB certainly drew strategically on ideas of American exceptionalism, often celebrating the Statue of Liberty and the idea of the "Nation of Immigrants." But at the same time, foreign-born spatial transnationalism led to organizational internationalism in the organization. Monisha das Gupta traces the ways that migrant advocates create what she calls "a transnational complex of rights" that do not rely on "the contingencies of citizenship." The ACPFB worked strategically, sometimes deploying patriotic conceptions of citizenship and other times relying on such alternate formations to defend immigrant rights.[37]

The internationalist and antiracist strands that informed so much of the work of the ACPFB prepared it to play a role in ongoing struggles for civil rights and against neoliberal capitalist formations. In the 1970s, the organization recognized racial bias in INS detention and deportation for Haitians fleeing the regime of Jean-Claude "Baby Doc" Duvalier; it also joined in protesting immigration raids in new Latinx communities in New

York and Chicago. Such advocacy advanced internationalist ideas of citizenship and solidarity that persisted in the organization. Through this work, the ACPFB developed relationships with new migrant organizations, forming the political core of what would become the twenty-first-century immigrant rights movement.

Tracing connections between migrant and civil rights advocacy has led to some of the best recent scholarship on the ACPFB. In his magisterial work untangling the complex relationship between Mexican Americans and new migrants from Mexico, historian David Gutiérrez notes the significance of the founding of the LACPFB. For Gutiérrez, the multiracial organization facilitated a critique linking the racist treatment of Mexican Americans to the harassment of new immigrants by the INS and the Border Patrol. In key articles, historians Jeffrey M. Garcilazo and George J. Sánchez delve into LACPFB records, illuminating the intertwined histories of the organization and Mexican American and multiracial community work for civil rights during the early Cold War period. These historians assert the entwined nature of Latinx civil rights, labor organizing, and broader campaigns for social justice in twentieth-century Los Angeles. Their work traces the emergence of particular community voices, such as those of LACPFB chairwoman Rose Chernin, Luisa Moreno, and a group of activists dubbed the "Santa Ana Four" and their struggles against deportation. (See Chapter 4 for more on the LACPFB.)[38]

More recently, Natalia Molina has analyzed the ways in which the multiracial coalition of the LACPFB worked against what she deems the "racial scripts" undergirding the INS's and the Border Patrol's harassment of Mexican American communities in California. In her work on multiracial coalitions in Los Angeles history, Gaye Theresa Johnson explores the "constellations of struggle" that connected Black and Latino communities. She writes about the antiracist work of African American newspaper editor Charlotta Bass and Guatemalan American labor organizer Luisa Moreno. Both of these women were involved in the struggle for civil rights broadly, and in the founding of the LACPFB in particular. At the seventh anniversary of the LACPFB's founding, Bass said, "Our coming dinner symbolizes the unity of the Negro peoples and the foreign born, both striving for first class citizenship."[39]

The historical work of Gutierrez, Garcilazo, Sánchez, Johnson, and Molina uncovers the significance of immigrant rights advocacy in Latinx communities, particularly Los Angeles. It recovers the stories of key organizers, such as Luisa Moreno, Josefina Yanez, Bert Corona, and Rose Chernin, as well as neighborhood coalitions of different migrant cohorts. While some of these organizers, such as Moreno, were deported, and the

LACPFB did not persist as an organization very long into the period of the "New Left," their immigrant rights advocacy played a role in shaping social justice advocacy in southern California.

In another vein, legal historian Marc Stein has explored the ways in which the ACPFB's legal strategies against deportation of the foreign born influenced lawyer Blanche Freedman's 1967 arguments before the U.S. Supreme Court in *Boutillier v. Immigration and Naturalization Service*. Clive Boutillier was denied citizenship and deported because the court found that his engagement in "homosexual acts" constituted an excludable "psychopathic personality" under immigration and nationality law. As the chief counsel for the ACPFB between 1955 and 1967, Freedman had argued previously before the Supreme Court, attempting to prevent deportations. Stein argues that legal strategies applied by Freedman in her work defending the rights of the foreign born created a "template" for the defense of other kinds of rights, gay rights included. While Boutillier lost his case before the Supreme Court, Stein is among contemporary historians who see the case as ultimately advancing the cause of gay rights. Margot Canaday argues that the court's identification of "homosexual acts" as excludable "raised the possibility that homosexuality might be an occasional act among aliens who otherwise had the potential to become good citizens." Stein also cites the case as an example of collaboration between advocates for gay and foreign-born civil rights.[40]

Such creative scholarship about the ACPFB looks frankly and without historiographical paranoia at the involvement of active Communists in the organization. But this has been only one, among many, of its avenues of inquiry. The scholarship described above uses the many stories found in the long history of the organization to outline the long struggle for immigrant rights in the twentieth century and beyond and to connect the history of immigrant rights to broader struggles for civil rights and social justice. *Against the Deportation Terror* resurrects the long subaltern past of immigrant rights and connects it to twentieth- and twenty-first-century social movements and political formations.

Its longevity as well as its origins in the internationalism and antiracism of the "Old Left" prepared the ACPFB to respond to continued but changing assaults on the civil liberties of the foreign born throughout its existence. The loose, networked structure of the organization forced it to continually create Chantal Mouffe's "chain of equivalence." This framework kept the ACPFB from becoming too rigid, allowing it to respond to the needs of changing constituencies as they emerged and/or migrated to the United States. As it turned out, the very internationalism and concern for immigrants as workers that led the ACPFB to face persecution during the Red Scare also enabled the organization to anticipate and respond to key political and economic shifts in the later twentieth and early twenty-first centuries.

This book fills in a long-standing gap purposively created by anti-Communist counterinsurgency. The stakes are high: we need to know this story. As Camp explains:

> When these protests are obscured, the state's attempts to crush radical social movements are aided and abetted. In other words, the historically specific form of racist social control coincident with the emergence of neoliberal capitalism maintains its hegemony through the misrepresentation of social protest against it.[41]

Overview

Excavating the subaltern past of immigrant rights, this book follows the story of the ACPFB from its founding in 1933 to the closing of its office in 1982. I have used the records of the organization as a trail to uncover much broader formations in this period.

A partial accounting of my research into these records gives a sense of the diffuse nature of the organization. Because the ACPFB was organized into different chapters and regions, its papers exist in several archives. The main collections of the organization's papers are housed at the Labadie Special Collections Library at the University of Michigan and the Tamiment Library at New York University. The papers of Ira Gollobin, a key figure throughout and after the duration of the organization, are at the Central Public Library in New York City, and his files on his work with Haitian refugees are housed at the Schomburg Center for Research in Black Culture; Gollobin also contributed to the collections at the Labadie and the Tamiment. The Southern California Research Library in Los Angeles contains the papers of the LACPFB as well as those of lawyers who played important roles in defending those in deportation proceedings; the Immigration History Research Center in Minneapolis has the records of local lawyer Kenneth Enkel, who was the counsel for the Minnesota Committee for the Protection of the Foreign Born. The ACLU papers, housed at the Seeley J. Mudd Manuscript Library at Princeton University, contain extensive records on the ACPFB. I found pieces that connect to this subaltern past in the archives of longtime labor and immigrant rights activist Bert Corona at Stanford University and in the Sophie Smith Papers at Smith College.

This book's organization is chronological and topical. The chapters proceed from the origins of the organization to the closing of its doors in 1982. However, because immigrant rights struggles were broadly diffused, with crises occurring in different migrant communities over time, the book has topical chapters that focus on particular struggles and their relationships to the ACPFB.

Chapter 1, "Aliens, Refugees, Citizens: The American Committee for the Protection of the Foreign Born, 1933–1959," traces the deportation efforts against Nicaraguan-born Humberto Silex in southern Texas and Polish-born Stella Petrosky in Pennsylvania. These cases were key to the early development of the ACPFB. This chapter also looks at the organization's development through the Cold War. I argue that its connection to migrant temporal and spatial imaginaries allowed the organization to survive repression during the Cold War.

From its inception, the ACPFB worked to defend foreign-born individuals against deportation. Early on, much of this work took place in seaports, as maritime laborers and longshore workers organized multiracial and international unions. Chapter 2, "Becoming Alien: The March Inland Blows Up the Cold War Space-Time Continuum," focuses on the March Inland staged by the International Longshore and Warehouse Union (ILWU) on the West Coast, starting in 1934. Focusing on the case against Australian-born labor organizer Harry Bridges, this chapter explores this well-known deportation case of the era, along with those of lesser-known Filipinx American organizers Ernesto Mangaoang and Chris Mensalves. In organizing workers along a vertical chain that linked agricultural, freight, and shipping interests, the ILWU created multiracial alliances along the West Coast, including the then-territories of Alaska and Hawai'i. The migrant imaginary of the March Inland, in turn, led the ACPFB to spatial and temporal innovations that helped it defeat deportation and denaturalization charges against Bridges, Mangaoang, and Mensalves.

Chapter 3, "Ports of Entry, Exclusion, and Removal: 'Alien' Seamen," follows the story of maritime workers. Distinguished as heroes because of their valiant and largely successful attempts to keep key shipping lanes open during World War II, maritime workers became suspect during the early Cold War. Maritime workers organized for better working conditions, including fighting segregation on board ship. As the United States cemented international alliances with new regimes in such nations as Greece and Portugal, the State Department responded to the insistence of its allies by blacklisting anarchist and Communist sailors and attempting to deport them to their countries of origin. Greek, Jamaican, and Chinese American labor leaders fought deportation in this period; the ACPFB expanded as it represented their struggles. At a time of enhanced repression, the ACPFB and maritime workers succeeded in expanding the rights of foreign-born workers at sea. The collapse of these rights in a 1963 landmark court case, *McCullough v. Sociedad Nacional*, paved the way for the reign of "flags of convenience" ships: American-owned ships chartered off shore, granting few if any rights to the workers on board. I argue that the flags of convenience system anticipated the 1965 Border Industrialization Program by outsourcing jobs and diminishing the ability of workers to advocate for themselves. Representing maritime labor was a capacity-building endeavor for the ACPFB, as it expanded the organization's network among foreign-born communities.

Representing workers on ship and on shore—those literally at the margins of the nation—resulted in the expansion of the ACPFB; the organization developed in dialectical relationship to racialized state repression of the foreign born. Similarly, the largest and most significant regional chapter of the organization was founded in Los Angeles as a response to deportation campaigns predominantly targeting Mexican Americans in southern California and the Southwest—another borderland. Chapter 4, "Counterinsurgencies: Global Militarism and Immigrant Rights in Los Angeles," examines the founding of the LACPFB and looks at the interracial alliances that undergirded the organization. While Operation Wetback's expansion of border control into urban areas targeted Mexican Americans and other Latinx in Los Angeles, diasporic Koreans faced persecution because of their opposition to the U.S.-backed regime of Syngman Rhee in South Korea. The raids that followed the passage of the McCarran Act in 1950 also focused on foreign-born labor leaders of diverse national origins. Forged out of this distinct milieu, the LACPFB created a multiracial political culture. I argue that the LACPFB influenced the national ACPFB, educating the East Coast–based organization on the issues particular to Mexican American migrants and creating lasting alliances that eventually shaped advocacy for immigration reform in the 1960s and 1970s.

Chapters 5 and 6 turn to the national context of immigration advocacy. Chapter 5, "'Creating Dangerously': Foreign-Born Writers and Crimes of Persuasion," draws on Haitian American writer Edwidge Danticat's admonition to immigrant artists to "create dangerously."[42] The chapter examines the creative work of those facing deportation throughout the period of the ACPFB's existence, analyzing the work of Trinidadian American feminist author Claudia Jones, bilingual newspaper editors Diamond Kimm and Knut Heikkinen, and successful Los Angeles architect David Hyun. All of these people were involved with the ACPBF. In examining their work, the chapter investigates the ACPFB's articulation of a political culture of immigrant rights that discursively opposed the deportation terror.

Chapter 6, "*The Names of the Lost*: Cold War Deportation Cases in the Mass Media," looks at the ways in which the mass media broadcasted ACPFB advocacy narratives during the early Cold War. But, just as Operation Wetback created a sea change for immigrant rights advocacy, it also represented a turnabout in mass-mediated representations of those facing deportation. As Kelly Lytle Hernandez has argued, the success of Operation Wetback was predominantly in drawing public attention to the INS. In the national media, Operation Wetback coincided with the rise of the term "illegal alien," which displaced prior, comparatively more sympathetic coverage of immigrants facing deportation, making it much more difficult for such immigrant rights advocates as the ACPFB to convey their message. This racialized term in many ways eclipsed other mass-media narratives, transforming public perception and advocacy narratives. It took activist responses to successive crises in the 1970s and 1980s to rearticulate immigrant rights in the national mass media.[43]

Chapter 7, "Repurposing Immigrant Rights Advocacy, 1959–1982," looks at this resurgence of immigrant rights. It takes up the historical narrative begun in Chapter 1, looking at the persistence of the central chapter of the ACPFB into the 1970s and 1980s, a time when New York City was demographically transformed by "new immigration" from Asia, Latin America, and the Caribbean. I argue that the ACPFB's multiracial national network allowed it to survive the Cold War and made it a source for immigrant rights organizing for newly arrived migrant cohorts after 1965. Advocacy for Haitian refugees in this period transformed the ACPFB and broader national networks, creating conditions for the emergence of a renewed national movement in the late 1980s and early 1990s.

The Conclusion further draws parallels between the history of the ACPFB and contemporary immigrant rights formations. Interracial solidarity during the era of the ACPFB was built on alliances of workplace and neighborhood. Through these alliances, the organization advocated for policy change. Many "not yet white ethnics" remained in the movement because of their investment in such alliances and their investment in changing immigration policy. In the Cold War era, such interracial solidarity drew suspicion as "un-American." While immigrant rights advocacy was affected by repression, it also survived the Cold War, anticipating new formations, such as capital flight and neoliberalism. The history of the ACPFB illuminates the significance of interracial solidarity and highlights the importance of the transnational insights of the foreign born in responding to political and economic changes.

Filling a gap in the record, this book offers a little-known story of migrants organizing against deportation and repression throughout much of the twentieth century. Creating a background for the current ascendance of vital immigrant rights formations, this story draws on a many-stranded subaltern past. The following chapter begins this story by recounting the origins of the ACPFB in the fluorescence of popular resistance during the 1930s.

A Note about Terminology

This book traces a long, dialectical struggle between the foreign born and the evolution of militarized and racialized immigration enforcement over the course of the twentieth century. To clarify and make the stakes of this contest clearer, I use certain terms throughout. I employ the terms "migrant" or "foreign born" to describe the constituency of the ACPFB: those affected by immigration policy. Accordingly, I use the term "immigration" to describe the work of the nation-state to regulate the actions of migrants.

The term "foreign born" has an important historical resonance, as it is the term most often used in ACPFB advocacy literature. Also, as I have argued above, this expression alludes to the randomness of birthplace and the alienness of the foreign born with respect to the assimilation project demanded by the "Nation of Immigrants" paradigm. At times, I refer to these same people as "migrants." I choose this term instead of the word "immigrant," because it connotes ongoing movement. Entry into the United States constitutes one stop among many; only sometimes is it a final destination. This is in part because of the agency of migrants and in part because of the power of immigration enforcement to enact the deportation terror and send them away.

I employ the terms "Latinx" and "Filipinx" for the adjectival and plural forms describing these groups of people. These words represent an evolution of the English language that moves beyond gender binaries and gestures toward the complexity of identity. Their use indicates multiple gender possibilities, at the same time freeing the prose of this book from slightly more cumbersome terms, such as "Latino/a" and "Filipin@."[44]

I hope that these writerly choices help make this book clear and readable.

ALIENS, REFUGEES, CITIZENS

*The American Committee for the Protection
of the Foreign Born, 1933–1959*

The relief administrators properly pay no heed to
whether a person needing relief is an alien or not: for
aliens too have a stake in this country. Did they not in
recent decades do much of the heavy and dirty work in
the building of America as it stands today? Are they not
entitled to aid in continuing their mere existence now
that the country has stumbled into a crisis?
—Louis Adamic, "Aliens and Alien-Baters," 1935

Writing in *Harper's Review* in 1935, Slavic American writer, laborer, and immigrant rights activist Louis Adamic weighed in on the then-much-debated question of whether noncitizen, foreign-born workers should receive federal assistance in the form of Works Progress Administration (WPA) jobs. Adamic viewed foreign-born workers as American, regardless of their citizenship status. In his migrant imaginary, their presence in the country was evidence of their Americanness; their labor served as immediate naturalization. Denying them work during the economic upheaval of the Great Depression, to Adamic, constituted "reactionary anti-alien baiting." But this vision contradicted the "Nation of Immigrants" narrative of slow assimilation and eventual citizenship. In 1938, "non-resident aliens" were barred from the WPA.[1]

Fears about the foreign born claiming jobs and relief at the expense of citizens during the Great Depression had consequences for many migrants, but particularly Mexican Americans. Immediately following the stock market crash of 1929, the Immigration Service responded to political pressure by deporting Mexican Americans from California and the Southwest. Because most Mexican American communities in the country included individuals of U.S. and Mexican birth, it was difficult to be certain that federal agents deported only noncitizens. As Secretary of Labor Frances Perkins hesitated to continue federal deportation drives, many states and localities coerced Mexican Americans to leave and "return" to Mexico.

Close to 20 percent of the Mexican American population of the United States departed, the combined result of federal deportation sweeps and state and local initiatives. This number included American as well as Mexican nationals. Historian Mae Ngai estimates that of the four hundred thousand deported from California and the Southwest, about 60 percent were American citizens.[2]

Depression-era deportation drives targeted Mexican Americans. Other foreign-born workers also faced deportation, particularly as a result of their participation in growing labor mobilizations. Strikes and unions drew local as well as federal authorities; the Immigration Service often initiated deportations as a way of subduing striking workers. By one estimate, 180 foreign-born workers were deported from the anthracite region of Pennsylvania alone during the early 1930s.[3]

This chapter looks at the founding of the American Committee for the Protection of the Foreign Born (ACPFB). It follows two early deportation cases that shaped the organization's national network during its first two decades as well as crucial Cold War legislation affecting the foreign born and the ACPFB. Migrant imaginaries and restrictive federal policies influenced the development of the ACPFB as an immigrant rights organization. I argue that the broad foundation of the organization in diverse migrant communities across the United States allowed it to survive the repression of the Cold War years.

The liberal American Civil Liberties Union (ACLU) and the Communist International Labor Defense (ILD) collaborated to found the ACPFB in 1933. A Popular Front organization, the ACPFB brought together such civil libertarians as Roger Baldwin and such progressive lawyers as Carol Weiss King and Ira Gollobin; advocates for foreign-born communities, such as Adamic, Leonard Covello, New York State Congressman Vito Marcantonio, and journalist Carey McWilliams; African American civil rights organizers, such as W. E. B. Du Bois of the National Association for the Advancement of Colored People (NAACP), Max Yergan of the Council on African Affairs, and George Murphy of the *Baltimore Afro-American*; and other progressive intellectuals and religious leaders, including John Dewey, Alaine Locke, Thomas Mann, William Carlos Williams, Melville Herskovits, and Ernest Hemingway. The organization promoted itself as "an independent, non-partisan, affiliated body, composed of representatives of trade unions, fraternal and cultural societies, etc." An early explanation of the organization focused on three objectives:

1. To ensure equal rights for the foreign born in the United States.
2. To preserve the traditional right of asylum in America for political and religious refugees.

3. To combat discrimination against the foreign born because of race, nationality, political opinion, or religious beliefs.[4]

The ACPFB existed as an organization until 1982, when it folded back into the ACLU. Throughout its existence, it maintained a central office in New York City, although local chapters around the country were operative at different times. The first executive secretary of the organization was Dwight C. Morgan. Originally from Colorado, Morgan had worked as a miner before moving to New York.[5]

The ACPFB was part of the politically charged context of the mid-1930s, in which local and national conservative reaction consistently contested the innovations of the New Deal and Popular Front organizations. Advocates from the ACPFB viewed their work in defense of the foreign born as a democratic imperative, parallel to struggles around the globe. A 1935 report explained:

> As the Jewish people were selected by Hitler as the target for the attack of the Nazis in Germany, so William Randolph Hearst, the United States Chamber of Commerce, etc., have directed their drive upon the "aliens," in an attempt to divide and pit sections of the mass of people against each other in the United States.[6]

The position of the foreign born as, variously, freedom seekers, antifascists, or dangerous fifth-column infiltrators bent on undermining the nation from within held particular significance in the period around World War II. As historian Rebecca Nell Hill points out, "antifascist" in this period could take on a variety of meanings, depending on the political orientation of the speaker. "Fascist totalitarianism" could refer to the ascendance of Nazism in Germany, but it could also point to Soviet authoritarianism. Critics of the New Deal conflated "fascism" with federal intervention in the economy in the form of social programs. Further, fascism and Communism were perceived as "foreign" ideologies, so limiting their influence often entailed restrictions on the foreign born.[7]

ACPFB advocates drew on and often benefited from discourses of antifascism. In 1941, ACPFB national chair Hugh DeLacy introduced a radio address by Marcantonio by drawing on the metaphor of Nazism in America: "The growth of a native Hitlerism in America means for us what Hitlerism meant for the German people—suppression, substandard living, and wars of foreign conquest." Marcantonio went on to inveigh against the repression brought about by the restrictions on free speech and registration of the foreign born required by the Smith Act, comparing the antisubversive law to Nazi totalitarianism.[8]

Similarly, in 1939, Representative Thomas F. Ford of California criticized the proposed Smith "Alien Registration" bill as "un-American," because he saw its "alien-baiting" as parallel to Adolf Hitler's treatment of German Jews. In the same year, the Hollywood Anti-Nazi League for the Defense of American Democracy was founded; the organization worked to prevent refugee anti-Nazi Germans from being deported. Anti-Nazism had an understandable power in the late 1930s; however, the specter of national socialist totalitarianism did not always overwhelm fears of Communist subversion. The ACPFB advocated for leftist German and Italian antifascist refugees, with mixed results. The Florida Sub-committee of the ACPFB intervened in the deportation of Rudi Muller and George Piermont to Italy; Mexico granted them asylum.

Otto Richter, a Jewish anti-Nazi who had been beaten by brownshirts on the night of the Reichstag fire, lived in hiding in Germany before shipping out to Seattle in 1933 as a maritime laborer. When the captain discovered Richter's identity and threatened that he would be sent to a concentration camp on his return to Germany, Richter jumped ship. Immigration and Nationalization Service (INS) agents found him in July 1934, working at a soup kitchen in a San Francisco workers' center. They promptly charged him with illegal entry and sent him to Ellis Island on a deportation train. The ACPFB advocated for him, organizing legal support as well as a letter-writing campaign; Richter was granted asylum in Mexico and ultimately crossed the border back into the United States without papers. Historian Yael Schacher points to tensions between the ACPFB and the ACLU around strategies for Richter's defense, given his professed Communist leanings.[9]

Anti-Communism could trump anti-Nazism. Ascendant anti-Communists before the war often connected a foreign, "alien menace" with broader threats to the American way. Hill explains the ways in which Congressman Martin Dies, the chair of the House Un-American Activities Committee (HUAC), connected immigrants to "European collectivism" and other scourges of civilization. Dies proposed a bill in 1935 that would effectively have made participating in a strike a deportable offense.[10]

Existing in a charged field in which ideas of democratic rights were delimited by fears of subversion by totalitarianism, immigrant rights advocacy could be controversial. Some advocates attempted to disentangle particular aspects of the struggle, hoping that some might be more publicly palatable than others. A 1937 radio address by Congressman Emanuel Celler displayed some of the contradictions of immigrant rights advocacy. Eventually a co-sponsor of the landmark 1965 Hart-Celler Act that bears his name, Celler carefully balanced an argument for immigrant rights in the name of American freedom with caution about exactly who should benefit from such rights. He argued that offering asylum for political and religious refugees was consistent with what was to him a uniquely American role of being a harbor for the oppressed. At the same time, he insisted on the necessity of distinguishing between such refugees and what he called "the general deportation cases."[11]

While he was a powerful advocate for immigrant rights, Celler's separation of refugees from deportees contrasted with ACPFB rhetoric, which linked refugee and asylum rights to "the oppression of minorities" and refused to sever the cases of "deserving" refugees from an implicitly less deserving cohort of "general deportation cases." Because they were influenced by the internationalism of the Popular Front and by migrant imaginaries like Adamic's, ACPFB advocates recognized the connections between different struggles. They understood how the labor and civil rights work of Cuban cigar workers in Tampa or of the Congress of Spanish-Speaking Peoples in Los Angeles affected the rights of the foreign born. In contrast to the limited rights proposed by Celler, the ACPFB's vision drew on migrant imaginaries to propose alternate senses of space and time, beyond the frameworks of partial rights leading to eventual Americanization. This vision afforded the organization broad coalitions and alternative conceptions of citizenship.

For example, a 1936 resolution of the ACPFB drew parallels between the African American struggle for civil rights, full labor rights, and rights for the foreign born. It proclaimed:

> We demand full social, economic and political rights for the foreign born in the United States. We are convinced that deportation of foreign-born workers and the persecution of minorities does not solve the economic problems from which the multitude of the people suffer but rather stands in the way of the solution of these problems.[12]

This argument drew on Popular Front and Communist antiracism stances, grounding the case for immigrant rights in broad struggles.

The ACPFB broadcasted such visions of rights throughout its existence. Advocating for immigration reform meant representing the interests of migrants who were involved in labor unions and in transnational organizations that could be construed in some contexts as "anti-American." It would have been safer to do what Representative Celler and other more mainstream advocates did: to select a particular group of migrants and argue that they were more deserving than others of protection and legal enfranchisement. This strategy has been a key structuring principle for many immigrant rights movements throughout the twentieth and into the twenty-first century. As ethnic studies scholar Lisa Marie Cacho explains, representing particular migrants as deserving of rights creates discourses of "respectability" that often erase shared histories of struggle.[13]

By and large, the ACPFB took positions advocating for the broadest definitions of rights for the largest numbers of migrants possible. This vision gained some traction before and during World War II. At an event commemorating the ninety-second anniversary of Emma Lazarus's birth, President Franklin Delano Roosevelt commended the ACPFB's work in a comment often reprinted in the organization's programs and pamphlets throughout the difficult Cold War period:

> I am glad to greet the American Committee for the Protection of the Foreign Born. It has undertaken the task of assuring fair play to the foreign born within the United States.[14]

This 1935 presidential affirmation of the importance of "assuring fair play to the foreign born" constituted a high watermark for the acceptance of immigrant rights. It was ratified in large part by the Popular Front coalition among labor, immigrant, and civil rights constituencies. After World War II, the prior existence of this coalition itself became grounds for suspicion.

Throughout its existence, the ACPFB responded to deportation crises. Because the ACPFB represented migrants struggling against deportation, the rights of those deemed most undesirable and threatening determined the history of the organization. The committee's national network included a wide array of civil rights, labor, and ethnic organizations, so it represented a variety of individuals contending with deportation. Many of these individuals had been accused of being "Communists." But, in the context of ascendant anti-Communism, many people could be accused of a broadly conceived anti-Americanism. The next section follows the case of Stella Petrosky, a foreign-born labor and welfare rights activist targeted for deportation because of her alleged Communist associations. As an immigrant, Petrosky became American through her involvement with radical politics. Her Americanization conflicted with the prescribed process of assimilation and eventual naturalization: the mythical "Nation of Immigrants" story. Broadcasting Petrosky's claim to remain in the country, the ACPFB devised advocacy strategies that shaped later campaigns for immigrant rights.

"The Only Real Protection [Is] Membership in Working-Class Organizations": The Radical Temporality of Stella Petrosky[15]

The title of this section comes from a pamphlet published by the ACPFB in 1935 about its ultimately successful defense of Pennsylvania labor and welfare rights advocate Stella Petrosky. Her case serves as an example of the alternative, migrant temporalities infusing the coalition work and advocacy practices of the ACPFB in the 1930s.[16]

Born within Russian borders, Polish-speaking Petrosky came to the United States as a young girl in 1914. She appears to have come without family, settling in Wilkes-Barre, Pennsylvania: coal-mining country. In 1917, she married Thomas Petrosky, a coal miner who drank heavily. At the time when deportation proceedings were initiated against her in the mid-1930s, Petrosky was divorced and in her mid-thirties. She had eight children, including a set of triplets. The family struggled to survive while Thomas and Stella were married and Thomas was working: after Thomas lost his job and the couple divorced, Stella and the children subsisted on $4 a week from the Luzerne County Relief Board.

The Great Depression brought widespread misery, poverty, and unemployment to Pennsylvania's coal country. Drawn to improve the lives of her families and others like them, Petrosky became active in the region's Unemployment Council. The Luzerne County Workers' Alliance fought for unemployment insurance and against discrimination and deportation for foreign-born workers. Historian Christina Heatherton writes of the expansive and charged nature of struggles over relief during the Depression:

> This working-class struggle for relief also promoted a collective consciousness, wherein a radical redistribution of resources supplanted individualized notions of success and failure. Conversely, in the hands of growers and the region's capitalists, relief had a different meaning: it could be strategically denied or supplied to break strikes, damage workers' leverage, coerce labor, provoke police repression, or trigger deportation efforts.[17]

This convergence of relief, labor, and immigrant rights describes the evolution of Petrosky's activist work. When the United Anthracite Miners Union went on strike in 1935, Petrosky worked to support the strikers. Four hundred high school students left school to join the picket line, Petrosky's older children among them. Her activism focused on basic human rights and survival, a horizon of mutual support and solidarity that was crucial to the survival of coal-mining families. She explained:

> When I joined the Workers' Alliance and the Committee for the Protection of the Unemployed[,] I had a sincere desire to help my children get food and to help my fellow citizens. Deep in my heart[,] I know it's not subversive to want better living conditions.[18]

On April 24, 1935, INS inspectors visited the Petrosky home. They arrested Stella and accused her of anarchism and membership in the ILD, which was active in the area. She was held at the Luzerne County Jail; bail was set at $1,000.

By the time of her arrest, Petrosky was well-connected among unions and unemployment councils in the region. Local allies organized the Stella Petrosky Defense Committee, which also drew support from the local chapter of the ACLU. The Defense Committee pressured county authorities to lower bail. Subsequently, the ACLU paid $500, and she was released. The Defense Committee then solicited support from the ACPFB, which sent lawyer Irving Schwab down to coal country from New York.

At her hearing on May 16, 1935, Petrosky was charged under the 1918 Immigration Act with advocating the violent overthrow of the U.S. government on the basis of her work with the Unemployed Council, the Workers' Alliance, the International Workers Order, and the ILD. Four witnesses testified against her: Charles Santee of the Pennsylvania State Police; Warren Bader, a Pennsylvania state trooper assigned to assist the INS; John Burke, a Wilkes-Barre police officer; and Stanley R. Henning, a high school principal, who accused Petrosky of being the organizing force behind the high school strike. The four presented evidence from raids on local Young Communist League and Communist Party homes and offices linking Petrosky to these organizations. Burke reported that the Petrosky home was festooned with pictures of Karl Marx, while Bader claimed that Petrosky had attended a mass meeting right before the school strike at which she stood up and shouted repeatedly, "Communism must prevail!" (Petrosky said she was not at that particular meeting, and those familiar with her case commented that "prevail" did not seem to be in her vocabulary. Additionally, those who had visited the Petrosky home noted that movie stars, not Marx, held pride of place in the small dwelling.)

After the initial hearing, the Stella Petrosky Defense Committee became the Luzerne County Committee for the Protection of the Foreign Born. Working with the New York ACPFB headquarters, advocates publicized the charges facing Petrosky. In her defense, they created a highly gendered rhetoric that emphasized her hard work and sacrifice for her children. A pamphlet published about the case by the ACPFB inverts the charges against her as "dangerous" to the nation. *"A Dangerous Woman"* emphasizes her stubborn work ethic and her skills as a cook and homemaker. It speaks of her work with labor unions and unemployment councils in the area but frames her activism as courageous mothering, proclaiming that "Stella Petrosky's children are not starved and not without clothes because this loving woman put herself forward for her children."[19]

The portrayal of Petrosky as a dutiful mother was a self-conscious and

"A Dangerous Woman"
Stella Petrosky Held for Deportation
by Sprad

Published by **AMERICAN COMMITTEE FOR PROTECTION OF FOREIGN BORN** 100 Fifth Ave., N. Y. C. Tel.: AL 4-2334

Price 3c

"*A Dangerous Woman*": Stella Petrosky and her children. (American Committee for the Protection of the Foreign Born Records, Joseph A. Labadie Collection, University of Michigan Library [Special Collections Library].)

largely successful advocacy strategy. It framed her struggles to survive as a component of her maternal decency rather than as an un-American effort to ensure the victory of Communism. Emanating from a migrant temporality, this strategy defined virtue outside the terms of the "Nation of Immigrants" narrative.

Morgan requested a photo of Petrosky and her children from the Defense Committee. Subsequently, this photograph was widely circulated in the national mass media. The pamphlet *"A Dangerous Woman"* attracted the attention of the New York immigration commissioner, Byron H. Uhl, who sent it to Washington with a note warning the INS about the potentially subversive activities of the committee. After months of publicity, the ACPFB organized a visit by Petrosky to the Department of Labor in Washington, DC; there, she met with Labor Secretary Perkins, who dismissed all charges against her. These charges were revived again in 1953, under the "past-membership" clause of the McCarran-Walter Act. Ultimately, a federal court found that there was no evidence of Petrosky's ever having been a member of the Communist Party. The court stayed her deportation once and for all in 1956; by then, she was a grandmother.[20]

Through her activism and her fight against deportation, Petrosky asserted an alternate trajectory of citizenship and belonging. Rejecting the discipline of assimilation, she said, "This is not my country and I am a better citizen than many women born here." Her articulation of a migrant imaginary, in turn, shaped the ACPFB's emergent rhetoric and its ability to connect with diverse foreign-born communities around the country.[21]

The following section looks at the deportation case against Nicaraguan-born labor organizer Humberto Silex. As with the Petrosky case, the ACPFB's defense of Silex shaped the organization's development. Legal work in defense of Silex connected the New York office to Mexican American labor and immigrant rights advocates in the Southwest and Texas. These connections infused the organization's work throughout the early Cold War and into the 1960s and 1970s, anchoring the ACPFB in antiracist work against the deportation terror in Mexican migrant communities.

"Terror in Texas": Transborder Organizing in El Paso

> There is a lot of talk about human rights today[,] but I say the first human right for a worker is the right to a job.
>
> —Humberto Silex, quoted in Frank Arnold,
> "Humberto Silex: CIO Organizer from Nicaragua"

Educated in Managua, Humberto Silex left for the United States in 1921, seeking adventure and fortune. Working at shipyards and smelting plants in the Midwest and the Southwest, he was struck by the appalling conditions there as well as the intense discrimination against Spanish-speaking people. In Chicago, he participated in protests against the execution of foreign-born anarchists Nicola Sacco and Bartolomeo Vanzetti. The occupation of Nicaragua by U.S. Marines in 1925 also troubled Silex, and he attended rallies and meetings supporting Augusto Sandino's resistance to the occupation.[22] In his first few years in the United States, Silex was affiliated with political movements for labor and civil rights and against what many at the time called U.S. imperialism. This internationalism shaped Silex's migrant spatial imaginary, eventually bringing him into conflict with authorities in Texas.[23]

After working at a variety of jobs around the country, Silex settled in El Paso in 1930, finding work at the American Smelting and Refining (ASR) Company there. Border crossing was a regular feature of life in El Paso. Many Mexican Americans maintained family and social ties in Mexico, and many found additional work there when they could. Like many denizens of El Paso, Silex crossed the border routinely for work as well as personal reasons: his wife, Maria de Jesus, a legal resident of the United States, was a native of Chihuahua, Mexico. Their seven children, all born in El Paso, were U.S. citizens.[24]

Soon after he began work at ASR, Silex sought to improve conditions there. He had been passed over for promotion a few times and was once asked by the company to train an Anglo-American to be promoted above him. Recognizing that the existing American Federation of Labor (AFL) union would do little for Mexican American workers, Silex worked with Congress of Industrial Organizations (CIO) organizers from the Packinghouse Workers Union, the only CIO union in El Paso. Although he was Central American, Silex was perceived and treated as "Spanish speaking" or Mexican American because of his association with preponderantly Mexican American low-wage smeltery workers. Newspaper coverage of Silex's legal travails often referred to him as a "Mexican American Labor Leader."[25]

In 1939, workers at the ASR plant in El Paso voted to create a CIO union affiliated with the International Union of Mine, Mill and Smelter Workers: Local 509. As the CIO worked to organize the smelteries, Silex collaborated with the Mexican labor organization Confederación de Trabajadores Mexicanos (CTM). Mexican unions in this period saw cross-border organizing as key solidarity work; they acknowledged Mexican Americans as part of their constituency. Silex crossed the border into Juarez frequently, working with Mexican organizers. He made a speech at a May Day celebration in 1939; on May Day in 1942, Mexican American members of the CIO Mine, Mill and Smelters Union marched with Mexican unions in Juarez. Silex's cross-border organizing and his presence at

Silex family (undated photo). (American Committee for the Protection of the Foreign Born Records, Joseph A. Labadie Collection, University of Michigan Library [Special Collections Library].)

such events was later used against him in attempts to deport him and to deny his application for citizenship.[26]

Historian David Gutiérrez points out that, given their concentration in low-wage and dangerous occupations, Mexican Americans in the period between the two world wars created labor organizations that also advocated for immigrant and civil rights. Gutiérrez points to the emergence of what he calls "new forms of political analysis and organization" at this time. These new forms combined the sociality of traditional mutual aid societies with advocacy for better work conditions as well as equality under the law. Transborder organizing in El Paso connected Mexican American civil rights struggles to Mexican labor struggles. Such connections were a component of the new forms of political analysis and organization Gutiérrez describes, bringing questions of labor and civil rights into an international framework. And this border-crossing component of Silex's union activities eventually evoked questions of immigrant rights, as Silex and others struggled against deportation.[27]

In 1940, Silex was fired and then reinstated at the behest of the National Labor Relations Board (NLRB). He was fired again by foreman Victoriano Tapia in 1945 and subsequently got into a fistfight with him. In its brief, the INS asserted that the 1945 charge against Silex for "aggravated assault" because of the fistfight with Tapia constituted "a crime of moral turpitude" and therefore made him ineligible for citizenship. In 1946, the INS presented a warrant for Silex's arrest and deportation. In 1949, Silex's application for citizenship was rejected.

The deportation effort and the denial of citizenship to Silex came out of a concerted effort by local and federal authorities to sanction foreign-born labor organizers, locating them outside the developmental temporality of assimilation and citizenship. From New York, the central office of the ACPFB participated in Silex's defense.[28]

In El Paso and throughout the Southwest, anxieties about the foreign born in this period were racialized, primarily focused on Mexican Americans. Threats of Communist subversion combined with long-standing racial animus against Mexican Americans. During the 1933 strike at the Phelps-Dodge coal mine in Gallup, New Mexico, the INS held one hundred foreign-born workers for deportation; eventually, Mexican American labor leaders Jesus Pallares and Liga Obrera were accused of being Communists and deported to Mexico.[29]

As El Paso County sheriff Chris Fox told the NLRB in 1940, "I don't see any difference between the CIO and the Communist Party." Fox testified further that he had personally arrested CIO organizers at the ASR plant and turned them over to immigration authorities. In this context of intimidation, many in the Mexican American community feared reprisals for any kind of union activity or political affiliation. In its annual report for the years 1937–1938, the ACLU decried the domination of the El Paso Police Department by a corrupt political machine with a "long record of attacks on the rights of Mexican workers and the unemployed."[30]

Mexican Americans in El Paso and the Southwest connected civil, political, labor, residential, and immigrant rights. Smeltery workers struck in 1946, gaining some improvements in working conditions as well as a raise of 18.5 cents per hour. The strike was supported by the CTM; Silex administered the CIO Strike Relief and Citizens' Committee. Because the majority of union members were Mexican American, they experienced residential and educational discrimination, and because many Mexican Americans were not citizens, the threat of deportation loomed over strikers and the community alike.[31]

The coalition that mobilized to defend Silex reflected the entwined nature of labor and civil rights in South Texas. Asserting her support for Silex, Guatemalan-born organizer Luisa Moreno explained that the struggle for labor rights in El Paso was part of "Operation Dixie," the attempt by unions to organize the South after World War II. (Moreno herself faced deportation for her political activities and left for Mexico in 1950.)[32] The Texas Civil Rights Congress, primarily concerned with questions of African American civil rights, worked on Silex's defense; the New York office of the ACPFB was closely allied with the national Civil Rights Congress (CRC).

In Denver, Isabel Gonzalez, the executive secretary of the Committee to Organize the Mexican People, identified the deportation cases of Silex and Chicago packinghouse worker Refugio Ramon Martinez as crucial to the cause of Mexican American civil rights. Gonzalez wrote:

Deportation [markings in margin]

> The threat of deportation has served as a very effective weapon to keep the Mexican people as a whole in bondage because, as soon as a leader arises among them, deportation proceedings are immediately used to remove him from such leadership.[33]

The ongoing deployment of what the ACPFB referred to as the "deportation terror" in the Southwest was part of a broader arsenal of racialized violence used against people of color in the region. Assertions of the rights of migrants not to be deported relied on organizational as well as rhetorical connections between Mexican American civil rights, labor rights, and political rights more broadly. As Gonzalez explained, the targeting of such leaders as Silex, Moreno, and Martinez had direct impacts on the mobilization of Mexican American communities for desegregation and for better labor conditions. Silex Defense Committee organizer and union member Nathalie Gross explained to the New York ACPFB office that many union members were not citizens and were afraid to even distribute leaflets to support the presidential campaign of Henry Wallace, because it might affect their citizenship or their very right to remain in the area. Gross described the situation in El Paso:

> The increasing political activity of the Mexican people in El Paso is encouraging many to apply for their papers. We are aware of intimidation by the immigration authorities and feel that a more aggressive attitude on our part and insistence that Silex be given his citizenship papers would in some measure help to overcome this.[34]

Mobilizing support for Silex, the ACPFB disseminated pamphlets; coverage of the case was featured in the ACPFB newsletter, *The Lamp*. Further, the ACPFB conducted a letter-writing campaign, addressing appeals to INS commissioner Ugo Caruso. Letters poured in from a wide array of labor and faith-based groups across the nation.[35]

The coalition that worked on Silex's defense kept him from being deported; at one point, he received a pardon from the Texas governor for the aggravated assault charge. Charges against Silex eventually included association with "Communist-front" organizations, including the CRC, the ACPFB, and his own defense committee. But, despite the fact that Federal Judge R. E. Thomason proclaimed that he could find no evidence that Silex had ever belonged to a subversive organization, Silex was unable to natu-

TERROR IN TEXAS

WHAT WILL HAPPEN TO

HIS SEVEN CHILDREN?

26 YEARS IN THE

UNITED STATES

OUTSTANDING TRADE

UNION ORGANIZER

CHAMPIONED CAUSE OF

MEXICAN-AMERICANS

PREVENT THE DEPORTATION OF HUMBERTO SILEX

Humberto Silex was born in Nicaragua 43 years ago. He entered the United States legally in 1920. He has lived in the United States continuously since his original entry. In 1922 Silex enlisted in the United States Army, serving seven months, after which he received an honorable discharge. From 1922 until 1931 he lived and worked in Dallas, St. Louis, Joliet and Chicago. In 1931, he went to El Paso, Texas, where he married a legal resident native of Mexico. They have seven children. The oldest child is 13 years of age and the youngest was born in June 1946. All the children were born in the United States. Silex has worked all the time he has been in the United States and provided a good home and supported his family.

Humberto Silex is acknowledged to be the outstanding labor leader in El Paso, Texas. He has been associated with the labor movement since its inception in El Paso. He was one of the first persons to become interested in establishing a CIO union in that city. He was employed in the El Paso plant of the American Smelting and Refining Company when

Local 509 was established in 1940. His organizational work on behalf of the union was so outstanding that he was singled out by the company and discharged for union activity in July, 1940. Silex was reinstated to this job with back pay by the NLRB after an unfair-labor-practice-and-discharge complaint had been filed against the company.

Humberto Silex was elected secretary of Local 509 in 1940 and held that office for 2 years. In 1942 he was elected secretary-treasurer; in 1943 and 1944 he was elected president of the local. He was also head of the grievance and negotiating committee for the workers at the American Smelting and Refining Company plant. Silex carried on his organizational activity and union work without compensation. In recognition of his devotion to the interests of labor, he rose from office to office and in 1945 he became the national representative and organizer for the International Union of Mine, Mill and Smelter Workers, District 2, which covers Texas, New Mexico, Arizona, Utah and Nevada.

There are two major plants in El Paso, Texas. One is

"Terror in Texas," ACPFB flyer. (American Committee for the Protection of the Foreign Born Records, Joseph A. Labadie Collection, University of Michigan Library [Special Collections Library].)

ralize. In a climate of intense anti-Communism in southern Texas, his lack of citizenship meant that he could not work as a labor organizer. Further, the Union of Mine, Mill and Smelter Workers was eventually blacklisted as a "Communist-front" organization. Silex himself was blacklisted and supported his family with a series of temporary jobs after 1951.[36]

As a foreign-born labor organizer, Silex was immersed in struggles over different kinds of rights: labor rights in the smelteries; civil rights for Mexican Americans in southern Texas; the right to remain in the country to which he immigrated; and the right of his home nation, Nicaragua, to political self-determination rather than rule by the U.S. Marine Corps. His transborder, internationalist spatial imaginary created broad alliances for labor and civil rights in southern Texas.

After a lifetime of hardship brought on by his political blacklisting, Silex insisted on the central significance of labor rights. The statement that opens this chapter comes from an interview with Silex conducted by labor historian Frank Arnold in the late 1970s. Silex understood the confluence of struggles for civil, immigrant, and labor rights and the ways in which these domestic struggles were connected to labor rights in Mexico and political sovereignty in Nicaragua and Central America.

Like Petrosky, Silex avoided deportation by federal pardon; in his case, the NLRB rejected the claim that his altercation with his former boss constituted "moral turpitude" and was, therefore, a deportable offense. Although Petrosky was not blacklisted for employment as Silex was, like him, she supported herself and her family with fairly menial work after successfully resisting deportation; in 1956, she was working for a company that packed lunches. The work lives of Silex and Petrosky are typical of those of workers without papers throughout the twentieth and into the twenty-first centuries. These conditions underscore the motivation of both organizers to promote labor rights for citizens and foreign-born workers.

Growing up in El Paso during the same years when Silex was active there, future labor and immigrant rights organizer Bert Corona experienced the segregation and violence that characterized Mexican American life in southern Texas. Like many of his generation, Corona became politicized around a migrant spatial imaginary:

> By the time I was about twelve, I saw myself as belonging to a people who possessed a right to be in the Southwest and who believed this was our land, too, despite the Anglo invasion. I felt that we had to redress our grievances here and not in Mexico and that the Anglos owed us at least equal treatment and recognition.[37]

Corona's articulation of rights based on migrant experiences of space paralleled assertions by civil rights organizations like the Congress of Spanish-Speaking Peoples, which drew such activists as him and Moreno. Corona moved from El Paso to Los Angeles in 1936, finding a Mexican American community there wracked by the repatriation drives. In Los Angeles, Corona became involved with labor organizing, working for Local 26 of the International Longshore and Warehouse Union (ILWU). Through labor organizing, Corona also became involved with the Mexican American movement and immigrant rights organizing in Los Angeles. Working for the CIO, he put together organizing committees that comprised Mexican Americans,

Russian Jewish immigrants, African Americans, and native-born white Californians.[38]

As a native-born citizen, Corona did not face deportation himself, but he remained acutely aware of the connections among civil, labor, and immigration rights. As it had in El Paso, defending worker rights in Los Angeles meant contending with the deportation raids often used to suppress worker militancy. This awareness led Corona to advocate for rights for migrants throughout his long political career, which lasted well into the 1980s. Corona's work with the Community Service Organization (CSO) and the Asociación Nacional México-Americana (ANMA) targeted issues of Mexican American community empowerment, inevitably confronting questions of immigrant rights as part of this work. ANMA worked closely with CIO unions, including Silex's Mine, Mill and Smeltery Workers.[39] In the early 1950s, these organizations became part of the founding coalition of the Los Angeles Committee for the Protection of the Foreign Born (LACPFB).

The organizing trajectories of Silex and Corona point to the ascendance of deportation as a technology to control not only labor militancy but also communities of color. Many repatriated Mexican Americans passed through El Paso during the early 1930s, en route back to Mexico. As Cold War laws like the Smith Act (1940) and the McCarran Act (1950) expanded the use of deportation against the foreign born, the ACPFB worked to oppose deportation by fighting for individuals like Silex and by mounting political challenges to such repressive legislation.

Emerging from this confluence of labor and civil rights struggles, the ACPFB was shaped by migrant spatial and temporal imaginaries like those of Corona, Petrosky, and Silex. Foreign and native-born individuals of disparate backgrounds resisted the deportation terror together. Just as the Silex case united Mexican and African American civil rights groups with labor and immigrant rights advocates, the ACPFB created a national movement for immigrant rights that worked through networks and coalitions. Through these connections, they asserted ideas about American citizenship informed by labor and civil rights struggles. The alternative senses of time and space came under fire as un-American during the early Cold War years.

Persistence and Repression during the Cold War

A spirit of democratic struggle against domestic as well as international fascism animated the founding years of the ACPFB. Along with many other progressive organizations worldwide, the ACPFB supported the Allies during World War II. Jewish advocates, such as Abner Green, King, and

Blanche Freedman, who were among the early founders of the organization, were not alone in discerning the urgency of the war against fascism. For many foreign-born communities with ties to Asia and Europe, concern for the fates of families, friends, and nations abroad ran high during the war years. Historian Donna Gabaccia notes the "strenuous but invisible" advocacy of immigrants for their relatives abroad during the war and their subsequent involvement in founding organizations for refugee relief after the war. As with transborder organizing among Mexican Americans in El Paso, concern for their "foreign relations" compelled immigrants to think internationally. Such internationalism attracted suspicion in the climate of patriotic anti-Communism after the war.[40]

After the war, anti-Communism captured much of the political impetus of antifascism. The two discourses had always been entwined, so "antifascist" could simultaneously mean general opposition to totalitarianism, including Soviet state socialism, and a progressive critique of the kinds of political coercion faced by such workers as Silex and Petrosky. As Allied victory was followed quickly by tension between the Communist Soviet Union and the "free world" of the United States and Western Europe, anti-Communism became a political imperative in American foreign and domestic policy. The terms "totalitarian" or "fascist" came to refer almost exclusively to repression by state socialist regimes.

For the ACPFB, the post–World War II period was marked by increased repression and a concurrent expansion of foreign-born communities fighting the deportation terror. The committee continued to define fascism as repression against human and worker rights in any country, the United States included. Unpopular in the context of the anti-Communism of the period, this definition incurred governmental repression. At the same time, the organization expanded because of the acceleration of persecution of the foreign born. It took on more cases and added regional and ethnic chapters around the country. A significant chapter, the LACPFB, was founded in 1950 to contend with deportations of longtime area activists as well as the depredations of Operation Wetback, which targeted Mexican Americans in California and the Southwest.

As the organization was expanding, it faced repression at the hands of state and federal agencies. Although many Democratic politicians had endorsed the work of the ACPFB before the war, the organization experienced increasing suspicion and surveillance after the war because of its internationalism and association with the leftist Popular Front. In the politically charged climate of the early Cold War, the risk of being publicly associated with such an organization led to the defection of many former supporters. A shrinking base of support, in turn, led to financial and legal challenges.

But unlike many other Popular Front–era organizations, the ACPFB survived the harsh repression of the early Cold War period. The war on current and past associations made many leery of such organizations as the ACPFB, because association with them could bring down surveillance, and sometimes sanctions, on individuals. But precisely because the Cold War targeted the foreign born as primary suspects of "un-American" activities and associations, the ACPFB found itself forming new alliances during this difficult period.

Internationalist concern for their "foreign relations" continued among the foreign born after the war. Regime changes in many nations and the transformed status of former colonies in Asia and the Caribbean led many to monitor the situations in their former homelands. The concern of many Euro-Americans during this period for their relatives abroad was ratified by both U.S. and UN responses to the postwar crisis of "displaced persons."[41] Yet unlike refugee rights, immigrant rights did not emerge as a central issue in the postwar period. Just as Celler and others had successfully argued in the 1930s that some migrants deserved more rights than others, one effect of the new category of refugee was to elevate the status of particular migrants over that of others. National and international law defined "refugees" as those fleeing religious persecution or political persecution. In the United States, Cold War diplomatic prerogatives determined what constituted political persecution. That left those struggling with repression by the United States or its allies without legal refuge. The ACPFB represented many who found themselves facing political repression in their homelands but unacknowledged by U.S. foreign policy as deserving of refugee status.

Green, who became the executive secretary of the ACPFB after Morgan's death in 1941, noted the contradiction of using Ellis Island as a place for deportation rather than entry:

> Today, Ellis Island is no longer an Island of Happiness, a stopping-off place to a new world. Today, Ellis Island has become an Island of Tears. Today, Ellis Island has become a prison—and the worst kind of prison in the world[,] because no other jail anywhere is made bright at night by the lighted torch of the Statue of Liberty.[42]

Here, Green deployed the "Nation of Immigrants" narrative strategically, referencing the hope that Ellis Island represented for immigrants globally. The use of Ellis Island as a space of internment indicated profound changes in mainstream ideas about immigration during the Cold War.

The ACPFB had long opposed the anti-alien provisions enacted by the 1940 Smith Act as anti-immigrant and undemocratic. For the organiza-

the
legacy
of
ABNER GREEN
a memorial journal

ISSUED BY THE AMERICAN COMMITTEE FOR THE PROTECTION OF THE
FOREIGN BORN, FOR THE 27th NATIONAL CONFERENCE, DEC. 19-20, 1959

Abner Green. (American Committee for the Protection of the Foreign Born Papers, #086, Tamiment Library/Robert F. Wagner Labor Archives, New York University. Used by permission of Ruth Gollobin-Basta.)

tion's Fifth Conference, in Atlantic City in 1941, co-chairmen McWilliams, Walter Rautenstrauch, and Yergan presented a "Declaration of American Principles." In it, they decried deportation sweeps as well as the discharge of noncitizens from employment, and they connected the general persecution of the foreign born with segregation and discrimination against Mexican and Asian Americans on the West Coast. This statement of unity between the foreign and native born echoed wartime rhetoric even as it asserted a vision of full rights for the foreign born.[43]

The multiracial advocacy represented by organizations like the ACPFB came under further federal scrutiny as a result of the McCarran Internal Security Act of 1950. The McCarran Act significantly honed the antisubversive provisions of the Smith and 1918 Immigration acts. It reiterated the time frame for subversive activities as "at the time of entering the United States or at any time thereafter." Further, it granted wide discretion to federal authorities to determine whether there was "reason to believe that such aliens would, after entry, be likely" to engage with such organizations or otherwise advance subversion. These two provisions gave the INS legitimacy to effectively act as historians and soothsayers, searching the past and future for evidence of subversion.

Under the McCarran Act, the INS initiated deportation proceedings against many foreign-born individuals in their fifties and sixties. Many of these individuals had been politically engaged during the 1930s, although most had been far less involved than such activists as Petrosky and Silex. No matter that such individuals as Petrosky had already been exonerated of all suspicion of subversive activities—the McCarran Act created the context for further investigation of all associations, past, present, and conjectural. Immediately after the McCarran Act took effect, the INS conducted a series of "midnight raids" around the country, detaining hundreds for deportation. Many were sent to Ellis Island on the East Coast; others were detained at local jails. In Los Angeles, the "Terminal Island Four" were detained in the old military base in Los Angeles Harbor. These raids targeted some individuals with minimal political experience, many of whom had joined unions or obtained insurance from the International Workers Order, along with seasoned organizers; it brought lifetime Communist Party activists, such as Trinidadian-born Claudia Jones, together with advocates for Korean self-determination, such as David Hyun and Diamond Kimm. The McCarran Act authorized the INS to pursue such imaginative dragnets.[44]

Under the McCarran Act, the INS confined foreign-born suspected subversives to "supervisory parole." Supervisory parole conditions included the following: submitting to psychiatric and medical examinations, reporting in person to Ellis Island on a weekly basis, giving information under oath about associations and activities, remaining in an area covered by a fifty-mile radius of Times Square, and discontinuing past "subversive" associations, particularly with the Communist Party or its suspected associates. Supervisory parole was used widely, but particularly in cases against Eastern Europeans, including Jews and non-Jews, whose nations no longer recognized them as citizens.[45]

Passed in 1952, the McCarran-Walter Immigration and Nationality Act resurrected and reinvigorated the restrictionist national origins quotas of 1924, which had closed the door to immigration from Asia and limited the flow of migrants from southern Europe and the Middle East. The McCarran-Walter Act continued the direction of the McCarran Act in enhancing the power of the federal government to detain and deport the foreign born. The McCarran-Walter Act also established the principle of preventive arrest and deportation at the attorney general's discretion.[46] Like much Cold War antisubversive legislation, many of these provisions remain law into the twenty-first century.

The ACPFB opposed the McCarran-Walter Act as white supremacy. Analysts noted the danger of the law's assessment that belief in particular doctrines, such as Communism, constituted a deportable offense. The organization joined a coalition of civil rights, ethnic, and religious groups, including African and Asian American groups, that opposed the restrictionism inherent in the new immigration legislation (its tendency to "ancestor hunt," in the words of Harry S. Truman); the tiny quotas set for newly decolonized nations, which, along with restrictions on immigration from colonies still existent, provided for the virtual exclusion of West Indians, Vietnamese, and Asian Indian immigrants; and the law's method of shutting the door on large parts of a war-torn Europe that World War II had supposedly been fought to liberate. While it repealed the long-standing ban on the naturalization of Asians, the McCarran-Walter Act created an "Asiatic-Pacific Triangle": each nation in a triangular-shaped region ranging from Afghanistan to Micronesia was assigned an annual quota of one hundred migrants to the United States. China and Japan were exceptions, with quotas of 205 and 185, respectively. Under the McCarran-Walter Act, many transnational spatialities of the foreign born became suspect.

The ACPFB contended with issues relating to its supposedly subversive nature throughout the 1940s and 1950s. In 1941, Yergan wrote to Carl White of the Cleveland Department of Law on the latter's resignation from the Ohio Conference for the Protection of the Foreign Born:

> I am absolutely convinced that many people raise false issues, particularly political issues, in order to distract attention from real issues of discrimination and persecution. During my long experience[,] I have observed this not only with regard to Negroes but other minorities and often majorities in Europe, Africa and India.[47]

In 1959, Green died of a brain tumor at the age of forty-seven. The ACPFB published a memorial journal honoring him. Edited by Harry Carlisle, one of the "Terminal Island Four" whose deportation had recently been legally overturned, the journal depicts the composition of the ACPFB. It contains statements from leftist journalist I. F. Stone as well as Du Bois commending Green's tireless work against repression and racism. Sponsorship for the ACPFB poured in from ethnic and community organizations across the nation.[48]

After Green's death, Wellesley College theology professor Louise Pettibone Smith became the executive secretary of the ACPFB. As the co-chair of the ACPFB's annual conference from 1950–1956, Smith had abundant experience with progressive and migrant advocacy. She had worked with refugees in Palestine during and after World War II. After the war, she was active in the defense of Julius and Ethel Rosenberg and later opposed the war in Vietnam as well as becoming co-chair of the Angela Davis Defense Committee of New York. Born in Ogdensburg, New York, in 1887, Smith came from a political family; her father was a newspaper editor, and her mother was a teacher. Her maternal grandfather had been a founder of the Abolitionist Society of central New York State and had traveled to Georgia during Reconstruction to organize schools for the Freedmen's Bureau. Smith headed the ACPFB until 1968. Subsequently, she became the honorary chair, while Paul Lehman took over as executive secretary, with the indefatigable Gollobin serving as general counsel.[49]

How did the ACPFB survive McCarthy-era repression? Historian John Sherman's account of the organization has it closing its doors in 1959; Robert Justin Goldstein echoes Sherman's periodization by claiming the organization was essentially defunct by that date.[50] But, while Cold War repression affected the organization, the ACPFB continued to act as an immigrant rights organization throughout the 1960s and 1970s, until it actually did close its doors in 1982, dissolving and becoming part of the National Emergency Civil Liberties Committee of the ACLU.[51]

The ACPFB outlived many other Popular Front organizations, partly because it was protected by its decentralized structure—local and regional committees for the protection of the foreign born were largely autonomous from the central New York office. Further, somewhat ironically, the same enhanced Cold War repression that sanctioned and delimited the organization kept a steady stream of deportation and denaturalization cases coming, necessitating advocacy work.

Their critique of the white supremacy of deportation policy enabled ACPFB advocates to identify the racism of Cold War immigration policy. Speaking in New York in 1955, ACPFB annual conference secretary Alec Jones connected the racist repression of the McCarran-Walter Act with the continuation of raids in California and the Southwest:

> We have seen the continued terrorization of Mexican communities across this land and have witnessed a continuation of General [Joseph May] Swing's military operation of rounding up Mexicans for deportation and denying them the most elementary facets of due process of law. Likewise there has been a rise in attempts at intimidation in the West Indian community.[52]

This recognition enabled the ACPFB to draw on its networks and forge alliances with emergent organizations contending with the threats posed by the deportation raids of Operation Wetback. During the Cold War, the bulk of the ACPFB's work consisted of defending leftist Euro-Americans against deportation. Corona remembered that the left, including the ACPFB, was much slower to defend Latinx deportees, such as Moreno and Silex, than it was to defend "those of European descent." For Corona, the organization's efforts on behalf of Latinx organizers was "too little, too late."[53]

The LACPFB was founded in 1951. Previously, ANMA and the CSO had collaborated with the CRC of Los Angeles to handle legal defense of the foreign born in close cooperation with the ACPFB's central office. With the passage of the McCarran Act, the CRC identified a need for an organization specifically devoted to advocating for immigrant rights and convened a founding conference in October 1950. The LACPFB emerged from this conference; Hyun, a labor and peace activist and one of the "Terminal Island Four" arrested during the McCarran Act raids, headed the new organization (for more on Hyun, see Chapters 4 and 6).[54]

While the LACPFB continued to work closely with the ACPFB's central New York office, the Los Angeles committee differed from the parent organization. Both were founded as a response to crises; while the ACPFB had challenged the antilabor deportation raids of the 1930s, the LACPFB contended most immediately with the racialized mass deportations of Operation Wetback. The LACPFB was particularly responsive to the needs of communities of color. Unlike the central organization, which generally had Jewish and non-Jewish white men and women in positions of power, the LACPFB was led by people of color, including Hyun and Josefina Yanez. While the LACPFB worked against antiradical deportation and denaturalization cases, most notably that of its second chairperson, Russian Jewish activist Rose Chernin, the organization was most directly shaped by the Mexican American struggle. At the organization's 1951 conference, Alfredo C. Montoya, the president of ANMA, explained the investment of Mexican American organizations in the newly formed LACPFB:

> We are proud to join with you in the struggle for the protection of the rights for the foreign born. We the Mexican people have a particular interest in this Conference. We have been the victims on a mass scale, of deportations[;] we have long been denied our civil, economic, and political rights. We are very grateful for the special attention being given by this Conference to the problems of the Mexican people, though we realize that this is done not only in our interest but also in the interest of preserving the rights of all.[55]

Also present at this conference were representatives from the CSO, the NAACP, and the National Negro Labor Council. While Corona does not mention the November 1951 conference explicitly in the memoir he coauthored with historian Mario Garcia, he was deeply involved with two of the organizations present. If he was not present that day in Alhambra, it is more than likely that he was aware of the goings on. Certainly, Corona was among the Angelenos who worked with the LACPFB and collaborated with the New York office on issues of concern to Mexican American and foreign-born people in his adoptive city. Historian Jeffrey Garcilazo notes the long collusion of the Los Angeles Police Department with the INS in deporting Mexican Americans there. Organizers from the "Mexican American generation," such as Corona, were deeply concerned with the effects of such constant dragnets on their community.

For the ACPFB, the founding of the LACPFB solidified an alliance against immigration policies the organization had long viewed as racist. Speaking at the Fourth Annual Conference for the Protection of the Foreign Born in 1940, Moreno linked deportation and the denial of welfare benefits to noncitizens with the exploitation of migrant labor in the fields of Texas, California, and the Southwest:

> But why have "aliens" on relief while the taxpayers "bleed"? Let me ask those who would raise such a question: what would the Imperial Valley, the Rio Grande Valley, and other rich irrigated valleys in the Southwest be without the arduous, self-sacrificing labor of those non-citizen Americans? . . . These people are not aliens. They have contributed their endurance, sacrifices, youth and labor.[56]

Because the LACPFB emerged from multiracial activism anchored solidly in California communities of color, the alliance between the New York and Los Angeles offices pulled the parent organization toward what emerged later as the community control and empowerment politics of the New Left.

The next chapter looks at the March Inland: the organizing campaign of the International Longshore and Warehouse Union linking West Coast ports to cannery and agricultural workers. Foreign-born activists in this campaign were targeted for deportation under the Smith, McCarran, and McCarran-Walter acts. Their ingenuity in fighting the deportation terror drew on migrant senses of time and space and created new alliances that sustained the ACPFB and extended its capacity among transnational migrant communities on the West Coast.

A native of Brooklyn, Green had worked in a waterfront pharmacy as a teenager, where he became familiar with the particular situation of foreign-born maritime laborers. Under his tenure as the ACPFB's executive secretary, which lasted until his untimely death in 1959, the circumstances of marine laborers was a signal concern of the organization. And because marine laborers were a uniquely multiracial, transnational workforce, advocating for them greatly expanded the work of the committee, expanding the volume and diversity of its advocacy. Chapter 3 takes up the vital role of foreign-born maritime labor in expanding the capacity and constituency of the ACPFB.[57]

BECOMING ALIEN

The March Inland Blows Up
the Cold War Space-Time Continuum

And when the United States relinquished its
sovereignty over the Philippine Islands and proclaimed
its independence on July 4, 1946, respondent became
an alien for all purposes.
—SUPREME COURT OF THE UNITED STATES
in *Mangaoang v. Boyd*, 1953

O riginating in mid-1930s labor militancy at West Coast ports, the
March Inland organized maritime and longshore workers, connecting
them along the agricultural commodity chain with teamsters, packers,
cannery laborers, and field workers. The success of this strategy on the
mainland eventually spread to the territories of Alaska and Hawai'i, where
workforces previously divided by race, language, and national origins had
long frustrated organizing attempts. While the March Inland did not result
in the formation of one big union along the commodity chain, it succeeded
in creating imaginative possibilities for alliances among a multiracial, polycultural workforce. As the spread of this vision led to enhanced repression
through deportation and denaturalization proceedings initiated against
labor organizers, the March Inland of necessity became a dynamic site of
immigrant rights organizing.[1]

Longshore work is transportation work—longshore workers load cargo
onto ships. Up and down the West Coast and into Alaska and Hawai'i,
much of the cargo they loaded consisted of agricultural products harvested
by farm laborers, packed by cannery workers, shipped to the docks in
trucks and trains operated by teamsters and railroad operators, and stacked
and stored in facilities maintained by warehouse workers. Significantly,
many of these workers were Latinx and Asian American migrants who did
not enjoy the benefits of collective bargaining ensured by the Wagner Act,
which had specifically exempted agricultural and domestic work from federal protections.

Wagner Act
→ exempt from
federal protections

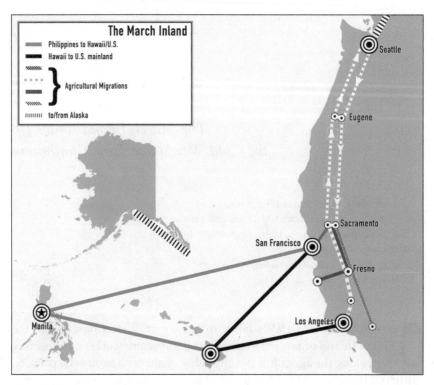

The March Inland. (Map by Milo Miller.)

Spatially structured by migrant trajectories around the West Coast, the March Inland coalesced around alternate conceptions of space, power, and time. As this diverse cohort of workers organized, they also asserted migrant imaginaries: alternate practices of acculturation and Americanization.

This chapter relates the entwined stories of two foreign-born organizers involved in the March Inland: Australian-born longshoreman Harry Bridges and Filipinx cannery and agricultural worker Ernesto Mangaoang. Both were targeted for deportation because of their activism, although the cases against them deployed racialized differences based on their national origins. In challenging these deportation cases, the American Committee for the Protection of the Foreign Born (ACPFB) and its allies successfully drew on the alternative relations of space, time, and power proposed by the March Inland. Drawing on these alternative imaginaries, they challenged the imperial space-time continuum, undergirding federal attempts to make these organizers into "aliens." As a result, the March Inland also transformed immigrant rights advocacy, creating new strategies, coalitions, and possibilities that influenced the ACPFB's subsequent development.

A broad cohort of foreign- and native-born Americans imagined new horizons of space and time in the March Inland. The strategy of organizing east from Pacific ports represented a collective reimagining of the West Coast by workers often spatially constrained by racial segregation and restrictive immigration laws. Where political distinctions formulated in far-off Washington, DC, bounded discrete states, and territories, laborers along the commodity chain affirmed alternate geographies that more closely reflected their histories of migration across national and territorial boundaries.[2]

Filipinx constituted a particularly important cohort of workers affected by the March Inland because of their numbers and their unique status with respect to American citizenship. As a result of laws implemented in the early twentieth century limiting the migration of other Asian workers, Filipinx were sought after for agricultural work in Hawai'i and the U.S. mainland as well as for cannery work in Alaska. Because the Philippines had become an American territory at the conclusion of the Spanish-American War in 1898, Filipinx occupied what historian Rick Baldoz has characterized as an "anomalous political designation that placed them in a political twilight zone between citizenship and alienage." Their status as American colonial subjects meant that they were not subject to laws excluding other Asians; at the same time, they were subject to naturalization laws prohibiting Asians from becoming citizens. This "twilight zone" allowed Filipinx migrants to work in the United States even as it limited their access to rights and labor protection. Therefore, labor contractors sought these workers, recruiting them in the Philippines as well as Hawai'i. By the 1920s, Filipinx constituted the main labor force in the Alaskan salmon industry. The "twilight zone" status of Filipinx workers, their location between colonial subjects and American citizens, enabled them to become part of the migrant chain linking the West Coast. This in-between status also came to inform the March Inland's migrant imaginary.[3]

In his famous autobiography, *America Is in the Heart*, Carlos Bulosan imagines an arc connecting his early life in the Pangasinan province in the Philippines through his subsequent migration into the life of an itinerant worker on the West Coast and Alaska. Bulosan connects the struggles of his family with rural poverty after the American occupation of the Philippines with his later involvement with migrant labor organizing among Filipinx on the West Coast. Arcs of migration and empire span Bulosan's Pacific, linking his two homes; the struggles of the Filipinx people in both places are contiguous. Bulosan's spatial imaginary contrasts the narrow coordinates of "America" with the broader horizons of Filipinx migrations.[4]

Bulosan's arc, with its mapping of territory and space, also suggests an alternate temporality that influenced the culture of the March Inland. The origins of many migrant laborers as "foreign born" cast them outside a national "American" family maintained and reproduced by proper and monogamous relations between citizens. In the "Nation of Immigrants" timeline of assimilation, such foreign-born origins could be eventually overcome by progress toward Americanization. Because of their "twilight zone" status with respect to citizenship, Filipinx migrant workers inhabited an alternate temporality, which eventually became central to defending the March Inland against repression.

The March Inland took place at a time of increased nativism and heightened attention to the distinctions between territorial and national status. Asian American and Latinx itinerant laborers contended with racial violence against them, ranging from local vagrancy laws to vigilante actions and race riots, such as those in Watsonville, California, in 1930, to federal and state-supported repatriation campaigns. The 1934 Tydings-McDuffie Act initiating independence for the Philippines was largely motivated by nativist desires to close the immigration loophole that allowed Filipinos to migrate as American subjects.[5]

The success of the March Inland in uniting workers along the commodity chain of West Coast agricultural production brought about great resistance on the part of agricultural and shipping interests and their allies. Such groups as the Associated Farmers, the Hawaiian Sugar Planters' Association, and the chamber of commerce castigated the March Inland as dangerous subversion. These campaigns heightened already existing tensions around the presence of foreign-born, nonwhite workers on the West Coast. This backlash countered the temporal and spatial imaginings of the March Inland by heightening the importance of political boundaries between states, territories, and nations and by casting these workers as alien and unassimilable: outside linear progress of the national temporality.

This chapter begins by considering the assault against Bridges and the International Longshore and Warehouse Union (ILWU) in some detail, connecting the deportation case against Bridges with the ILWU's multiracial organizing on the West Coast and Hawai'i. It examines the deportation and denaturalization cases against lesser-known Filipinx labor organizer Mangaoang. Along with other Filipino cannery workers, Mangaoang was refused reentry to the continental United States from Alaska after Philippine independence in 1946 made Filipinx in the United States newly subject to Asian exclusion laws. The ACPFB and its West Coast allies contested deportation efforts against activists and worked toward earning citizenship for Filipinx Americans. The tribulations of foreign-born workers connected to broader contemporary questions around "insular subjectivity," or citizenship, for the denizens of U.S. territorial possessions.

To a great extent, immigrant rights advocates recognized the connections between the case against Bridges, the assault on organized labor, and the implications for racial justice domestically and internationally. Familiar with the politics of denaturalization, the ACPFB also recognized the centrality of the Filipinx citizenship issue after Philippine independence in 1946. And, aware of the connections between domestic repression and imperial reach, the ACPFB fought the McCarran-Walter Act, with its grim implications for foreign-born progressives, workers of color, and denizens of U.S. territories. Taking place in the context of emergent Hawai'ian and Alaskan statehood and Philippine nationhood, the March Inland challenged exclusionary constructs of citizenship, establishing new kinds of relationships between workers from different national origins and racial groups. These new connections made imagining new horizons possible for workers previously excluded from citizenship and labor rights.

The Many Trials and Tribulations of Harry Bridges

Bridges faced more than twenty years of successive attempts to deport and denaturalize him between 1934 and 1955. Accused of being a Communist largely because of his successful organizing work, the Australian-born longshoreman became a well-known figure in labor and immigrant rights circles. Eventually, Bridges and the ACPFB defeated four attempts by the federal government to rid the nation of him. The defeat of the high-profile case against Bridges was a significant victory for the ACPFB. When the federal government abandoned denaturalization proceedings against him in 1954, it reflected the alternate temporal and spatial horizons created by migrants in the March Inland.

While the accusations against Bridges alleged his past and/or present membership and/or association with the Communist Party, these accusations targeted much more than one Australian-born, left-leaning dockworker and labor organizer. At stake was the project of interracial alliances represented by the March Inland. The federal attacks on Bridges constituted part of larger conflicts around questions of citizenship and power, issues that were being renegotiated in the immediate post–World War II period. As Congress of Industrial Organizations (CIO) president Philip Murray explained in 1945, Bridges was "'guilty' of the 'crime' of organizing the unorganized."[6]

The case against Bridges took place in the context of a profound narrowing of access to citizenship. While the March Inland proposed new organizations of space and time, a Cold War, anti-Communist imaginary consistently attempted to regulate the spatial boundaries of the American empire and delimit the boundaries of acceptable speech and association by

Harry Bridges at CIO
Organizational Meeting,
Huntington Park, California,
1950. (Los Angeles Committee
for the Protection of the
Foreign Born Collection,
Southern California Library
[Los Angeles, California].)

making laws that applied to past as well as current conduct. The resulting
narrowing affected immigrants and "insular subjects" as well as citizens,
redefining ideas of legitimate American identity.

Bridges's struggles were widely documented in the popular and progressive press. As a handsome "regular Joe," Bridges made good copy. In
the mass media, his story could be read either as evidence of the dastardly
ability of Moscow to infiltrate even such normal-looking faces or as an
illustration of the ineptitude of the federal government as it wasted time
and taxpayer dollars to harass a hard-working man. In progressive circles,
the Bridges case came to symbolize the persecution suffered by many in
this period.

The twists and turns of Bridges's legal tribulations alone made for a
good story. Further, as an English-speaking white man, Bridges came
across as decidedly less foreign and less "un-American" than many other
immigrants facing deportation and denaturalization. Part of the publicity
given his case at the time, then, seemed to present the issue of political
anti-Communism on its merits rather than targeting Bridges on the grounds
of other "un-American" affiliations with foreign-born or civil rights orga-

nizations. Similarly, much of the treatment of Bridges in the historical literature has focused on the way his case epitomized the red-baiting of labor, particularly after the anti-labor Taft-Hartley Act of 1947.

Anti-Communism definitely played a key part in Bridges's many tribulations. The persecution of foreign-born organizers, such as Bridges, and the blacklisting of unions, such as the ILWU, transformed the possibilities for labor organizing after World War II. In the charged context of anti-Communism in the immediate postwar period, the CIO went from being a powerful force that redefined class politics to an organization fearful of radical leadership and dependent on cooperation with management. Attacks on foreign-born organizers and progressive unions were a key part of this transformation.

In 1920, the Australian ship Bridges was working on docked in San Francisco. Bridges paid the head tax required to immigrate and became a resident of the United States and a member of the American Federation of Labor (AFL) Sailors' Union of the Pacific (SUP). In 1921, he also became a member of the Industrial Workers of the World (IWW). Where the SUP excluded nonwhite laborers, the IWW was antiracist. In New Orleans, Bridges built levees on the Mississippi. He lived with other Wobblies, as IWW members were known, in an African American neighborhood. White Wobblies looked for opportunities to combat segregation, sitting in the Black sections of buses and movie theaters. Bridges later credited the IWW with transforming his views on race. As an SUP member, Bridges took part in a 1921 strike.[7]

After 1922, Bridges settled in San Francisco. He married and sought work on the docks, loading ships. In this period, longshore work operated through the shape-up: those wanting work would gather at the docks early in the morning to jostle and compete for a job or a day's labor. Crowds of laborers clamoring for work would often be moved by police to allow commuters to board the ferries. To get steady work, longshoremen were forced to join a company or "blue book" union; shops were closed to other unions.[8]

The shape-up has a particular place in the history of foreign-born workers. Just as it exists in many contemporary U.S. communities as places where undocumented workers find daylong or job-based employment, the shape-up on the docks before the successful organizing campaigns of the ILWU offered casual employment for those ineligible for other kinds. Bridges remembered that the shape-up had particular importance for those who were blacklisted because of their union activities or for those who were not citizens and thus not eligible to work at the army transport docks. Possibly because of this experience, Bridges remained responsive to the particular circumstances of noncitizen laborers throughout his career.[9]

In 1953, an ILWU member remembered the shape-up system on the docks in the 1920s:

> We had to shape-up for work[,] and only those who were favorites of the hiring boss and kicked back to him ever got a day's work. If we were "lucky" and got taken on, we had to break our backs[,] because hundreds of hungry men were willing and eager to take over our jobs. We couldn't squawk, we just had to take it.[10]

This system created ample discontent among longshore and warehouse workers, although it worked to the benefit of the owners by providing a surplus of labor, which kept wages low.[11]

In the early 1930s, Bridges was among longshore workers who organized a chapter of the International Longshoremen's Association (ILA), an AFL affiliate, on the Bay Area docks. The ILA organized a major strike in 1934, closing all Pacific ports. In San Francisco, workers shut down the entire city. The National Guard was called in, resulting in the deaths of eight strikers, including two longshore unionists. Workers walked off the job and stayed off for almost three months; the general strike included more than one hundred thousand workers from the San Francisco and Alameda areas. Bridges was elected leader of the ILA strike committee.[12]

Before the strike had even been settled, the question of Communist influence on the docks was raised by adversaries of unionization. The ship and warehouse owners, the chamber of commerce and the American Legion, and the Associated Farmers all opposed the growing power of labor on the Pacific Coast. At the time, the American Legion was also involved in attempts to exclude the entry of Filipinx laborers from Hawai'i and the Philippines; the Tydings-McDuffie Act passed Congress the same year of the San Francisco strike.[13]

The San Francisco Chamber of Commerce wrote a letter to President Franklin Roosevelt, raising questions about influence and affiliations. These allegations dogged Bridges and the ILWU for two decades. Widely printed in the press, the letter explained the conflict on the docks:

> The strike is not a conflict between employers and employees—between capital and labor—it is a conflict which is rapidly spreading between American principles and un-American radicalism. . . .
>
> The longshoremen are now represented by spokesmen who are not representative of American labor but who desire a complete paralysis of shipping and industry and who are responsible for the bloodshed which is typical of their tribe. . . .

There can be no hope for industrial peace until communist agitators are removed as the official spokesman [*sic*] of labor and American leaders are chosen to settle their differences along American lines.[14]

Articulating an ideal horizon of "industrial peace" obstructed only by "un-American" organizers, the chamber of commerce letter conflated labor militancy with un-Americanism. "Un-Americans," who could be radical, foreign born, or both, stood in the way of progress toward industrial peace. Harper Knowles of the Subversive Activities Committee of the California American Legion, a former secretary of the Associated Farmers, continued to work on formulating a legal case against Bridges throughout the 1930s. Knowles was assisted in this work by the Portland and Los Angeles Police Departments.[15]

In the wake of the strike, the blue book union and the shape-up were replaced by an ILA union-run hiring hall. Workers up and down the Pacific Coast commemorated "Bloody Thursday" each July 9 to remember those who died in the strike. Longshore organizers quickly realized that the strength of their union depended on a strong alliance with warehouse workers, who packed the cargo that came to the docks. Many warehouse workers had participated in the 1934 strike. In 1936, freight handlers began a March Inland to organize warehouse workers on the Pacific Coast. This marked the origin of the March Inland, with its spatial strategy of commodity chain integration. In 1937, West Coast longshore workers voted to leave the AFL for a new CIO union. They were joined by warehouse workers, creating the ILWU.[16]

As historian Harvey Schwartz explains, the March Inland was "a dream of labor unity on the broadest scale."[17] This vision of labor unity contrasted with the chamber of commerce's horizon of "industrial peace." In turn, the conflict between these two visions and related temporal regimes created the conditions for the many trials and tribulations of Bridges.

While he worked closely with Communists and was influenced by reading Marxist labor history, Bridges insisted throughout his career that he was never a member of the party or any Communist organization. He took the ample evidence around him as indication of the existence of a class struggle. For Bridges, the labor unity represented by the ILWU projected a horizon of empowerment and freedom:

We take the stand that we as workers have nothing in common with the employers. We are in a class struggle, and we subscribe to the belief that if the employer is not in business[,] his products will still be necessary[,] and we still will be providing them when there is no employing class. We frankly believe that day is coming.[18]

At the apogee of CIO power, this conflict between horizons of "industrial peace" and "labor unity" alarmed many. The prospect of a March Inland uniting otherwise disparate workers intimidated West Coast agricultural and shipping interests, who were closely allied with the "Big Five" sugar producers in Hawai'i. After surveying the situation in San Francisco in 1936, Assistant Secretary of Labor Edward F. McGrady reported to President Roosevelt: "The shipowners have joined with organizations consisting of farmers, wholesale businessmen, manufacturers and industrialists. . . . All of them are determined to 'smash radicalism and communism' but, in reality, to destroy the maritime unions."[19]

Labor Secretary Frances Perkins received many letters alleging that Bridges was a Communist and should be investigated and/or deported. Finally, in 1936, the Immigration Service on the West Coast came up with four witnesses who claimed to have seen Bridges at Communist Party meetings.[20] These allegations eventually led to the first deportation cases against Bridges in 1938. Knowles was a central witness against Bridges in this and subsequent trials.

Time and association were key questions linking Bridges's legal trials and tribulations. Authorized by the Immigration Act of 1918, the first case against him was based entirely on allegations that he had, in the past, been a member of as well as associated with organizations that advocated the overthrow of the government. While the Labor Department proceedings against Bridges were taking place, however, the Supreme Court was working on the question of whether past membership and/or association actually constituted a deportable offense. The original 1918 statute had been written in a broad legal present tense, deeming deportable "belief in, advocacy of [,] . . . membership in [,] . . . [or] affiliation with an organization advocating or distributing literature containing proscribed views."

The 1938 deportation case against Bridges on the grounds of "past membership" in the Communist Party failed when the Supreme Court ruled in another case, *Strecker v. Kessler*, that persecution on the grounds of past activities were unconstitutional. Immediately following the Supreme Court decision in *Strecker*, the Immigration Service changed its charges to allege that Bridges was currently a Communist. After several months of testimony, Harvard University Law School dean James M. Landis found that Bridges was innocent of membership or association with the Communist Party. Consequently, Secretary of Labor Perkins dismissed the charges against him.[21]

A political furor ensued from this exoneration of Bridges. In Congress, a bill providing for the singular deportation of Bridges passed the House of Representatives in 1940. On the same day that the bill passed the House, President Roosevelt moved the Immigration Service out of the Department of Labor and into the Department of Justice, hoping to facilitate the removal of subversives like Bridges. When the bill failed to pass the full Congress, Attorney General Robert Jackson agreed to open another investigation of Bridges.[22]

As Jackson was initiating this second investigation, Congress passed the Smith or Alien Registration Act of 1940, which reversed the *Strecker* ruling on past associations. Section 23 of the Smith Act provided for the deportation of "aliens" for "past membership or association" with organizations that advocated the overthrow of the government. Because it altered temporality, making suspected prior associations grounds for contemporary accusations, this change had broad ramifications for the rights of the foreign born. Most immediately, it gave weight to new deportation charges against Bridges.

Questions of time in the trials of Bridges and other foreign-born activists led naturally to the issue of affiliation. Although freedom of association is often broadly interpreted as a civil liberty, the 1918 Immigration Act had made a deportable offense of "affiliation with an organization advocating or distributing literature containing proscribed views" by noncitizens. Further, the Smith Act made the crime of affiliation retroactive. In Bridges's case, he had worked with the Marine Workers Industrial Union (MWIU), a Communist-affiliated organization, during and after the 1934 strike; earlier in his career, he had joined the IWW. The case against Bridges turned on four points of association: his acceptance of help from Communist organizers; his ongoing work with such organizers; his public denunciations of "red-baiters"; and his work as the editor of a newsletter, the *Waterfront Worker*, originally started by the MWIU. In all four of the cases against him, the question was whether such alliances constituted a deportable offense.

Immigrant rights advocates worked to delimit the potentially broad application of the Smith Act. Carol Weiss King of the ACPFB, the lead attorney for Bridges in the first two cases, argued that neither the Immigration Act of 1918 nor the Smith Act made Bridges's acts deportable. He had worked with the MWIU, an organization that was affiliated with another organization—the Communist Party—that held "proscribed views." Although Bridges freely admitted to working with Communists and to being influenced by Marxist doctrine, King argued that his activities were a degree removed from affiliation with the actual party, mediated as it was through his work with the MWIU. Further, King drew on older jurisprudence distinguishing between "spasmodic or casual" and "permanent" relations, asserting that Bridges's relationship to the party was best described by the former and therefore did not fall under the Smith Act.[23] Essentially, King argued that Bridges's affiliation with the Communist Party took the form of transient liaisons rather than a long-term, committed relationship and that such sporadic affiliations did not make him guilty of subversion.

Led by King, the ACPFB fought the case of Bridges's Communist affiliations all the way to the Supreme Court. A *Yale Law Journal* article points out that the charges of affiliation violated a fundamental idea of punishment only for personal guilt. Further, the article also notes that many of the witnesses against Bridges were, as former Communists themselves, guilty of crimes of past association. Murray of the CIO argued that if Bridges could be found guilty of crimes of affiliation, "Every alien who seeks to build a labor organization in this country is in jeopardy and with him the labor organization that he leads."[24]

Ultimately, the Supreme Court found in 1945 that Bridges had never been a member of or associated with the Communist Party. Having been cleared of charges of past and present membership in the Communist Party, Bridges naturalized and became a citizen. A year later, he faced perjury charges for lying about his Communist Party membership during his citizenship oath. Bridges and the two ILWU organizers who stood witness for him during his naturalization ceremony, Henry Schmidt and J. R. Robertson, were convicted of conspiracy to defraud the federal government in 1950. Once again, this conviction rested on assertions about temporality and intent: that based on their supposed behavior in the past, Bridges and his friends did not plan, in the future, to be loyal Americans. While waiting for legal appeal, Bridges's bail was revoked, because a judge deemed his criticism of American involvement in the Korean War a potential danger to national security. He served three weeks of jail time.

It was precisely such "aliens" who, along with Bridges, were under attack in his many trials. The 1949 indictment against Bridges, Robertson, and Schmidt for "fraud and conspiracy" came during an important ILWU strike in Hawai'i; all three men were involved in organizing there. Attorney General Tom Clark commented, "If we are successful in our prosecution of Bridges, it may be that we can break the Hawai'ian situation without any other intervention."[25] Paying attention to changes in Hawai'i, Clark recognized that Bridges and the ILWU were involved in a profound refiguring of relationships in the territory. Like many of his contemporaries in the Cold War state, Clark feared the implications of the interracial organizing

Pecks Park gathering in San Francisco, 1946. The photo includes Harry Bridges (left center, behind the people seated in chairs, in front of the row of people standing); Joe and Doris Kaewe of the ILWU, Hawai'i (fourth and fifth from the left, at the top); and Lou Goldblatt, also of the ILWU, Hawai'i (bottom right, with the lower part of his face obscured). (Los Angeles Committee for the Protection of the Foreign Born Collection, Southern California Library [Los Angeles, California].)

and alternative spatial and temporal orders proposed by the March Inland. And, in fact, the March Inland in Hawai'i transformed politics in the territory.

The March Inland in Hawai'i

The March Inland in Hawai'i brought workers previously divided by language and loyalty together to organize for better conditions in the fields, packing houses, and docks that provided sugar to much of the world. As Asians, Europeans, and native Hawai'ians worked together to improve their access to labor rights, they also questioned the limits imposed by the colonial status of the islands, instead imagining new horizons of equality and freedom. Some workers projected a trajectory of Hawai'ian sovereignty, away from the settler-colonialist past. For others, it meant moving toward full American citizenship for the multiracial denizens of Hawai'i. The legal assault on Bridges and the other organizers was part of a broader attempt to forestall the realization of such horizons. The coalition to defend Bridges, which included the ILWU and the ACPFB, noted that the timing of renewed assaults against him coincided with the gathering momentum for interracial worker organizing in Hawaiʻi.[26]

Just as the March Inland triggered hostility from powerful shipping and agricultural interests on the West Coast, the unprecedented interracial mobilization of workers in Hawaiʻi incurred the wrath of the territory's ruling elite. Hawaiʻi was dominated by the Big Five plantation-owning families; the Big Five also controlled the Matson Navigation Company, which maintained trade between the West Coast and the territory. Matson had been affected by the 1934 strike. Its owners were concerned because of the participation in the historic San Francisco labor action by Hawaiʻian longshore organizers, such as Harry Kamoko and Levi Kealoha, and because of a sympathy strike by the Honolulu Longshoremen's Association in 1936. Historian Gerald Horne argues that Hawaiʻian labor organizers provided crucial support for the operation of the ILWU on the West Coast and for Bridges's legal defense.[27] "Marching Inland" connected workers in disparate locations in territory and mainland, forging relations of mutual aid and interdependence.

Historically, plantation owners had frustrated labor-organizing attempts among agricultural as well as transportation workers by playing different ethnoracial groups against one another. This tactic had been particularly effective against Japanese and Filipinx workers during the Oahu Sugar Strike of 1920. Together, these workers represented 77 percent of the workforce on Oahu; their different unions came together in planning the strike, which was successfully defeated by the Hawaiian Sugar Planters' Association (HSPA) and the local constabulary. Wallace Farrington, the editor of the *Honolulu Star Bulletin*, characterized strikers as "un-American" and warned of the potential power of the nonwhite majority on the islands.[28]

Subsequently, asserting the need to protect the territory against potentially hostile foreign interests, territorial authorities moved against Japanese-Hawaiʻian organizations, attacking the Japanese schools that had flourished on the islands and promoting suspicion of Japanese-Hawaiʻian disloyalty in light of the rise of Japan as an imperial power in Asia. Citing economic necessity, the HSPA shipped 11,670 Filipinx workers home during the Great Depression. During the early 1940s, anti-Japanese sentiment was deployed against further labor organization. Martial law during World War II made organizing difficult while fomenting worker discontent.[29]

Compounding repression and ethnic division in Hawaiʻi, AFL affiliates, such as the ILA, did not charter Hawaiʻian workers' unions. Historian Moon-Kie Jung credits the formation of the ILWU, which was led by Hawaiʻian as well as mainland organizers, such as Bridges, as changing the "class capacity" of Hawai'ian workers. The ILWU held meetings in multiple languages, including Japanese, English, and the Filipinx dialects of Ilocano and Visayan. It provided legal defense to leaders of the Filipinx labor organization Vibora Luriminda. After the ILWU petitioned the National Labor Relations Board (NLRB) to investigate the conditions of plantation workers on the island, Congress passed the Hawai'i Employment Relations Act, which extended the rights of collective bargaining to all agricultural laborers in Hawai'i. Where the Wagner Act of 1934 had specifically exempted agricultural and domestic workers from collective bargaining, Hawai'ian unions had succeeded in their efforts to claim labor rights for all workers.[30]

The 1946 sugar strike and the 1949 longshore strike created the first interracial labor organizations in Hawai'ian history. Jung explains that the formation of the ILWU, with its insistence on racial equality, "signaled a seldom recognized turning point in relations among Hawai'ian workers."[31]

The formation of the ILWU in Hawai'i featured current and former Communists in central roles. According to Horne, the Communist Party provided key antiracist leadership in multiracial Hawai'i, along with mainland organizers, including Louis Goldblatt, Bridges, Thompson, and Schmidt. Many Asian Hawai'ians drew on radical backgrounds from their homelands. Japanese Communists with experience in the Japanese Workers and Peasants Party immigrated to Hawai'i after the party was dissolved on the Ryukyu Islands in 1920; similarly, laborers from Okinawa brought their experiences in radical organizations there. Japanese Communist intellectual Sen Katayama wrote extensively on Hawai'i; Communist Party member Karl Yoneda became a union leader. Some of the Filipinx brought to Hawai'i as contract laborers were veterans of the Huk Resistance against the Japanese occupation of the Philippines during the war and against the government of the Philippine Republic after 1946. Filipinx labor leader Pablo Manlapit was active in the Anti-Imperial League, resulting in accusations throughout his career of being a Communist.[32] Diasporic Korean Hawai'ians, although a small population, were actively engaged in the struggle for the liberation of their homeland from Japanese and later American occupations. Peter and David Hyun, for example, participated in labor organizing in Hawai'i and advocated for the liberation of Korea from colonial rule.[33] The ILWU drew on multiple radical traditions and diverse organizers in Hawai'i.[34]

For many indigenous Hawai'ians, the ILWU addressed their long-standing sense of grievance at the hands of the Big Five and the territorial government. ILWU organizer Goldblatt described the disposition of native Hawai'ians in the 1940s:

They had lost the islands to the missionaries and to the haoles, and they wanted them back. They saw the union as the first effective fighting organization to come along.[35]

Hawai'ian natives made up a small but substantial portion of rank and file and leadership in the new unions. Many nonnative Hawai'ian laborers adopted the idea of Hawai'ian sovereignty as a part of the horizon they were working toward.[36]

While many laborers supported increased independence for Hawai'i, the ILWU also advocated granting U.S. citizenship to Filipinx in Hawai'i. The question of "insular," or territorial, citizenship was particularly pressing for Filipinx; because they had lost their ability to naturalize after Philippine independence in 1946, these workers were increasingly vulnerable to the depredations of the labor market. Sugar planters and labor contractors could deport them more or less at will. ILWU organizer Ricardo Labez argued for American citizenship for Filipinx to accompany Hawai'ian statehood. Manlapit noted that the lack of legal status among Filipinx led to the manipulation of these workers in their homeland as well as in Hawai'i; as noncitizens who were not excluded under the U.S. laws that proscribed other Asians from entering, they could be recruited in the Philippines by labor contractors and then summarily deported from Hawai'i.[37]

Claims of labor rights led to broader visions of citizenship and political subjectivity in multiracial Hawai'i. In light of postwar questions around the fate of the territory and its denizens, these claims were controversial. In Congress, opposition to statehood had long turned on the multiracial nature of Hawai'ian society. Objecting to the entry of a mixed-race, majority nonwhite territory as a state was good politics for many on the mainland. But, as pressure grew in the early Cold War period to demonstrate the racial equality of American democracy, Hawai'i became what Horne calls "a Cold War racial symbol" of democratic mixing and harmony. Farrington, who had long been an advocate for Hawai'ian statehood, elevated an interracial unity that was illegal in many states of the union at the time:

> The mingling of other races with the Hawaiian has probably furnished the foundation for the high character of American citizenship in the Hawaiian islands, citizenship where representatives of pure blooded families of the Occident and pure blooded families mingle freely on terms of social equality with pure blooded Hawaiians, and where there are mixtures of ancestry that in some instances combine in one family ancestral strains from New England, Europe, Hawaii and China.[38]

In context of an insurgent but not yet widely powerful campaign for civil rights on the mainland, the notion of Hawai'i as a paragon of mixed-race democracy was hard for some in Congress to swallow. Further, southern Democrats, such as James O. Eastland, feared the potential for Black militancy in Gulf ports—some of the same ports that Bridges had attempted to organize with the IWW. The rise of the multiracial, left-influenced ILWU precipitated a panic in Washington about Communist influence on the islands. Horne argues that fear of a Red Scare was entwined with racial anxiety about the influence of Asian Hawai'ians; fear of Asian Hawai'ians, primarily the Japanese, had long found traction in Congress and in the territory. Combined, the threats resulted in successive visits by representatives of the House Un-American Activities Committee (HUAC) to Hawai'i, the Smith Act trials of many Hawai'ian ILWU leaders, and the ongoing persecution of Bridges.[39]

In the face of these assaults, Hawai'ian laborers kept up the pressure, striking to protest the Smith Act proceedings in Honolulu as well as the jailing of Bridges in 1950. Horne writes that it "was difficult to convince the Hawai'ian working class that the Smith Act trial was about subversion of the colony, as opposed to subverting a radical movement that had uplifted the dispossessed."[40]

The many trials and tribulations of Bridges were part of a Cold War backlash against the achievements of the March Inland. Commercial interests worked alongside anti-Communists and overt white supremacists to undermine the enfranchisement of the multiracial workforce represented by the ILWU. Even Hawai'ian statehood, originally controversial because of the territory's multiracial population, eventually triumphed, in part as a way to forestall "Communist" aspirations toward sovereignty and racial democracy. In the post–World War II period, this collaboration passed itself off as patriotic Americanism, claiming the necessity of defending the nation from anti-American subversion.

Successful multiracial labor struggles in Hawai'i transformed the territory from experiencing near-feudal labor conditions to having stronger and more inclusive worker protections than the continental United States. The March Inland projected a horizon of solidarity, progress, and possibly even sovereignty for the territory. While some labor advocates supported Hawai'ian statehood as the best way to solidify labor rights, others recognized the dangers and losses that accompanied the entry of Hawai'i into the union. Multiracial solidarity, according to historian Gretchen Heefner, provided images used by statehood advocates to portray Hawai'i as a "new frontier" of racial tolerance that would contrast images of violence and repression circulating around the world. At the same time, of course, statehood forestalled many of the horizons projected by the ILWU.[41]

Militancy in the territories precipitated the persecution of labor organizers as well as a broad federal reaction in the form of new immigration legislation. Concerning itself with questions of subversion from within and of management of an ascendant American empire, the McCarran-Walter Act of 1952 reinstated national origin quotas and provided additional legal basis for the deportation of foreign-born subversives. Assuming an ongoing global U.S. military presence, the act asserted a particular vision of imperial space. The law contained detailed treatment of questions of citizenship and empire, ruling that, for example, a child born abroad to one U.S. military parent had a right to citizenship. At the same time, this law contained a specific provision aimed at foreign-born Asian workers in the territories: Section 212(d)7 restricted the entry of any "alien who shall leave Hawaii, Alaska, Guam, Puerto Rico or the Virgin Islands of the United States, and who seeks to enter the continental United States or any other place under the jurisdiction of the United States." The act specifically referred to the Tydings-McDuffy Act of 1934, which had ended Filipinx access to legal entry. As advocates at the time pointed out, the McCarran-Walter Act essentially considered Alaska and Hawai'i to be foreign countries, pointedly and only for the purposes of the immigration of Asian American workers.[42]

The advent of the McCarran-Walter Act and its immediate use to initiate deportation proceedings against Filipinx Americans caused a crisis for the ILWU and its affiliates, including the ACPFB. The next section looks at the ways in which this coalition responded to this crisis. The defense mounted by Filipinx advocates and their allies against deportation ultimately caused a rupture in the formidable Cold War space-time continuum. This rupture also enabled the final defeat of charges against Bridges.

Becoming Alien

> 1952, therefore, is the year for the great offensive of the people everywhere—in Europe, in Asia, in America, in Africa. Everywhere[,] the working people all over the world are fighting back. This struggle is carried on in various forms: by mass democratic action for more and more democracy, or by force and rebellion when the people are forced to fight for their liberation, as in Korea.[43]

Writing while fighting his deportation, journalist and cannery organizer Chris Mensalves, the president of ILWU Local 37 in Seattle, proclaimed 1952 a year of victory. Mensalves's article appears in the *1952 ILWU Local 37 Cannery Workers Yearbook*, edited by his close friend Bulosan. In it, Mensalves celebrates the formation of the union; its resistance to "the most vicious anti-labor legislation of modern times—the Taft-Hartley Law"; and the many achievements of the March Inland. Founded in the 1930s, the union affiliated as Local 7 of the United Cannery, Agricultural, Packing, and Allied Workers of America (UCAPAWA) and after 1950 as Local 37 of the ILWU. Mensalves's celebration of "the best traditions of the American people" is consistent with the broad horizon projected by the March Inland and with the migrant imaginary expressed in Bulosan's literary work.[44]

Bulosan and Mensalves met on the West Coast in the early 1930s. Both worked as transient laborers in the fields of the West Coast, traveling to Alaskan canneries for contract labor during the summers. Together, they became active in the Filipino Labor Union's efforts to organize Filipinx agricultural workers, which culminated in 1934 with strikes in Salinas, El Centro, and Vacaville, California. While these strikes were met with violence, they were also successful in organizing workers and winning small pay increases.[45]

After the strikes of 1934, Bulosan and Mensalves shared an apartment for a while in Los Angeles and published the short-lived literary magazine the *New Tide*. Bulosan was hospitalized for tuberculosis from 1936 to 1938. During this time, Mensalves continued organizing, becoming the business agent of the Portland, Oregon, cannery local and later becoming the president of Local 7 in Seattle. When he recovered enough to be discharged from the hospital, Bulosan continued to write for small magazines; he also became involved with the ACPFB's campaign for Filipinx citizenship. Bulosan moved to Seattle in 1952, editing the Local 37's 1952 *Yearbook*. He lived with Mensalves's family until his death in 1956.[46]

In his essay "The American," Bulosan articulates a broad horizon of migrant identity, tracking the agonies and losses of Americanization as well as the violence of poverty and exclusion. Like many Filipinx, the central character in "The American," Bulosan's cousin, fought on the U.S. side during World War II. He returned unwell and died shortly after learning that he would finally be allowed to naturalize. Bulosan writes, "He lives again in my undying love for the American earth. And soon, when I see the last winter coming to the last leaf, I will be warm with the thought that another wanderer shall inherit the wonderful dream which my cousin and I had dreamed and tried to realize in America."[47]

Baldoz explains the patriotism embraced by Bulosan and other Filipinx migrants during the war as "part of a larger effort launched by the Filipino American community aimed at projecting a new meaning onto the term *patriotism*, replacing its uncritical embrace of national chauvinism and the American ruling system with an aspirational allegiance to the principles of multiracial democracy and class solidarity."[48] For some, like Bulosan's cousin, service during the war resulted in citizenship; for others, it constituted defense of their Philippine and American homelands. For such activists as Mensalves, Mangaoang, and Bulosan, labor organizing was part of their patriotic commitments to their transpacific homelands; their affiliations were with the March Inland and the transnational communities it represented.

Bulosan's work on the 1952 *Yearbook* reflects the migrant imaginaries of the March Inland. On one level, the *Yearbook* documents the formation of a predominantly Filipinx American labor organization, a watermark in Filipinx American history. The *Yearbook* recounts the history of the local and the efforts to organize cannery workers in Alaska—efforts in the 1930s, a successful strike in 1946, and eventual affiliation with the ILWU in 1952. But in telling the history of the local, the activist-authors in the *Yearbook* reference broad histories of struggle. Consonant with the spatiality outlined by Bulosan's transpacific arc, an article by union secretary Mattias Lagunilla commences the history of Local 37 by talking about the anticolonial leadership of José Rizal and Apolinario Mabini. Local 37 board member and former Stanford University research associate Trinidad Rojo surveys the multiracial history of salmon canning in Alaska. Importantly, the *Yearbook* contains messages of solidarity to and from Bridges as well as in-depth coverage of the March Inland in Hawai'i. An essay about deportation by ACPFB director Abner Green is reprinted, and there is an article specifically discussing Filipinx deportability by Seattle lawyer C. T. Hatten, who represented many of the Filipinx American activists in their deportation cases. The *Yearbook*, then, documents the union and asserts the itinerant horizons of the March Inland.

Historian Dorothy Fujita-Rony explains that Filipinx migrants arrived in the United States with an understanding of labor struggles back home. On the West Coast, labor organizing brought them in contact with other workers of color as well as Euro-Americans. The acculturation of these migrants, then, was into the "March Inland," with its multiracial solidarity among itinerant agricultural and cannery workers. Nayan Shah argues for the liberatory potential of transient alliances like these:

> The unconventional yet widespread sociability of migrants reveals neglected models for democratic livelihood and distributions of ideas, resources, and social well-bring. Exchanges between strangers of feelings, beliefs, ideas, and actions have the capacity to create new ethical, political, and social formations of civil living and participation.[49]

In contrast to this multiracial migrant solidarity, the coordinates of the McCarran-Walter Act, passed in 1952, attempted to bound the nation in space and station it along a progressive temporality of assimilation into patriotic loyalty. For the purposes of immigration policy, the law converted Alaska and Hawai'i into foreign territories occupied by "aliens" whose potential entry threatened the American body politic. The law also reiterated the nativist impetus of the Tydings-McDuffy Act: the Philippines, once a colony, was now to be considered a foreign nation for the purposes of immigration. The McCarran-Walter Act removed the ban on Asian naturalization but set national origin quotas very low; migration from the Philippines was capped at one hundred per year. Filipinx who had previously entered the United States under the special imperial provision for them as "non-alien nationals" now became solely aliens. Despite their acculturation, such migrants as Bulosan and Mensalves now had no legal standing in their adoptive homelands.[50]

The McCarran-Walter Act also implemented substantial antisubversive provisions, barring the entry of suspected subversives and expanding the grounds for deportation because of "past membership" in proscribed organizations. This law made the position of Filipinx who identified with the broad horizons of the March Inland particularly precarious. Bulosan was blacklisted, greatly reducing the limited income he had managed to receive as a writer. Accused of "past membership" in the Communist Party and now viewed as "aliens" excludable on reentry from Alaska, such labor leaders as Mangaoang and Mensalves faced deportation charges.

The ACPFB fought their deportations, and Mensalves and Mangaoang eventually won their cases. Mangaoang's was the more protracted struggle, becoming a cause célèbre in labor and immigrant advocacy circles. Except in Filipinx and advocacy circles, the case had a far more limited circulation than did the Bridges case. Even though the ACPFB united foreign-born activists of different national origins, the broader Cold War racial context created divisions between them. The notion of Filipinx and other migrants as "alien" undermined popular sympathies for the struggles of the foreign born against deportation. Persistent racial divisions limited the impact of immigrant rights advocacy on mainstream popular discourses. Still, the Mangaoang case had profound implications for the rights of the foreign born.

Like Bridges, Mangaoang was accused of "past membership" in the Communist Party because of his success in organizing Filipinx migrant laborers. Local 37 provided key leadership to Filipinx workers. The union hall in Seattle served as a kind of community center, offering an alternative to work in the fields for itinerant laborers during the summer months.

Along with thirty other Filipinx, Mangaoang was arrested on the grounds of subversive activities in 1950. Subsequently, the Department of Justice issued deportation orders for Mangaoang and other labor leaders. The timing of these initial arrests is noteworthy, because it corresponded with widespread raids against foreign-born organizers after the passage of the McCarran Act and because 1950 was also the year when the cannery union affiliated with the ILWU as part of the March Inland. These deportations threatened the progress and interracial solidarity of the March Inland. Earl George of the Seattle Chapter of the National Negro Labor Council explained, "We view the persecution against Ernesto Mangaoang as a threat to the civil liberties of every Negro citizen in America."[51]

Mangaoang's potential deportability as an "undesirable alien" was enhanced by the passage of the McCarran-Walter Act. After 1952, the federal case against Filipinx reentering from Alaska treated them as "aliens" coming from "foreign" territory rather than as "non-alien nationals" returning home. These deportation cases, then, were part of the attempt by the McCarran-Walter Act to remap the relations between territories and empire and purposely denaturalize itinerant Filipinx American laborers.

In 1949, Filipinx laborer Arcadio Cabebe sued to have a passport issued so that he could travel from Hawai'i to Guam. The Ninth Circuit Court of Appeals found that Cabebe had no right to travel as a U.S. national. In explaining its decision, the court asserted the sovereignty of the United States and the Philippines, erasing a historical and ongoing colonial relationship:

> In light of the un-deviating, non-imperialistic policy of the government of the United States, it seems to us that the expression, "people of the Philippines" is all-inclusive excepting only those who have by their own volition taken authorized steps to separate themselves from a national relationship to the government of the Philippines.[52]

The court's decision in *Cabebe*, like the deportation cases against Local 37 organizers, categorized Filipinx as undesirable aliens. Both created rigid and impermeable national boundaries, denying the transpacific experiences of migrant workers as well as their interconnections. Further, in asserting an "un-deviating, non-imperialistic" federal policy, these cases necessarily tinkered with temporality, changing the historical record to create neat geographic boundaries not muddied by the history of empire. As transients, Filipinx workers inhabited a temporality that, as it turned out, was uniquely positioned to disrupt this federal imagining of long-term, seamless national boundaries.

Mangaoang was born in the Philippines in 1902, four years after the Treaty of Paris ended the Spanish-American War and Puerto Rico, Guam, and the Philippines became U.S. possessions. Like Bulosan, Mensalves, and many other migrants of his generation, he came to the United States in 1926 and never left. Working as a transient agricultural laborer, Mangaoang became involved in attempts to better labor conditions during the 1930s, as had Mensalves and Bulosan. He headed the Portland UCAPAWA during the early 1940s, a time when cannery work was becoming increasingly dominated by Filipinx labor. In 1944, when the Portland local was absorbed by the Seattle union, Mangaoang moved to Seattle, becoming the business agent for Local 37. Together, Mangaoang and Mensalves led the successful 1948 asparagus workers strike in Stockton, California.[53]

Work conditions in the Alaska canneries were grim. Workers depended on contractors for their wages, for food and shelter during their time in Alaska, and for transportation to the territory. They encountered rundown, segregated barracks and difficult and dangerous work conditions. As with the "blue book" system on the docks in West Coast ports, cannery workers were coerced into joining company unions. Cannery workers struck unsuccessfully in 1946, signing a contract for substantial wage increases after a long period of negotiation in 1947. Ted Daddeo, a Local 37 trustee, wrote:

> I have known years when cannery workers worked in Alaska, lived like pigs, and came back to Seattle with nothing. Those were the years of labor racketeering and exploitation. . . . Those were the years when the unorganized worker had no chance to ask for higher wages and better living conditions.[54]

As with the case against Bridges, the case against Mangaoang and the other Local 37 organizers turned on questions of time and space. In pursuing these cases, the federal government denied the connections forged through empire: Bulosan's transpacific arc. Further, these cases attempted to turn the clock back on the March Inland. By targeting migrants whose acculturation had brought them into the collective itinerant imaginary, these deportation cases denied the multiracial horizons of the March Inland, attempting to impose a temporality of assimilation and loyalty instead. By winning the Mangaoang case, then, the ACPFB recast the horizons of the March Inland, broadcasting the itinerant imaginary into the early Cold War period.

In combatting his deportation, Mangaoang asserted that he could not be deported, because he was not an alien; as a "national" born in U.S. territory, he had never "entered" the United States. This assertion defied the McCarran-Walter Act's careful separation of the world into nation and territorial foreign countries. Further, in refusing to recognize national boundaries, it ratified Bulosan's transpacific geography. Essentially geo-

precedent for residency rights

graphic in nature, this argument created a precedent for residency rights for the Filipinx Americans who had arrived before Philippine independence in 1934.[55]

Because the case against Mangaoang turned on the vexed issue of "past membership" in the Communist Party, Mangaoang and his advocates also took on the issue of time. Defense attorney John Caughlan revisited the *Strecker* decision, which had held deportable only "aliens who *are* members" [emphasis added]. Neither the Smith nor the McCarran Act had succeeded in making past Communist Party membership by legal residents or citizens a deportable offense. His legal team argued that Mangaoang had never been a member of the Communist Party *and* an alien *at the same time.* As an ACPFB press release explains: "Appellant next says that even if he has been an alien since 1946, he was not an alien but a national of the United States prior to that time and particularly in the years 1938 and 1939[,] when he was a member of the Communist Party."[56]

If Mangaoang had not been, simultaneously, an alien and a subversive, then this legitimated the alternative claims of the migrant imaginary. Advocate C. T. Hatten argued that "Filipino Americans who have spent their lives under the American flag in useful work and endeavor according to due principles of democracy should not now be treated suddenly as unwanted foreigners."[57]

This reversal of coercive Cold War temporal and spatial forces was significant, because it undermined not only the federal case against Filipinx leaders, such as Mangaoang and Mensalves, but also the temporality of the entire assault against foreign-born "past members." Victory in the Mangaoang case affirmed the alternate temporality of the March Inland and created a space for "twilight zone" Filipinx to claim citizenship. Further, this affirmation of alternate temporality may well have set the stage for the final exoneration of Bridges; in the fourth and final case against him, the Supreme Court dismissed a long-standing attempt to denaturalize him, on the grounds that the statute of limitations on such accusations had long expired.

Of course, victory in the Mangaoang and Mensalves cases did not stop the persecution of foreign-born activists for good, or even for long. Many of the antisubversive protocols of the McCarran Act remained on the books, to be mobilized against foreign-born and even domestic activists during the 1960s. And the USA PATRIOT Act added to the playbook. So, what do we learn from the stories of Mangaoang and Bridges?

For one thing, these stories point to connections between the struggles of different foreign-born people. The case against Bridges, an Anglophone white man, received national publicity, whereas the struggles of Mangaoang circulated only in the Filipinx and immigrant rights communities.

However, advocacy for Mangaoang by the ACPFB was successful in not only defending him against deportation but also temporarily disrupting the Cold War order, to the benefit of many actual and potential deportees around the country.

The stories of Bridges and Mangaoang and the March Inland further point the way toward thinking about "rights" in a transnational, migrant context. Rather than being grounded in the nation, migrant rights claims are contingent and contextual; as Monisha das Gupta writes, it is often the "constant, versatile encounters with these co-constituated contradictions rather than their resolution" that invigorate social movements for justice.

The March Inland organized workers who had migrated from across the Pacific, from such U.S. territories as the Philippines and Hawai'i and from other settler-colonial nations, including Australia. Defying repressive and racially exclusive ideas of Americanization, the March Inland proceeded east, from the docks to the trains and the trucks, to the packing houses and the fields. As this chapter explains, the success of this campaign resulted in deportation campaigns against many organizers. Although it was targeted by the antisubversive campaigns of the Cold War, the ILWU survives today as an exceptionally progressive organization that is concerned with the global politics of workers and cargo.

The next chapter reverses the motion of the March Inland, focusing on struggles over the rights of workers at sea. Foreign-born maritime laborers existed in a gray zone quite similar to the "twilight zone" inhabited by Filipinx after 1934. Just as work with the March Inland expanded and transformed the ACPFB, representing the struggles of a multiracial maritime labor force created new challenges in a global arena traversed by sailors and remapped by postwar geopolitical imperatives.

PORTS OF ENTRY, EXCLUSION, AND REMOVAL

"Alien" Seamen

Free men should be treated as free men.
Merchant Seamen are the ambassadors
of good will throughout the world.
—JOSEPH CURRAN, president,
  National Maritime Union, 1953

In October 1945, 171 Indonesian sailors employed by Dutch and British fleets refused to ship out of New York. Many of them had seen service in war zones; some had only recently been released from Nazi concentration camps, where they had been held as prisoners of war. Well aware of the civil war raging in their homeland, these maritime laborers "refused to work on ships . . . taking men and munitions to murder their families in Indonesia."[1]

The National Maritime Union (NMU) provided support during their strike. Because strikers feared white supremacy in New York, the NMU found quarters for them at the Harlem Salvation Army United Service Organization on 124th Street; they received a warm reception in Harlem. Paul Robeson and Jamaican-born NMU leader Ferdinand Smith joined the strikers on one of the Dutch ships. Subsequently, the NMU voted to boycott all ships carrying military cargo to the Dutch in Indonesia.[2]

While Indonesian sailors struck international ports, including New York, Baltimore, Los Angeles, and San Francisco, republican forces in Indonesia fought against the Dutch colonial government. These anticolonial forces were led by Sukarno, who later became the first president of independent Indonesia in 1949. A broad strike of marine and dock workers in Australia, supported by the Australian Communist Party, resulted in the return of Indonesian strikers from Australia to republican territory.[3]

After the New York strikers' thirty-day transit visas expired, the Immigration and Naturalization Service (INS) detained them at Ellis Island.

As Asian "aliens ineligible to citizenship," the Indonesian sailors had no right to enter the country. As the strike spread, other Indonesian sailors were interned at Terminal Island in Los Angeles Harbor, which had previously served as temporary lodgings for Japanese Americans en route to internment camps and would subsequently be used to house foreign-born dissidents pending their deportation hearings. Arguing that the strikers' visa overstay constituted illegal entry, U.S. Attorney General Tom Clark petitioned for the deportation of detained Indonesians to the custody of the Dutch East Indian government.

The American Committee for the Protection of the Foreign Born (ACPFB) defended the detained Indonesian sailors against deportation, publicizing their cases in its newsletter, *The Lamp*. The ACPFB also advocated for a small cohort of Indonesian Americans, such as Philip Sumampow, who had arrived as a sailor in the Dutch fleet, jumped ship, and settled in the United States, later finding himself targeted for deportation. The coalition supporting the strikers also included the NMU and its parent union, the Congress of Industrial Organizations (CIO); the National Lawyers Guild; the Civil Rights Congress (CRC); and Indonesia American ethnic organizations, such as the Indonesian League of America, the American Committee for Indonesian Independence, and the Indonesian Association of America.

Together, these groups created the Emergency Committee for Indonesian Seamen, which was chaired by Max Yergan, the codirector with Robeson of the Council on African Affairs. Protests against the deportations of the Indonesian sailors took place across the country; the largest, at Webster Hall in New York City, drew a crowd of eight hundred.[4]

These strikes attracted international attention. At a meeting in London, George Padmore, writing for the Pan-African federation, called for all seamen of color to join in the strike against Dutch shipping. In the same vein, a *Chicago Defender* editorial recognized the significance of the strikes in New York and Sydney and pointed out the parallels between antiracist and anti-imperialist struggles:

Whether the strike is to protect a native government or a dislike to again return under the colonial yoke is insignificant. Both causes are akin and are of high moral value. The important feature is that the action clearly demonstrates a re-awakening of the native seamen, and shows their determination to oppose a vicious system of white exploitation.[5]

In its public advocacy, the coalition drew on a wartime grammar of heroism in the service of democracy, reminding readers of the sacrifice of

Indonesian seamen during the war. They argued that the service of these workers to the cause of world democracy justified their actions in support of democracy for Indonesia. A letter written by the Indonesian Club of America explained, "They are revolting against undemocratic rule, monopolies, slave wages (20 cents a day), discrimination, and concentration camps, which the Dutch practiced before the war."[6]

The Supreme Court refused to hear arguments against a court of appeals ruling to deport the seamen back to Indonesia, despite the defense's position that "the U.S. was born out of a revolution like the one in Indonesia." Because the seamen had no right to enter the country, their visa overstays constituted illegal entry. But the INS eventually responded to arguments honed by the ACPFB that this deportation would violate U.S. policy against returning political refugees back to their homelands. The ACPFB drew on the new language of international refugee policy to assert that Indonesian strikers had a "well-founded fear" of persecution by the Dutch colonial government.[7] Although they were not able to prevent deportation, advocates gained enough traction to moderate it. In Indonesia, the Red Cross gave the deported sailors food and clothing and then turned them over to republicans rather than to the Dutch colonial government. Little is known about what happened to them after their return to Indonesia.[8]

The strike of the Indonesian sailors and their ensuing struggle against deportation reveals the emergence of an immigrant rights movement that linked the global process of decolonization to domestic struggles over civil rights. Just as the migrant trajectories of the March Inland shaped the immigrant rights advocacy that successfully defended Bridges and Mangaoang from deportation and cleared space for Filipinx citizenship, this postwar immigrant rights coalition emerged out of a multiracial, anticolonial imaginary. Striking Indonesian sailors and the coalition defending them against deportation linked the liberation of their homelands to their fight for rights on board ships and in docks around the world. Premised on an oceanic, connective sense of space, this nautical imaginary contested the enhanced securitization of national boundaries and insurgent multinational corporate formations in the early Cold War period.

The ACPFB represented the foreign born as deserving of rights and respect because of their status as workers and their denizenship in American fields and ships. In the case of maritime labor, the ACPFB had advocated for a "Seaman's Bill of Rights" since 1940. Consistent with the "expedited naturalization" made available to noncitizens in the armed forces by the 1942 War Powers Act, this legislation would have guaranteed citizenship to any foreign-born sailor serving in the U.S. merchant marine for three years or more. After the war, the ACPFB's advocacy of onboard rights began to conflict with more mainstream ideas about gradual assimilation through residence on land. The nautical imaginary of marine labor shaped the immigrant rights work of the ACPFB; it also put the organization at odds with insurgent Cold War practices regarding borders and time.[9]

Transnational maritime laborers and the immigrant rights coalition waged struggles at the docks and at sea over rights as workers, citizens, and denizens. They asserted an internationalist practice of citizenship that certified portable rights at sea and on land, regardless of national origins. For a brief moment after World War II, they succeeded. In the immediate postwar period, this coalition created an extraordinary exception in American labor history: the extension of protections modeled on the rights of presumptively white citizen-workers to foreign-born, even nonresident, maritime laborers. This radical model of citizenship and rights presented alternate conceptions of space and time infused by the oceanic imaginary.

As they had during the March Inland, shipping interests reacted against radical innovation. Pressuring for the deportation of organizers, they prevailed on the federal government to delimit the power of labor organizing. This opposition took place in the context of heightened global concern about the power and subversive infiltration of maritime unions, so that deportations of foreign-born sailors were often in response to transnational pressure through diplomatic channels.

Shipping owners also pushed back against the radical spatiality of the oceanic imaginary, increasingly resorting to registering their vessels as "flags of convenience" ships in nations lacking protections for maritime workers. Yet while they pressed the federal government to enforce borders, shipping interests and their allies deployed Cold War geopolitical alliances to elude them, creating onboard workplaces that avoided regulation.

The coalition for maritime labor rights achieved temporary success in the immediate postwar period, forcing ship owners to consolidate an extranational "flag of convenience" system. Eventually, the prevalence of these "runaway ships" cleared the decks for "runaway shops" in other industries, providing a means for American-owned companies to continue to exploit the legal vulnerabilities of foreign-born and increasingly stateless workers. Postwar struggles at the docks took place in the contradictory context of a profound narrowing of citizenship on the one hand and extranational innovation on the other. Cold War political pressure narrowed definitions of national citizenship through such laws as the McCarran and McCarran-Walter acts at the same time the flag of convenience system transformed domestic commercial shipping into an international fleet.

An intrinsically global enterprise, shipping was also the site of coercive intervention against the transnationalism of the nautical imaginary. This intervention presaged later neoliberal developments, such as the Border

Industrialization Program, which rendered economic borders porous at the same time that national borders and citizenship practices remained rigid and exclusionary.[10]

The oceanic imaginary of transnational migrant labor transformed immigrant rights advocacy. As a workforce, maritime labor was ideologically diverse, multiracial, and polycultural. It included Communists, anarchists, nationalists, and sailors who did not think of themselves as political. Expanding to represent this multinational, migrant workforce changed the ACPFB's capacity and alliances. Working in coalition with maritime labor unions and ethnic organizations, as it did in the case of the Indonesian sailors, the ACPFB made new alliances in migrant communities. The coalition supporting the Indonesian strikers in the United States emerged out of Communist-influenced Popular Front organizations, such as the ACPFB, the CRC, and the CIO. But the nautical imaginary of maritime labor influenced these organizations and the trajectory of immigrant rights organizing in the postwar period.

This chapter tracks the entwined development of the ACPFB and maritime labor unions from the origins of the NMU in the mid-1930s through the 1963 Supreme Court decision that ratified the essentially rights-less status of maritime laborers on "flag of convenience" ships. While this ruling represented a significant blow to the rights of this transnational workforce, I argue that the oceanic imaginary of maritime labor crucially shaped immigrant rights organizing during this period. Assertions of transnational rights expanded the immigrant rights network in the immediate postwar period, laying the groundwork for ongoing struggles of migrants for justice throughout the twentieth and into the twenty-first centuries.

The Oceanic Imaginary

The twentieth-century growth of commercial shipping in the United States drew laborers from around the world. On the East and Gulf Coasts, workers from the Caribbean and Latin American were a growing minority as early as 1915; Asian sailors made up a substantial part of the crews of Pacific vessels. Even as their labor became more crucial to the shipping industry, these workers faced discrimination based on their race and national origins on board ship as well as in port.

Sailors were a uniquely international labor force. On board ship, sailors were often divided by race and nation of origin. Scandinavians were traditionally the deck sailors, with English-speaking workers, including the Irish, working in the engine room. Asian and Black sailors were often confined to serving as stewards. The employment of Asian and Afro-diasporic workers sometimes occasioned divisions on ships and in maritime unions. The International Seamen's Union advocated Asian exclusion and decried the employment of Chinese and Filipinx workers as bringing down wages and conditions for white workers. Asian and Black seamen experienced discrimination in such ports as Johannesburg, Durban, Galveston, and Wilmington.[11]

Typical of many Caribbean migrants to the United States, Jamaican-born Ferdinand Smith first migrated to Panama and Cuba in search of employment. Leaving a virulently anti-Back climate in Cuba, which included deportations of many Jamaican workers, Smith found work on an American ship as a steward and came first to Mobile, Alabama, in 1918. In Gulf ports, Smith found work opportunities in a very segregated context. Many Gulf ports, such as Galveston, denied Black sailors shore leave or required that they be incarcerated in city jails while their ships were in port.[12]

Like Smith, West Indian–born Hugh Mulzac confronted many kinds of racism over the course of his career at sea. His first encounter with U.S. racism came on his first voyage as an ordinary seaman, in 1907. The ship docked in Wilmington, North Carolina, where Mulzac was forbidden to enter church on a Sunday because of a state law against the integration of congregations. Mulzac went on to serve in the U.S. merchant marine during World War I, after which he became a U.S. citizen and took the exam to become a ship's captain, becoming the first African American to obtain captain's papers. After much searching and many rejections based on his race, he captained his first ship in Marcus Garvey's Black Star Line, which went out of business in 1922. He went on to become the captain of the merchant marine ship *Booker T. Washington* in 1942.[13]

Mulzac and Smith proclaimed oceanic imaginings of labor and rights. Communist organizers stood against Jim Crow on ship and on shore; they also recognized the uniquely precarious position of Asian seamen because of immigration restrictions. Both men were drawn into the NMU, where Smith became an important organizer. Eventually Smith and Mulzac became involved in the ACPFB as it took on individual cases and broader issues involving foreign-born maritime laborers.[14]

As the U.S. commercial fleet expanded under the Merchant Marine Act of 1936, many of its workers lacked representation. The maritime labor unions that existed excluded nonwhite sailors from membership. Even among sailors permitted to join, union membership declined during the 1920s due to the open-shop incentive, which made it more difficult to organize maritime workers. Influenced by the formation of the International Longshore and Warehouse Union (ILWU) and the March Inland, maritime laborers began to organize during the mid-1930s. In 1934, Al Lannon of the Marine Workers Industrial Union organized a centralized shipping bureau in Baltimore. The lack of a centralized place to obtain jobs had long been a key issue among maritime laborers, as it was among longshore workers. The shipping bureau rationalized the hiring process, eliminating often exploitative middlemen, called crimps, and ending the frenzy of the shape-up, in which hundreds of men at the docks competed for the favor of work on board ship.[15]

In March 1936, the crew of the New York–based SS *California* docked in San Pedro, California, and demanded conditions equal to the ones prevailing on the Pacific Coast. The ship was owned by J. P. Morgan's International Merchant Marine. Led by Bo'sun Joe Curran, sailors on the *California* initiated an unauthorized strike. Secretary of Labor Frances Perkins promised that their grievances would be adjudicated when they returned to their home port of New York City. On return to New York, however, crew members had their pay docked, and many of the leaders of the action were not rehired for further voyages. The International Seamen's Union declined to represent the fired sailors.[16]

Port organizers formed a Seamen's Defense Committee in New York in response to this incident, and Smith and Curran were two of the nine men elected to it. Smith was the only African American elected. Subsequently, marine laborers on the East Coast struck again, in solidarity with another Pacific Coast strike. As the National Maritime Union emerged on the East Coast, Smith became a union leader. Along with other sailors of color, Smith put the issue of desegregating ships and of ending the Jim Crowing of Black sailors in Gulf ports at the forefront of the new union's agenda.[17] Mulzac writes:

> Most important for me was the inclusion of a clause in the [NMU] constitution providing that there should be *no discrimination against any union member because of his race, color, political creed, religion, or national origin.* . . . [I]t is to the lasting honor of the NMU that, like the ILWU among shoreside workers, it was the first maritime union to establish this basic principle and to enforce it. [Emphasis in original.][18]

The internationalism of marine labor enabled the emergence of the NMU by the late 1930s.

During World War II, the NMU pledged to "keep 'em sailing," despite the rigors of life on board ship and the high mortality rate: close to six thousand sailors perished during the war. In the context of the wartime labor shortage, adherence to restrictions regarding the nationality and citizenship of marine workers proved tricky. While a 1943 estimate noted that only 10 percent of graduates of the U.S. Maritime Service Schools set up as a component of the Merchant Marine Act were naturalized Americans, transnational marine laborers anxious to vie for the comparably better wages and living conditions on U.S. ships abounded on the docks.[19]

These conditions created a wartime version of what literary scholar Claudia Sadowski-Smith describes as an "illegality spiral." A vast undocumented or, in the parlance of the time, "alien seamen" labor pool took on the dangerous work of ensuring the delivery of military materiel along with the overall preservation of international business transactions during the war. An "illegality spiral" was created by the combination of demand for labor and for jobs on the one hand and political crises over the existence of noncitizen workers on the other.[20] Further, during and briefly after the war years, the labor rights conferred by the Merchant Marine or Jones Act of 1920 on citizen seamen were broadly construed to extend to all maritime workers toiling on U.S. and Allied ships.

By 1942, an estimated eight thousand "alien seamen" were sought by the U.S. Maritime Commission to work on U.S. and Allied ships. The NMU organized these as well as native-born maritime laborers. While nonnational marine laborers were sought during the war years, the federal government made a concurrent effort to deport "deserters" from Allied ships who overstayed their shore leave, becoming undocumented workers in the United States. During the war, the Department of Justice set up a "Foreign Seamen's Program" to stop desertion, regulate deportation, and ensure the continued operation of the U.S. merchant marine and allied fleet. The ACPFB supported this program during the war, even though it contained provisions for the detention and deportation of foreign-born sailors who came ashore in the United States and did not choose to ship out. As the U.S. left came to see the war as a global struggle against fascism, the ACPFB rallied ethnic communities in support of the war effort, even backing the deportation of foreign-born sailors who were not willing to serve in the merchant marine. Like the Indonesian strikers after the war, many such "deserters" were detained at Rikers Island and at Ellis Island, which was transitioning in this period from being a port of entry to a detention station.[21]

While serving in the war effort, Asian seamen struggled against the limitations on their rights to shore leave, which essentially rendered them prisoners on board ship. A provision of the Immigration Act of 1924 stipulated that no alien seamen excludable for admission would be permitted to land for any purposes but temporary medical treatment.[22] Asian maritime laborers were caught between the Seaman's Bill's certification of a human right to desert and the prerogatives of national immigration policy. New York had effectively become the home port for many Chinese seamen during the war, yet they were forbidden to disembark there.

In the wake of several incidents during which Chinese crew members attempted to disembark, even in one case coming to blows with the British ship's captain, the New York–based Chinese Association of Labor negotiated improved wages and working conditions as well as shore leave for Chinese seamen with the British merchant marine. Chinese workers serving in the British fleet continued to allege harsh treatment and racial discrimination. The lack of shore leave in American ports also remained an issue. Chinese workers were still "aliens ineligible to citizenship" and therefore unable to leave ship except under a guard provided by ship agents.[23] In response, by the summer of 1942, the War Authority had initiated a policy of "free gangway" for Chinese seamen. This policy, however, contributed to the illegality spiral among marine laborers, as an estimated fourteen to fifteen thousand Chinese workers employed in the British and Dutch merchant marine came through New York, with its possibilities of alternate employment.[24]

The status of Asian seamen remained uncertain throughout the war. On the one hand, the high rate of desertion resulted in the War Authority's attempting to prohibit the employment of Chinese seamen on U.S. and Allied ships. On the other hand, the ACPFB and Chinese American organizations pressed for broader rights and set up seamen's clubs to welcome Chinese marine laborers—when they were allowed shore leave. These organizations were part of the coalition pressing for immigrant rights after the war.[25]

Many Asian seamen recognized parallels between their struggles and those of other seamen of color. Chinese seamen rioted against discrimination in Capetown in 1942. A *Chicago Defender* editorial notes:

> The men held that nowhere in the world had they been discriminated against on color grounds except in Durban and Capetown. Their country was an ally of Britain and America, they argued, and they deserved better treatment from the white races they were helping as much as China's in risking their lives carrying war supplies.[26]

For maritime labor, the war was a heady moment of transnational unity, power, and possibility. A journalist commented at the time, "Since a great proportion of the shipping affected falls within the lend-lease provisions, and since it is operated in a single cause, seamen insist that equality in wages and living conditions should be the obvious answer to equality in purpose and the dangers faced at sea."[27]

The ACPFB and the NMU advocated for the labor rights of foreign crews on American and foreign flag ships. Curran identified the particular need for organizing on foreign registry ships in 1940: "Ships are transferred to foreign flags primarily in order that the companies may avoid paying American wages and establishing American working conditions."[28]

Recognizing oceanic connections, Abner Green argued against the deportation of British sailors in the United States illegally in 1943. In opposing these deportations, Green acknowledged the internationalism of the maritime workforce:

> [The bill allowing for deportation] would help freeze existing low wages and intolerable working conditions on foreign flag ships to the detriment of American working conditions and our war program for victory. It would be a precedent easily applicable to similar conditions in American industry.[29]

Using the exigencies of wartime, the ACPFB and the NMU created space to assert rights for maritime workers, regardless of race or national origin. Even in the context of their wartime heroism, the oceanic, internationalist affiliations of this workforce occasioned repression. While the ACPFB continued to argue for labor and citizenship rights for foreign-born laborers after the war, insurgent anti-Communist sentiment challenged the alternate Americanism of maritime labor and the political coalition it relied on.

Fighting Deportation on the Docks

In its postwar advocacy for rights for maritime labor, the ACPFB emphasized that the war had been won by international cooperation and that transnational marine laborers had played a heroic role in the struggle against fascism by keeping Allied shipping lanes open. Advancing the expansion of rights of foreign-born sailors after the war, the ACPFB favored legal entry into the United States for alien seamen with at least a year's service in the merchant marine and the option of naturalization with three years of service. A 1945 article in *The Lamp* exhorts against extending the Foreign Seamen's Program after the war:

> Foreign seamen are entitled to at least equal treatment to that of all other aliens. Many of them have performed great and heroic service to the United States during the war.[30]

Supportive legislators, including Representatives Claude Pepper of Florida and Vito Marcantonio and Emanuel Celler of New York, introduced several bills in Congress to grant marine laborers these rights. Pepper recognized the international nature of the maritime war effort: "Our Maritime Service is perhaps the most international of all our services. Men

ACPFB flyer advocating for foreign-born maritime labor. (American Committee for the Protection of the Foreign Born Papers, #086, Tamiment Library/Robert F. Wagner Labor Archives, New York University. Used by permission of Ruth Gollobin-Basta.)

from countries overrun by the enemy who have lost family and friends have found it possible to contribute to victory in this way." In 1947, President Harry Truman signed a bill granting waivers to noncitizen seamen that allowed them to remain in port.[31]

But by the late 1940s, the central struggle in U.S. political discourse had changed. It emphasized the threat of global Communism rather than the one posed by fascist totalitarianism. Successful strikes in the immediate postwar period evidenced the strength of labor as it emerged from the war. The backlash against these strikes targeted the labor movement through restrictive legislation, such as the Taft-Hartley Act of 1947, and through repeated scares about Communist union leadership. As labor advocacy became suspect, foreign-born workers were vulnerable to deportation for "un-American activities." The patriotic case for rights for transnational marine laborers began to crack at its foundation. The Department of Justice, for example, went out of its way to oppose a bill to grant citizenship and legal entry for service that had been introduced in the House by Representative Celler in 1948.[32]

Maritime laborers responded to the realignments of the postwar period. They opposed the political narrowing of the Cold War and fought for transnational alliances and human rights. Foreign-born organizers, such as Smith, recognized the connections between rights for the foreign born, the desegregation of maritime labor, and global struggles against colonialism. Mulzac writes about his growing awareness of the function of global racial capitalism during his tenure as chief cook on board the cruise ship *Polk* before the war:

Was not our fight for a decent life for ourselves inseparable from the struggle of Indonesians against the Dutch? The Congolese against the Belgians? The Algerians against the French? The Kenyans against the British? Or the Cubans against Batista and his American cohorts? Or the Haitians and Dominicans against their respective dictators? The essential thing to grasp seemed to me then, and seems to me still, that we are *one people* in *one world, and that our battles are inseparable.* [Emphasis in original.][33]

Having experienced ports all over the world, rank-and-file sailors recognized these parallels between liberation struggles. The increased internationalism of the war years and the success of maritime organizations in obtaining better work conditions and control expanded the political awareness of maritime workers.

The formation of the Federation of Greek Maritime Unions (FGMU) in 1943 had been a high-water mark of wartime internationalism.[34] By October 1942, Greece was occupied by the Nazis, with the national government in exile in London. Half of the prewar Greek fleet had been lost to the fight against the Axis powers. Greek maritime laborers began during the war to press for union terms in their labor, hoping to end the unsanitary living conditions, low wages, and poor food prevalent in the Greek fleet. In 1943, the FGMU, representing about 80 percent of Greek international seamen, signed a historic contract with Greek ship owners. Although this agreement met with opposition from the Greek government in exile, international support for maritime laborers as heroes bolstered the cause of unionization. The union went on to establish offices in New York, Cardiff, Buenos Aires, London, and Durham, South Africa, and allied with the International Transport Workers' Federation (ITF).[35]

As early as 1945, however, the FGMU was reporting an effort, backed by the Greek Consulate in Britain, to discharge more militant union members in favor of more compliant workers. The Voulagaris government reinstated a state union, the "Piraeus Seamen's Federation" or Panhellenic Federation (PNO), which it approved to represent seamen. FGMU members taken off ships in Britain were then refused employment on other ships, becoming, essentially, undocumented migrants. In South Africa, in January 1945, twenty-nine Greek seamen were taken off two ships and sent to detention. These seamen were eventually transferred to Britain for trial by the Greek Maritime Court, which had by that time disbanded. They too became stateless in Britain, blacklisted from signing onto Greek ships and dependent on the public relief they could obtain.[36]

By 1947, the Greek government had signed an agreement with national shipping companies annulling the 1943 FGMU contract. The FGMU was outlawed, its offices in Greece closed, and its leaders arrested and sentenced to death. The government outlawed demands for overtime pay, extra pay for extra work, and better food conditions, all components of the 1943 agreement. Deploying transnational diplomacy against the FGMU, the Greek Consul circulated to U.S. and British governments a list of seamen who had been active in the FGMU or violated the new laws. This list went over and above the ongoing existence of the despised "fink book," papers that every seaman was required to carry to ship out. By transmitting its list to the State Department, the Greek government inaugurated a transnational practice of blacklisting that became commonplace during the decades that followed. This practice worked against the oceanic transnationalism of maritime organizing.[37]

Transnational repression of oceanic organizing entailed a Cold War imagination of a world divided into Communist and democratic zones. The FGMU had been politically inclined toward anarchism, but in a climate charged with anti-Communism, the idea promulgated by the Greek government that the FGMU was dangerously subversive found an attentive audience in Washington. Attorney General Tom Clark wrote in 1949:

> The [State] Department is in the possession of satisfactory evidence, of a nature that it would not be in the public interest to disclose, concerning the character and objectives of the Federation of Greek Maritime Unions. The character and objectives of this organization are plainly contradictory to the public interest of the United States. That being the case, it is the general policy to effect a formal deportation of alien members of such organizations who have rendered themselves subject to deportation, in order that they may be barred from reentering the U.S., and in order that if they do attempt to reenter after such deportation, without obtaining prior permission, they may be subject to criminal persecution.[38]

Edward J. Ennis, working with the ACPFB to defend the seamen, wrote to INS commissioner Watson B. Miller:

> There has been no hearing to determine whether the Greek Maritime Union is an anarchist organization. Mere membership in the Federal [sic] Greek Maritime Union is thus deemed sufficient evidence upon which to term a man a menace to public safety. The organization concerned has never been granted a hearing on the merits of its contentions and it has insisted to us that it is not a Communist organization. These proceedings, on their face, appear to be the use of deportation procedures in a discriminatory way to aid the Greek government and Greek shipping interests in a strike-breaking movement.[39]

In 1946, forty-one U.S. and international organizations, including the ACPFB and the NMU, protested the threatened deportations of Emmanuel Pitharoulis and Nicholas Kaloudis, the secretary and the organizer-treasurer, respectively, of the New York office of the FGMU.[40] Kaloudis, who was married to an American citizen, spent ninety-two days detained on Ellis Island before being released on $1,000 bail.[41]

Kaloudis entered the United States in 1944 on shore leave and exceeded his twenty-nine-day leave limitation. Deportation proceedings against him were initiated in 1946, his appeals were dismissed in 1949, and a deportation order was issued in 1952. Drawing on legal defense strategies from before the war, the ACPFB argued that he would be executed if he were forcibly returned to Greece. Antonios Ambatielos, a former FGMU official in New York, was in Athens at the time, sentenced to death (the sentence was commuted, and Ambatielos was finally released in 1964 after an international campaign). Free Greek Radio reported in 1949 that four thousand men and women had been sentenced to death by the Athens regime since 1946. UN action had halted the execution of ten FGMU leaders in 1948. The argument against Kaloudis's deportation succeeded in the UN International Labor Organization (ILO) court. In a move that would become a trail for many deportees, Kaloudis took "voluntary departure," leaving the United States for Poland in August 1952.[42]

The blacklist targeted rank-and-file sailors as well as leaders, such as Kaloudis. In January 1949, the Greek Consul sued in the U.S. District Court for the Eastern District of Pennsylvania for the removal and repatriation of four seamen on board the Greek ship *Syros*, which was docked at the time in Philadelphia. Georgios Therianos, Manolis Kasmas, Andreou Mihail, and Spiridon Zannos had all signed onto the ship in 1948 but had been discharged by order of the Greek Merchant Marine Ministry. The sailors were charged with "refusal to perform services, mutiny, etc.," for activities violating the 1947 agreement on other ships as well as on the *Syros*.[43]

The 1943 FGMU agreement stipulated extra pay for such work as opening and closing the hatches in port when longshoremen or others did not do it. In 1948, the crew refused to open the hatch without additional pay. Eighteen men in all, including deck sailors and firemen, and sometimes the entire crew, joined the protests on board. Such protests were widespread among Greek sailors, who had very recent memories of the guarantee of compensation for the extra labor. In Wabana, Newfoundland, the chief officer of the ship agreed to pay an additional $100 per worker, and the sailors opened and closed the hatches. But on the remainder of the stops, in Norfolk, Virginia, and in Cherbourg and Rouen, France, the crew was denied the extra pay. Crew members refused to open the hatches, forcing officers to perform this labor. The crew testified that it was united in this purpose and wanted to avoid the targeting of any particular members. But Zannos, Mihail, Kasmas, and Therianos were already blacklisted as troublemakers and were summoned to the offices of the Greek Consul in New York.[44]

The Greek Consul requested repatriation under a 1902 treaty between Greece and the United States, which ratified control of internal affairs on a vessel by the nation under which it was flagged. But the district court found that the issues in the case pertained more closely to questions of wages and compensation and did not fall within the jurisdiction of the treaty. Further, the court invalidated the attempt of the consul to intervene in politics on board the *Solis*.

Surprising considering the antiradical cast of the period, the court's finding was consistent with the broader legal history governing the rights of nonnational workers in the United States. Since the era of Chinese exclusion, courts had asserted the plenary power of Congress to regulate immigration over the claims of international treaties. The development of the plenary power doctrine since that time affirmed the sovereignty of the United States and the more or less exclusive prerogative of Congress over immigration policy. The ACPFB deployed these arguments in its attempts to legally defend the rights of the foreign born.[45]

Given the antisubversive climate of the times, however, not all the cases against foreign seamen in U.S. ports ended so well. As the Truman Doctrine allied the United States with right-wing regimes around the globe, the NMU and the ACPFB came into conflict with the federal government. In Greece in 1947, three Black sailors were beaten, robbed, and imprisoned. One of the seamen, Thomas Groves, said that a "U.S. Coast Guard officer urged the Greek court to jail him solely because he [was] a Negro and a union representative on the ship." The U.S. Consul in Greece was of little assistance in this incident. Union members had similar problems in Portuguese Mozambique and South Africa, bringing maritime labor and its advocates into conflict with the State Department's Cold War priorities.[46]

In 1949, fourteen Greek sailors were seized by a combined effort of the INS and the Federal Bureau of Investigation (FBI) in New York as they were boarding the Polish ship *Batory*. The INS said that the seamen had overstayed their shore leave, violating immigration law. But the FGMU issued a statement, claiming that the U.S. government was following a policy of terrorizing seamen on the Greek government's blacklist.[47]

Another case involving Greek sailors featured a spectacular photo that was widely reprinted in newspapers around the country in November 1949. The picture showed three sailors sitting high up in the rigging of their ship,

Aristocratis, in Baltimore harbor. Immigration inspectors had claimed that Sarantis Xanthopolus, Antonios Fafalios, Stellos Larentzakis, and Antonios Margaziotis did not have the correct papers, or "bona fides"; therefore, they became "malafied," unable to sail and vulnerable to deportation. After being apprehended by the dock agents and locked in a cabin, they broke out and climbed the mast. They stayed there in the rain, with the crew slipping them food and whiskey by night. After several days in Baltimore, the *Aristocratis* sailed with three men still sitting on the mast. The ship changed its route to get to Greece as quickly as possible, where the seamen were likely to face imprisonment and persecution at the hands of the government there.[48]

The vicissitudes of Greek sailors seeking asylum from repression by their own governments highlight the partial successes of the immigrant rights coalition in the immediate postwar period. In this period, the ACPFB drew on support from the NMU and other labor organizations to make the case for rights for foreign-born workers. While it met with uneven results, the work strengthened the coalition for immigrant rights.

The Oceanic Imaginary and Anti-Communism

Just as the State Department was responsive to requests from its international allies for the deportation of troublemakers, the Department of Justice was careful to police the presence of foreign-born labor leaders in the United States. The political climate of the late 1940s and early 1950s continued to focus on the potential for subversion, particularly by the foreign born. The Taft-Hartley Act of 1947 targeted Communist influence in the labor movement. As early as 1946, Louis Russell emphasized to HUAC the particular risk posed by Communists in shipping: "In a war against a communistic aggressor, communistic control of American vessels on the high seas and the means of communications between these vessels means that no supplies will be delivered to the American army in foreign ports."[49]

During the 1940s, the ACPFB advocated for the rights of an ideologically diverse maritime labor force. The organization's advocacy for maritime labor expanded its caseload to include many sailors accused of subversion by the United States or by governments in their nations of origin. Many of these laborers did not hold Communist sympathies themselves; the presence of Greek anarchists, Finnish social democrats, Indonesian nationalists, and Issei fisherman in the case files of the ACPFB attests to the ideological diversity of cases the organization represented.[50]

As anti-Communism emerged as a significant political force in the late 1940s, the organization found itself fighting this sentiment on the docks and on ships as well as within the coalition working on behalf of foreign-born sailors. Tensions developed within the NMU over the issue of anti-Communism, dividing and crucially weakening the organization. Black and foreign-born seamen, in particular, lost ground during this time. The Port Security Act of 1950 allowed the Coast Guard and the FBI to bar the employment of seamen and dock workers whose loyalties were suspect. By one estimate, about 75 percent of the marine cooks and stewards and 65 percent of longshoremen barred from work under this act were Black or Puerto Rican. Mulzac was among those banned from sailing. In the South, infighting in the NMU resulted in violence. An emergent anti-Communist, anti-integrationist faction within the union hired Ku Klux Klan members to beat and intimidate Black union members in South Atlantic and Gulf ports. Anti-Communism in the NMU translated directly to the decline of the status of Afro-diasporic, Asian, and Latinx laborers.[51]

As the NMU transformed from a progressive, internationalist union to an Americans-first organization, its advocacy for the foreign born also declined. In 1950, Neal Hanley, the national secretary for the NMU, characterized the organization as "an American trade union for Americans only" and praised the "increasingly nationalistic spirit of membership." The ACPFB deplored this shift, invoking charged language to assert that "alien seamen [were] deserted by the NMU."[52]

While anti-Communism put pressure on the coalition working for the rights of foreign-born marine labor, ship owners used the centrality of the merchant marine for national security to press their interests. Like farmers and ranchers at the U.S.-Mexico border, ship owners recognized the utility of a foreign-born, noncitizen, and therefore vulnerable workforce. In a letter to Senator Warren G. Magnuson (D-Washington), the chair of the Senate's Interstate and Foreign Commerce Committee, George W. Morgan, the president of the Association of American Ship Owners, argued that American crews were better but that "foreign crews" would serve "in a pinch."[53]

Recognizing the potential permeability of U.S. ports by foreign agents, the McCarran-Walter Act required all foreign seamen to have newly issued identification cards before leaving ship. It also forbade shipmasters from paying alien seamen in port without explicit and specific permission from the INS. Policing of national boundaries on docks and at sea paralleled the McCarran-Walter Act's renewed attention to transnational Filipinx workers traveling between the mainland United States and the territories of Alaska and Hawai'i. As with the Filipinx cannery workers of the March Inland, the McCarran-Walter Act impeded the occupational migration of maritime laborers.[54]

Ferdinand Smith entered the United States legally in 1918 but departed multiple times after his first entry, because he was working on board ship. Although he attempted to become a citizen in 1945, he never formally naturalized. The government initiated deportation proceedings against Smith along with other activists in early 1948. In New York, Smith was detained on Ellis Island with Gerhart Eisler, Communist Party leader John Williamson, and United Chemical Workers vice president Charles A. Doyle. The men were segregated from other detainees. Together, they wrote a letter protesting their deportations and treatment to Attorney General Clark; they began a hunger strike to protest their deportations and their treatment as detainees. Green and the ACPFB's chief legal counsel Carol Weiss King worked with other advocacy organizations to organize protests and letter-writing campaigns. Opposing the deportation drive and calling for bail for the detained activists, ten thousand people marched on the INS building in New York; labor unions organized a picket line lasting a week in San Francisco. As the case gained political traction, labor leaders in St. Louis and Buffalo joined Hollywood personalities, such as Dashiell Hammett and Uta Hagen, in pressuring for the release of the detained activists. This activism notwithstanding, the hunger strikers were kept at Ellis Island, even after they had to be transferred to the hospital there. After a long legal battle, Smith was deported back to Jamaica in 1951.[55]

The increased surveillance of maritime workers in U.S. ports imposed by the McCarran-Walter Act antagonized laborers as well as ship owners. By Christmas 1952, the status of the crew of a French ship docked in Manhattan harbor created a high-profile, international incident. The new law stipulated that each seaman had to be cleared for shore leave by being screened by an INS agent before disembarking. Further, the INS made it clear that any seamen who did not answer all required questions, including ones about their political views, would be denied shore leave. Many of the French seamen were Communists and refused to answer. More than 250 of the seamen on board the ironically named *Liberté* were declared ineligible for shore leave. This decision drew an international outcry, with many North Atlantic Treaty Organization (NATO) allies, including France, Norway, the United Kingdom, and the Netherlands, objecting to the enforced Christmas on board ship. A similar incident affected the crew of the *Ile de France* in January 1953.[56]

By February 1953, a *New York Times* writer argued:

Whatever the McCarran Walter Immigration and Nationality Act as it applies to alien seamen may have gained for the country in the way of security has been more than lost in the ill will, anger, and

outright disdain it has fostered among the thousands of foreign
seafarers put through the wringer of the law's strict shore leave
provision.[57]

Ship owners complained about the inconvenience and expense the law
caused them; if aliens were detained entering through an airport, they rea-
soned, they would be stuck at the airport. But workers detained on ship
cost ship owners food and time, and the ship owners were liable for the cost
of their detention. Further, if ship owners discharged alien seamen without
the permission of the attorney general, they were fined by the INS.[58]

A temporary coalition emerged between maritime labor and ship owners. In 1953, Senator Magnuson introduced a bill to prevent alien seamen
from being signed onto American flag ships in foreign ports. It was common
practice for ship owners to get around the law requiring three-quarters of
the crew to be citizens by recruiting workers at foreign ports. The National
Federation of American Shipping, Inc., responded that it was sympathetic
to the problems posed by alien labor but that Magnuson's bill was simply
impractical, as ship owners could not do without foreign workers.[59] At the
same time, the NMU and other unions continued to advocate for the working conditions of alien seamen, attempting to extend shore leave and continuing to push for their access to naturalization.[60] If foreign-born sailors
could replace American sailors at a cheaper wage and lesser working conditions, they would undermine the position of all maritime workers.

Working for the ACPFB, Ira Gollobin successfully litigated the case of
Chinese American seaman Kwong Hai Chew to the Supreme Court, which
established rights for laborers on American ships in 1953. Chew, a legal
permanent resident married to an American citizen, shipped out on the SS
Sir John Franklin in 1950. Chew had served in the merchant marine during
the war and subsequently filed for naturalization. The Coast Guard approved him for service. Chew was detained on his return to San Francisco
and denied entry on grounds that his admission would be "prejudicial to
the public interest," based on information possessed, but not revealed, by
the attorney general, as written in the Immigration Act of 1918. He was
transferred to Ellis Island to await deportation and interned there for more
than two years without bail.[61]

The secret evidence in the case against Chew was based on INS assessment of the potential fallout in Chinese American communities from the
success of the Chinese revolution, and from two former Chinese American
Communist witnesses, both of whom were seamen who needed certification by the Coast Guard to work. Chew had been politically active in New
York Chinatown during the 1940s, serving as the president of the Kang Jai

Association, one of the benevolent organizations for seamen that pressed for shore leave rights during the war. In addition, he was involved in NMU politics and ran successfully for office in 1948. The Kang Jai Association refused to sign a loyalty oath in 1951, resulting in the rounding up of forty-two members for deportation. Chew was at sea during the arrests but was detained as soon as he returned to the country. As Carlene Cho writes, "In other words, the INS attempted to politically deport him because he was Chinese and allegedly susceptible to Communism, instead of basing the deportation on evidence of subversive intent."[62]

Gollobin sued for habeas corpus in the Eastern District Court of New York and then appealed the denial to the Court of Appeals for the Second Circuit. Both courts found that Chew's detention and deportation were legal. However, in 1953, the Supreme Court stayed Chew's deportation orders. The court recognized Chew as a legal permanent resident who had traveled abroad as a seaman on an American vessel, therefore retaining his right to reenter the country. The court also granted Chew the right to naturalize.

In this decision, the court affirmed the rights of legal permanent residents to due process and specified their rights when on an American-owned ship registered under an American flag. The court was careful to define what it meant by an "American ship." This definition subsequently became crucial, as the incidence of American-owned ships registered under foreign flags increased. In defending Chew from deportation, the ACPFB affirmed the rights of foreign-born, Asian American seamen in a difficult political context.[63]

The question of the legal rights of noncitizens became important to questions of marine labor as the merchant marine began to shift to flags of convenience ships in the 1950s. The transnational character of the NMU brought the union scrutiny as a potential internationalist den of subversion. At this time of enhanced suspicion of Communist activism, the ACPFB fought to expand the grounds for noncitizen rights.

The successes of the ACPFB in representing nonnational marine laborers laid important foundations for immigrant rights activism during the Cold War. Potential deportees and their advocates deployed politically charged questions around their return destinations, gaining some traction in terms of public relations and in sometimes being able to control the timing and location of deportation. This strategy was one response to the increasing use of deportation against the foreign born in the postwar period. In the struggle at the ports, immigrant and labor advocates pressed the inherently internationalist question of maritime labor rights. Their success elicited an internationalist response of a different kind.

Runaway Ships and Elusive Protections

> I am especially interested and share your concern with your problems
> and in particular the "runaway ship" threat to the high standards
> which you and your union have fought for and established over the
> years. The "runaway ship," like its counterpart, the "runaway shop,"
> is a hit-and-run operation which should be stopped.
>
> —JOHN F. KENNEDY, telegram to Joe Curran, October 30, 1960,
>   quoted in Rodney Carlisle, *Sovereignty for Sale*

> The basic concept of the merchant marine policy of the United States
> is the private ownership of vessels. One of the attributes of ownership
> is the right to dispose of the property.
>
> —SINCLAIR WEEKS, Secretary of Commerce, 1957, quoted in
>   "Panlibhon Registration of American-Owned Merchant Ships"

The emergence of global and domestic anti-Communist networks in the
postwar period limited the expansion of rights for foreign-born maritime
laborers. As the United States created alliances with right-wing governments, it became increasingly difficult for advocates to defend the rights
of foreign nationals of these governments in U.S. courts. At the same time,
domestic anti-Communism facilitated the blacklisting of foreign-born labor leaders, such as Smith. But even in the context of the repression of the
Cold War years, the ACPFB and its allies had some success in defending
and expanding the rights of maritime laborers. If the maritime workforce
had remained a matter of U.S. jurisdiction, these advocates may have succeeded in promoting broader access to citizenship and rights.

But after the war, maritime laborers increasingly worked aboard ships
licensed abroad. This development situated sailors as a transnational pro-
letariat in the emergent postwar order of global racial capital, essentially
taking their labor rights out of national jurisdiction. An oceanic internationalism forged on board ship infused the advocacy for these rights by the
ACPFB and its allies. They pressed for practices of citizenship and rights
that corresponded with their mobile, transnational labor on American
ships. In countering these emancipatory claims, shipping interests and
anti-Communists created another kind of internationalism, one in which
ownership and power moved unimpeded by federal regulation, while the
rights of workers were limited by the strict enforcement of national boundaries.

Anthropologist David Harvey writes of the emergence of coalitions
between public and private interests as one of the hallmarks of neoliberalism. For Harvey, the emergence of neoliberalism deliberately undermines the power of organized labor and other forms of opposition to
corporate power. Harvey situates the emergence of neoliberalism in the

early 1970s, but in the global shipping industry, this transformation began much earlier.[64]

The neoliberal response to maritime organizing had its roots in transnational developments taking place well before World War II. Beginning in 1919, a few American ship owners registered their vessels in Panama, mainly to avoid Prohibition. During World War II, more ship owners transferred their registrations to Panama to avoid requisition or regulation under the Neutrality Acts. Modeled after Colombian law, the Panamanian Fiscal Code allowed for the registration of foreign ships at Panamanian Consul offices worldwide. Transactions were conducted in English.[65]

After World War II, the 1946 Ship Sales Act allowed for the sale of 1,113 U.S. "liberty ships" to foreign flags. These were privately owned ships that had sailed in the merchant marine. Decisions about the sales as well as the profits were left to the owners. Of the "liberty ships" sold, 152 were registered in Panama. As shipping continued to be a national security priority after the war, the Maritime Commission recognized the evolving opportunity for ship owners to take advantage of the comparatively lower wages and costs of foreign registries. At the same time, the Department of Defense articulated an idea of "effective control" of foreign-registered but American-owned vessels. In a case of wartime emergency, these ships would revert to complete American control. In 1947, a Joint Chiefs of Staff memo explained:

> There are certain countries in this hemisphere which, through diplomatic or other arrangements, will permit the transfer of their registry to United States ships . . . and allow United States citizens or corporations to retain control of these vessels. . . . Such a case can be considered to be within the meaning of the term "effective United States control."[66]

The practice of foreign flag registry was grounded in transnational collaboration between private shipping interests, the American national security complex, and foreign governments. While they remained an economic asset to U.S. shipping companies, the "liberty ships" came to represent not only the democratic freedoms promoted by the war effort but also the liberty of shipping interests to elude national regulation through the emerging flags of convenience system. The freedom to elude national regulation is one of the hallmarks of neoliberalism.

Transnational collaboration intensified with the founding of the Liberian ship registry. With the return of Arnulfó Arias to power in Panama in 1949, the State Department and the ship owners became concerned about the stability of the Panamanian government. Under the Effective

Control Doctrine, this concern encompassed the private interests of the ship owners as well as U.S. national security.

In 1947, former Secretary of State Edward R. Stettinius created a charitable development venture in Liberia: Stettinius Associates. Citing Liberia's "special relationship" with the United States, Stettinius went on to help author the Liberian Maritime Code in 1948. Stettinius Associates and the Liberian government shared the profits of this venture with the American Overseas Tanker Corporation, which was owned by General Julius Holmes, Admiral William Halsey, and Stettinius.[67]

Like the ACPFB and its allies, Stettinius recognized the significance of shipping to the global postwar order. Looking out over what appeared to him to be a raging sea of African decolonization, Stettinius saw Liberia as America's "sole beachhead in Africa." Cooperation between the United States and Liberia would provide the Central Intelligence Agency (CIA) with a steady stream of informative reports. By 1955, Liberia had surpassed Panama as a foreign flag registry. Politicians like Stettinius saw the threats posed by decolonization to the economic and political health of global as well as U.S. capitalism and implemented transnational regimes, such as foreign flag registries, in response. The emergence of the "flags of convenience" system policed the order of global racial capital against anticolonial uprisings as well as labor protections.[68]

The ACPFB and maritime labor organizers protested the threat posed by the emergence of foreign flag registries. Green emphasized this point in 1943 when he said, "It is the responsibility of Congress and the government to enforce minimum health, working and safety conditions on foreign-flag ships that use American ports."[69]

In 1947, Philip Murray of the CIO estimated that Panamanian registration had resulted in the loss of sixteen thousand union marine jobs. In Portland, the Marine Firemen's Union boycotted the Panamanian-registered *Don Anselmo*. In response, the Panamanian embassy protested to the State Department, characterizing the boycott as contrary to Panamanian sovereignty and illegal under U.S. law, because it was not based in a shipboard union.[70]

Undeterred, Scandinavian unions prevented members from working on Panamanian flag ships.[71] In 1949, the ILO investigated Panamanian registry ships, finding older ships, problems with labor conditions, poor accommodations, no worker's compensation, and an absence of clear labor contracts.[72]

Conflicts over the status of workers on foreign registry ships involved issues of national sovereignty as well as the nationality of seamen. In 1953, Kaj K. Larsen, a Danish worker injured on a Danish ship of Danish national registry while in Havana, sued for worker's compensation under the Jones Act. He had signed his contract in New York, so a federal district court in New York found in his favor. The Danish ship owners appealed the case to the Supreme Court, which found in their favor, arguing that allowing remedy under the Jones Act would contradict Danish sovereignty, as the seamen's contract clearly stated that his rights would be governed by Danish national law. In *Laurtizen v. Larsen*, the court invoked established maritime practice recognizing the "law of the flag" on board foreign ships, except where the issue at hand might involve the "peace and tranquility" of the port, or the United States in general. In the confusing new world of American ships flying foreign flags and employing international crews, the Supreme Court in this case attempted to set forth a rational framework to negotiate issues of sovereignty and rights.[73]

In 1957, the Senate Committee on Interstate and Foreign Commerce investigated the issue of foreign flag registries. Senator Magnuson proposed legislation to eliminate the foreign transfer of U.S. vessels. The House of Representatives also held hearings regarding the activities of the Maritime Board. Labor representatives argued that the concept of effective control endangered the American merchant marine, calling the notion that foreign flag ships would be a national resource in a time of crisis "a figment of vivid and unrealistic imaginations." But the national security establishment and the shipping interests defended effective control and foreign registry as being crucial to national security. Little effective regulation came out of these hearings.[74]

International bodies also attempted to regulate flags of convenience ships. A Law of the Sea Conference held by the International Law Commission of the UN in 1958 ended with a weak resolution that regulations on board ship should be linked to the ships' flags of registry; the resolution contained no definition of what this was to mean. The United States, Panama, and Liberia together scuttled a "recognition of national character" clause for all ships. Similarly, at a meeting of the Inter-Governmental Maritime Consultative Organization in London in 1959, the traditional maritime powers attempted to exclude Panama and Liberia from membership, arguing that neither owned sufficient maritime tonnage to participate as voting members. The United States pressured for the inclusion of these two nations, which were seated in 1960. Predictably, little regulation of foreign flag ships emerged from this meeting. The ILO did pass a resolution in 1958 discouraging seamen from working on foreign flag ships without contracts. But in part because international law does not recognize the concept of a foreign flag ship, and in part because of the activism of the United States and international shipping interests, the labor conditions on these ships remain largely unregulated to the present day.[75]

Ship owners organized to assert their interests. In 1958, the American Committee for Flags of Necessity elected Norwegian whaling ship owner

Erling Naess as its president. A transnational figure himself, Naess was the first Norwegian ship owner to move parts of his fleet to Panamanian registry in the 1930s. Naess hired a public relations team, and soon "flags of necessity," the term the ship owners preferred, began to appear in American periodicals. Unions tended to call the same ships "runaway ships," while military spokespeople referred to them as "flags of survival."

The ITF called for a four-day worldwide boycott of Panamanian, Liberian, and Honduran (PANLIBHON) ships in 1958. A central objective of this boycott was to equalize pay for all seamen. The NMU and the Seafarers International Union (SIU) participated in this boycott; in the United States, it affected 125 vessels, with 38 more held up worldwide. Subsequently, many legal cases presented U.S. courts with questions of jurisdiction over marine union activity.[76]

In 1958, the SIU organized the predominantly Cuban crew of the Liberian flag ship *Florida*. The *Florida* initially operated under an American flag but switched, hiring Cuban laborers at reduced wages. The SIU argued, "The mere fact that a majority of the employees are non-resident aliens does not take the case outside the coverings of the NLRB [National Labor Relations Board]." Through court cases pressed by marine workers, seamen's unions were able to organize nonnational, nonresident workers throughout the 1950s.[77]

The NLRB backed the union's work among nonnational seamen. Important Supreme Court decisions, such as *Marine Cooks v. Panama SS Co.* (1960), upheld the application of American labor laws to prohibit the restraint of union activities at the docks. The NLRB drew on these success stories to consolidate its jurisdiction on foreign flag ships. In 1961, the NLRB heard the case of *West India Fruit and Steamship Corporation and Seafarers Union of North America, Atlantic and Gulf Division, AFL-CIO*. Cuban crew members asserted that ship officers had exerted unfair labor practices, interrogating them about their union activities, offering them incentives not to organize, and threatening them with termination if they joined a union, in violation of the National Labor Relations Act.[78]

The ship in question, the *Sea Level*, was registered under the Liberian flag, and none of the seamen were U.S. residents or nationals. West India Fruit and Steamship was incorporated under Virginia law. All the officers, directors, and stockholders were citizens of the United States. The company's main operating offices were in West Palm Beach. It maintained offices in New York and New Orleans and employed a general shipping agent in Havana. The *Sea Level* had been built in Britain in 1928 and was transferred to American registry in the 1930s. The company purchased the ship from its prior owners in 1954 and registered it in Liberia to save money. As such, the *Sea Level* was subject to only minimal inspection in U.S. ports.[79]

The NLRB found in favor of the crew. The board's majority argued that a strike on the *Sea Level* would affect national commerce, bringing the issue well within federal jurisdiction. Further, the board explained that the National Labor Relations Act did not contain exclusionary language about nationality or residence. The decision held that "it would be anomalous at best to base jurisdiction on the citizenship and residence of the parties involved, rather than upon their relationship to the protected commerce of this nation."[80]

Because of the lack of a bill to provide naturalization or even the limited rights of permanent residence to marine laborers, protection under the NLRB was a matter that was dependent on court jurisdiction. Like ranchers on the U.S.-Mexico border, ship owners were more than willing to hire nonnational laborers, but they were less concerned with the access of these workers to decent conditions and workplace democracy. Flexibility for ranch and ship owners depended on the purposive stripping of the rights of foreign-born workers. In both cases, the ACPFB recognized the vulnerability of transnational laborers by working to limit deportation and broaden access to citizenship.

Shipping interests had complained bitterly about previous deportation policies. Detaining crews on board ship was costly, as was paying the fine for discharging alien seamen in port. The ship owners wanted to end federal jurisdiction over labor disputes on foreign flag ships. They found allies in some parts of the federal government, specifically the Maritime Administration and the State and Defense Departments.[81]

While ship owners made common cause with the Defense Department over the issue of "effective control," this coalition had its fissures. Ship owners were content to hire foreign seamen if it resulted in lower labor costs and wanted to keep costs low by preventing unionization. In contrast, the Defense Department worried that foreign flag ships sailed by nonnational crews would be less likely to be loyal in case of a national emergency. Although foreign seamen had been the heroes of the U.S. merchant marine in 1945, by 1959, they looked like potential subversives, apathetic at best to the national interests of the United States. The activities of American unions among these seamen were of particular concern to the national security state. The Defense and State Departments joined with shipping interests to press for a judicial remedy for the continued activities of the unions on the docks.[82]

Seeking to solidify its progress, the NMU in the early 1960s focused its organizing efforts on United Fruit, a New Jersey–based international corporation with ships registered in Honduras. The Honduras case was slightly different from those of Panama and Liberia. After a massive, successful strike in the banana plantations in 1954, labor unions won the right to organize in Honduras. Under the leadership of the Nationalist Party, Honduras consolidated a limited autonomy within the hemisphere.[83] While U.S. domination, by United Fruit in particular, looms large in Honduran history, Honduras was not quite the same client state as Liberia and Panama. Claims of state sovereignty against the interference of NLRB jurisdiction had more traction in the case of Honduras, where sailors were required to join a Honduran union, and where national law held "that no foreign union can represent the interests of seamen who work on ships sailing under the Honduran flag."[84]

Believing that they would fare best in court, the ship owners and their allies in the government pressed for a Supreme Court hearing. The NMU filed a petition in 1959 against United Fruit, alleging that it was the majority owner of the shipping line Empresa. Empresa and the Honduran marine union, Sociedad de Marineros de Honduras, sued the NLRB in federal district court to prevent the NMU from organizing Empresa ships. The case against the NLRB asserted that "the overriding consideration is that the Board's assertion of power to determine the representation of foreign seamen aboard vessels under foreign flags has aroused vigorous protests from foreign governments and for our government."[85]

In 1963, the Supreme Court decided the landmark case *McCulloch, Chairman, National Labor Relations Board, et al. v. Sociedad Nacional de Marineros de Honduras*. In this case, the court affirmed a lower court decision by the U.S. District Court for the District of Columbia. These decisions decisively ended the rights of workers on foreign flag ships to petition for redress under U.S. labor law: "The court held that the Act [National Labor Relations Act, 1935/National Labor Management Relations Act, 1947] as written was not intended to have any application to foreign registered vessels employing alien seamen." Attorney General Robert F. Kennedy agreed that the NLRB should not have jurisdiction in this case.[86] President John F. Kennedy, too, appeared to have been convinced by his advisers of the salience of the case against the use of labor rights for the foreign born.[87]

In reaching this conclusion, the courts deferred to Honduran sovereignty, in effect reversing more than seventy years of federal law and jurisprudence on the rights of foreign-born seamen in U.S. ports. The Honorable Celeo Davila, the ambassador to the United States from Honduras, cowrote an amicus brief with the State Department, reminding the court of a 1927 treaty between the two nations. This treaty supported the "law of the flag" on Honduran ships in American waters as well as on the high seas. The court found for the sovereignty of Honduras over its previously developed "contact theory." It disregarded the work of the NMU and previous decisions acknowledging the American ownership and interests of United Fruit.

Further, rather than limiting the decision in *McCulloch v. Sociedad* to the case of Empresa or Honduran shipping, the court extended the case to include organizing on *all* foreign flag ships. The outcome summary of the case reads: "The court affirmed the judgment that enjoined petitioner National Labor Relations Board from ordering an election involving seamen on vessels owned by a foreign subsidy of an American corporation where the jurisdictional provisions of the National Labor Relations Act did not extend to maritime operations of foreign flag ships employing alien seamen."[88]

This sweeping decision nullified much of the work of supporting rights for foreign-born seamen. This invocation of national sovereignty over the rights of migrants would have returned Kaloudis to certain death in Greece, exiled Chew from his life in New York City, and sent more than two hundred Indonesian sailors who had publicly opposed a colonial regime back to the tender mercies of the Dutch. *national sovereignty in an*

The language of the decision in *McCulloch v. Sociedad* strains around *international* a historical contradiction: this document affirms national sovereignty in a *terrain* case regarding an international field of economic activity. Harvey observes the use of international bodies against the local in the development of neoliberalism. In this early case of neoliberal policy, the U.S. Supreme Court, a national actor attempting to adjudicate an international field, asserted the law of nations, recognizing Honduran sovereignty against the claims of the oceanic international. The results have been consequential for the rights of maritime workers, consigning them to labor without protections.[89]

Justice William O. Douglas commented on *McCulloch v. Sociedad*, "The practical effect of our decision is to shift from all the taxpayers to seamen alone the main burden of financing an executive policy of assuring the availability of an adequate American-owned merchant fleet for federal use during national emergencies." Douglas's idea is consonant with Nobel Prize–winning economist Joseph Stiglitz's observation that "free trade" policies have shifted much of the risk and much of the economic burden of economic development to the world's poor. In the years after this decision, Panamanian and Liberian registries steadily increased their share of the percentage of global marine tonnage. Overall, the value of goods and services traded internationally by sea has increased since 1945. Ninety-five percent of international trade relies on shipping.[90]

Since the 1963 decision, flags of convenience ships have enticed ship owners with few if any regulations on labor conditions and exceedingly low wages. These ships have featured "crews of convenience," who are often prohibited from joining unions. Sources of marine labor have shifted over time. Shipping is often an occupation of last refuge, pursued by those who

few labor regulations

have few options elsewhere. Asian seamen went from being 15 percent of the world's seafarers in 1960 to 47 percent in 1987. Their nations of origin have shifted over time, with the predominance of Korean and Chinese workers shifting in the 1980s to the dominance of Filipinx marine laborers.[91]

In Francisco Goldman's 1997 novel *The Ordinary Seaman*, the main character, Esteban, and his Central American crew mates inhabit an unregulated and hellish ship, moored on a rotting dock in New York City. To go ashore is to risk living in the shadows of undocumented migration. The maritime workers in this book have no documents, and their rights as foreign seamen are not protected by any local, national, international, or transnational statute. They are, therefore, vulnerable to local, state, national, or international forces of policing.

Paul Chapman cites the nonfictional case of Honduran seafarers on the Carnival Cruise Line. More than two hundred workers staged a work stoppage in April 1981 after two of their coworkers were dismissed without cause. While the ship was docked in Miami, the ship owner fired them and, with the collaboration of the local INS, had them all declared undocumented and summarily deported. Neither the Honduran government nor the Supreme Court stepped in with reminders about Honduran sovereignty and the rights of Honduran subjects.[92]

Faced with the dire situation in the global shipping industry, it is tempting to see contemporary seafarers confronting Giorgio Agamben's state of exception and nil political subjectivity. Migrant rights advocates have deployed a discourse of a "new slavery" to describe the conditions of foreign-born laborers who fall outside the jurisdiction of national rights but whose labor is necessary for economic development. Writing about the lives of foreign-born domestic workers in the United States, Charles T. Lee argues that the distinction between rights and non-rights-bearing subjects can obscure the agency of the latter. Monisha das Gupta questions whether, in the case of domestic workers in New York, redress can ever come from a city and a nation so deeply involved in neoliberal development.[93]

One of the hallmarks of neoliberalism is the collusion of national governments in rendering such industries as shipping free of regulation; these same governments, then, seem unlikely to enforce labor and human rights standards on board "flags of convenience" ships. The rise of the flags of convenience system and its endorsement by the Supreme Court constitute a loss for immigrant rights organizing among maritime workers. However, as this chapter demonstrates, advocacy for foreign-born sailors has often contended with the contradictions inherent in an international labor force. In concert with the ACPFB, foreign-born maritime workers pressed their interests throughout the early Cold War period. In the repressive climate of mounting anti-Communism and the enhanced use of deportation, they pressed for new conceptions of citizenship and rights. Animated by the internationalist oceanic imaginary, the success of this inherently transnational coalition evidences the possibilities for organizing even after the juridical ascendance of the flags of convenience ships. International solidarity for decent conditions and workplace democracy enabled the ACPFB to articulate a global, antiracist politics and to defend against the deportation terror, at sea and on the docks.

Foreign-born workers were central to the March Inland and maritime organizing. In turn, advocacy for the rights of these workers shaped the ACPFB, bringing the organization into close alliance with a multiracial, transnational workforce. Many of these workers saw their citizenship status further undermined by Cold War realignments of global racial capitalism. The next chapter turns to the ways that a transnational, multiracial workforce joined forces to fight the deportation terror on land, in Los Angeles.

COUNTERINSURGENCIES

Global Militarism and Immigrant
Rights in Los Angeles

M oving away from the industry-specific focus of the previous two chapters, this chapter takes Los Angeles as a central site of struggle over immigrant rights in the post–World War II period. A West Coast port and urban hub that was home to many maritime and agricultural laborers, Los Angeles became a postwar epicenter of repression against the foreign born as well as resistance to this repression. This chapter looks specifically at the Los Angeles Committee for the Protection of the Foreign Born (LACPFB). Founded in 1950, the LACPFB responded to deportation campaigns against foreign-born activists and to Operation Wetback, which targeted the Mexican American community.

Federal deportation policy in this period evolved in concert with counterinsurgency campaigns in Latin America and Asia. In Los Angeles, refugees from these counterinsurgency campaigns and their allies created a political culture that defended individuals targeted for deportation and contested the racialized repression of the foreign born. The political understandings of these migrants had been forged in the struggles of their homelands: these foreign-born understandings imprinted the political culture of immigrant rights. With their inherently transnational geographic imaginaries, immigrants often recognized the connections between disparate instances of U.S. militarism. The experiences of these cohorts in their homelands formed their understandings of possibilities in Los Angeles.

Institutionally, the LACPFB emerged out of labor, civil rights, and antiracist organizations in Los Angeles, including the local chapter of the

Communist-affiliated Civil Rights Congress (CRC). Migrant radical imaginaries drew on prior struggles over labor and power in Los Angeles as well as the international experiences of migrants. The LACPFB was an affiliate of the New York–based American Committee for the Protection of the Foreign Born (ACPFB). It brought together the primarily Jewish and European-origin leadership of the ACPFB with Latinx and Asian American organizers on the West Coast. These connections continued long after the LACPFB disbanded in 1965, becoming foundational to a revived, national immigrant rights movement in the 1980s.

Jewish leadership

Historian Scott Kurashige asks how we can comprehend the transformation of Los Angeles from a "white city," in which the forces of white supremacy controlled the boundaries of neighborhoods, employment, and citizenship, to a multicultural "world city" situated at the crossroads of the Pacific Rim and the Mexican Border. Foreign-born activists and the campaigns against them were pivotal to this process. The radical migrant imaginaries deployed in the creation of the LACPFB responded to a history of militarism that radiated from Los Angeles west, toward Asia, and south, toward Mexico. This chapter foregrounds the parallel struggles of foreign-born Korean Americans and Latinx, as they contested white supremacy and created the grounds for alternative visions of racial solidarity. At the same time, the evolution of deportation as domestic counterinsurgency perpetuated the great power asymmetry foundational to white supremacy in Los Angeles.[1]

After World War II, deportation policy evolved as domestic and international counterinsurgency, enforcing the postwar global racial capitalist order. Besides regulating the labor supply and purging the country of radical influences, the deportation of foreign-born dissidents became an important way for the State Department to cement alliances with foreign governments. Historically, deportation had been used against indigenous insurgencies within the United States and in imperial campaigns abroad. On errands occasioned by the Cold War, troops and advisers advanced into Asia and Latin America, regions already being transformed by struggles over imperialism and national liberation. Cold War global militarism created conditions under which many people were compelled to leave their homelands, while U.S. military encounters with counterinsurgencies abroad increasingly came to inform domestic immigration enforcement. Abroad, the military learned about the nature of the enemies they faced and about counterinsurgency in general.

Because Cold War military adventures were contiguous with prior conflicts, many of the foreign born had already experienced dislocation and, in some cases, deportation during struggles around empire and liberation. Their experiences in their homelands shaped their understanding of poli-

Pattern of migracion

tics in the United States. Many Koreans living in Los Angeles worked for the liberation of their homeland from Japanese occupation after 1910. This activity forced many to flee Korea, first departing for political exile in Manchuria or Shanghai and later moving to the United States. Those who found themselves in California joined refugees from the long upheaval of the Mexican Revolution in the rapidly expanding Los Angeles metropolitan area. Many Mexican refugees had been displaced by the revolution; some Yaquis joined the exodus north, fleeing the deportations of their people from Sonora to the Yucatan in the early twentieth century.

The securitized context of the early Cold War occasioned enhanced repression of the foreign born. Guatemalan-born labor organizer Luisa Moreno was targeted by the California legislature's Tenney Committee on Un-American Activities for her activism. The Immigration and Nationalization Service (INS) issued a deportation warrant for Moreno in 1948. She and her husband, Gray Bemis, departed for Guatemala in 1950, becoming involved in the short-lived democratic socialist government of Jacobo Arbenz. After a 1954 coup backed by the Central Intelligence Agency (CIA), Moreno and Bemis fled Guatemala for Mexico City. Moreno had been involved with the ACPFB. While she left Los Angeles before the founding of the local chapter, her activism in southern California helped set the stage for the progressive, multiethnic coalition embodied by the LACPFB.[2]

On October 17, 1951, INS officers swept barrios in the citrus town of Santa Ana, California, in Orange County, outside Los Angeles. They arrested four Mexican-born community activists in their late fifties: Justo Cruz, Augustin Esparza, Elias Espinoza, and Andres Gonzalez. The "Santa Ana Four," as they came to be known, were interned at Terminal Island with other foreign-born Angelinos suspected of being subversive.[3] At almost the same time, the Justice Department issued deportation orders for Korean American intellectuals David Hyun and Diamond Kimm in Los Angeles and Chungson and Choon Cha Kwak in New York City. All four were involved with the bilingual newspaper *Korean Independence*, an organ of the Korean Nationalist Revolutionary Party that was published in Los Angeles and distributed in the United States, Hawai'i, Asia, and Europe. Simultaneously, the INS expanded the U.S.-Mexico border focus of Operation Wetback inland, targeting the Los Angeles Mexican American community. These efforts brought militarized, federal force to bear against foreign-born activists well aware of the broader, global context in which such repression took place. These cases, along with many other similar instances of repression, led to the emergence of the multiracial immigrant rights movement represented by the LACPFB.

Global Contexts

Routes to Los Angeles

This section traces the routes migrants took from Mexico and Korea to California in the early twentieth century. Many of those subject to deportation at mid-century had experienced militarized operations in their nations of origin. As Korean and Yaqui migrants found themselves laboring together on the plantations of the Yucatan, a broad cohort of Mexican migrants, including Yaquis who had escaped the brutal deportation regime, later encountered Korean intellectuals and labor migrants, many of them fleeing Japanese rule, in Los Angeles.

In early twentieth-century Mexico, thousands of Yaquis were deported from what had been their homelands in the Mexican state of Sonora to work in the henequen plantations of the Yucatan. Fearing ongoing resistance to the confiscation of Native lands, the Porfirio Díaz regime jailed and executed many, promoting forced relocation as a solution to the problem of ongoing Native insurgency. After 1907, these deportations had full support from American officials previously inclined to welcome migrants as political refugees and as a ready supply of labor for the mines of Arizona.[4]

Joining the Yaquis on the brutal plantations of the Yucatan were contract laborers from Europe and Asia: Italy, Spain, the Canary Islands, Cuba, China, Korea, Japan, and Java. Contract laborers came from Korea in two cohorts. The last Korean laborers came aboard a ship that left Inchon harbor in April 1905 with 1,033 contract workers headed for the Yucatan. The contract was arranged by U.S. labor recruiter David Deschler, who had been granted the right by the Korean government to arrange for the exportation of Korean workers to Hawai'i only. The presence of Korean and Yaqui laborers working side by side in the Yucatan demonstrates the unlikely convergences of imperial projects, global labor flows, and, along with them, migrant imaginaries.[5]

Yaquis able to escape forced removal joined a massive migration of Mexicans north. Recruited by labor contractors, moved by newly developed railroad networks, and often fleeing the turmoil of the revolution, this generation moved north and west, repopulating and transforming Mexican American communities in California and the Southwest.[6]

In the early years of the twentieth century, Mexican authorities negotiated with the United States to turn away fleeing Yaquis at the Arizona border. In 1906, the Arizona territorial government agreed to forbid Yaquis without papers from crossing into Arizona. Subsequently, in 1908, the Department of Commerce and Labor intervened, compelling the Immigration Service to deport the many Yaquis who had fled to Arizona back to Mexico. A consequence of U.S. concern for stabilizing Mexico and maintaining order in the borderlands, this activity took place well before the establishment of the U.S. Border Patrol in 1924 and demonstrates how the regulation of the Yaquis at the U.S.-Mexico border also led to the transformation of New Mexico and Arizona from territories to states in 1912—the federal government rewarded the territories for deporting and excluding Yaquis with their sovereignty as states. The deportation of Yaquis, some of whom were suspected supporters of the revolutionary Mexican Magon brothers, was an early instance of what would become common practice in the United States after World War I: the deportation of suspected subversives.[7]

Despite counterinsurgency efforts, many Yaquis crossed the border, escaping deportation to the Yucatan. They created substantial settlements in Arizona, near Tucson. There, they maintained close connections with Yaqui communities in Mexico, frequently crossing the border for social as well as military purposes. Many Hispanicized their last names to escape detection. Many young Yaqui men found work on the railroads, eventually migrating west to Los Angeles, where they found refuge in Mexican American communities. These Yaquis were part of the large Mexican Revolution–era migrant generation, many of whom rode or worked on the railroads en route to California. Yaquis who became part of the revolution-era generation of Mexican migration to Los Angeles were later subject to the regime of Operation Wetback, implemented by the INS to regulate southern California labor markets as well as to maintain control over ethnic communities. Many Mexicans, such as the four men who became known as the "Santa Ana Four," entered the United States during this time. At the same time, Moreno came from Guatemala City to New York in 1928, becoming engaged with the labor organizing that eventually brought her to Los Angeles and earned her the attention of the INS.[8]

Fleeing Japanese repression in their homeland, many Koreans arrived in the United States during a period of mounting agitation over Asian immigration. About seven thousand Koreans, mostly urban laborers, signed contracts to work on the plantations of Hawai'i before 1905. In contrast to Japanese contract laborers to Hawai'i in the same period, few Koreans returned to their homeland because of ongoing political repression and upheaval there.[9]

Emigration from Korea was one consequence of Japanese occupation. Many Korean intellectuals and students in particular were forced into political exile after the brutal suppression of the March 1, 1919, uprisings. Many took refuge in Manchuria or China before moving farther west. Between 1910 and 1918, 541 Korean refugee students were admitted to the United States through Angel Island; another 115 women arrived as "picture brides." While the INS stopped admitting Korean students after 1917, another one thousand Korean women entered as picture brides between 1910 and 1920. These migrants, along with secondary migrants leaving the brutality of Hawai'ian plantation life, formed the Korean American community in the mainland United States. Los Angeles and San Francisco became the urban centers of the Korean American community.[10]

As with the Yaqui deportations under Díaz, the restriction of global Korean mobility was a tactic used to control a newly conquered population. In a climate charged by calls on the American West Coast for Asian exclusion, the Japanese government tended to view Korean laborers in the United States as competition for transnational Japanese workers. The potential migration of workers from the plantations of Hawai'i to the comparatively more open labor markets of California was chief among the concerns of American exclusionists and Japanese diplomats. Negotiating a "Gentlemen's Agreement" for Japanese in the United States also meant restricting the migration of Koreans. While the Japanese were concerned with maintaining the lucrative business in contract labor, colonial officials worried about exporting an already transnational movement for Korean independence. By restricting Korean emigration, they attempted to limit the momentum of this movement.[11]

Among Koreans taking passage to Hawai'i in 1905, Soon Hyun was a recent graduate of Jen Den Kiu Ko Sat, a Japanese college. While studying in Japan, Hyun had converted to Christianity. Like many in his generation of Korean converts to Christianity, Hyun heard in the words of Jesus invoked by missionaries a distinctly anti-imperial message.[12] He later explained, "The basic reason for this close alliance between the religious and political interests of the Korean people is that Christianity reached Korea at a time when Korea was brought under Japanese subjugation, and the Korean people sought the church as a sanctuary. Furthermore, the Korean people came to identify the Christian concept of brotherhood as freedom and equality."[13]

Hyun signed on in 1903 as a labor recruiter for the East-West Development Company. Many Korean-run schools were closed during the initial occupation by Japan. Hyun, his wife, Maria, and their daughter, Alice, left Korea for Hawai'i, where they became deeply involved in Korean diasporic nationalist politics. Soon Hyun found work in the sugarcane fields as an overseer. He founded a "Self-Rule Association" to advance Korean cultural identity in Hawai'i and to maintain the transnational struggle for Korean liberation. Subsequently, he became a minister to widely dispersed Korean-Hawai'ian plantation settlements, eventually founding and leading the first Korean church on Kauai in 1905. While the Hyuns lived in Hawai'i, they had two more children: Elizabeth and Peter. Because they were born in Hawai'i, Elizabeth and Peter were American citizens under the Organic Act of 1900.[14]

By 1907, the Hyuns were compelled by patriotic conviction to return to Seoul. There, Hyun taught at a Methodist Mission high school, Pai Jai School, and immersed himself in nationalist politics. During this time, the Hyuns added five more children to their family: Soon Ok, Paul, Joshua, David, and Mary. These Korean-born children were subjects of the Japanese empire and, under the U.S. laws of the time, were "aliens ineligible to naturalize." In Korea, Hyun was involved in the planning of the March 1, 1919, uprisings, which took place two months after the funeral for the last Korean monarch, Emperor Kwang Mu. Just before the uprising, Hyun fled Korea for the comparative safety of the émigré Korean community residing in the French sector of Shanghai. The rest of his family eventually joined him in Shanghai. Later, they moved together across the Pacific back to Hawai'i.[15]

The Hyun family's serial exiles and reunions were typical of the transnational migrations of many Koreans during the Japanese occupation. The Hyuns were initially able to emigrate as contract laborers during the slim margin of time between 1903 and 1905. After this period, Koreans migrated from Hawai'i to California; a small number of students and picture brides were able to come from Korea. Many of this generation left from points outside Korea, such as China, Manchuria, and elsewhere in the eastern portion of the Soviet Union. Many from this generation remained politically active, founding a tradition of diasporic political engagement.[16]

In Hawai'i and the United States, the Hyun family remained engaged with the transnational politics of homeland liberation. Hyun worked for the Korean Provisional Government abroad throughout the 1920s and 1930s, incurring the lasting enmity of Syngman Rhee through bitter political conflicts in Washington and Hawai'i.[17] Of the Hyun children, Peter, Alice, and David, in particular, were politically involved with Korean as well as American domestic politics throughout their lives. But the mixed status of the Hyun family, as foreign-born and American citizens, had grave implications for the consequences of their ongoing transnational political engagements. David Hyun, who eventually prevailed in his long struggle against deportation, was a founding member of the LACPFB.

On their routes to Los Angeles, Mexicans and Koreans encountered familiar and new adversaries. In the process, their identities and affiliations broadened and changed. The next section looks at the ways in which migrants drew on homeland experiences of repression to resist the segregation they encountered in Los Angeles and the deportation drives waged against them by a militarized INS.

Radical Migrant Imaginaries in Los Angeles

Coming to Los Angeles in the early twentieth century, Korean and Latinx migrants created imaginaries charged with their memories of prior struggles as well as their adaptation to their new environments. These imaginaries, in turn, transformed the political culture of Los Angeles.

For example, popular Mexican American musical versions of the border struggles familiar to the revolutionary generation of migrants celebrated "banditos" who fought against injustice and repression with pistols in their hands as heroes. These corridos reframed border struggles not as the legitimate operation of sovereign Texas, New Mexico, and Arizona but as the daring exploits of border crossers dauntlessly seeking adventure and opportunity. Corridos, many of which were written as political satire during the Mexican Revolution, flourished as a popular urban art form in Los Angeles.[18]

Just as corridos recast the racial logic of the encounter between the military/border patrol and the indigenous/migrant, Korean American activist Peter Hyun, in his autobiography, parodies the embodiment of American power in Asia by mocking Douglas MacArthur's famous return to the Philippines at Corregidor. En route to Korea to work for the American Military Government in 1945, Hyun visited Corregidor. He viewed the devastation wrought on much of the town by the U.S. infantry, learning from a Filipino longshoreman that the one standing tower was a brewery that turned out to be owned by MacArthur. Hyun discerns a decided "disaffection" toward MacArthur among the GIs stationed in the Philippines, which he credits to the loss of lives in the saving of the brewery, along with GI awareness of the phoniness of MacArthur's return:

> When the Japanese forces were nearly wiped out in the Philippines, to be safe, General MacArthur staged a landing of U.S. forces on the Leyte beaches far North of Manila. And when assured of absolute safety, he staged the historic 'I shall return' scene for posterity. The camera crews were ready. . . . The general had indeed returned. I didn't hear a single kind word from any GI.[19]

In communities made up of substantial populations of the foreign born, such alternative narratives of empire gained particular currency in the context of early Cold War repression.

This section situates the struggles of these communities against deportation in the postwar period in the context of the cultural politics of Los Angeles in the 1940s and 1950s. It locates a group of Mexican Americans targeted for deportation, known as the "Santa Ana Four"—Cruz, Esparza, Espinoza, and Gonzalez—as part of the large cohort of Mexican Revolution–era migrants and places Guatemalan American activist Moreno in the context of her participation in Los Angeles radical migrant imaginaries of the period. It also situates the Korean diasporic activists involved in producing the newspaper *Korean Independence* in the context of a transnational, migrant imaginary.

Participation in immigrant rights organizing by the foreign born in Los Angeles constituted what historian George Sánchez calls "a new politics of opposition." Sánchez explains this "new politics of opposition" as necessary for foreign-born communities to engage with local struggles. He describes a reorientation of the Mexican American community in Los Angeles toward workplace- and community-based struggles after the repatriation campaigns of the 1930s· While they were still engaged in transnational struggles, Mexican Americans in Los Angeles recognized the significance of local politics and alliances. Comparatively new to Los Angeles, many Koreans were also drawn into local and national politics in the United States.[20]

The development of radical migrant imaginaries after World War II drew on prior political formations. According to historian Mark Wild, the Communist Party of Los Angeles maintained a decentralized structure throughout the 1930s, supporting satellite organizations often organized along the lines of ethnic and racial identity. Labor organizing in agricultural and cannery work brought workers of different national origins together. Historian Vicki Ruiz argues that their experiences working together in the United Cannery, Agricultural, Packing, and Allied Workers of America (UCAPAWA) gave Jewish and Mexican women a sense of solidarity in southern California. Like Filipinx cannery workers farther north, UCAPAWA members were engaged in the March Inland during the 1930s and 1940s. While many such organizations were targeted for repression and destruction after the war, the decentralized, multiethnic political climate of progressive Los Angeles fostered new organizations, such as the LACPFB, that drew on bonds of solidarity and the collective migrant imaginaries of prior connections.[21]

Migrant imaginaries also drew on specific diasporic histories of struggle. In 1909, the Korean National Association (KNA) was founded in California to advance the cause of national independence and to advocate for Korean immigrants in the United States. The KNA often negotiated directly with the State Department, opposing Japanese attempts to restrict Korean emigration. David Lee of the KNA wrote to Secretary of State William Jennings Bryan in 1913, "We, the Koreans in America, are not Japanese subjects, for we left Korea before the annexation of Japan, and we will never submit to her as long as the sun remains in the heavens."[22]

The KNA was a key organization in a broad spectrum of diasporic Korean American politics that, in time, ranged from left-leaning organizations, such as the Korean Revolutionary Nationalist Party, to more centrist alliances with the U.S government. Korean migrants arrived during the exclusion period and were barred from naturalization. The deportation case against David Hyun rested on his inability to become a citizen; his American-born family members, including his brother Peter, had the comparative safety of their birthright citizenship. Many Korean Americans like David Hyun acculturated to life in the United States in the context of their exclusion from full citizenship. At the same time, many maintained affective ties to the struggle for national independence in Korea. As historian Richard Kim points out, the virtual exclusion of Koreans from political participation in U.S. society meant that "mobilization around homeland-related causes represented the only means to exercise a meaningful voice within the U.S. polity."[23]

After the war, many diasporic Koreans turned to U.S. politics while still maintaining their commitment to the national liberation struggle in Korea. Asian American communities were transformed by changes in immigration policy as well as the aftershocks of Japanese internment. These communities were also targeted during Operation Wetback and the expanded deportation of suspected subversives. Deportation had long been a racialized operation in Asian American communities, as Asian "aliens ineligible to citizenship" under federal law had been targeted for suspicion of illegal entry since the late nineteenth century. But during the Korean War period, the deportation of Asians, and specifically Korean Americans, was also a component of a global militarization.[24]

Kim describes the development of "Constructive Americanism" in Korean communities during the 1930s and 1940s. KNA leader Kilsoo Haan advocated a dual strategy of engagement in U.S. society and continued work for Korean independence. Kim explains, "Korean nationalism facilitated the development of a collective identity as ethnic Americans. This identity was not solely rooted in cultural ties to the homeland or imagined notions of a Korean nation-state, but also emerged from the daily experiences of living in the United States." In these daily experiences, diasporic Koreans contended with some of the same forces arrayed against other immigrant communities in Los Angeles, including Mexican Americans as well as Japanese American leftists opposed to the imperial state.[25]

Many of the Mexican migrants later targeted for deportation entered the Los Angeles area at a time of expansion in key industries requiring a steady supply of cheap labor. They were part of a massive migration of Mexicans north. Recruited by labor contractors, moved by newly developed railroad networks, and often fleeing the turmoil of the Mexican Revolution, this generation moved north and west, repopulating and transforming Mexican American communities in California and the Southwest.[26]

Historian David Gutiérrez points out that the extreme repression of Mexicans in California during the late 1920s and into the 1930s resulted in the diminishing of distance between native-born and migrant Mexican Americans. The narrowing of the gap between the native born and migrants represents an acculturation that is often ascribed by historians as part of the "cycle of assimilation," in which new migrants form ethnic communities en route to assimilation and Americanization. But, as Gutiérrez's work clearly demonstrates, Mexican American communities in Los Angeles could not gather many of the fruits offered by Americanization. Like Korean Americans, many Mexican Americans acculturated into broader struggles. In founding El Congreso de Pueblos de Habla Española, Moreno linked immigrant rights to civil rights, arguing that "a people who have lived twenty and thirty years in this country, tied by family relations with early settlers, with American-born children, cannot be uprooted without the complete destruction of the faintest semblance of democracy and human liberties for the whole population."[27]

Many of the Mexican migrants who were later targeted for deportation entered the Los Angeles area at a time of expansion in key industries requiring a steady supply of cheap labor. Most found work in agriculture, on the railroads, or in domestic service. In Orange County, between 1910 and 1920, the Mexican population had increased by 175 percent. In 1920, the Los Angeles metropolitan area, which included barrios and colonias in Orange, San Bernardino, and Riverside Counties, had the second-largest population of Mexicans in the United States.[28]

Throughout the 1920s, despite economic downturns and increased regulation at the border, Mexican migrants continued to enter the Los Angeles area. According to historian Zaragosa Vargas, three-quarters of Mexicans in Los Angeles during the 1930s worked in unskilled jobs. By 1940, there were close to half a million Mexicans in California; one-third of them were foreign born. Agricultural and domestic workers were left out of the collective bargaining rights ensured by the National Labor Relations Act of 1934; the majority of Mexican American workers lacked federal protections.[29]

The revolution-era generation of migrants from Mexico faced unique struggles in Los Angeles and the rest of the United States, confronting segregation in schools and housing, discrimination and marginalization in the workforce, and recurring regimes of surveillance and deportation, from the repatriation campaigns of the 1930s, to urban police campaigns against young people identified as "zoot suiters" or pachucos/pachucas, to the militarized terror of Operation Wetback in the 1950s. Migrants engaged in these struggles in light of their positions as foreign-born workers with the least access to redress from the state and as transnational political subjects with memories of and investment in a homeland changed by the revolution. In the words of scholar Mary Lisbeth Haas, "Chicano labor struggles had roots in the Mexican ideological and political traditions of anarchism, revolutionary syndicalism, and the Mexican Revolution."[30]

Significantly, Mexican migrants to Los Angeles quickly entered labor struggles. In part, they did so because of appalling workplace conditions and the comparatively powerless position of union efforts unaided by federal collective bargaining rights. Historian Matt Garcia describes the struggle to organize the citrus industry as a "long revolution" that only became more difficult during the war years.[31] Such groups as El Congreso brought a Popular Front opposition to global capitalist imperialism to bear on local struggles, including those for the desegregation of housing and schools. This global awareness allowed labor activists, such as Bert Corona, to see themselves as transnational actors while they struggled for citizenship rights in a highly racialized context.

Just as Mexican Americans organized in Mexican as well as multiethnic unions in the fields, industrial workers collaborated with African Americans during the 1930s and 1940s. Initially, they demanded protection by the Fair Employment Practices Commission, and later they fought for access to war work and the federal housing afforded to war workers. In the late 1930s and during the war, Mexican American organizations fought threats of deportation while they worked with African Americans to demand equal opportunity for defense work. The practice of forging interethnic alliances also characterized the immigrant rights movement after the war.

In Los Angeles, Vargas points out, the struggle for labor rights also became a struggle for civil rights. Like ongoing attempts to organize the fields, canneries, and factories, the struggle for civil rights was characterized by multiethnic alliances as well as the palpable presence of the foreign born. In the citrus community of Lemon Grove, Mexican parents organized a group to press for desegregation of the public schools, El Comité de Vecinos de Lemon Grove, and won an early victory against segregation in 1931. Eight years later, the first assembly of the Congress of Spanish-Speaking Peoples called for immigrant rights and for desegregation of housing, work, and schools.

The struggle to desegregate schools in Orange County pitted Mexican American and other civil rights activists against the powerful citrus growers' organization, the Associated Farmers. Many of the community leaders who were active in the struggle for school desegregation during the 1940s had previously been active in attempts to organize citrus work. In the struggle for school desegregation, the Mexican migrant imaginary shaped by the revolution continued to inspire activists. Activist Hector Tarranga explained at the time, "The Fifth of May stands for the beginning of political independence for all the people of Mexico[;] so[,] too, may the 5th of November go down in history as the day that California Mexican Americans struck the blow that brought them freedom."[32]

Like the struggle for labor rights, the struggle for school desegregation was multiethnic. The case for the plaintiffs in *Mendez v. Westminster* (1947) featured several amicus curie briefs. Featured among the authors were the American Jewish Congress; the American Civil Liberties Union (ACLU), the parent organization of the ACPFB; the Japanese American Citizens League; and the National Association for the Advancement of Colored People (NAACP), whose brief was, in part, the work of the young Thurgood Marshall. Alliances formed in this struggle infused later immigrant rights formations. Similarly, progressives around Los Angeles came together around the defense of Mexican American youths in the racially charged Sleepy Lagoon case. Moreno was active in this case; California state legislator Jack Tenney accused her of "anti-Americanism" and may have called on the INS to deport her as a result of her advocacy. Kurashige describes how, even though interethnic alliances in Los Angeles in this period were complicated by racial categories anchored in of white supremacy, these alliances were a site where "progressive activists of all races repeatedly sought to develop a counterhegemonic vision of racial solidarity."[33]

"Constructive Americanism," like Sánchez's "new politics of opposition," constituted a kind of alternative, radical acculturation through which Korean and Mexican Americans drew on migrant imaginaries to assert political subjectivity in the circumscribed context of racialized repression in Los Angeles. And new forms of political organizing became crucial as a militarized INS increasingly turned its attentions to the presence of foreign-born radicals in cities after 1945.

The Racial Education of Joseph May Swing

The INS pursued the mass deportations of Mexican Americans as well as those of leftist Korean Americans under the leadership of Joseph May Swing, who retired as the commanding general of the Sixth Army immediately after the withdrawal of U.S. troops from the Korean Conflict in 1953. Under Swing, the expansion of deportation as a tool of "post-entry social control" was part of the great concern for loyalty and the overall narrowing of ideas of appropriate political citizenship characterizing the Cold War period overall.

As Daniel Kanstroom explains, the expansion of deportation from an operation denying entry at the border to a sweeping form of coercion aimed at the foreign born constituted a weakening of immigrant political status—a kind of "eternal probation." Such postentry social control had been deployed in the United States against first the Chinese and then, gradually, other immigrants since the inauguration of Chinese exclusion in 1875. Deportation had also been utilized, postentry, against other immigrants in specific incidents, such as the Bisbee Deportation of 1917, in which the Immigration Service essentially responded to alarms sounded by mining interests about worker radicalism and against a multiracial contingent of Industrial Workers of the World (IWW) members active in San Diego and Tijuana during the Mexican Revolution and Free Speech conflicts. Under Swing's tenure as INS commissioner, heightened scrutiny of the political affinities of the foreign born became standard operating procedure.[34]

In its mid-twentieth-century incarnation, deportation was also inspired by military campaigns against indigenous counterinsurgencies in the Americas and in Asia, which is why it is significant that Swing was the first career military man to serve as INS commissioner. In an era of expanding U.S. military presence overseas, Swing brought with him an understanding of conflict based on his experiences in military campaigns against indigenous insurgencies in Mexico, the Philippines, and Korea. Under his tenure, deportation was part of an increasingly militarized approach to policing immigrant communities.

Swing was a West Point graduate and a classmate of Dwight D. Eisenhower. In 1916, right after their graduation, he and Eisenhower participated in the "Punitive Expedition" into Mexico. Led by General John "Black Jack" Pershing and Lieutenant George Patton, the Punitive Expedition, also known as the Mexican or Pancho Villa Expedition, ventured across the border to quell Mexican Revolutionary activities and stop their spread into the United States. Responding to Francisco "Pancho" Villa's raid north of the border into Columbus, New Mexico, in 1916, the Punitive Expedition marked the last of a few small, direct U.S. interventions into the Mexican Revolution. Well before the formation of the U.S. Border Patrol in 1924, President William Howard Taft dispatched special military forces in 1911 to protect the borderlands from the chaos of the Mexican Revolution. He did so, in part, at the behest of ranchers in the United States, many of whom were afraid of the influence of the Mexican anarchist Magon brothers in southern California. Militarization of the border region responded to fears about the potential reach of Magonista sympathies within the United States, particularly in Mexican American communities, at the same time that the troops protected communities against the possibility of external threats from Mexico.[35]

By 1913, Woodrow Wilson's government, while publicly abjuring "gun boat diplomacy," was secretly backing the ascendance of the Mexican Constitutionalist Party, led by wealthy Sonoran plantation owner Venustiano Carranza. After American soldiers protecting U.S. interests in Tampico oil refineries were detained in April 1914, President Wilson sent the Atlantic Fleet to Veracruz, where marines fought Mexican forces in the streets. Wilson's support of Carranza and his Constitutionalist Party marked a decided switch from his administration's prior backing of Villa as an acceptable ally based on Villa's ability to stabilize the country and respect U.S. property holdings.[36]

Historian Sterling Evans argues that Wilson's active support of Carranza was in part motivated by North American concerns for the sisal exported from the Yucatan and made into the crucial twine that bound the wheat produced in U.S. and Canadian farm states. As a northern plantation owner, Carranza seemed to the Wilson administration to be capable of stabilizing the border and the crucial sisal trade.[37] The raid perpetrated by Villa and his men on the small military town of Columbus, New Mexico, in March 1916 was, in part, retaliation for the occupation and for the U.S. government's defection from its former alliance with Villa. Five hundred Villistas attacked the town and were pushed back by the Thirteenth Cavalry, garrisoned in Columbus. At the time, Columbus was the largest Black military garrison in the West. In the fighting, one hundred of Villa's troops and seventeen Americans were killed.[38]

In the wake of Villa's raid, the 1916 National Defense Act allowed for the mustering of 110,000 National Guard troops to protect the U.S.-Mexico border. Many of these troops remained at the border; others were dispatched into Mexico. A week after the raid, Wilson ordered Pershing to pursue Villa and prevent further actions north of the border. General Frederick Funston, in charge of the Southern Department of the Army, cabled the War Department after Villa's raid:

> I urgently recommend that American troops be given authority to pursue into Mexican Territory hostile Mexican bandits who raid American territory. So long as the border is a shelter for them they will continue to harass our ranches and towns to our chagrin.[39]

Wilson approved the Punitive Raid, and the army chief of staff selected Pershing, who had a long record of counterinsurgency work, to lead it. Pershing had served in the frontier Native American wars and the Philippine Insurrection and had observed the Russo-Japanese War. He had commanded Buffalo soldiers on the western frontier, and he was familiar with the border intrigue that marked the revolutionary-era Southwest.[40]

The Punitive Expedition operated in northern Mexico from March 1916 through February 1917. It constituted a force of more than fourteen thousand troops, including Black soldiers of the Tenth Calvary and Twenty-Fourth Infantry units, backed up by National Guard troops patrolling the border. Many of the troops mustered for the Punitive Expedition were Buffalo soldiers who shared Pershing's background in counterinsurgency through their experience fighting Indians as well as insurgents in the Philippines.

The Punitive Expedition was a militarized border expedition. The racialized understanding of borders and insurgencies that characterized the experience of career military men like Pershing was not limited to the military. In a 1916 article in the *American Journal of International Law*, for example, editor-in-chief James Brown Scott of the Carnegie Endowment for International Peace ultimately condemns the raid for violating principles of sovereignty. But as he struggles to reconcile the clear need to "secure a reparation for the violation of American sovereignty" (338) with international principles, Brown initially justifies the expedition as a reprisal against raids comparable to Indian raids, noting that the right of the United States to cross the international border in reprisal for the depredations of Mexican Indians had been clearly established in 1856. Speaking of Villa, Brown explains, "A bandit is a bandit, whether he be an Indian or not."[41]

Such a militarized border expedition constituted a racial education for a recent West Point graduate like Swing. The chain of command of the Punitive Expedition contained its own racial logic, with Black soldiers relegated to defending lines of communication and working on the difficult issue of transportation, as Carranza forbade the U.S. Army the use of Mexican railroads. Anti-Black riots in Brownsville in 1906 had reinforced the fraught position of African Americans in uniform, while rumors of relaxed attitudes toward interracial relations west of El Paso, let alone south of the border, made white officers concerned about maintaining proper order among soldiers of color. Additionally, Pershing's command conveyed a sense of the Villistas as "bandits" prone to the primitive violence and itinerancy ascribed in the period to Indians and native Filipinx. What became Cold War counterinsurgency policy in immigration as well as foreign policy was founded on this key notion of indigenous peoples as lawless and prone to violence.[42]

The Punitive Expedition trained Swing to see the border as a dangerous place requiring military intervention against insurgencies perpetrated by excitable banditos who were comparable to wild Indians. Because the Expedition ultimately traveled three hundred miles south of the border in pursuit of Villa, it also provided the lesson that border enforcement did not necessarily have to be restricted to the physical border between nations. It was likely during his service on the Punitive Expedition that Swing acquired a taste for the countryside of northern Mexico. While Carranza's army was divided, with some defecting to join Villa and others collaborating with the Americans, Swing managed to make friends among the Mexican officers. These friendships would later inspire sustained cross-border collaboration in immigration enforcement.

Carranzistas shared a racial common sense about the border remarkably similar to that of career U.S. military men. As American troops made their way southwest through Chihuahua and then into Sonora, Sinaloa, and Durango, they traversed territory only recently dispossessed from Yaquis. The massive deportations of Yaquis under Díaz from Sonora to the Yucatan to provide cheap labor for the sisal plantations to the south were part of what Evans calls the "henequen-wheat complex," facilitating hemispheric economic interdependency. American investors in Mexican railroads aided the deportation efforts in the name of pacification, supplying weapons from across the Arizona border. It was common in northern Mexico at the time to refer to Yaqui rebels with the same criminalizing dismissal used against Villistas: "banditos."[43]

Swing's INS administration was marked by controversy over his use of government resources to conduct hunting expeditions in Mexico. Swing explained these hunting trips, along with the barbecues he sponsored in Mexico for border guards on both sides, as important social events in which he promoted collaboration between Mexican and U.S. Border Patrols. Such collaboration was one characteristic of Swing's internationalist vision. Many of the Mexican generals who hosted these hunting expeditions, according to Swing, had been lieutenants he encountered during the Pershing expedition.[44]

Historian Kelly Hernandez notes the significance of such transnational collaboration in modernizing the Border Patrol and in implementing Operation Wetback. But the regulation of cross-border migration had an older history: it was anchored in the dispossession of Native lands and forced migration of Native people as laborers. Swing's Sonoran friends would have been familiar with the technology of deportation, since portions of their lands had only recently been carved out of formerly Yaqui territories. While Swing was lampooned by the press for these visits during his tenure as INS commissioner, his use of government property for recreational hunting trips south of the border was a component of a developing, transnational culture of counterinsurgency.[45]

During his subsequent military career, Swing served under General Peyton March in World War I in Europe. He was decorated for his participation in the liberation of the Philippines from the Japanese at Luzon during

World War II. Under his command, the Eleventh Airborne Division liberated the Los Baños prisoner of war and civilian internment camp. This raid is widely credited with revolutionizing airborne operations through careful planning—the same concern for efficient operation that would subsequently distinguish Swing's tenure as INS commissioner. After the Pacific war ended with the bombing of Hiroshima-Nagasaki, the Eleventh Airborne moved to Okinawa, where it helped facilitate the occupation of Japan.[46]

From 1951 to 1953, Swing served as the commanding general of the Sixth Army, which was deployed during the U.S. intervention in Korea. By 1953, the United States was strongly allied with Rhee in South Korea. For the State Department, Rhee represented a stable anti-Communist leader in Asia. Because of the timing of Swing's career move from the military to the INS, and because the implementation of Operation Wetback overlapped with the Korean War, this police action in Asia emerges as a key moment in postwar militarization and its impact on immigration enforcement in the United States. For Koreans in the diaspora, Rhee's ascendance also marked the ascendance of a particular transnational vision. Many opposed the American alliance with the Korean Republic. Like the Korean American deportees who were targeted for deportation after the Korean Conflict, Rhee had long been involved in émigré Korean nationalism in the United States and Hawai'i. He had been working for Korean liberation in Washington, DC, since the 1920s. His Korean American enemies in the United States, including but not limited to the Hyun family, suffered the consequences of his rise to power and influence. Swing was uniquely positioned to understand the necessary connection between maintaining stability in Korea through supporting Rhee and backing up this support by policing Koreans in the United States.

Because of his experiences in Mexico and in Asia, Swing was an expert in what today would be called counterinsurgency. After Swing retired from the U.S. Army in 1953, President Eisenhower contacted him to ask for help with "the wetback problem." Harlon B. Carter of the U.S. Border Patrol met with Swing to request military assistance in getting rid of undocumented Mexican nationals and securing the border. The Border Patrol proposed Operation Cloud Burst, which would have increased the number of fences along highly traveled areas of the border, maintained roadblocks on major thoroughfares crossing the border, and performed "mopping up" operations in cities and known migrant labor camps. The generals were enthusiastic. Swing in particular saw the operation as good training for troops bound eventually for Korea. Eisenhower, however, chose not to override the Posse Comitatus Act of 1878 to allow the army to be utilized for domestic enforcement.[47]

At the request of Eisenhower, Attorney General Herbert Brownell visited Swing in San Francisco during the summer of 1954. Initially, Brownell asked Swing to use the Sixth Army to help with the "illegal Mexican problem." In a 1971 interview, Swing recalled his initial response to Brownell:

> I explained to Brownell that the great majority of the so-called Sixth Army was recruits undergoing training for combat, and being pepped up to go into combat, with the idea that anybody they had to stop, they had to kill him; and to put these youngsters down along the border, particularly out on those lonely spots in Southern California and Arizona and the Big Bend in Texas, with very little training, the impulse to shoot should be at any sound, and after they'd killed a few hundred Mexicans, I thought we'd be back in the same situation we were in when [General] Winfield Scott went into Chapultepec.[48]

While retrospectively inventing a care for collateral damage that he lacked in 1954, Swing also indicated in his remarks how strongly his memory of the Punitive Expedition of 1916 informed his understanding of Mexican migrants. His reference to Winfield Scott's military triumph and execution of the Irish San Patricios loyal to Mexico at Chapultepec indicates his awareness of the long history of counterinsurgency at the Mexican border.

Instead of having Swing conduct a military excursion against Mexican Americans at the border, Eisenhower appointed him commissioner of the INS. Swing served in this position until 1961. The militarization of immigration enforcement by the INS under Swing included Operation Wetback and a particular interest in transnational Korean activists. This emphasis paralleled shifting American policy in Asia, in which Swing had played a significant role. Swing's international military experience made him particularly fluent with the increasingly transnational demands on the INS by a State Department responsive to foreign governments like that of Rhee and concerned with maintaining the security of the U.S.-Mexico border without sending troops across it.

Under Swing, immigration enforcement was a racialized counterinsurgency against suspected Communists and "wetbacks" infiltrating the United States. But many of those targeted by the expansion of deportation in this period were familiar with the politics of counterinsurgency. The next section considers the formation of the LACPFB as a response to the militarization of immigrant life in the early Cold War period.

Race, Repression, and Immigrant Rights

In October 1950, a group of progressives in Los Angeles who had been working with the CRC on immigrant rights issues formed the LACPFB.

David Hyun was the chairman of the organizing committee; soon after, Rose Chernin, a Jewish émigré from czarist Russia, became the first director of the organization. Drawing on the cultures of opposition existing in multiethnic Los Angeles, this autonomous branch of the ACPFB contended with the repression of the early Cold War period. As Alicia Schmidt Camacho writes, the LACPFB "brought together Jewish and Latino/a radicals who shared a pluralist vision for the incorporation of migrants into U.S. society." Because people of many national origins were targeted for harassment, intimidation, and deportation, the LACPFB drew a wide variety of migrants into its legal defense and political organizing work. These migrants contended with the militarization of Operation Wetback as well as ongoing harassment of foreign-born radicals. This section follows the development of the LACPFB as an immigrant rights organization.[49]

Immigrant rights activists understood the militarization of global security and immigration critically; they had access to an internationalism that challenged the Cold War perspective dominant in the United States. Many of the Mexican migrant generation targeted for deportation in the 1950s had left the same revolution-era turmoil that Swing was involved in pacifying in 1916. In opposing deportation, activists drew on these alternative understandings, creating a discourse of immigrant rights to oppose the predominant narrowing of citizenship and nationality. Anticolonial as well as antiracist, these immigrant rights discourses contested "the deportation terror" by formulating a transnational political consciousness and local interethnic alliances.

In its culture, the LACPFB practiced a blithe, Popular Front inclusion, in English, featuring a "Festival of Nationalities" with food and entertainment from different national groups and neighborhoods each year. The loose structure of this immigrant rights organization left individual communities sovereign, while forging antiracist, anti-imperialist, and anticapitalist ties. In 1957, for example, publicity for the seventh annual testimonial dinner featuring Paul Robeson proclaimed:

> The basic unity developing between the Jewish, Negro and Mexican people, together with all other decent Americans, will lay the ground-work for Peace and the shelving of all such un-American legislation as the Walter-McCarran law.

When the LACPFB held a Cinco de Mayo celebration, as it did in April 1954, the celebration of Mexican decolonization held echoes of the revolution and the generation who came to Los Angeles. *The Torch* celebrated the "heroic" battle of the Mexican people while making parallels to current struggles in the United States:

Cinco de Mayo is a holiday that can and should be understood by
the people of the United States, whose day of triumphant struggle
for independence is similar in important respects. It also has a
great meaning for the entire foreign-born, who are struggling in
the face of the racist, hateful Walter-McCarran Law to keep alive
in traditions of freedom.

This embrace of the Mexican Revolution made transnational connections
at the same time it hearkened to the struggle to desegregate Los Angeles
schools and workplaces during the 1930s and 1940s.[50]

Among the early cases taken up by the LACPFB were those of the "Santa Ana Four" and the circle around *Korean Independence*. The LACPFB
recognized the links between the unconstitutional sweeps of foreign-born
communities, including the internment of Japanese Americans; a long history of racialized repression against Mexican Americans in the Southwest
and California dating back to the Treaty of Guadalupe Hidalgo in 1848;
and the militarization of policing in urban communities as well as international proxy wars.[51] Nationally, the ACPFB had an explicitly antiracist
stance on U.S. immigration policy and foreign relations. Because of this, the
LACPFB could be a space for collaboration across lines of race and neighborhood and the creation of a multiracial politics of opposition.[52]

Where the INS under Swing saw migrants as potential counterinsur-
gents, immigrant rights activists understood deportation sweeps as part of
global militarization. Under Operation Wetback, the oppression of Mexican Americans extended into the cities. The dangerous militarization of
communities of color alarmed Los Angeles immigration attorney Josef
Widoff in 1954:

> A condition prevails here that is tantamount to martial law and . . .
> no person has any guarantee that he can obtain a hearing under
> legal process to determine whether or not he has any rights to re-
> main in the U.S. . . . . Only in war have the constitutional rights of
> people been so suspended. There is no guarantee that attacks be-
> gun against Latin-Americans cannot repeated . . . against all
> Americans.[53]

Under what immigrants and activists called Operation Terror, the urban arm of Operation Wetback, Elysian Park became a temporary holding
station for potential deportees, "a concentration camp, if you please,"
according to a pamphlet published by the LACPFB: *Shame of a Nation:
Police-State Terror against Mexican-Americans in the U.S.A.* The pamphlet describes INS activities in the city:

Business places were raided and their owners—many of them long-time U.S. citizens—were pushed about; customers and employees were dragged away by immigration authorities. Street cars and buses were stopped and their riders interrogated. U.S. planes swooped down upon fields at near-ground level to "spot" terrorized field workers who, thus fingered, were picked up by deploying U.S. deputies.[54]

The integration of political subversion with the ongoing "Mexican problem" of agricultural labor represented an expansion of the border and allowed for the militarization of deportation procedures in urban areas through the technology of "post-entry social control." The INS sought to extend its reach into urban neighborhoods; in 1951, a federal court decision blocked an attempt to allow for local supervision of those in deportation proceedings by deputized American Legionnaires. In 1957, the LACPFB reported that General Swing had admitted that "of 34,634 residents expelled from the US[,] 22,326 Mexicans were held in detention before departure and 7,683 in county jails, in violation even of the Walter-McCarran law." Swing succeeded in streamlining the efficiency of the deportation process and militarizing relations with urban immigrant communities.[55]

The cases of the "Santa Ana Four" and the Korean American intellectuals involved in publishing *Korean Independence* were pivotal to the formation of an immigrant rights community in Los Angeles. These were some of the first cases taken up by the organization's legal defense team. Additionally, the LACPFB recognized the dangerous militarization of Operation Wetback. It defended Mexican Americans targeted for deportation under this operation and critiqued it. In *Shame of a Nation*, the LACPFB notes the powerful convergence of the McCarran Act of 1950, the McCarran-Walter legislation of 1952, and Operation Wetback. It links contemporary repression against Mexican American workers to the Treaty of Guadalupe Hidalgo and the subsequent "despoiling" of Mexican American lands at the hands of Anglo landlords, the repatriation efforts of the 1930s, and the bracero guest worker program. Like the rhetoric of Moreno, Emma Tenayuca, and other labor organizers, the LACPFB asserts the rights of Mexican workers living in the area and identifies the deportation campaigns as racist and antilabor: "With this law, under pretext of hunting 'illegals' and 'subversives,' immigration service officers serve as a terroristic police force in Mexican communities, as a strike-breaking, union-busting force in the fields, shops and factories."[56]

Shame of a Nation also elaborates on the wide coalition protesting the raids on migrant communities. In particular, it points to "representatives of the Los Angeles Jewish community, whose 300,000 members recall with horror other pogroms and other concentration camps" and "Japanese residents, which number 110,000 in Los Angeles [and] remembered the U.S. Relocation Camps where they were imprisoned during World War II." This kind of coalition work drew on prior civil rights organizing in Los Angeles: Jewish, Japanese, and African American organizations had also contributed amicus briefs for *Mendez v. Westminster.*

Multiethnic organizing characterized the LACPFB. The organization drew on the progressive coalitions formed in Los Angeles around labor and civil rights activism during the 1930s and 1940s. For example, the program of the 1954 Fourth Annual Conference reports on cases against Mexican Americans in the area as well as a surge of deportations of Black workers from British Honduras. A special committee to protect the rights of these Hondurans was formed under the title of People's Defense Committee. The report explains: "This is fully in keeping with the policy of the Immigration Service to harass, arrest and deport Mexicans, West Indians, and other Negro workers, in a permanent campaign to deny them civil rights and pave the way for lower wage-scales."[57]

The LACPFB defended many Mexican Americans against the deportation sweeps of Operation Wetback. In addition, it represented migrants from around the globe, including Korea, Yugoslavia, Armenia, Greece, Japan, Okinawa, El Salvador, and the Philippines. In many cases, the LACPFB defended those charged under the McCarran and McCarran-Walter acts as "aliens" who had been associated in some way with the Communist Party or other subversive organizations. Arthur Dmytrick, for example, was an Austrian-born steelworker who had helped organize Local 1549 in 1937. He had never been able to naturalize, and the INS began deportation proceedings against him in 1947. Petros Lezos was a Greek sailor from Corfu Island who had jumped a Japanese ship with his entire crew in 1940. At that time, they were invited by the U.S. government to seek asylum from Nazi-occupied Greece. He became the editor of the *Greek-American Tribune* in Detroit and worked with the Greek Radio Club, which was supported by the Office of War Information as an antifascist organization. Lezos married an American citizen and tried to naturalize. He lost his registration card and applied for another one shortly before he was apprehended and ordered deported to Greece, his antifascist organizing work having become suspect in the context of the postwar Red Scare. The LACPFB defended him, arguing that he would face physical persecution if he were returned to Greece.[58]

Frieda and David Diamond, both Russian Jews, emigrated in the early twentieth century; they married in 1917 and had two children. David was active in trade union struggles in New York City between 1910 and 1922; he moved to Los Angeles in 1922, where he trained as an electrician and remained active in electrical trade unions. Blacklisted out of the electrical trade after the war, he became a small business owner. Frieda worked in the needle trades and was a shop representative for her dressmaker's union. Both had managed to naturalize in 1943 but found themselves fighting denaturalization after the war because of their politics. In a statement to the LACPFB in 1956, David explained:

> There are so many things to tell about our life and our dreams in the new country, the United States. When I was a child in Russia[,] I dreamed so much about the United States, where people can live in peace and get together, work together, and have the freedom to organize to make life worth living. . . . Naturally, when we came here[,] we tried to live up to these ideas of freedom and progress. Is there any crime in that?[59]

The LACPFB primarily defended left and labor activists from deportation. Political defendants ranged ideologically: some had been Communist Party members in the 1930s; others were active in trade unions; still others, like Lezos, identified as anarchists or, like Sang Ryup Park, as philosophical Communists. But in other cases, it defended migrants charged with violating the rapidly multiplying technicalities of immigration law. Okinawan activist Paul Shinsei Kochi was born in Japan in 1892 and entered the United States in 1918. In 1937, he published *Imin No Aiwa* (*An Immigrant's Sorrow Tale*). A self-employed gardener, he served in the Office of Strategic Services, as did Kimm, during the war. He worked in Japan after the war, on the Atomic Bombing Survey Corps, and was awarded a certificate of appreciation on his return to the United States in 1946. Subsequently, Kochi was active in the Okinawa Relief Committee. The deportation case against him was based on allegations that he had entered illegally through Calexico in 1918 after the "Gentlemen's Agreement" stipulated the exclusion of Japanese workers. The case was ultimately judged by the Supreme Court to be "non-political," and he was able to remain in the country.[60]

While the LACPFB functioned as legal defense for a wide-ranging community of the Los Angeles foreign born, it is clear that deportation targeted people on suspicion of their engagement in a broadly conceived counterinsurgency that threatened to undermine the stability of the U.S. government. Taken together, these deportation cases indicate the broad ideological, local, and transnational scopes of what was known as a "Red Scare." Just as migrants created radical imaginaries to sustain their struggles in Los Angeles, the INS under Swing envisioned the threats posed by immigrant communities.

The INS was suspicious of the multiracialism of the movement. In 1953, for example, Henry Martinez, a Mexican-born furniture worker facing deportation, was unable to attend the funeral for his infant child held in Tijuana. His wife, Alicia, was refused readmission to the United States. When Martinez went to the immigration office to report monthly, he was asked by INS officials, "Where did you get that Jew lawyer?"[61]

In the case against Jose Noreiga, the INS pointed to "his union activities; his work in the San Bernardino community among 'Hooverville' dwellers, impoverished victims of the Great Depression; the books he read, [which] made him suspect. . . . They even questioned the presence on his wall of a picture of the great Mexican liberator Benito Juarez."[62] This laundry list makes clear that part of what made Noreiga and other Mexican Americans in Los Angeles suspect were their political affinities, which allied them with the local Popular Front as well as broader, transnational constituencies. Operation Wetback targeted foreign-born Mexican Americans who had been active in civil rights and labor struggles.

This was also the case for the "Santa Ana Four." Two of the four had been political; two had not. Espinosa had been an organizer in the citrus fields in the 1930s, and he had organized neighborhood meetings during the 1940s. Cruz came to the United States at age nineteen and found work building railroads and working in fields and orchards. In 1933, he joined the Workers' Alliance, which played a key role in supporting organizing in the citrus fields during the major strike efforts of that period.[63] Cruz also fought to integrate schools. He was a member of the Orange County Community Chest, one of the organizations that played a key role in *Mendez v. Westminster*, the case that desegregated schools in Orange County.[64]

When Cruz joined the Workers' Alliance, it was a legal organization. But under the 1950 McCarran law, it was declared subversive. Membership therefore became punishable retroactively, with deportation for noncitizens or naturalized citizens and a fine for the U.S.-born.[65] Immigration officers went to Cruz's employer, trying to get him fired, but the employer defended him. Consequently, INS agents arrested him and took him to Terminal Island in Los Angeles Harbor, where he was held on $5,000 bail.[66]

At a benefit for Cruz's defense in 1951, his son, Ladislao, told of how Cruz had earned the enmity of the Associated Farmers of Orange County, who saw his struggles for full citizenship as undermining their need for cheap migrant labor:

> Mexican American workers who fight against this policy [the use of illegal Mexican workers and the need to keep them as second-class citizens] are made victims of political deportation charges, under the McCarran Act, which is being used more and more

against foreign-born workers who have lived here for most of their lives. Many who have fought against oppression and are being persecuted by the Immigration Service have lived here for thirty or more years, and have American-born children and sometimes grandchildren.[67]

The Associated Farmers of Orange County worked in the 1930s with the Orange County Sheriff's office to break strikes in the citrus fields, blacklisting many organizers and suspected troublemakers. Deportation was used as a weapon during these strikes.[68] In addition to their intimidation of citrus workers, the Associated Farmers agitated for the cheaper labor provided by the federally subsidized bracero program, eventually replacing a Santa Ana barrio community center with a labor camp for contract laborers.[69]

More than twenty years later, after the arrest of the "Santa Ana Four," the Associated Farmers warned of subversive activities led by Cruz, Esparza, Gonzales, and Espinosa. When Consuela Espinoza, Elias's wife, contacted Arizona Congressman James B. Utt, the congressman "intimated that he had received many requests from his constituency asking him to do something for Mr. Espinoza, but he regretted that at this moment he could do very little because the Associated Farmers of Orange County did not approve of Mr. Espinoza. He advised Mrs. Espinoza to see if she couldn't convince the Associated Farmers to change their minds about Mr. Espinoza."[70] The illegal blacklisting of workers in the 1930s migrated in the 1950s to the INS's use of the blacklist against suspected foreign-born subversives.

The use of the blacklist by the State Department had grave implications for Korean Americans in Los Angeles. With the occupation of Korea in 1946 and the partition in 1948, *Korean Independence* became quite critical of the United States. An editorial by Park in 1951 argues:

Let the Korean people alone. Let them decide what they want— whether they would choose the cause of "the free world" or the cause of "atheistic Communism." It's entirely up to them.

Withdraw foreign invading troops from Korea as speedily as possible. This is the prelude to peace and security of the world.[71]

After 1948, references to the United States as an "imperialist aggressor" in Korea abound in the pages of *Korean Independence*. With the overthrow of the Woon-hyung Lyuh government and the assassinations of Lyuh and Kim Koo, the United States was no longer seen as a potential liberator but as an obstacle to national self-determination. Just as the State

Department began to recognize Korean American "patriots," including Hyun, Kimm, the Kwaks, and Park, as potential subversives, these transnational activists understood the threat posed by the United States to their political objectives and their survival.

The LACPFB recognized the ways that Operation Wetback particularly targeted activists for civil rights and the precarious situation for transnational activists. *The Torch* noted how dangerous the visit of Rhee to Los Angeles in 1954 was for Korean Americans in the midst of deportation proceedings. The newsletter linked the militarization of overseas foreign policy to that of immigration enforcement.[72] After the United States withdrew south of the thirty-eighth parallel in Korea, the engagement of these Korean American activists with national liberation struggles challenged the internationalist project of the emergent transnational security state.

As part of the transition from supporting the general cause of Korean national liberation to its anti-Communist alliance with the new Republic of Korea, the State Department focused on the threat posed by the alliances of transnational Korean American activists. Many in the Korean diaspora had worked for the military effort in Japan. But, as the comparatively open culture of the Office of Strategic Services (OSS) was replaced by the secretive, hard-line climate of the CIA, the patriotism of Korean Americans committed to the liberation of their homeland came to seem dangerous.

Among Korean Americans who found themselves increasingly opposed to the U.S. partition and the Rhee government, Kimm, also known as Kim Kang, was born in what later came to be called North Korea in 1902. He was active in anticolonial uprisings against the Japanese in Korea and, like many young patriots of his generation, subsequently spent time in exile in Manchuria. Kimm came to the United States in 1928. He majored in geology at the University of Southern California and in 1936 obtained a degree as a metallurgical engineer at the Colorado School of Mines. He remained in the United States instead of following his wife and young son back to Korea, explaining, "In 1937, when I was about to leave the United States for Korea, Imperial Japan started war in China. I changed my life plan and joined in the struggle for peace and democracy, while working as a testing chemist in a nonferrous metal refinery."[73]

In 1939, Kimm was hired by the U.S. government to test naval and aircraft supplies. The U.S. government initiated deportation proceedings against him in 1941 for failing to maintain a continuous student visa, but these proceedings were suspended, likely because Kimm went to work for the OSS. Along with other "Korean patriots," as they were called by the military, he worked at the Catalina Island experimental station, preparing for the invasion of Japan and then, presumably, Korea. The Korean Americans in the OSS taught other soldiers to speak Japanese and advised officers on Korean geography and culture. Kimm said of his work for the OSS, "We were trained to help prepare for the invasion of Korea, then occupied by the enemy Japan. We were to camouflage ourselves, and be dropped by plane as paratroopers, or land by submarine, before the invasion. We were to supply advance information to the Army, to open the way for Army invasion."[74]

During one of his many deportation trials, Kimm was asked why he had not become a citizen during his long residence in the United States. He explained that when he first came to the United States, he was not eligible to naturalize, under the Asian exclusion policy. Later, in the OSS, his supervisor offered citizenship to the Korean Americans working at Catalina Island. Kimm explained:

> He asked our advice as to whether we would be more effective if we entered enemy-occupied Korea as Korean citizens. Our group decided that we would have the people's confidence more if we went in as Korean citizens.[75]

Kimm here expressed his attitude toward citizenship in the pragmatic terms of an OSS operative. Denying citizenship in the Japanese empire had been a key strategy of diasporic Koreans throughout the twentieth century; the KNA had used this argument to try to claim exemption for immigrant Koreans at Angel Island. In the context of the Cold War, the failure to naturalize could be made to seem tantamount to disloyalty. But Kimm's refusal to become a citizen either of the United States or, later, of South Korea was also an expression of a radical migrant imaginary. Embracing a unified Korea that no longer existed politically, Kimm insisted on a political subjectivity outside the imperial reach of the American Cold War. He eventually took voluntary departure for Czechoslovakia, where he and his second wife, Fania Bernstein, obtained visas for the Democratic People's Republic of Korea.[76]

Political subjectivity [handwritten marginal note]

Like the "Santa Ana Four," David Hyun was persecuted for his labor activism and political associations. In 1950, he was one of eleven aliens in Los Angeles named as active members of the Communist Party.[77] After voluntarily serving in the University of Hawai'i ROTC, Hyun worked his way through college in the sugarcane fields and eventually graduated from the university. He participated in the struggle to organize workers in the cane fields. After the war, Hyun worked as an architect-engineer in Honolulu, becoming a member of the Federation of Architects, Chemists, Engineers and Technicians. He was active in union politics and was appointed to the Congress of Industrial Organizations (CIO) executive board. At this time, the CIO in Hawaiʻi was deeply engaged in organizing in the cane fields; Hyun took part in supporting the successful strike of 1946 as well as the CIO Political Action Committee. Like Cruz and Espinosa, Hyun earned the enmity of the growers—in this case, the "Big Five," as the major owners of plantations, canneries, and shipping were known in Hawaiʻi.[78] In 1947, Hyun and his wife, Mary, left Hawaiʻi so he could pursue further architecture education at the University of Southern California. Hyun became a successful architect in Los Angeles; indeed, much of his work was given civic prominence at the same time that he was fighting deportation (see Chapter 5). In 1949, Hyun was arrested as an "undesirable alien"; these charges were dismissed, but he was arrested again after passage of the McCarran Act of 1950. This initiated a long legal battle, accompanied by several periods of incarceration, before Hyun was finally exonerated.

Although Hyun tried to naturalize and was allowed to file "first papers," he could not become a citizen because of his Korean birth. Perhaps because of the mixed citizenship of his family, Hyun's political identity was firmly grounded in his claim to American citizenship. A pamphlet put out by "Friends and Neighbors of David Hyun" asserts:

> He was convinced of his essential American citizenship, despite denial to him of his formal right to vote or hold political office. He was an American, husband of a native-born wife and father of a young American-born son; his was the right to petition for a redress of grievances.[79]

Hyun asserted his rightful claim to citizenship through his engagement with American politics. This attitude very much paralleled the radical imaginary expressed by other Angelenos, such as Moreno. These migrants believed that their work and political strivings made them already a part of America.[80] While they were accused of participating in "un-American" activities, migrants like Hyun and Moreno turned the tables, insisting on the vitality of their work for justice to true Americanism. Faced with deportation in 1949, Moreno proclaimed, "This Latin American alien came here to assist you in building and extending American democracy."[81]

Newspaper coverage of these stories of deportation, militarization, and repression appeared in the ethnic press, such as *Korean Independence*; the left press, such as the *Guardian*; and even the national press. These stories became part of the articulation of immigrant rights discourse. Immigrant advocates in the LACPFB conveyed ideas about global citizenship and human rights at a time when notions of citizenship and rights were profoundly narrowed in the name of national security. These articulations give historical depth to the emergence of the contemporary immigrant rights movement. Because many of these stories came from multiethnic organizations, they also point to ways in which different communities forged bonds of solidarity across racial divisions.   bonds of solidarity

The LACPFB, like the editors of *Korean Independence* and the small Mexican American civil rights organizations of Cold War Los Angeles, was part of a broad antiracist and anti-imperialist movement during the 1950s. Retaining transnational ties to communities and struggles outside the United States, these groups of necessity confronted the racialized repression targeting the foreign born in this period. The LACPFB continued to defend immigrant rights throughout the 1950s and 1960s. Because of their ongoing antiracist and anticolonial internationalism, the radical migrant imaginaries of this organization provide a bridge between historiographical understandings of the "Old" and "New" Left.

Although the LACPFB closed its doors in 1965, other organizations adopted its intersectional politics of immigrant rights. In 1968, Corona was among the founders of the Center for Autonomous Social Action (CASA), which featured this invocation in its charter: "To build an independent organization which believes that Latino or immigrant workers, with or without documents, must unite together in an organization that will defend their rights." Taking up this piece of the LACPFB's work, CASA became central to the Los Angeles Chicano Movement, expanding to include community and labor organizing efforts.

Founded during the crises of the Cold War and Operation Wetback, immigrant rights organizations in Los Angeles have continued to respond to the militarization and racialized terror of immigration enforcement. Today, immigrant rights organizations thrive in southern California and elsewhere; marches and public actions fill the streets with thousands of supporters. The origins of this movement lie in the work of the small, stalwart LACPFB.

The next two chapters pan out a little bit to look at dialectical cultures of immigrant rights during and after the cold war. Chapter 5 looks to the creative work of ACPFB writers and artists and the ways in which they drew on migrant imaginaries to create narratives of belonging in the face of the deportation terror. In contrast, Chapter 6 examines the ways in which the ACPFB was able to broadcast sympathies for "red aliens" in national newspapers until Operation Wetback foreclosed on such advocacy with its creation of the "illegal alien" threat. Despite this foreclosure, Chapter 7 looks at the work of the ACPFB during the 1970s and how it created conditions for the emergence of a much larger national immigrant rights movement in the 1980s and 1990s.

"CREATING DANGEROUSLY"

Foreign-Born Writers and
Crimes of Persuasion

The people are not alien
one to the other.
And the day will come,
when,
In letters of fire and love,
this consuming fact
is written
and spoken
and sung
by the people
to the people.

—Unattributed [David Hyun?],
   "To Four Who Stand but Do Not Wait,"LACPFB,
   Los Angeles Committee for the Protection of the Foreign Born Papers

"A Virtual United Nations": Midnight Raids

Trinidadian American writer Claudia Jones described the "McCarran wing" of Ellis Island where she was detained as a "virtual United Nations" because of the diverse crew incarcerated there. The "midnight raids" that followed the 1950 McCarran Internal Security Act targeted foreign-born writers and intellectuals in particular. Chapter 1024(G) of the act specifically referred to "aliens who write or publish, or cause to be written or published" materials calling for the overthrow or opposition to government, including destroying property or advocating Communism.[1]

This chapter investigates the creative work of foreign-born writers accused of violating chapter 1024(G) of the McCarran Internal Security Act. Contemporary Haitian American writer Edwidge Danticat writes about the precarious position of the immigrant artist. Fleeing danger in their home nations, migrant writers, artists, and journalists are constantly impelled between worlds, between their ties to histories of violence and their ongoing efforts to "create dangerously," to "remake the world" they see. Danticat writes of the murdered journalist Jean Dominique and of the ex-

[handwritten margin note: immigrant artists]

ecution in Port-au-Prince of the freedom fighters Louis Drouin and Marcel Numa. Like Danticat, these figures lived between Haiti and its diaspora, haunted by each. She writes, "The nomad or immigrant who learns something rightly must always ponder travel and movement, as the grief-stricken must inevitably ponder death."[2]

Like the contemporary Haitian American figures Danticat describes, the foreign-born artists, writers, and intellectuals targeted by the McCarran Act conjured migrant imaginaries that referenced the histories that occasioned their migration from their homelands as well as conditions in the United States. Born of these migrant imaginaries, their creative work framed alternate horizons. Literary scholar Nadia Ellis writes about the "deterritorialized belonging" conjured by diasporic writers: "a future-oriented belonging, a feeling for a place that relies on the belief in a surely finer place to come." Under the McCarran Act, imagining such horizons constituted a crime of persuasion against a "Nation of Immigrants" sure of where it stood and devoid of conflict or multiple loyalties. Writers whose work created a sense of "deterritorialized belonging" were incarcerated in detention facilities, such as Ellis Island; many of them were eventually deported.[3]

How did the creative efforts of migrant artists seem to stand in the way of the secure horizons promised by Cold War Americanism? What were the ambitions and achievements of their work? Despite the deportations of many of these artists, their creative work continued to circulate, functioning as a resource for imagining other futures and ways to belong outside the strictures of Cold War citizenship. The American Committee for the Protection of the Foreign Born (ACPFB) deployed their language and images in its advocacy, making the work of these foreign-born artists become part of the culture of the Cold War immigrant rights movement.

Some of those detained in the raids were from communities defined by language and national origin. Knut Heikkinen, for example, had long played a central role in the radical Finnish American press in the northern Midwest; in Los Angeles, Diamond Kimm, David and Peter Hyun, and Sang Ryup Park edited the bilingual, diasporic newspaper *Korean Independence*. And, of course, there were those, like Jones, who worked from the many media platforms provided by the Communist Party USA (CPUSA). Writing in the Finnish language newspaper *Eteenpäin* in 1950, the year of the McCarran Act, Heikkinen explains the stakes of deporting foreign-born writers:

> This kind of politics can only lead to the loss of the concept of freedom of the press, and to prohibiting millions of Americans from reading publications in their own languages. . . . [T]his ha-

rassment of editors of foreign-language newspapers [is] a dangerous precedent, which puts in danger the fundamental democratic
rights of all Americans.[4]

For Heikkinen and other foreign-born writers, the enhanced threat of
deportation under the McCarran Act countered the highest principles of
the nation. As leftists, these writers were engaged in scrutinizing manifest
national ideals and contrasting them to the realities of ongoing inequality
and violence. Their engagement constituted the grounds of their acculturation, the way they chose to become Americans.

Literary scholar and Jones biographer Carole Boyce Davies situates
Jones's essays and poetry from immigrant detention, federal prison, and
her eventual exile to London within a long tradition of African American
prison writing. Boyce Davies explains that incarceration and deportation
constitute denials of citizenship rights: those detained, incarcerated, and/
or deported write from a particular, vexed relationship to national citizenship.[5] This chapter looks broadly at the work produced by foreign-born
writers and intellectuals before as well as after their arrests, detentions,
and removals. I argue that, as much as their work spoke to the depredations of incarceration and deportation, their "dangerous" creativity also
worked to create a literary and artistic horizon of alternate Americanism,
as reflected in the Heikkinen editorial quoted above. Broadcasted in advocacy campaigns, this dangerous creativity was part of the movement culture of the ACPFB.

That juridical anti-Communism targeted writers directly engaged with
the CPUSA is not surprising. But many journalists from the foreign-
language press outside the party also found themselves caught up in the
McCarran Act dragnet. Each of these individuals engaged in progressive
journalism. Each imagined democratic, multiracial horizons and criticized
injustice, segregation, and global imperialism. These activities attracted surveillance and persecution. But the scale of the McCarran Act dragnet, and
the multiracial and mixed ideological cast of its victims, indicates that the
raids had a broader mark than individual dissenting journalists. These writers illuminated alternative spatial and temporal trajectories, pointing to the
possibility of immigrant acculturation into an alternately imagined, truly
democratic nation. Their literary work created a democratic horizon that
contrasted with coercive Americanization into a white supremacist order.
Their participation in transnational newspapers and journals put them in
dialogue with each other and with activists around the world. Even more
than the existence of an active Communist party, these networks and imaginings were subversive to the ascendant Cold War order.

The ACPFB represented foreign-born activists experiencing persecution. In doing so, it engaged with multiracial, internationalist networks of writers and activists. The journalism of immigrant rights advocacy therefore placed itself within the sights of juridical anti-Communism. Federal persecution of ACPFB leaders, such as Abner Green, Rose Chernin, and David Hyun, attempted to curtail the advocacy of the organization. As historian George Sánchez points out, migrant organizing in response to detention and deportation is an act of remembering in the face of erasure and enforced forgetting. Such remembering ran counter to the story being told at the time; it also created alternative futures.[6]

"What Is an Ocean between Us? We Know How to Build Bridges":[7] The Transnational Migrant Imaginary of Claudia Jones

The dangerous creativity of foreign-born writers is best framed by drawing on the pioneering theoretical work of Trinidadian American writer Jones. The ACPFB took part in the coalition opposing Jones's deportation, ultimately helping her secure "voluntary departure" to England rather than deportation back to the Caribbean.

Like Danticat's migrant Caribbean artists, Jones was impelled between various claims on her identity. Her biographer, Boyce Davies, writes that "Claudia Jones lived and organized at the intersection of a variety of positionalities (anti-imperialism and decolonization struggles, activism for women's rights, the critique of appropriation of black women's labor, the challenge to domestic and international racisms and their links to colonialism) and was therefore able to articulate them earlier than many of her contemporaries." Jones drew on the work of other Black leftist writers, such as Grace Campbell, Louise Thompson Patterson, and Esther Cooper Jackson, to theorize what these writers called "triple oppression": the intersecting burdens imposed by race, class, and gender. Because she was also foreign born and conscious of events unfolding in her native Caribbean, Jones theorized triple oppression in the context of a particularly internationalist perspective.[8]

Jones expressed the migrant aspects of her identity much more directly during her residence in the United Kingdom, before her untimely death in 1964. But an internationalist migrant imaginary always framed her intersectional analysis of power and politics in the United States.[9]

Jones's work on triple oppression, along with her consistent and evolving understanding of the internationalism of the struggle against white supremacy, illuminates what seemed particularly un-American and threatening about the work of foreign-born intellectuals during the Cold War. Jones was a writer her entire life. Her father was an editor of what she referred to as "an American West Indian newspaper" before he lost his job during the Depression. Jones wrote a weekly column in a Black nationalist newspaper before she joined the CPUSA in 1936; subsequently, she edited and wrote for party organs the *Weekly Review* and the *Daily Worker*. After her forced relocation to Britain, she founded a newspaper, the *West Indian Gazette*.

Writing constituted Jones's acculturation, her migrant imagining of American life. Historian Erik McDuffie points out that she changed her name from Claudia Vera Cumberback to Claudia Jones after joining the Communist Party in 1936. She did not change her name again, even during her brief marriage to fellow Communist Party member Abe Skolnick. She applied for citizenship in 1938 but was denied. Jones's naturalization, then, was into an intersectional migrant imaginary: her self-naming was as an activist and a writer.[10]

The postwar Red Scare targeted membership or association with the CPUSA as subversive. Jones's 1951 arrest was on the basis of prior Smith Act charges as well as new McCarran Act charges that an article she had published in *Public Affairs* constituted subversion. Her article, "Women in the Struggle for Peace and Security," promotes the kind of internationalist, intersectional analysis that government readers found so dangerous. In it, Jones heralds the International Women's Day disarmament protests of 1950, linking sectarian left activism with campaigns joined by mainstream, white Protestant organizations; women's antiwar groups, such as the Women's International League for Peace and Freedom; and "Negro civic and middle class led" clubs. Further, she asserts that the "sex antagonism" between returning GIs and women workers was the result of capitalist antiworker reaction, likening it to the antilabor Taft-Hartley Act. Jones's genealogy of resistance links Rose Pastor Stokes, Williana Borroughs, Elizabeth Cady Stanton, and Elizabeth Gurley Flynn with German Communist Clara Zetkin and Soviet women; she also writes about the struggle for school desegregation in "Negro, Puerto Rican, Mexican and other working-class communities." This article adheres to the Fosterite party line of the CPUSA, asserting that the full emancipation of women "will be achieved only in Socialist America." Throughout her writing career in the United States, Jones asserted that triple oppression, the "special oppression she faces as Negro, as woman, and as worker," constituted the true "iron curtain."[11] Describing the long struggle of Black women workers, she illuminated an often-repressed American history and imagined a path toward freedom.[12]

At her trial with twelve other Communist leaders arrested under the McCarran Act, Jones pointed out that the prosecution had declined to introduce her writing as evidence of subversion. Further, she explained that the exclusion of her writing constituted a violation of her constitutional rights consistent with her experience of violence and humiliation as an American of African descent: the lack of her writing eviscerated her power, her "fragile agency." Jones said:

> Is this not a tyrannical violation of the American dream of life liberty and the pursuit of happiness? . . .
> It was here on this soil . . . that I early experienced experiences which are shared by millions of native-born Negroes—the bitter indignity and humiliation of second-class citizenship, the special status which makes a mockery of our Government's prated claims of a "free America" in a "free world" for 15 million Negro Americans.[13]

Here, Jones positioned herself as American and pointed to her trial as un-American for the evisceration of her agency through the exclusion of her written work and for the long U.S. history of crimes against African Americans. Jones asserted that she did not import radical ideas from some far-flung homeland, but that the experience of becoming African American trained her to be critical, catapulting her into political activism.

Before being deported to England in 1955, Jones rarely discussed her foreign-born origins in her published writings or in her personal correspondence. She identified rhetorically as well as emotionally with local struggles grounded in race, class, and gender. But as she experienced detention and removal from the United States to the different racial context of Great Britain, Jones's migrant, exilic identity came to play a greater role in her writing and activism. Adding migrant identity to Jones's pioneering work on the intersections between oppressions based in race, class, and gender provides a framework to understand the foreign-born writers targeted by the McCarran Act raids of 1951.[14]

On board *Queen Elizabeth* in December 1955, Jones confronted uncertain horizons. Her always poor health worsened during her prison term at the segregated federal facility in Alderson, West Virginia, where she was denied basic medical care. Active advocacy for her case failed to allow Jones to remain in the United States. However, these advocates persuaded the State Department to allow her to travel to England rather than be returned to Trinidad, then experiencing political upheaval on the eve of independence.[15]

As she had in prison, Jones wrote poetry on board ship. In these confined spaces, she was forced to imagine new horizons for herself. Literally facing into the unknown on the ship's deck, Jones wrote this "Paen to the Atlantic," which reads like an ode to migration:

CALL

TO A CONFERENCE

TO DEFEND

CLAUDIA JONES

AGAINST DEPORTATION

AND TO DEFEND THE

CIVIL RIGHTS

OF BLACK and WHITE
NATIVE and FOREIGN BORN

AMERICANS

Saturday, February 21, - 1 P. M.

ELKS HALL

160 West 129th Street   New York, N. Y.

Near 7th Avenue

"They have rights who dare maintain them".
—JAMES RUSSELL LOWELL.

"The limits of tyrants are prescribed by the endurance of those whom they oppress".   —FREDERICK DOUGLASS.

Flyer from the coalition to defend Claudia Jones against deportation, which included the ACPFB. (American Committee for the Protection of the Foreign Born Records, Joseph A. Labadie Collection, University of Michigan Library [Special Collections Library].)

Oh, rest wide Atlantic
Path of nations old and new
Asylum path of peoples
Bound to social progress true[16]

Like "The New Colossus," the famous poem by American-born Sephardic Jewish writer Emma Lazarus that is inscribed at the base of the Statue of Liberty in New York Harbor, Jones's "Paen to the Atlantic" does not speak of the United States, or even of the idea of America, by name. And, of course, where Lazarus's poem celebrates the coming of migrants through the "seawashed, sunset gates" into the safe harbor, Jones's poem speaks of departure and uncertainty: "mankind's search for freedom's clue." Poetic closure in Jones's poem moves with the pitch of the ocean rather than ending with the certainty of arrival. Linking "asylum" with "progress," Jones centers the figure of the migrant, whose search for safe harbor drives the poem. The poem brings the question of place to bear on Jones's thinking about justice, marking an important evolution in her social theory.

The transnational migrant imaginary that Jones describes in her "Paen to the Atlantic" largely sustained her in exile in London. The Communist Party of Great Britain helped her out initially with some introductions and employed her briefly at its New China News Agency. But historian Marika Sherwood argues that the British Communist Party's refusal to acknowledge the centrality of race ill-prepared them to understand Jones, her intersectional work, or its importance to global struggles for social justice.[17]

Jones arrived in England during a time of racial and political transformation there. Passage of the McCarran-Walter Act in the United States in 1952 meant diminished admissions for West Indian migrants, who were no longer able to enter under the immigration quota for Great Britain. In Jones's well-worn copy of the ACPFB publication *The Walter-McCarran Law: Police-State Terror against Foreign Born Americans*, by Green, she bracketed the sentence: "This is an obvious attempt to prevent the immigration of Negro people from the West Indies." While the ACPFB had been involved in Jones's legal defense, immigrant rights were not central to her political analysis until after her deportation. Reading this pamphlet in exile, Jones applied the internationalist, antiracist analysis of the ACPFB to her ongoing work in Britain.[18]

With the obstacles posed by the McCarran-Walter Act to their migration to the United States, many West Indians used their Commonwealth passports to travel to England instead. Increasing numbers of Caribbean migrants came to Great Britain during the postwar "Windrush" migration, benefiting from the newly passed British Nationality Act of 1948, which placed all holders of Commonwealth passports on equal footing in terms of migration. This cohort of migrants and their children were the first sizeable cohort of Black Britons. They clashed with a society fundamentally based on white supremacy, precipitating a deeply racist and nativist reaction to their presence.

Racist backlash against the Windrush migration took many forms. London newspapers published claims that West Indian migrants came to England only to take advantage of welfare benefits and did not want to work. White resistance groups, such as like Sir Oswald Mosely's Union League, the British Union of Fascists, the Ku Klux Klan, and the White Defence League, began organizing in London, particularly in such cities as Nottingham and such London neighborhoods as Notting Hill, where many new migrants lived.[19]

In 1958, white racist organizations led youths in attacking Caribbean residents, homes, and businesses, precipitating two weeks of open racial conflicts that came to be known as the Notting Hill Riots. A leaflet distributed during this time advised white residents to "take action now. Protect your jobs. Stop coloured immigration. . . ." Official and popular response to the riots, in turn, called for the restriction of immigration from the Commonwealth. As a Black deportee, Jones had personal experience with the connection between white supremacy and nativism that was emerging in Britain. In this context, analysis that would have been familiar to her from her work with the ACPFB took on new power.[20]

After the Notting Hill Riots galvanized the colonial diasporic community in Britain, Jones joined a circle of Black exiles in antiracist organizing. She worked with Amy Ashwood Garvey, the first wife of Marcus Garvey, to found the Association for the Advancement of Colored People. A pan-Africanist who frequently traveled between Africa, the Caribbean, and London, Amy Garvey was living in the Ladbrooke Grove neighborhood, which was adjacent to Notting Hill and similarly affected by racial conflict. Amy Garvey and Jones were also involved in initiating an Inter-Racial Friendship Coordinating Committee.[21] With support from Paul and Essie Robeson, Jones founded the first Caribbean newspaper in Britain, the *West Indian Gazette*, in 1958. The *Gazette* became a center for Caribbean and, more broadly, diasporic culture and resistance. In a 1958 memo, Jones explains her impetus for founding the newspaper:

The present status of the *WIG* may be summarised as (1) having established the need for a paper for Afro-Asian-West Indians in the UK with emphasis mainly on the West Indians, who are the most numerous of the coloured population in Britain[;] (2) having contributed to developing a sense of identification with the struggles

of colonial and ex-colonial peoples everywhere for peace and freedom[;] (3) showing the relationship of the coloured people to their
allies who fight for similar aims of peace freedom and equality and
self determination for culturally oppressed peoples.[22]

Jones's work on the *Gazette* drew on her internationalist background
to link imperialism and racism in England, as evidenced by Jones's analysis
of the purpose of the newspaper. At the same time, Boyce Davies explains,
"The needs of the Caribbean community and their links with other communities and nations of Afro-Asian, African and Latin American peoples
necessitated a politics even more internationalist in scope than was possible
in her prior journalistic endeavors." Her experiences as a deportee and her
familiarity with the internationalism of the ACPFB provided some of this
scope.[23]

Internationalism had always been part of Jones's political analysis. After her forced migration from the United States, internationalism became a
central, daily part of her experience. Previously Jones's analysis had converged around the figure of the triply oppressed African American woman.
Her work in England maintained this intersectionality while expanding to
incorporate migrant dynamism. While Jones had spent her political career
in the United States writing against imperialism and white supremacy, the
figure of the "Afro-Asian-West Indian" began to appear in her work only
during her years in England. This new trope was a component of Jones's
postdeportation migrant imaginary. Historian Paul Warmington points out
that "blackness" in postwar Britain was a strategic, migrant invention:

> [It was] partly a creative appropriation of American civil rights les-
> sons; partly the organic product of struggles over work, education,
> immigration and racism in Britain. True, it was also a response to
> the mainstream political discourses of the 1950s and 60s, wherein
> migrants from former colonies, the New Commonwealth, were rou-
> tinely grouped together under descriptors such as "coloured" and
> "immigrant."[24]

In this charged field, Jones drew on the internationalist imaginary of the
ACPFB to articulate an intersectional, diasporic Black British migrant
identity.

In England, Jones is best remembered for her central role in establishing the annual Notting Hill Carnival. As with the *Gazette*, Jones's involvement in the carnival constituted a political response to the violent racial
context. The first carnival in 1959 was organized by a committee run out
of *Gazette* offices. The event was in part a fundraiser to benefit West In-

dian youth facing stiff fines for their roles in conflicts in Notting Hill. Sociologist Colin Prescod explains that Jones deployed the Caribbean cultural tradition as a way to transform the racial landscape of postwar Britain.[25] Such repurposing of homeland tradition is a classic act of migrant imagination—something the ACPFB had long practiced in its movement culture of ethnic festivals.

While she participated in Black migrant organizing in England, Jones maintained her connections with the civil rights struggle in the United States. The first edition of the *West Indian Gazette* features her review of James Baldwin's first novel, *Go Tell It on the Mountain*. In 1963, Jones responded to Baldwin's call to organize in solidarity with the March on Washington in the United States, leading a crowd of about three hundred people—"mostly Negroes and Indians," according to the *London Observer*—through Notting Hill to rally in front of the American Embassy against racial discrimination in the United States and the United Kingdom. Banners at the march engaged struggles on both sides of the Atlantic: "Equality for Negroes in the USA"; "No colour bar on immigration."[26]

Just a few weeks before her untimely death in December 1964, Jones hosted Martin Luther King Jr., who was in London en route to Oslo to accept the Nobel Peace Prize. King spoke in London, decrying the Commonwealth Immigration Bill as a component of a global racist order. In her last editorial for the *Gazette*, Jones reflects on King's charge to the diasporic community in London: "That is why Dr. Martin Luther King's answer had to be a dual one, namely, the necessity for all decent Britons to challenge every case of racial discrimination and for the Commonwealth citizens to organize and unite—the better to effectively challenge the disabilities confronting us."[27]

Jones's migrant imaginary left a powerful legacy on both sides of the Atlantic. In England, the Notting Hill Carnival continued to be a site for Afro-diasporic invention and solidarity. The work on race, culture, and politics that Jones initiated in the *West Indian Gazette* anticipated and set the stage for the crucial interventions of the Birmingham Centre for Contemporary Cultural Studies. Like Jones, Jamaican-born writer Stuart Hall arrived in England in the early 1950s; his work was deeply influenced by the diasporic, antiracist political formations that responded to the Notting Hill Riots.[28]

In the United States, Jones's work on intersectional and multiracial analysis managed to survive the Cold War despite her deportation, influencing politics and alliances among progressives. McDuffie points to the persistence of the triple oppression analysis forged by Black feminist leftists, such as Jones, and the influence of this work on subsequent generations of activists, such as Angela Davis. He describes a 2009 conference on Black Women and the Radical Tradition during which Davis gestured to the influence of Black Communist women, such as Charlene Mitchell and Jones, in helping her learn "what it meant to be a Communist, what it meant to be a citizen of the world."[29]

Jones's migrant imaginary and her experience of deportation also had lingering effects on the ACPFB. The ACPFB defended Jones as part of its advocacy on behalf of foreign-born political radicals. As has been discussed throughout this book, this immigrant rights advocacy invariably engaged questions of civil rights, bringing the ACPFB into alliance with diverse struggles for social justice. While the ACPFB is often viewed as part of the "Old Left" because it confronted allegations of Communist and subversive ties during the Cold War, these civil rights alliances continued to shape the work of the ACPFB and its allies. In 1971, Louise Pettibone Smith, who had been centrally involved with the ACPFB throughout the Cold War, served as the executive secretary of the New York committee to free Davis.[30]

Jones's dangerous acts of creativity and persuasion caused her deportation and, quite possibly, her early demise because of the damages done to her health by her many incarcerations. The radical horizons she projects in her work create an insistent belonging out of her marginalization and eventual deportation. The next section considers the work of the Los Angeles Korean American writers who advocated for the liberation of their homeland. Drawn into the Los Angeles Committee for the Protection of the Foreign Born (LACPFB) because of the deportation cases against them, these writers, like Jones, deployed their "fragile agency" against repression.

"A Priceless Treasure of the American People": Horizons of Liberation and *Korean Independence*

At roughly the same time that Jones looked out over the Atlantic, facing east into uncertainty, a group of Korean Americans in Los Angeles looked west, considering their occupied, partitioned homeland. The bilingual newspaper *Korean Independence* was founded in Los Angeles in October 1943 to advocate for national liberation. Distributed on three continents, the newspaper was produced, written, and edited by a group of Korean Americans in California, including Diamond Kimm, John Juhn, David and Peter Hyun, and Sang Ryup Park.

Maintaining the central concern of this chapter with the literary and cultural politics of migrant Americanisms and the ACPFB, this section examines the editorial trajectory of *Korean Independence*. While Jones developed much of her migrant imaginary of intersectionality after her exile from the United States, the circle of Korean Americans around the bilingual paper convened around a common, diasporic investment in the liberation of Korea from first Japanese (1905–1945) and then American (1945–1948) occupation. The central project of *Korean Independence* was to advocate for a united, sovereign, and democratic Korea, even when that reality did not exist on any map. In the context of the American occupation of and subsequent alliance with South Korea, this advocacy eventually involved acts of "dangerous creativity." As they experienced increasing repression in the post–World War II period, these Korean American writers came into broad alliance with other foreign-born artists and activists through the LACPFB).

The editors of *Korean Independence* engaged in political work with the broad left coalition that eventually founded the LACPFB in 1950. David Hyun participated in the organizing drives of the International Longshore and Warehouse Union (ILWU) in the sugarcane fields of Hawai'i during the 1940s, which were later linked by crimes of association to Communism; on moving to Los Angeles, he became involved in the Westlake Communist Party as its educational director. Juhn, who was married to an American citizen, worked as a maritime laborer and printer and was a member of the American Federation of Labor (AFL) typographers' union. One of the founders of the paper, Park, entered the United States as a student in 1937, leaving his wife and young son in Korea. He attended Ohio Wesleyan and worked at Boston University, supporting himself as a translator. Peter and Alice Hyun were active in the peace movement. Affiliated with Popular Front political activities, these Korean Americans also worked transnationally toward what they viewed as liberation of their homeland.[31]

Except for Peter Hyun, who was born while the Hyun family lived in Hawai'i, none of these diasporic Koreans was eligible for citizenship because of the ban on Asian naturalization in effect, ironically, until the passage of the McCarran-Walter Act in 1952. Eventually, this lack of citizenship made Kimm, Juhn, David Hyun, and Park subject to deportation. As they combatted these deportation campaigns, the circle around *Korean Independence* was drawn further into left Los Angeles politics, becoming involved with the multiracial immigrant rights coalition of the LACPFB. This coalition responded to the linked threats of the McCarran Act, the McCarran-Walter Act, and Operation Wetback. For the circle around the newspaper, the LACPFB was a key site of acculturation into the United States. Like Heikkinen and Jones, they Americanized through their engagement in the antiracist, coalition politics of the immigrant rights movement.[32]

Korean Independence was published for fifteen years, from 1943 to 1958. From the paper's beginning and throughout World War II, the editors of the English-language pages placed their hopes in a U.S.-led liberation of Korea from Japanese imperial rule.[33] Kimm and Park worked for the wartime Office of Strategic Services (OSS), preparing to serve as linguistic and cultural translators in the event of a U.S. invasion of Japan. Relations between the newspaper and the OSS were cordial enough that the newspaper circulated a petition from the North American branch of the Korean Revolutionary Party asking that Park be allowed to remain as editor-in-chief during his work for the service. After the request was granted, the paper proudly ran an article about Park's new appointment.[34]

During the first two years of its publication, *Korean Independence* was exceedingly pro-American. In its first issue, published on October 6, 1943, the editors extol the virtue of a free press. An op-ed by "the Korean Methodist Church in Los Angeles"—likely written by its minister, Key H. Chang—marks the occasion:

> We rejoice over the birth of a paper—*The Korean Independence*—conceived in the spirit of freedom and dedicated to the hope of national independence. It is said that the pen is mightier than the sword. True![35]

This quote extolls U.S. civil liberties, including freedom of the press. In their enthusiastic deployment of such terms as "freedom" and "freedom of the press," the writers of *Korean Independence* embraced an American national identity founded on similar use of these very terms. They assumed that the centrality of these terms in U.S. political discourse would mean ongoing support for their cause of Korean national liberation; for them, the war's popular front as a fight against fascism had specific application to their homeland.

As part of their embrace of freedom in U.S. terms, the paper advocated for Korean American citizenship, enthusiastically covering the progress of ultimately unsuccessful bills to allow for Korean racial eligibility for naturalization introduced first by Hawai'ian territorial representative Joseph Farrington and then by Senator Claude Pepper (D-Florida). These were bills also supported by the ACPFB. In March 1945, the paper wrote of these efforts in Congress:

> This gesture along with the recent issuance of the five cents Korea commemorative stamp is nothing more or less than a bona fide recognition by the American people of Koreans' magnificent fight against Japanese militarism for the past three and more decades.

The same article saluted the United States as "a haven for many Korean political refugees," thus aligning the paper with the contemporary idea of the United States as global champion of democracy. As they did with the issue of national liberation, the editors assumed that the U.S. discourse of freedom ensured their ongoing security as migrants.[36]

In the early years of its publication, *Korean Independence* expressed hope that the United States would assist in the liberation of its occupied homeland and would make good on its democratic promise by granting full citizenship rights to Korean Americans. The Korean Americans who edited the paper linked the liberation of their homeland to the project of becoming American citizens. But this changed after the war. In the name of fighting Communism, the State Department made alliances with established dictatorships in Greece and Portugal and supported the rise of despotic, if anti-Communist, leaders in other nations, including Syngman Rhee in South Korea.

Domestically, as historian Carol Anderson points out, this shift led to a narrowing of civil rights possibilities. As liberal senators such as Pepper were red-baited and as the House Un-American Activities Committee (HUAC) convened special hearings in Hawai'i to detect a purported Communist presence there, repeated attempts to expand Asian American racial eligibility through congressional action failed. Eventually, the McCarran-Walter Act of 1952 lifted the ban on Asian naturalization, but this law simultaneously reinstated the Asiatic Barred Zone, setting symbolic, tiny quotas for Asian immigration at the same time that it enhanced the deportability of foreign-born "subversives." So, while citizenship for Asian Americans was theoretically possible after 1952, it became much more elusive for the circle around *Korean Independence*. While these intellectuals found themselves impelled to criticize U.S. policy in their homeland, their rights as foreign-born writers narrowed, making their creative work considerably more dangerous.[37]

Shifting U.S. practices abroad transformed the attitudes of the circle around *Korean Independence* toward the United States after 1945. Titled "A Hope of Koreans for 1945," the first editorial appearing in *Korean Independence* that year envisions the United States and the United Nations working together to end the Japanese empire. When Korea was denied representation at the UN Conference on International Organization in April, diasporic Koreans convened to petition for their national sovereignty, holding a conference of Koreans living in North America, Hawai'i, and Mexico at the Korean National Association (KNA) hall in Los Angeles. A *Korean Independence* editorial rails against the denial of Korean sovereignty:

> Why do not the Big Powers recognize the Korean people, a people who for the past more than thirty years have helplessly been trampled underfoot by the Japanese tyranny[,] as a member of the U.N.?[38]

The editorial goes on to urge that "all the Koreans in the United States, regardless of their political opinions, should unite to have themselves properly and effectively heard." Ultimately, the U.S. State Department agreed to have two representatives of the Korean diaspora, Park and Kilsoo Haan of the Sino-Korean People's League, seated as "correspondents" at the conference.

At the war's end in August 1945, the United States and the Soviet Union partitioned Korea into north and south. The United States occupied South Korea, first administering the country through the American Military Government and then aiding in Rhee's ascendance to leadership in 1948. A diasporic Korean himself, Rhee had worked to build alliances with the State Department since the 1930s. During the years he lived in Hawai'i, he also incurred the enmity of Soon Hyun, who viewed him as a traitor and a despot. After 1945, the editors of *Korean Independence* became increasingly wary of the U.S. presence in the region. The small Korean American community living in the United States was divided over events in their homeland.

As Rhee purged South Korea of political dissidents, murdering and imprisoning thousands, the editors of *Korean Independence* protested, aligning themselves with alternate spatialities by endorsing the Democratic People's Republic to the north while also maintaining hope for a unified, sovereign Korea. They criticized American support for Rhee, claiming that he represented the same business interests that had profited from the Japanese occupation and pointing to his political purges in the name of anti-Communism. Repeatedly, they called on the United States to live up to its promises to liberate Korea from occupation and despotism. In an editorial titled "The Fourth of July, 1946," the editors summon a fading definition of freedom as national liberation against

> the arrogance and stupidity and platitudes of some American brass hats as military dictators in the conquered or occupied foreign countries. . . . [T]he greatness of the American people is destined to light a candle for the dark world with a spirit of the freedom and equality of the promise of liberty and the pursuit of happiness for all.[39]

As the U.S. occupation gave way to the consolidation of Rhee's power—he ruled as president of the Republic of Korea from 1948 to 1960—*Korean Independence* criticized the government of South Korea as well as its American backers. In the context of shifting rhetorical definitions of freedom and slavery, this criticism could easily be viewed by anti-Communists as subversion.

In 1947, editor Park responded to charges against *Korean Independence* published in the *Los Angeles Examiner*. Anti-Communist activist
Walter S. Steel had testified before the HUAC that several Korean American organizations, including *Korean Independence*, wanted to bring about
the recall of U.S. troops from the Korean peninsula to advance Soviet
domination in the region. In an editorial, Park reiterates the paper's support for American efforts during World War II, recounting the shock of
the Korean people when they discovered that the occupying American
Military Government

> came as the guardian of pro-Japanese Korean collaborators, na-
> tional traitors, reactionaries, pro-fascists, and a minority of feudal
> landlords, industrialists and capitalists (but) as another tyrant
> against the majority of the Korean people who had suffered, starved
> and fought under the Japanese reign of terror.[40]

In this editorial, Park invokes prior definitions of freedom and slavery that
were outmoded by 1947. Under the new rubric, *Korean Independence*'s
advocacy for alternate conceptions of Korean sovereignty could be called
"un-American" because of its opposition to Rhee. The California State
Senate Committee on Un-American Activities listed the newspaper as a
Communist front in 1948. By 1955, Roger Baldwin of the American Civil Liberties Union (ACLU) was describing *Korean Independence* as being,
"for all practical purposes, a Communist Party organ" in his affidavit
against the deportation of Kimm. Their transnational allegiances and particular political perspectives on liberation brought the circle around *Korean Independence* increased scrutiny and persecution. Historian Cindy
I-Fen Cheng writes that "the Cold War effectively transformed into 'subversive activities' the nationalist efforts of Korean Americans to establish
an independent Korea that did not cater to the interests of the wealthy
landowning Korean elites."[41]

Developments in 1950 decisively alienated the circle around *Korean
Independence* from their prior embrace of the United States as an advocate
of freedom. While Jones faced escalating efforts to deport her because of
her opposition to the Korean War, the persecution of Korean Americans in
the McCarran Act raids resulted from their work against escalating U.S.
militarism in their homeland. The war represented these diasporic Koreans'
worst fears about the American presence in Asia, and it was accompanied
by repression against foreign-born intellectuals. The U.S. government initiated deportation proceedings against Kimm in 1941 for failing to maintain
a continuous student visa, but these proceedings were suspended, likely
because of Kimm's work for the OSS. In October, Kimm and Juhn were

David Hyun and
family. (Los Angeles
Committee for the
Protection of the
Foreign Born
Collection, Southern
California Library
[Los Angeles,
California].)

among the Angelenos arrested in the McCarran Act midnight raids. David
Hyun was also arrested and imprisoned at Terminal Island in Los Angeles
Harbor with three other suspected subversives, who came to be known as
the "Terminal Island Four" (see Chapter 4).[42]

In New York, Chungson and Choon Cha Kwak, a married couple who
were allies of *Korean Independence* and who wrote for the paper as correspondents, were fired from their positions at Voice of America at the same
time that their applications for permanent residence were converted by the
Immigration and Nationalization Service (INS) into deportation orders. In
the fall of 1950, the Kwaks were arrested and detained at Ellis Island;
likely, they were fellow denizens of Jones's "virtual United Nations."[43]

Increasingly after 1950, *Korean Independence* covered deportation
cases. In part, this was because most of the small staff of the newspaper
had been targeted by the midnight raids. Working to defend the Kwaks,
Juhn, Kimm, Park, and David Hyun against deportation to South Korea,
the circle around *Korean Independence* entered into the multiracial immigrant rights advocacy of the LACPFB. And as immigrant rights became
a more central concern of the newspaper, it transformed some of the prior
ideas about citizenship and identity important to these diasporic Koreans.
They continued to advocate for a liberated homeland, but in light of postwar global alignments, their loyalties were to a deterritorialized and imagined Korea. Their understandings of American citizenship also shifted.

Korean Independence covered the ACPFB before the passage of the Mc-
Carran Internal Security Act and the related deportation cases against the
paper's staff. As early as January 1948, the paper featured articles about the
ongoing tribulations of Nicaraguan American labor organizer Humberto

Silex (see Chapter 1) as well as the cases of other foreign-born activists confronted by deportation, including Ukrainian American newspaper editor William Zasuliak. Initially, this connection may have been facilitated by the ongoing engagement of the Hyun family in progressive politics in southern California. When the LACPFB was formed in 1950, David Hyun was its first chairperson.[44]

Covering the struggles of the foreign born influenced the ways in which *Korean Independence* wrote about questions of citizenship and rights. In October 1948, for example, the paper ran a story that it had gotten from the San Francisco–based newspaper *Chung Sai Yat Po* [*Chinese American Daily*]. The story concerned a Chinese woman, Leong Bock Ha, who committed suicide after being detained in a downtown INS facility for four months. The wife of a Chinese American veteran, Ha was detained according to INS protocol governing the admission of Chinese and other Asians. A *Korean Independence* article points out the different treatments of the relatives of white and Asian Americans and draws on the *Chung Sai Yat Po* story to note that this incident took place at the same time that the United States prepared to admit thousands of displaced persons from Europe.[45]

As their hopes for U.S. liberation of Korea faded, the activist intellectuals of *Korean Independence* forged new visions of antiracist and transnational solidarity. Reporting on a dinner sponsored by the paper, a 1948 editorial proclaims:

> It was gratifying, particularly to the progressive Koreans in the country[,] to reassure themselves that they are not alone in their difficult struggle to maintain their voice for a free, united Korea.
>
> It was enlightening for them to rediscover their real friends among the Negro people, the Jewish people, and among all others who are waging the battle for equal rights and justice for all minorities.[46]

The discovery of their "real friends" by the activist intellectuals of *Korean Independence* paralleled Jones's courtroom description of how she became conscious of the violence and oppression of African American life. Like Jones, the editors of *Korean Independence* saw parallels between global events and their struggles in the United States. And, as with Jones, they acculturated into a particular, progressive subculture of the Cold War United States. Increasingly, their affinities were to alternate spatialities and diasporic horizons.

During the tumultuous year of 1950, the newspaper published protests against the Yoshida government's treatment of Koreans in Japan. The Japanese government imposed an "Alien Registration Act" parallel to the Smith

Act, banned Korean political organizations, shut down Korean schools, and deported six hundred thousand Koreans from Japan to South Korea. The paper editorialized against the deportation of Koreans from Japan, using a rhetoric of failed democracy similar to the one deployed to describe deportations in the United States. In addition to articles and editorials, the paper also published letters from the Civil Rights Congress (CRC) and from Japanese trade union leaders decrying these events. Resurrecting the earlier opposition between freedom and slavery, these writers criticized the deprivation of human and civil rights by the Japanese government, comparing the actions against Koreans in Japan to the deportation of Jews to concentration camps in Europe in the 1930s.[47]

After 1950, the editors of *Korean Independence* increasingly conflated their struggles against deportation with the conflict in their homeland. Where they had once seen the United States as an ally and potential liberator, they came to conflate the violence of the "deportation terror" with American militarism in Asia. A December 1951 "Report on the Deportation Drive" describes deportation drives against "practically all nationality groups, Mexican, English, Polish, Italian, Rumanian, Russian, Philipino [*sic*] and many more." The same article continues to extoll the national liberation struggle in Korea:

> Their resistance to the deportation hysteria is part of a dramatic story of the Korean peoples' resistance to the war in Korea. The story of the Korean Deportees makes definite and clear that the deportation drive against all national groups and its attendant hysteria aided against all Americans, is the result of the reactionary war policy of our present administration.[48]

For the writers of *Korean Independence*, the solution to discrimination and harassment in the United States and liberation at home was one and the same: the peaceful termination of the Korean War abroad. They urged their readers to get involved in the "Korean People's Movement"— the struggle for full access to citizenship and against deportation and militarism.[49] In context of ascendant anti-Communism, their transnational critique sounded like subversion.

Interned at Terminal Island, David Hyun wrote poetry and made art prolifically. He and his codefendants, Welsh American Harry Carlisle and Polish American Frank Carlson, staged "socialist poetry competitions." Hyun sketched the men's barracks and self-portraits. The LACPFB incorporated the products of this dangerous creativity into its advocacy literature. The midnight raids were pivotal in connecting the work of *Korean Independence* with broader progressive constituencies. Hyun's prison writ-

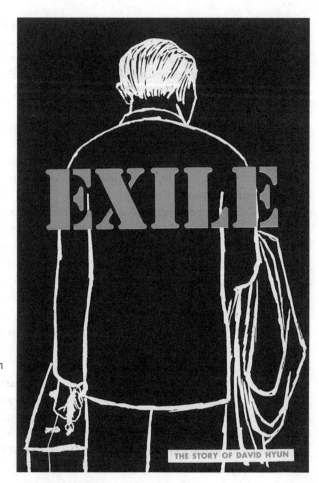

Exile pamphlet on the Hyun case, with sketches by Soon Hyun. (Los Angeles Committee for the Protection of the Foreign Born Collection, Southern California Library [Los Angeles, California].)

ings, exemplified in the lines of poetry that open this chapter, are less evidence of his "unbecoming" American, in Joseph Keith's terms, than of his firm belief in an alternative Americanism flourishing even in the repressive context of domestic repression and global militarism.[50]

As the staff of the newspaper fought their deportation during the last three years of its publication, the pages of *Korean Independence* featured increasing coverage of other immigrant communities. A Korean-American Defense Committee was formed in 1952, in cooperation with the LACPFB. The paper covered movement events, such as a dinner celebrating the release of Green from prison and the annual LACPFB Festival of Nationalities. The paper also began to cover events of concern beyond those of diasporic Koreans, such as the ninth anniversary of the Warsaw Ghetto Uprising and the long legal struggle of Julius and Ethel Rosenberg. A New Year's Eve editorial for 1952 reflects the immersion of

Korean Independence in the antiracist coalitions still surviving in this Cold War moment:

> We as peace-loving Americans have a chance and an opportunity to participate in such activities that are in the best interests of all peace-loving and peace-wanting peoples of the world.
>
> It all depends on us—our silence will make possible the continuation of the war in Korea with all its horrors; it will make possible the legal killing of Ethel and Julius Rosenberg for a crime they have never committed.
>
> But if we demand peace in Korea, if we will refuse to be scared and intimidated, if we will continue to fight for a place in the sun for every human being regardless of the color of his skin or the place of his birth, if we will just do that in 1953—we will save America to be America again.[51]

Ending with echoes of Langston Hughes's famous 1935 poem, "Let America Be America Again,"[52] this editorial exemplifies the ways in which these Korean American diasporic intellectuals chose to Americanize. Just as Hughes held out the hope that America could "be the dream the dreamers dreamed," and Jones remembered the struggles of migrants before her, the editors of *Korean Independence* maintained the possibility for "saving" America.

In a speech given after his release on bail from Terminal Island in 1951, David Hyun described his incarceration as "the richest and best experience of my life." In terms strikingly similar to Jones's prison writing about the "McCarran wing" of Ellis Island, Hyun mentioned his deepening relationships with codefendants Carlson, Carlisle, and Miriam Stevenson. Hyun's speech held up the fight for immigrant rights as part of a broader struggle for civil rights. He spoke about the broader context of the struggle for the "Terminal Island Four":

> Negro people supported us, the trade unionists supported us, Mexican Americans supported us, artists and cultural workers supported us, nationality and religious groups supported us. This support taught me that justice and oppression attacks all working people. . . . Thus I learned that clear lesson that civil rights is also a fight for peace, for trade unions, for the Negro people, for a better livelihood, as well as a fight for the foreign born.[53]

Working with the ACLU, the national and Los Angeles branch of the ACPFB fought the deportations of the Kwaks, Park, Kimm, and Hyun, seeking to prove that these Korean diasporic nationalists would be in danger of physical persecution if they were returned to the Republic of Korea. They prevailed in the case of Park, whose deportation order was stayed in 1951, despite the assurance of the ambassador from the Republic of Korea that Park would face no physical danger, "so long as he abides by the laws of the country."[54]

In the cases of Kimm and the Kwaks, use of the McCarran Act provision against physical persecution did not overturn their deportation orders; all three of these diasporic Koreans had to leave the country. Kimm and the Kwaks benefited from the national advocacy campaigns conducted on their behalf in that they were able to choose their destinations. This was crucial, because they had been branded as Communists by the U.S. State Department, which colluded closely with the Rhee government in the Korean Republic. In all probability, they would have faced imprisonment if not death there. All three took voluntary departure for Czechoslovakia, where the Kwaks, Kimm, and Kimm's second wife, Russian Jewish American Fania Bernstein, were able to obtain visas for the Democratic People's Republic of Korea. Kimm and Chungson Kwak were originally from up north, while Choon Cha was born in Seoul. Alice Hyun, David and Peter's sister, also took this route. Alice was eventually executed in North Korea as a spy, but the fates of the Kwaks and of Kimm and Bernstein are not known.

Because their abiding belief in Korean unification found no corollary in Cold War cartography, these diasporic activist intellectuals faced a difficult choice. Returning to South Korea was physically dangerous. Additionally, South Korea represented what they came to see as prolonged occupation by a corrupt ruler installed by the United States. In the extremely limited circumstances imposed by the deportation and Cold War militarism, they made the choices available to them. Their forced departures evidenced their deterritorialized loyalty to a liberated homeland that did not yet exist.[55]

After a protracted public struggle, the LACPFB won an "indefinite delay" of the case against David Hyun in 1958; the Board of Immigration Appeals withdrew his deportation order in 1966. Cheng argues that the LACPFB deployed familiar tropes of assimilation and Americanization in its advocacy for Hyun, downplaying his activist past in Hawai'i and emphasizing his appropriate conduct as a family man and professional architect. Further, she notes that Hyun himself refrained from criticizing U.S. participation in the Korean War throughout his many legal tribulations.[56]

Hyun had a longer history in domestic labor and left movements than did other members of the circle around *Korean Independence*. His involvement with *Korean Independence* constituted part of a long career in labor and civil rights advocacy, dating back to his work organizing the sugarcane field workers of Hawai'i, his union membership in both the ILWU and architects and engineers unions, his peace activism, and his work in the LACPFB.

During the sixteen years when he faced the possibility of deportation, Hyun's professional life as an architect brought him into prominence in the growing city of Los Angeles. An article about the arrest of "alleged reds" in 1950 notes that Hyun worked as a draftsman for "a Beverly Hills company." In the period after Hyun's release from Terminal Island, he was engaged in fighting deportations, including his own, and in building a career in the Buckeye Construction Company of Beverly Hills. By 1958, he was put in charge of Buckeye's Imperial Hospital project. Notably, this "alleged red," still under deportation orders, played a central role in designing the hospital, which was a component of the expansion of the Los Angeles Airport. In turn, the hospital and the airport were part of the civil defense plan for Greater Los Angeles. This project points to an interesting contradiction: as the chief architect of the hospital project, this accused subversive likely would have been privy to some paperwork deemed classified.[57]

Hyun was instrumental in founding the LACPFB, the organization that eventually prevailed against his deportation. He went on to become a prominent Angeleno: an award-winning architect, an advocate for Asian American community empowerment, and a supporter of the arts. The next section concludes my consideration of the "dangerous creativity" of foreign-born artists and writers by turning to Hyun's long and successful career in Los Angeles. What do the contradictions of Hyun's life in Los Angeles—reviled subversive, trusted insider—tell us? Why did Hyun's case succeed where others faced deportation? What was the price of his survival in the United States, and what might this tell us about the work of the deportation terror and about the circumstances delimiting migrant creative work?

"This House Lives Way beyond Its Walls": Belonging and Exile in the Career of David Hyun

Between 1950 and 1966, Hyun contended with the possibility of being deported to South Korea, which was under a regime that was not only politically but also personally hostile to him and his family. Depositions taken in Hawai'i attested to the personal enmity between Rhee and Soon Hyun and formed part of the ACPFB's legal argument against David Hyun's removal to the Republic of Korea.[58]

Hyun was instrumental in the formation of the LACPFB in 1950. Incorporating his talents as a draftsman and a writer, he worked for immigrant rights as well as for the broader cause of social justice. By the time ACPFB lawyers managed to prevail in his case in 1966, the white heat of anti-Communist persecutions under the McCarran Act had subsided a bit. And by that time, Hyun himself had also changed. He became engaged in the creation of an Asian American ethnic identity in Los Angeles, investing in a territorialized Korean American identity. While the Cold War context framed antiracist figures, such as Jones, Hyun, and the circle around *Korean Independence*, in the context of broad suspicion about their affiliations and loyalties, Hyun's Asian American activism in the 1960s and 1970s was framed and legitimated by an ascendant discourse of civil rights. This discourse largely explained the struggle for civil rights in a national rather than a global context.

Mainstream civil rights discourse focused on legal injustices, such as abuses of the Bill of Rights, rather than the broad anti-imperialist and antiracist agenda of the coalition represented by the LACPFB. Along with "New Left" organizations focused on community control and empowerment, these organizations maintained an internationalist analysis of white supremacy. The acceptance of civil rights as a mainstream discourse relied on the continued silencing of the multiracial, antiracist left. Further, as historian Gerald Horne argues, the Watts uprising fostered white reactions of fear and an attendant concern for urban and national security.[59]

As a veteran of the "Old Left," Hyun occupied a contradictory position during the time he was under deportation orders, and even afterward. Taken from a 1958 *Los Angeles Times* review of a house designed by Hyun, the quote in the heading for this section, "this house lives way beyond its walls," could be said to describe the architect himself. Confined by the looming possibility of deportation, Hyun "live[d] way beyond" these limits, continuing his artistic and professional work at a time marked by persecution and crisis. In 1961, he and another architect opened their own firm: Hyun and Whitney and Associates. But how did he manage these contradictions between the role of the subversive outsider and that of the trusted insider?[60]

The review of the house Hyun designed gives some indication. In four short paragraphs, the reviewer twice characterizes the design as "Oriental," possibly because of its garden plan and "interesting quality of extending indoor-outdoor living." An Asian American architect was unusual in Cold War Los Angeles. The year after the *Los Angeles Times* reviewed Hyun's design, Olympian Sammy Lee faced intransigent white resistance to his purchase of a home in nearby Orange County. While Hyun's status as a noncitizen ineligible to naturalize created the conditions for his deportation, ethnic identity was fungible in the context of the design market in an expanding, increasingly global city. Hyun's survival and his success were due in part to his adept deployment of a migrant spatial imaginary in his architecture: he translated these deterritorialized desires into richly designed spaces for a globalizing city. As Los Angeles saw increased global migration and the growth of large new cohorts of migrants from Asia, Hyun achieved renown as an architect and as an ethnic advocate. But his activist work increasingly differed from the labor-based, antiracist, and anti-imperialist political formations that he had previously been involved with. In fact, it was almost as though a condition of Hyun's eventually winning his case against deportation involved his willingness to remain completely silent about his political past through 1950.[61]

Historian Jordan Sand writes about the entwined transpacific migrations of people and fashion, linking the ideas of "civilization" embodied by domestic architectural forms, such as the bungalow, with political initiatives restricting the movement of Asian laborers. To Sand, the peregrinations of architectural styles are a component of migrant imaginaries as well as transnational security regimes. Policing dissent in Japanese and American empires involved monitoring the activities of suspected subversives as well as advancing particular forms of healthy, middle-class living. He writes:

> Although American architecture and design and the popular rhetoric of simple living were laden with images of Japan, the cultural trade across the Pacific was profoundly unequal. . . . Americans appropriated things Japanese for an air of Oriental decadence or as part of the game of temporarily escaping the bounds of civilization.[62]

Writing about imperial formations in the early twentieth century, Sand points to the ways that Koreans bore the burden of both empires, "plus the loss of their national sovereignty."[63] This of course was true for the circle around *Korean Independence* and very much describes the history of the Hyun family in Hawai'i and the continental United States. At the same time, a transpacific migrant imaginary linked Hyun's Korean ethnicity, his birth while the family was in exile in Shanghai, and his residence in Hawai'i and Los Angeles. This migrant imaginary informed Hyun's political activism and his artistic practice throughout his life.

Before the withdrawal of his deportation order, Hyun worked on public architectural projects, such as hospitals and parking garages. His designs for individual clients won notice for their Asian-influenced architecture, with its balance of California bungalow living and carefully de-

signed outdoor gardens.[64] Many years later, in 1993, Hyun designed his
Silver Lake home to emphasize his specifically Korean influences.

The final stay of Hyun's deportation order took place in 1966, a
charged moment in Los Angeles as well as in Asian American history. The
Immigration and Nationality Acts of 1965 decisively ended national origin
quotas and, mostly through a preference system based on family reunification and work preferences, facilitated greatly increased migration from
Asia for the first time since 1924. Between 1970 and 1990, Korean populations grew rapidly, resulting in the growth of a Koreatown in Los Angeles. Ethnic Studies scholar Glenn Omatsu points to the revitalization and
growth of Asian American neighborhoods during this period. The mid-
1960s also saw an increase in activism in Asian American communities
around issues of education and community control. Historian Scott
Kurashige explains the shift in Asian American politics in Los Angeles
from struggles over citizenship to creating "solidarity and coalition building" with Latinx and African Americans in multiethnic neighborhoods.[65]
At the same time, as Horne points out, the Watts uprising in 1965 resulted in the formation of a "multiracial coalition" that supported liberal
politicians, such as Tom Bradley, who was elected mayor in 1973. After
the uprising, municipal politics were driven by contradictory impulses to
secure the city for white business interests *and* to represent and contain its
ethnic and racial diversity. In this context, Hyun emerged as a creative
community leader.[66]

His involvement with the transnational municipal project of revital-
izing Little Tokyo in 1977 consolidated Hyun's status as an architect and
ethnic spokesperson of note. By that time, Japanese Americans had been
struggling for thirty years to reclaim and revitalize the neighborhood they
had been forced to abandon. Hyun's work in this politically charged context evidenced his transformation away from the anti-imperial, antiracist
politics of his LACPFB and *Korean Independence* days toward an embrace of ethnic representation and empowerment.

Returning from internment camps in the late 1940s, Japanese American Angelenos confronted attempts by the city to demolish Little Tokyo,
which had been populated during the war with African American migrants
seeking war work. These migrants created the neighborhood known as
Bronzeville during the 1940s. The city of Los Angeles also purchased property in the area, constructing the Parker Police facility on formerly residential blocks and a quarter of the area's retail space there in 1953. Crowded
postwar conditions led to conflict as well as solidarity among Japanese and
African American denizens of the area. In the 1960s, Japanese Americans
made coalitions with African Americans around fair housing issues and
against police brutality. Kurashige notes an invigoration of Afro-Asian

unity after the Watts uprising. While only a few Japanese Americans had been engaged with the LACPFB, this multiracial solidarity nonetheless hearkened to the alliances formed during the Cold War.[67]

Hyun was central to the Los Angeles Community Redevelopment Agency's Little Tokyo Project. Adopted by the city in 1970, this project worked to attract international investment from Japan as well as to lure back to the city Japanese Americans who had moved from the city to the suburbs—at least to shop. This well-financed, municipally endorsed vision of ethnic transnational solidarity eclipsed prior interracial solidarities, giving particular valence to the Little Tokyo project. Hyun was a strong advocate for the design as well as the community-building aspects of this project. In 1977, he explained:

> The central purpose behind this community project was the preservation of the rights, interest and livelihood of the people who historically lived here in Little Tokyo. The approval of our project by the CRA [Community Redevelopment Agency] means the little businessman displaced by the renewal of the area will have a place to go.[68]

In this context, "community" meant "Japanese American" rather than the previous multiracial community of Little Tokyo/Bronzeville. Municipal authorities in Los Angeles celebrated the success of the revitalization project in ethnic terms that erased not only the multiracial history of the area but also the specific struggles of Japanese Americans. A 1978 article about the opening of the shopping plaza explains that the residents of Little Tokyo had been there "since the close of World War II," neatly omitting where most of them had spent the war as well as their struggles to return. Similarly, celebratory coverage of "Nisei Week" in 1980 cited the festival's continuous existence since 1934 and featured Hyun congratulating city leaders for "not giving up" on keeping rents low enough to accommodate small shopkeepers.[69]

The Little Tokyo project marked Hyun's ascendance as a successful Los Angeles architect and as a player in Asian American politics in the city. The Japanese Village Plaza at the center of the area won the first Federal Design Award in 1983; it also received accolades from the federal Health and Urban Development Urban Design Administration and the Japanese American Citizens League. Hyun was involved in Korean American and Asian American organizations: the Korean American Coalition; the Korean Federation; the founding of the Japanese American National Museum and a planned Chinese American Center; and the political campaigns of Michael Woo, the first Asian American to serve on the Los Angeles City Council.

He supported summer camps for urban youth and appeared at arts benefits with other local Asian American celebrities, including George Takei and Lee. Omatsu characterizes this period in terms of the ascendance of Asian American professionals and the consolidation of community organizations; he also notes the power of the backlash against political radicalism, often symbolized by the election of Ronald Reagan in 1980.[70] In 1987, Hyun noted the achievement of Little Tokyo in specifically ethnic terms:

> The biggest visible change is the return of people to Little Tokyo. There are more people here than there were fifteen years ago and there's more pride in Little Tokyo by the Japanese Americans, especially the very young Japanese who come here and bring their girlfriends and boyfriends. Fifteen years ago the Sansei [third-generation Japanese Americans] rarely came here. They were ashamed of Little Tokyo.[71]

The migrant imaginary informing Hyun's work after 1977 drew on widespread rhetoric of community empowerment in this period. A powerful advocate for Asian American communities, he worked for the representation of Korean, Chinese, and Japanese American communities in Los Angeles and for collaboration among these different ethnicities in pan–Asian American organizations. He was celebrated in Los Angeles as an architect and as a community advocate.

This post-deportation-charge-era career was animated by a very different vision than the one driving Hyun's artistic and advocacy work with the LACPFB and *Korean Independence*. Neither these earlier achievements nor Hyun's background as a union organizer was ever mentioned in any of the abundant press coverage that he attracted over the course of his architectural career. An article noting a party held for Hyun's seventieth birthday party in 1987 talks about the family's venerable lineage, mentioning that Soon Hyun, David's father, was a minister. Soon Hyun's achievements as a "pioneer" and a "national hero" were sometimes noted in the Asian American press, but even articles focused on the Hyun family never mention Alice, who took voluntary departure to North Korea instead of deportation to South Korea.[72]

When David Hyun recreated himself as a successful professional and ethnic advocate, he dropped any mention of his radical past. At a personal level, this absence was understandable—sixteen years of fearing deportation to a country hostile to him and his family may well have taken their toll. But the loss of the migrant imaginary that had fueled the multiracial collaboration of the LACPFB undermined the crucial grounds for coalition and solidarity that had informed pre-1970 attempts to defend Little Tokyo/

Bronzeville as a Black and Asian urban space. Increasingly throughout the 1980s, Hyun adopted a multiculturalism that celebrated Asian American success as a key component of American global diversity. In an op-ed piece he wrote in 1983, he salutes the Asian American contribution to Los Angeles as "reversing urban decay . . . without federal aid." He celebrates the presence of refugees and immigrants as invigorating the economy and culture of the city, but the reference is strictly Asian-Pacific—no mention is made of African Americans or Latinx. The only trace of his past lies in the final paragraph, where Hyun looks to Hawai'i for a model of "the merging of East and West [that] has flowered into a blend of peoples, cultures and trades that is truly American." There is the smallest invocation here of Hyun's experience with the ILWU's triumphant multiracial organizing in the 1940s and the way it transformed the territory. But it is sedimented deep in a past that Hyun rarely referenced publicly.[73]

The absence of this multiracial imaginary transformed Hyun's activism. He opposed African American boycotts of Korean businesses after the Los Angeles riots of 1992, arguing that conflict between the two communities had largely been fomented by the mass media. At a conference held at the University of Southern California in 1993, Hyun recollected Watts and the more recent uprising. His talk centered on the Korean American experience, briefly referencing his work in the sugarcane fields of Hawai'i. While acknowledging the history of anti-Asian sentiment, particularly in California, he expressed skepticism about the existence of racism:

> Do not let the rhetoric of racist prejudice confuse us. It is not only White people who are prejudiced. We are all prejudiced. We all prefer our own. The prejudice of racism can be overcome, not by complaint and confrontation, but much, much better, by friendship and cooperation.[74]

Kurashige wrestles with the ways in which whiteness has triumphed in the "global city" of Los Angeles. He holds out hope for the ongoing possibilities of the multiracial city, hidden just under the newly poured pavement of the revitalized Little Tokyo. And while Hyun was proclaiming the insignificance of racism, new multiracial organizations working against inequalities were gaining traction in Los Angeles and elsewhere. These organizations had much to gain from knowing the full story of Hyun's past and that of the multiracial organization that fought for him and for so many others.[75]

Foreign-born writers "created dangerously" during the early Cold War period. As discussed in this chapter, many of them were deported as a result of their work. While Hyun successfully fought his deportation, the cost of his success as an architect and an ethnic advocate was the silencing of his earlier political and artistic work.

Despite their defeats in space and time, the migrant imaginaries and diasporic horizons proposed by the work of these writers persist. Ellis notes that diasporic affinities often fail, but she insists that "by failure we always understand there to be a utopian reach."[76]

Focusing on the mass media, the next chapter examines the failure of ACPFB advocacy narratives to persist in the face of the public relations campaign mounted by the INS Service during Operation Wetback. While the ACPFB was able to foster some popular sympathy for those in deportation proceedings before Operation Wetback, the use of the incendiary term "illegal alien" effectively foreclosed this option. Immigrant rights advocacy persisted, however, reemerging after 1965, as examined in Chapter 7.

THE NAMES OF THE LOST

Cold War Deportation Cases
in the Mass Media

When you grip
my arm hard and lean way out
and shout out the holy name
of the lost neither of us is scared
and our tears mean nothing.

—PHILIP LEVINE, "And the Trains Go On,"
   in *The Names of the Lost*

Introduction: The Deportations
of William Heikkila and Elvira Arellano

In April 1958, the Immigration and Naturalization Service (INS) kidnapped Finnish American draftsman William Heikkila on his way home from work in San Francisco. Long targeted by INS commissioner Joseph May Swing as a dangerous subversive, Heikkila was escorted by Northern California District INS assistant director Stan Olson to the airport. The two men flew to Vancouver, British Columbia, where Heikkila was detained and questioned, incommunicado. A friend phoned Heikkila's wife to let her know what had happened. Well aware of the long campaign against her husband, Phyllis Heikkila immediately began calling the press and the immigration courts.[1]

After staying overnight in Vancouver, Heikkila and Olson boarded a Canadian Pacific flight bound across the North Pole to Helsinki. On the plane, they sat next to a Finnish Canadian logger headed to visit relatives. Heikkila spoke to the logger in Finnish and related the story of his kidnapping. Subsequently, when the plane was delayed for mechanical repairs, all the passengers except Heikkila were allowed to deplane. The logger called his family, who alerted Finnish and Canadian media. When the plane landed in Helsinki, Heikkila and Olson were greeted by an international array of journalists. Thus commenced a high-profile scandal, in which the kidnapping of Heikkila became a symbol of abuse of power by the INS.

A collage of news coverage from the cover of a pamphlet on the Heikkila case, created by the ACPFB. (American Committee for the Protection of the Foreign Born Papers, #086, Tamiment Library/Robert F. Wagner Labor Archives, New York University. Used by permission of Ruth Gollobin-Basta.)

Fifty-one years later, in August 2007, Mexican American immigrant rights activist Elvira Arellano was arrested on the street outside Our Lady Queen of Angels Church in Los Angeles. She had taken refuge in a sanctuary church in Humboldt Park, Chicago, a year before. Arellano left Chicago to travel the nation and campaign for immigration reform. Upon her arrest, Arellano was taken to a federal detention center. She was then deported to her native Mexico, enduring separation from her eight-year-old American citizen son, Saul.

Sometimes referred to at the time as the "most famous undocumented immigrant in America," Arellano became an activist after she was among many undocumented airport workers arrested in Department of Homeland Security (DHS) sweeps in 2002. Working with the Illinois Coalition for Immigrant and Refugee Rights (ICIRR), Arellano intentionally drew publicity to her case. Her intent was to broadcast the dire situation of thousands of undocumented migrants targeted for deportation by the DHS.[2]

Arellano's deportation did not create a scandal of nearly the same proportion as did Heikkila's kidnapping. While it was noted in Mexican and U.S. media, coverage of Arellano's deportation was infused by a sense that her status as an "illegal alien" justified her deportation. In the words of Chicago Spanish-language radio host Javier Salas, "I'm not happy that this happened, but it was bound to happen, because she was challenging the system."[3]

Heikkila was an avowed Communist, a "red alien" living in the United States during a widely publicized national security crisis in which Communists were perceived to be the central threat. But despite contemporary legislation criminalizing the status of being a foreign-born Communist, the media depicted him as an individual deserving of justice. In contrast, Arellano professed no "un-American" ideology. Contemporary immigrant rights advocacy often deploys a language of patriotism and constitutional justice. But Arellano's status as an undocumented Mexican American woman meant that her very presence in the country was criminalized in mass-media accounts. By the early twenty-first century, Arellano's status as an "illegal alien" undermined her attempts to claim rights or to solicit popular sympathy in the press.

The difference in mass-media responses to these two deportations can be largely explained by the increased power and circulation of the term "illegal alien," first during Operation Wetback and then after the Immigration Act of 1965. This chapter examines the shift in mass-media representations of deportations displayed by the differing coverage of the kidnapping of Heikkila and the detention and deportation of Arellano. Focusing on the early Cold War era, it examines the ways in which advocates for immigrant rights—specifically, the broad coalition represented by the American Committee for the Protection of the Foreign Born (ACPFB)—were able to achieve a comparatively high level of visibility for foreign-born progressives' deportation proceedings before 1965. In contrast, immigrant rights advocates of the early twenty-first century, although much more numerous, struggle to broadcast stories of even comparatively well-known deportations, such as that of Arellano.

Since the 2017 escalation of federal threats to deport "all" of the more than twelve million unauthorized migrants present in the United States, immigrant rights advocates have worked to call attention to a handful of activists who have taken public sanctuary in churches. Part of the immigrant rights movement's sanctuary strategy is to draw mass-media attention to these individuals to highlight the often-concealed effects of deportation on broader communities. Jeanette Vizguerra, who took sanctuary in a Denver church in February 2017, received copious mass-media attention, being named one of *Time Magazine*'s "most notable people" of the year. Subsequently, in May 2017, she was granted a stay of deportation and was able to return to her family; three of her four children are U.S.-born citizens. The effective use of public sanctuary in Vizguerra's case highlights the importance of mass-media visibility to effective mobilization for immigrant rights. By taking public sanctuary, migrants claim the moral high ground as well as the spotlight: they risk arrest and deportation to bring attention to the crisis in migrant communities. This crisis goes largely unheralded because of a cultural logic about illegality that puts undocumented lives beyond the frame of most mass-mediated accounts.[4]

The mass-mediated emergence of the figure of the "illegal alien" in the mid-twentieth century was part of a broader struggle over race and rights in the postwar period.[5] The terms "red alien" and "illegal alien" are ideological distillations: they fix histories of struggle over belonging and rights into particular notions of threats to the body politic. Such "structures of feeling" condense social experience into small, affectively charged moments, such as shifting terminology to describe the foreign born struggling with deportation. Literary scholar Shelly Streeby writes about the ways in which sentiment and sensation operate in the mass media, "by provoking affect and emotional responses in readers and viewers and by foregrounding endangered, suffering, and dead bodies and separated families, often in order to make political arguments about races, classes, nations and international relations." This chapter examines the ways in which public, mass-mediated rhetoric about immigrants, informed by law and policy, eventually foreclosed on the representation of deportees as individuals deserving of having a story, in many ways necessitating the development of public sanctuary as a mass-media strategy. Before the public relations success of Operation Wetback in broadcasting an image of "illegal aliens" besieging the nation's borders, the ACPFB was able to disseminate a migrant logic by which foreign-born denizens had some rights.[6]

The move of federal immigration and naturalization services to the newly inaugurated DHS after 9/11 was accompanied by the acceleration of deportation sweeps. The evolving grammar of DHS conflated unsanctioned border crossing with potential terrorist activity. In turn, this grammar drew on prior understandings of the criminality of "illegal aliens," a figure conceived as part of the long, white supremacist history of immigration restriction. The punch packed by the term "illegal alien" in the era of the DHS conflates criminality, immigration status, and racial identity. The 2017 Executive Order on "Border Security and Immigration Enforcement Improvements" is replete with language conflating unauthorized status with criminality. This particular distillation originated during the Cold War assault on Mexican migration in Operation Wetback and gathered force after the Immigration and Nationality Acts of 1965. Periodic panics about "illegal immigration," from Operation Wetback to the present, indicate the ongoing power of the term and its harnessing to silence migrant resistance in an era of neoliberal economic consolidation.[7]

Red Aliens

During the early Cold War, the ACPFB drew on Depression-era structures of feeling infused by migrant imaginaries to conjure sympathy for the foreign born. In the repressive atmosphere of the period, the ACPFB was tarred by accusations that it was a "Communist front." However, advocates around the country managed to levy public sympathy for the foreign born. Historian Michael Denning explains the persistence of such sympathies as one effect of the long arc of what he calls the "cultural front": the alliance created during the 1930s between workers and intellectuals, many of them foreign born or from second-generation immigrant families. Many journalists working in the late 1940s and early 1950s had been shaped by the experience of this cultural front; many of these cultural workers had close ties to migrant communities. Further, Denning argues, the cultural front steeped mass-media audiences in a structure of feeling that sympathized with workers and immigrants, identifying them as true and deserving Americans.[8]

Cold War laws limiting freedom of speech and movement for the foreign born targeted immigrant communities for enhanced surveillance. A structure of feeling that associated those born outside the United States with what were deemed "un-American" activities informed these laws. This emergent discourse constructed such aliens as existing outside any possibility of citizenship, just as Soviet Communists were portrayed as lacking moral scruples. Aliens threatened the body politic, as demonstrated by the mobilization of the term to describe would-be invaders from outer space during the same period. Eventually, these discourses of political subversion and racial fitness for citizenship converged in the figure of the illegal alien.[9]

Although it drew on earlier ideas of the "enemy alien," the term "red alien" first appeared in media coverage of early Cold War deportation cases against foreign-born labor leaders. A 1950 front-page *New York Times* article proclaims: "Ex-Red Alien Loses Deportation Fight." The article describes the Supreme Court case against Greek American journalist Peter Harisiades, who was represented by the ACPFB. Harisiades had joined the Workers Party in 1925. He participated in strikes in Massachusetts and West Virginia during the late 1920s and 1930s. When the Workers Party became the Communist Party, Harisiades worked as a journalist and as the secretary of the Greek bureau. He left the party in 1939.

The article recounts how, at Harisiades's trial, Federal Judge Vincent Liebel read aloud from writings by Vladimir Lenin and Joseph Stalin to demonstrate that the Communist Party sought to overthrow the U.S. government "by force or violence." This interpretation allowed the court to decide that Harisiades's past membership constituted grounds for deportation.[10]

While the *Times* piece does not advocate for Harisiades's innocence, it portrays him as simultaneously a former Communist and an ordinary person, noting his marriage to an American citizen. Being a "red alien," then, did not necessarily preclude being depicted as a human being, particularly when the "alien" in question was domesticated by heterosexual marriage to a white woman. Harisiades's case eventually went to the Supreme Court, along with those of former Communists Luigi Mascitti and Dora Coleman; all were ruled deportable under the McCarran Law. Like many other progressives deported in this era, Harisiades chose "voluntary departure" to Poland because of his fear of persecution by the Greek regime.[11]

Similarly, in the case of *Galvan v. Press*, the Supreme Court ruled in 1954 that Robert Norbert Galvan, a Mexican American cannery worker who had been living in California since 1918, was deportable on the basis of his past membership in the Communist Party. Galvan had been a party member from 1944 to 1946. Justices William Douglas and Hugo Black dissented from the past association provision. Black writes, "This man may be driven from our land because he joined a political party that California and the nation then recognized as perfectly legal."

After the Supreme Court verdict made him imminently deportable, Galvan filed a writ of habeas corpus in federal court in San Diego, arguing that he was being deprived of the equal rights guaranteed to Mexicans under the Treaty of Guadalupe Hidalgo in 1848. This intervention drew on the historical imaginaries broadcasted by the ACPFB and the Los Angeles Committee for the Protection of the Foreign Born (LACPFB) in such publications as *Shame of a Nation: A Documented History of Police-State Terror against Mexican-Americans in the U.S.A.* (1954). But invoking this treaty against a hundred-year history of the depredation of Mexican American rights in California and the Southwest ultimately failed Galvan; he was deported in 1955.[12]

Harisiades and Galvan were among those targeted for deportation. Many of these individuals worked with the ACPFB to contest repression against them. Most of these cases ratified the new McCarran Act policy of deporting the foreign born on the basis of their past membership in the Communist Party. Effectively, the "past membership" clause of the law allowed the INS to heighten surveillance of the rights to free speech of the foreign born, allowing agents to become historians and editors in their search for subversion. At the same time, the ACPFB advanced the notion that the individuals facing deportation deserved justice.

As deportations for past affiliations with the Communist Party increased during the "Midnight Raids" of 1950, so did the use of the term "red alien." Fairly high-profile cases accused individuals of different national origins of past association with the Communist Party. As the pitch of these deportation drives heightened, increasing numbers of foreign-born activists were targeted for deportation. This wave spread throughout the country, as Abner Green of the ACPFB describes in an early 1951 pamphlet:

These deportations reach into every phase and facet of American life. Of the 160 non-citizens arrested in deportation proceedings to date, more than 25 are women—wives, mothers and grandmothers of American citizens; more than 30 are leaders and active members of trade unions; two are leaders of the Negro people; three are important leaders of Jewish communities; and more than 100 are active members and leaders of national group communities throughout the country. These deportations cut into the very heart and soul of the American community because the non-citizen is an integral part of our society and it is not possible to remove the non-citizen without injuring the fabric of society.[13]

A good proportion of the foreign born targeted were in their fifties and sixties; some had not been active in "subversive" activities for a decade or more. One example was the case of Polish Jewish migrant Abraham Malkin, who was targeted for deportation in 1948. Malkin said he joined the Communist Party in 1937 to maintain his position as the shop steward of the International Ladies Garment Workers Union but left it a few months later. Nevertheless, he was included in the deportation sweeps of October 1950.[14]

These campaigns against "red aliens" were struggles over memory. Trials often involved conflicting recollections of rallies and meetings held during the 1930s: the words of foreign-born activists turned government informers were pitched against those of immigrants accused of past membership and subversion. For many readers of the national press, lingering structures of feeling positively associated foreign-born activists with important American struggles, particularly civil and labor rights. The ACPFB drew on these structures of feeling in legal arguments as well as advocacy efforts. But the harsh light of the McCarran Act cast the struggle for equal education for Mexican Americans in Los Angeles as having been led by foreign-born subversives; it suggested ulterior motives for the Finnish-born organizers who helped create Minnesota dairy cooperatives. Two different structures of feeling coexisted for a brief time, before a powerful discourse about the foreign born as enemy aliens and race invaders came to dominate the mass media.

The outcome of this struggle had not yet been determined in the period immediately following World War II. Political theorist Jodi Dean argues that the uptick in sightings of UFOs in 1946 summoned widespread excitement about the possibility of flight and galactic companionship. It took concerted federal effort to contain this "populist agency" and to convert this excitement into anxiety about national security. Tellingly, the use of the term "alien" to describe visitors from outer space emerged in the 1930s, concurrent with the cultural front. Similarly, a popular investment in the foreign born, even in foreign-born "radicals," as true Americans persisted into the Cold War period. Immigrant rights advocates drew on the continued existence of this structure of feeling to frame their defense of "red aliens."[15]

In Defense of "Red Aliens"

In 1952, Irving Taffler of the Minnesota Committee for the Protection of the Foreign Born addressed a delegation of American citizen families of foreign-born individuals targeted for deportation. The delegation was headed to Washington, DC, to petition President Harry Truman, Attorney General Tom Clark, and others for clemency for their relatives. Taffler drew on tropes of national loyalty and antifacism that would have been familiar in the immediate postwar period:

> We who have served our country at the risk of our lives are especially sensitive to the persecution of our parents, because we know that it was their devotion to their adopted country which inspired us in the war against fascism. You, too, must be aware of the simple fact that, in your daily lives, you are better Americans because of the understanding your immigrant parents have given you of democracy and liberty.[16]

Taffler reminded the people gathered to petition for the rights of their relatives who were accused of subversion and disloyalty. These immigrants stood for "democracy and liberty." The notion that immigrants came to the United States seeking freedom was part of the Cold War "Nation of Immigrants" narrative; it was a way of celebrating the American dream and contrasting it with Soviet socialist totalitarianism. But the immigrants Taffler referred to were accused of sympathy with the Soviet Union, the apotheosis of un-Americanism. Even as the ideological mechanisms of counterinsurgency geared up to purge society of subversives, residual structures of feeling still conjured sympathy and alliance with accused "red aliens."

For one thing, memories of suffering and deprivation during the Great Depression persisted in the immediate postwar period. Advocates for "red aliens" accused of subversion often deployed such memories, turning accusations of Communist Party affiliation on their head. Where the Federal Bureau of Investigation (FBI) saw Minnesotan Finnish American newspaper editor Knut Heikkinen as "one of the key Communists of the nation," ACPFB lawyers created an idea of "Depression Communism."[17] Immigrants accused of subversion often countered with their own understandings of their political work.

Heikkila's extraordinary rendition to Helsinki made international headlines. The ACPFB used this case to broadcast unjust treatment of the foreign born. But Heikkila continued to face deportation charges, eventually dying before his case could be decided; his legal trials may well have aggravated his heart condition. After his death, the INS attempted to deny his American-born wife, Phyllis, Social Security benefits. During one of his trials, Heikkila defended his engagement with the Workers Alliance in Minnesota in the 1930s, invoking this idea of "Depression Communism" eloquently:

> As I see the Communist Movement, I have to judge it on the basis of what I know it to be, as I saw it; on the basis of that[,] I have to make my answer as during the time I was in it. We worked very hard for unemployment insurance and social security, against foreclosure sales on farms and homes; we worked for relief for people who needed relief so a lot of people wouldn't be kicked out of their home[s]. We went with people and spoke for them when they were unable to make themselves understood because of language difficulty. These were the things that I believed in, these were the things that the Communist Party, in my opinion, stood for; for improving and making it possible to have better living conditions for all in the United States. On the basis of that, I would have to say that I have done nothing in opposition to those ideals.[18]

Harisiades described his labor advocacy in very similar terms, asserting that his work for justice during the Depression had constituted his Americanization.[19]

The strategy of dismissing the "un-American" implications of past membership in the Communist Party was not surprising on the part of advocates for those in deportation proceedings. But what is surprising, in the context of the Cold War, is that it sometimes worked. While Harisiades was deported and Heikkila eventually died of a heart attack that may well have been partially brought on by continual INS harassment, others fared better. In 1957, ACPFB lawyers prevailed as the Supreme Court overturned the deportation case against former German American Communist Charles Rowoldt, who had admitted past membership as well as employment in a bookstore selling Marxist-Leninist literature. The court found that Rowoldt's membership could well have been economic rather than political. Lawyers for the Minnesota Committee for the Protection of the Foreign Born argued that because Rowoldt had joined the party to fight for daily needs, he was "not a member in the meaning of the internal security law and not deportable."[20]

Contextualizing the "past membership" provision of the McCarran Act in historical terms had some limited legal successes. More broadly, memories of the struggles of the Great Depression lingered enough in the early Cold War period to conjure mass-media sympathies for "red aliens" subjected to arrest as suspected subversives. Newspaper accounts headlined with the purple prose of Cold War counterinsurgency routinely included the voices of social justice advocates, including those targeted for deportation.

· While the defense of the foreign born mobilized a residual structure of feeling grounded in the 1930s, immigrant rights advocacy during the 1950s was increasingly cast in terms of what historian Susan L. Carruthers identifies as a captivity narrative. Drawing on the captivity narrative as "an enduring template for constructions of identity and difference," Carruthers asserts the centrality of what she calls "metaphors of enslavement" to popular understandings of Cold War geopolitics. This emergent structure of feeling connected the detention and deportation of the foreign born to limitations on mobility imposed by fascist governments, from the Axis Powers during the war years to the Socialist Bloc nations afterward.[21]

The Cold War captivity narrative tapped into deep wellsprings of historical imaginings of encounters between Euro-Americans and indigenous nations and into the enduring popularity of the captivity narrative as a literary form. Always gendered and racialized, the captivity narrative creates a cast of villains and victims. Just as American national identity emerged in distinction to a supposedly savage indigenous other, Cold War

identity emphasized the total struggle between democratic good and totalitarian Communist evil. These foundational stories posited an always
insurgent evil, perennially prepared to raid the freedom and security of
virtuous Americans. At the same time, the Cold War captivity narrative
transferred sympathy for those displaced or imprisoned at the hands of
fascists during World War II to ascendant anti-Communist animus after
the war. The Cold War captivity narrative, in other words, captured popular sympathies for displaced persons and mobilized them in service of Cold
War political alliances.[22]

The ability of ACPFB advocates to bend the Cold War captivity narrative to elicit sympathy for individuals targeted for deportation was a testa-
ment to their ingenuity and daring. For this strategy to work, immigrants
in deportation proceedings had to be portrayed as victims of undue state
power. Because of the racialized roots of the captivity narrative, this strategy worked better for some migrants than for others. In the increasingly
repressive political context of the time, the ACPFB had limited success on
a case-by-case basis in rallying support for those in deportation proceedings. Immigrant rights advocates drew on a tradition that had been established by the International Labor Defense (ILD) and antilynching
movements. According to historian Rebecca Nell Hill, "Both labor-de-
fense campaigns and anti-lynching campaigns historically have worked
primarily through appeals to public opinion in the media, used stories of
terror and heroism to build alliances across lines of class and race, and
have been formative in the creation of radical political identities."[23]

ACPFB pamphlets stressed the situations of individuals: their life histories, family and community connections, and the risk many faced if
deported back to repressive regimes. The media circulated many of the
tropes and stories disseminated by immigration rights advocates. In some
cases, this mass-media attention allowed for support and even clemency
for those targeted for deportation under the Smith and McCarran acts.

Immigrant rights advocacy worked at the intersection of memories of
collectivity during the cultural front, on the one hand, and imaginings of
totalitarian imprisonment, on the other. This position made it easier to
advocate for the rights of individuals than to successfully petition for
broader changes, such as policy reform, or a broad defense of the accomplishments of accused activists. It was not that ACPFB activists did not try
to make broader critiques or to stand up for immigrants as a group, as
evidenced by their ongoing efforts in support the rights of the foreign born
in general and of specific populations, such as Mexican Americans, in
particular. For the ACPFB, immigrant rights advocacy was part of broader international struggles against white supremacy and imperialism. But
popular structures of feeling meant that pleas for individuals who ap-

peared to be caught in the web of government repression got more attention in the mass media than advocacy for immigrants as a class or for
broader social change. Further, because sympathy for the foreign born was
increasingly forced to draw on the Cold War captivity narrative, these
sympathies were deeply racialized and gendered.

The ascendant discourse of national security compelled the increased
detention and deportation of the foreign born. But this discourse was rid-
dled with contradictions and popular ambivalence. The following sections
examine mass-media treatment of particular cases and cohorts of the foreign born.

Eastern European Immigrants: Shifting Geographies of Suspicion[24]

Shifting cognitive maps of the globe created an additional affective strand
allowing for sympathy with foreign-born immigrants from Eastern Europe. Immediately after the war, Winston Churchill's "Iron Curtain"
proclamation sundered prior alliances with the Soviet Union. Immigrants
from such countries as Poland, Hungary, Czechoslovakia, and Yugoslavia
were portrayed as seeking freedom from totalitarianism.

Just as advocates for maritime laborers drew on the famous heroism
of the merchant marine on the high seas during wartime (see Chapter 3),
Eastern European migrants elicited wartime mass-media interest and sympathy because of the precarious situations in their home nations. Writing
about Canadian "press narratives of migration," historian Franca Iacovetta notes the contradictions involved in eliciting a warm popular reception for Eastern European refugees while simultaneously warning of the
possible presence of dangerous Communists among them. This contradiction opened up space for advocacy for the foreign born, including those
deemed "red aliens."[25]

Popular sentiment welcomed the postwar influx of Eastern European
refugees. Many Americans from Eastern European backgrounds served in
the U.S. Armed Forces during the war. After the war, these "white ethnics" had access to assimilation and upward mobility through the education and housing benefits offered by the GI Bill. Increasingly, these Eastern
European ethnics were portrayed as democratic American citizens; at the
same time, they were shaped by a migrant imaginary.

The humanization and individual subjectivity granted to immigrants
from Eastern Europe was contradictory, in light of the Cold War sea
change. The "Eastern Bloc" of Soviet-allied nations became enemies of the
States, while individuals from these countries were perceived as

escaping freedom fighters, as white, and as ultimately assimilable. Some Eastern European "red aliens," then, were also human. An examination of the mass-media coverage of the cases against two immigrants from Eastern Europe—Slavic American activist George Pirinsky and Czech war bride Ellen Knauff—reveals some of the contradictions at play.

A 1948 *Chicago Tribune* article deploys the term "red alien" to describe Pirinsky, the executive secretary of the American Slav Congress (ASC). Pirinsky was arrested after this congress was declared to be affiliated with Moscow and therefore a "subversive organization" by the House Un-American Activities Committee (HUAC). But the article cites the Justice Department's claim that Pirinsky's arrest was based on his alleged affiliation with the Communist Party, not with the ASC. It quotes Pirinsky, who describes the organization as promoting "cultural activities of American Slavs, and friendship between the Americans and the Slavs" and emphasizes its activities in support of the Allies during the war. Further, the article notes that the fifteen hundred delegates to the ASC represented an estimated fifteen million Americans of Slavic ethnic descent.[26]

The ambivalence displayed in the *Tribune* piece indicates the contradictions involved in targeting the leaders of European ethnic communities immediately after the war. A broad coalition of American Slavs united behind the Four Freedoms, defined by Franklin Roosevelt as worth fighting for during the war, and Slavic American union members worked in defense industries, particularly on the East Coast.[27] But what looked like Slavic ethnic unity against fascism before 1945 could be reinterpreted as the community's potential to infiltrate national security a short three years later. The HUAC report alleged that the ASC represented Soviet infiltration:

> By means of a nationalistic appeal, [the ASC] strives to enlist our Slavic population in behalf of Russia's ambitious designs for world empire and simultaneously to incite American Slavs against the land of their adoption.[28]

The loyalties of Eastern European ethnics were suspect after the war, but there were a lot of them in the United States. The *New York Times* noted that support for the ASC came from smaller Slavic organizations centered around Pittsburgh, Detroit, Chicago, Cleveland, and New York; "Slavic" organizations included those for "Russians, Byelorussians, Ukrainians, Carpatho-Russians, Poles, Serbs, Croats, Slovenians, Macedonians, Czechs, Slovaks and Bulgarians."[29] Like Pirinsky, many Slavic Americans had engaged in antifascist activities during the war. In the context of ascendant anti-Communism, these activities increasingly came under scrutiny and fire.

Press coverage of Pirinsky's political activities and the deportation case against him reflected this ambivalence. When Polish resistance leader Lieutenant General Tadeusz Komorowski visited New York in 1946, the press noted protests against him by the Polonia Society of the International Workers Order and the ASC. That same year, the ASC held a "Win the Peace" Rally in Madison Square Garden, chaired by Louis Adamic. The rally drew cheers from the crowd of nine thousand for Henry Wallace and for a message from Stalin read by Pirinsky. The *New York Times* and the *Chicago Tribune* covered the rally fairly evenly, noting the HUAC assertions about the ASC at the same time they lauded the way in which a performance by Paul Robeson moved "a Russian general" to "kiss him on both cheeks, a salute that was fervently returned."[30]

Pirinsky's fight against his eventual deportation was covered closely by New York and Chicago papers. The Midwest and East Coast regions included large populations of Slavic American ethnics. The arrest of Pirinsky in 1948 came at a time of increased INS sweeps that included foreign-born labor activists and journalists. Pirinsky was held in detention at Ellis Island with many other clients of the ACPFB: Ferdinand Smith of the National Maritime Union (NMU), Claudia Jones of the Communist Party, Rose Lightcap of the International Workers Order (IWO), Carl Palvo of the Finnish Mutual Aid Society of the IWO, Harry Yarris of the Diamond Workers' Protective Union, and Harisiades.[31]

In context of the ascendant "Red Scare," newspapers allowed for the possibility that these were dangerous, dishonest subversives. Articles repeatedly insinuated that Pirinsky was lying by referring to his "true name": Nicholas Icholoff Zaikoff. At the same time, coverage of his case featured arguments by the ACPFB and by dissenting judges decrying "illegal" detentions at Ellis Island. The press also attended to questions of the rights of the detained, such as their ability to post a bond for bail and what appropriate bail should be.[32] Perhaps most importantly, media coverage of Pirinsky's case often included the voice of the accused himself.

The fact that Pirinsky's case was covered more or less fairly in the mass media did not prevent his removal from the United States. Ultimately, Pirinsky was deported with his American citizen wife, Pauline, and their three-year-old son, George Jr. The Justice Department sent them to Bulgaria, although Pirinsky had not renewed his passport and claimed to be a citizen of no country. The same fate befell many other immigrants of Eastern European origin targeted for deportation during this period.

While Pirinsky's case was covered in the mass media, the case of excluded war bride Ellen Knauff generated much more attention. Knauff, a German Jewish woman with Czech citizenship from a previous marriage, fled Adolf Hitler's regime and served in the Czech Red Cross and the

Royal Air Force in London from 1943 to 1946. After the war, she returned to Germany, where she worked for the U.S. Occupation Forces. There, she met and married an American soldier named Kurt Knauff in 1948. After she experienced a miscarriage, the couple decided that she should go to the United States and stay with relatives of her husband, under the War Brides Act of 1945. But Knauff was refused admission, detained at Ellis Island, and accused of "spying" for the Czech government. In 1950, the Supreme Court affirmed Knauff's exclusion and detention without trial as justifiable for "security reasons." Although Knauff was not represented by the ACPFB, her case provides a strong counterpoint to those of the "red aliens" broadcasted by the committee.[33]

Starting with her detention in 1948, Knauff's case took many high-profile twists and turns. She had two deportations scheduled and stayed, one with only twenty minutes to spare before she was to board the airplane. Apparently moved by her pluck, the *St. Louis Post-Dispatch* began an advocacy campaign on her behalf. Representative Francis Walter (R-PA) and Senator William Langer (R-ND) introduced bills in Congress calling for Knauff's admission. Finally, in 1951, an Immigration Service Board of Appeals cleared all charges against her and recommended that she be admitted for permanent residency.[34]

This was a compelling story in Cold War America, meriting close attention from news organizations around the country. As Carruthers points out, stories of prisoners of war, forced laborers, internments, and refugee camps circulated in the aftermath of World War II. Cold War narratives contrasted democratic "freedom" with Communist "enslavement." In cases like Knauff's, the fates of individual prisoners resonated with the overall U.S. defense of freedom against tyranny. The story of the plucky white brunette confronting the beast of unfair bureaucracy resonated with the Cold War captivity narrative.[35]

Knauff's story elicited widespread media attention on a different scale than the cases of "red aliens." Knauff was a young, white, presentable refugee from the horrors of the war; her story of unjust detention and last-minute stays of deportation had a *Perils of Pauline* quality to them. Newspaper accounts and the memoir she published in 1952 downplayed Knauff's Jewish identity in favor of her status as an attractive war bride and a would-be loyal American. In her memoir, she emphasizes her dependence on steady support from her husband and her lawyer, German American Gunther Jacobson. Knauff rarely speaks of politics, except to contrast her ordeal with the democratic principles she had expected from the United States.

While mass-media coverage of Knauff's captivity and bid for freedom deemphasized her Jewish identity, her status as a refugee interned at Ellis

Island conjured affective ties to the plight of European Jewry. Knauff was consistently described as "German-American," and by the *Atlanta Daily World* as "a brunet in her mid-thirties."[36] A *New York Times* review of Knauff's memoir makes no mention of her Jewish identity but refers to her "picture of Ellis Island as a high-class concentration camp within the shadow of the Statue of Liberty."[37] Consistent with the captivity narratives that Carruthers finds to be so central in mustering popular sentiment, Knauff's problems were presented as those of a plucky individual against an immigration bureaucracy out of control.

Part of the popularity of her cause, then, had to do with Knauff's ability to stand in for those displaced and interned in Europe without embodying a particular historical identity. Although she was accused of spying, which would seem to be somewhat more perilous to national security than having a brief membership in a Popular Front organization, her numerous defenders represented the incident as "a modern Zenger case—a document against giving arbitrary power to a government bureau." Unlike many of the "red alien" cases, Knauff herself professed no ideology. This reference to the eighteenth-century case affirming the right to freedom of speech of German-born John Peter Zenger signals Knauff's inclusion among wronged, but ultimately redeemed, victims.[38]

The media spun Knauff's case as a romance. Although she had married and changed her name more than once, the media did not point to the question of Knauff's aliases, as they did with Pirinsky and others. As a woman and as a war bride, she was expected to change her name. Knauff claimed that the attorney general's case against her drew on the testimony of a jealous rival for her husband's attentions back in Germany. This Cold War romance played well: Knauff's book was syndicated in the *Daily Sunday Compass*; ACLU lawyer Arthur Garfield Hays, who wrote the introduction, appeared on *Meet the Critics* on New York local television station WABD to discuss the book.[39]

Like the ethnic Slavs represented by Pirinsky in the ASC, Knauff was accused of fifth-column infiltration. But Pirinsky had a clear political past, featuring definite transnational ethnic loyalties and partisan struggles. Although the federal case against Knauff turned on her Czech citizenship and her unreliability as a war bride and a potential American, mass-media sympathy for her drew on assumptions about her gender and nationality and, in particular, her status as a captive.

The cases of Pirinsky and Knauff demonstrate quite different outcomes for Eastern Europeans accused of subversion and disloyalty. Like many Eastern Europeans in the immediate postwar period, both were effectively stateless. Pirinsky did not claim citizenship in socialist Bulgaria, and Knauff, no longer married to her first Czech husband, had no wish to return to her native Germany. But Pirinsky's migrant spatiality and his transnational Slavic political associations ultimately made his defense unsustainable. Knauff, on the other hand, claimed no loyalties to an ethnic group or a prior nation. Her captivity on Ellis Island was unpopular, and ultimately she was successful in her bid to claim legal entry and naturalization as a war bride. The McCarran Act facilitated both of these cases by opening season on the past associations of the foreign born. While newspapers complied with the new logic of suspicion, they also paid attention to the voices and fates of individual deportees. This contradiction created a space that advocates used to draw attention to injustices against the foreign born. The following section examines how this contradiction functioned in the case of nonwhite immigrants targeted for deportation and suspicion.

Red (and Nonwhite) Aliens

The widespread use of deportation against foreign-born political activists had particularly dire consequences for Asian, Afro-diasporic, and Latinx migrants. The civil rights component of the cultural front of the 1930s emphasized struggles for racial justice in the workplace, housing, and education. Many of the activists targeted for deportation in the early Cold War were veterans of these struggles. After the war, many people who had been affected by these struggles retained strong attachments to the antiracist priorities of the cultural front. This residual structure of feeling inclined many in these communities toward sympathy with the "red aliens" targeted for repression.

The INS sweeps that emanated from the passage of the McCarran Act targeted a multiethnic array of activists and former activists. These deportation sweeps included many foreign-born individuals who would have been considered nonwhite at the time, many of whom were represented by the ACPFB. These included, among many others, Filipinx David Vega, Chris Mensalves, Ponce Torres, and Ernesto Mangaoang; Mexican Americans Jose Estrada Castillo and Refugio Roman Martinez; Korean Americans David Hyun, John Juhn, Diamond Kimm, Sang Ryup Park, and Choon Cha and Chungson Kwak; Japanese Americans Shuji Matsui and Edo Heihachi Mita; Okinawan Paul Shinsei Kochi; Jamaican-born Ferdinand Smith; and Trinidadian-born Claudia Jones.[40] This section considers mass-media representations of some "red aliens" of color.

Popular sympathy for "red aliens" generally did not extend to Asian American activists. While the diasporic activities of some Korean American intellectuals paralleled those of Pirinsky in the ASC, transnational antifascist politics during World War II did not necessarily translate into an even presentation in the media after the war. The marginalization of

Asian American deportees by the popular media paralleled the exclusion of Asian Americans from access to citizenship. Further, in the case of Korean Americans, their resistance to repatriation to South Korea threatened to indict the Cold War narrative of liberation as well as the crucial project of containment in Asia.

On the West Coast, the LACPFB brought attention to the cases of the Mexican American community leaders known as the "Santa Ana Four" and the "Terminal Island Four," which included British screenwriter Harry Carlisle, Polish-born former Communist Party educator Frank Carlson, British dance instructor Miriam Stevenson, and Korean American architect David Hyun (see Chapters 4 and 5). The passage of the McCarran Act, along with the U.S. intervention in the Korean peninsula, intensified the deportation drive against diasporic Korean intellectuals involved in the publication of the bilingual Los Angeles newspaper *Korean Independence*. As a result, the newspaper took up the cause of Korean Americans targeted for deportation and gradually became involved with the multiethnic struggle for immigrant rights in Los Angeles.[41]

Mass-media outlets covered the case against the "Terminal Island Four" in Los Angeles because of the interest generated by the advocacy campaign on their behalf and because of the broad legal questions raised by the new McCarran Act. The *Los Angeles Times* took a local interest in the case, turning its vociferously anti-Communist lens on the struggles of the "Terminal Island Four" against deportation. The paper referred to the group using the name initially given to them by their supporters.[42] As in the case of Pirinsky, even the mainstream, anti-Communist press represented issues of legal fairness for accused "red aliens."

While the *Los Angeles Times* did cover the legal travails of the "Terminal Island Four," articles tended to endorse an anti-Communist position, undermining assertions by the accused. The paper reported that Judge Ben Harrison reacted to the petitions for release on bail by saying, "I'm not going to turn these people loose if they are Communists any more than I would turn loose a deadly germ in the community." Further, the paper impugned Hyun's loyalty, noting in an article about the continued legal struggles of the "Terminal Island Four" that Hyun "spoke of the Korean people's struggle for freedom but refused to say which side he was on in the Korean War." Although Hyun was a public intellectual and active in progressive politics in southern California, media coverage did not include his voice nor those of his codefendants. Because of this, it is significant that the *Los Angeles Times* saw fit to mention that the name "Terminal Island Four" had been given to them by "their supporters."[43]

While the cases of Hyun and the "Terminal Island Four" received some mass-media coverage, those against other Korean diasporic intellectuals were almost completely ignored by the national as well as the African American mass media. Similarly, the cases of Japanese American poet Edo Mati, Okinawan laborer and wartime OSS recruit Paul Shinsei Kochi, and Okinawan domestic worker Masui Shuji received little attention. These cases were publicized by the ACPFB and the LACPFB, so it is likely that local and national media received information about them in the form of pamphlets. Greater media attention to Hyun's case may have had to do with fact that his legal struggles were effectively merged with those of the other, Euro-American members of the "Terminal Island Four."

Most foreign-born Asian Americans had just become eligible for citizenship in 1952 when the passage of the McCarran-Walter Immigration Act eliminated the ban on their naturalization. The national imaginary that conjured support for accused "red aliens" did not include Asian Americans. In his autobiography, Peter Hyun, David Hyun's American-born brother, talks about his frustration with disregard for Asian artists in Federal Theater Project productions. Hyun believed that there was little place for him as an Asian actor in the cultural front. The residual structure of feeling that conjured popular support for the foreign born still excluded Asian Americans. As historian George Lipsitz points out, it may have been the Popular Front's deployment of American exceptionalism and virtue that allowed for the privileging of whiteness to be so unchallenged immediately after World War II.[44]

Racially and geopolitically, Asian Americans did not fit into the Cold War captivity narrative. The ACPFB had criticized the internment of Japanese Americans as an unjust deprivation of freedom, but this view was not widespread in the immediate postwar period. Internationally, the cause of "freedom" was used to justify the "police action" in Korea, as Carruthers points out. Carruthers argues that U.S. insistence on the freedom to refuse repatriation prolonged the war for eighteen months. The ensuing "liberation" of North Korean and Chinese prisoners of war made headline news and fed the ascendant Cold War captivity narrative. Stories of Korean Americans detained by the INS and threatened with forcible repatriation to South Korea did not jibe with the notion that the Korean War had been fought to free captives of Communist regimes in North Korea and China. Further, the refusal of these Korean Americans to recognize South Korea as a viable homeland, and the insistence of advocacy campaigns that they faced grave physical danger if they were forcibly repatriated there, contradicted the idea of the United States as an emancipator of captives.[45]

When Chungson and Choon Cha Kwak were deported in 1955, the New York Times carried only a three-paragraph article, noting that the couple had "failed by credible testimony to establish that they would suffer physical persecution if deported." The same Los Angeles Times article

PATRIOT

DIAMOND KIMM

FACES

EXILE

A PATRIOT'S REWARD!

The U.S. Supreme Court on June 13, 1960, in a 5 to 4 decision upheld the deportation order of Diamond Kimm, who now faces exile to South Korea, where possible physical persecution or death awaits him.

The MAJORITY of the court upheld the deportation order on the grounds that he had failed to prove that he was a person of good moral character, because he had invoked the Fifth Amendment in answering the question as to whether he was or ever had been a member of the Communist Party.

IN DISSENT Mr. Justice Douglas stated in part: "The import is underlined by the fact that there is not a shred of evidence of bad character in the record against this alien. He entered as a student in 1928, and pursued his studies until 1938. He planned to return to Korea, but the outbreak of hostilities between China and Japan in 1937 changed his mind. Since 1938, he has been continuously employed in gainful occupations. The record shows no criminal convictions, nothing that could bring stigma on the man. His employment since 1938 has been as manager of a produce company, as chemist, as foundry worker (metallurgist - Ed.), and as a member of the OSS during the latter part of World War II." He also was self-employed in the printing business, publishing a paper, Korean Independence. There is not a word of evidence that he had been a member of the Communist Party at any time. The only thing that stands in his way of being eligible for suspension of deportation by the Attorney General, is his invocation of the Fifth Amendment . . ."

"I had assumed that invocation of the privilege is a neutral act, as consistent with innocence as with guilt." "The Court in terms does not, and cannot, rest its decision on the ground that by invoking the Fifth Amendment, the petitioner gave evidence of bad moral character."

WHAT MUST BE DONE:

In view of the 5 to 4 decision, the Los Angeles Committee, which has defended Mr. Kimm for the past 10 years, has filed a motion for a rehearing to the U.S. Supreme Court, and urges all to write to Attorney General Wm. Rogers, Justice Department, Washington, D.C., and ask him to drop the Diamond Kimm deportation order.

WAR DEPARTMENT
OFFICE OF THE ASSISTANT SECRETARY OF WAR
STRATEGIC SERVICES UNIT
Field Experimental Unit
25th & E STREETS, N.W.
WASHINGTON 25, D.C.

9 November 1945

Mr. Diamond Kimm
909 West 36th Place
Los Angeles 7, California

Dear Mr. Kimm:

. . . . . You were one of those selected for particularly hazardous and difficult work, the full details of which may never be made public. The eager willingness you displayed in all phases of the program, and the unselfish patriotism which underlay your desire to serve, are particularly worthy of special mention.

I therefore wish to extend to you not only official commendation for having done in a superior manner a job that was complex and difficult, but also my personal thanks and appreciation for all you have done so unselfishly and efficiently "over and above the call of duty".

Sincerely yours,

Carl F. Eifler
Colonel, Infantry
Chief, FEU OSS

ACPFB flyer opposing Diamond Kimm's deportation. (American Committee for the Protection of the Foreign Born Records, Joseph A. Labadie Collection, University of Michigan Library [Special Collections Library].)

architect...

American...

THIS MAN IS BEING SENT TO HIS DEATH...

LACPFB pamphlet opposing David Hyun's deportation. (Los Angeles Committee for the Protection of the Foreign Born Collection, Southern California Library [Los Angeles, California].)

noting Hyun's refusal to reveal which "side" he had been on during the Korean War concludes by observing that Hyun also refused to comment on an advocacy pamphlet decrying the risk he faced at the hands of Syngman Rhee.[46] The freedom struggles of diasporic Koreans and Japanese contradicted the ascendant narrative of Cold War emancipation.

Popular sympathy for "red aliens," then, did not extend to Asian American activists. While the activities of the diasporic intellectuals around *Korean Independence* paralleled those of Pirinsky in the ASC, transnational antifascist politics during World War II did not necessarily translate into even coverage in the media after the war. The marginalization of Asian American deportees by the popular media paralleled the exclusion of Asian Americans from access to citizenship. Further, in the case of Korean Americans, their resistance to repatriation to South Korea threatened to indict the Cold War narrative of liberation as well as the crucial project of containment in Asia.

In contrast to the scant coverage of Asian American deportation cases, mainstream and African American newspapers covered the use of the McCarran Act against foreign-born Black civil rights activists in great detail. Newspapers on the East and West Coasts focused more on the cases against high-profile Afro-diasporic activists and less on cases against Asian and Mexican American activists, unless, as with Galvan, their cases went to high levels of the judiciary.

The African American press featured close coverage of the deportation sweeps, paying particular attention to the fate of foreign-born Afro-diasporic leaders, such as Smith of the NMU (see Chapter 3) and Jones, the former chair of the New York State Young Communists League (see Chapter 5). The Black press covered the deportations of non-Afro-diasporic "red aliens" only sporadically, although it paid attention to the 1950 "midnight raids." Historian Barbara Beeching points to the fraught position of the Black press during this period: newspapers enjoyed a high point of independence and an advertising base, while editors felt constrained by the repressive context of McCarthyism, as evidenced by the FBI investigation of the *Pittsburgh Courier*'s "Double V" campaign after the war.[47]

The persistent structure of feeling that inclined popular sentiment toward those in deportation proceedings provided for substantive interest in the cases of such leaders as Jones in the mainstream press. The *New York Times* had followed Jones's career as a Communist Party leader and her work as an editor of the party organ, the *Daily Worker*, throughout the 1930s and 1940s. Other mainstream newspapers picked up on these cases once they became part of the McCarran Act deportation sweeps.

A resident of Harlem, Jones, born Claudia Vera Cumberbatch, emigrated from Trinidad in 1924. Jones tried unsuccessfully in 1940 to naturalize. The press carried a story, disseminated by the ACPFB, that she had been prevented from filing first papers. She admitted Communist Party membership in an Alien Registration affidavit the same year.

Jones took that name when she joined the Communist Party. Where Pirinsky's use of an alias prompted insinuations of his deception, newspapers mentioned Jones's other names matter-of-factly. As with Knauff, this was partially an issue of gender: women were expected to change names. But where no mention was made of Knauff's name changes, Jones's name changes were included as part of her story. There was less media spin on her name changes than on Pirinsky's, but she did not get a free pass from the press, as Knauff did.

After Jones's arrest in 1948, her case became a cause célèbre. The same 1948 *New York Times* article that describes her as a "woman Communist leader" and "an alien in this country illegally in that she advocated and taught the overthrow of the government by force" includes an admiring description of Jones by William Z. Foster as "a leader of the Negro people." Unlike with the case of Knauff, the mainstream media constantly referenced Jones's embodied identity: few articles failed to note her race.[48]

The antiracist and pro-immigrant strand of the Popular Front was very much alive in the Black press in the 1940s and 1950s. Prominent African Americans, such as W. E. B. Du Bois and George Murphy, were involved in the ACPFB. The ACPFB central office in New York collaborated closely with the Civil Rights Congress (CRC).

The African American press recognized Jones's Communist Party activism as part of the broader civil rights struggle. When Jones spoke at a "Peace and Freedom Caravan" organized by the Manhattan CRC in 1950, the *New York Amsterdam News* linked "Red Scare" arrests and the death-row cases of Willie McGee and the "Martinsville Seven." Writing in the *Chicago Defender* in 1948, Walter White of the National Association for the Advancement of Colored People (NAACP) assailed the Justice Department's campaigns against Jones and Smith as "downright silly," even as he cautioned the foreign born to take care to naturalize. Overall, the Black press recognized that these deportation cases were part of a larger project of repressing civil rights activism.[49]

An *Atlanta Daily World* article titled "Protest the Deportation of Claudia Jones" urges readers to support the ACPFB's appeal of her deportation. The paper describes Jones as "a tireless fighter for Negro rights." An *Amsterdam News* piece picked up on Jones's sense of humor, quoting her as telling Federal Judge Edward W. Dimock that she could hardly have come to the United States with the purpose of conspiring against the government, because she was eight years old when she arrived.[50]

As with European-born "red aliens" like Pirinsky, mass-media coverage did not prevent the deportation of Afro-diasporic activists, such as Jones. But advocates had success at least in broadcasting their stories. This success was particularly striking in light of the almost complete mass-media black-out on cases of Asian and Mexican Americans facing deportation. As Operation Wetback generated attention for Mexican American deportations in the mid-1950s, the character of mass-media coverage of deportation and of immigrant rights in general underwent a profound shift.

"Red Aliens" Displaced by "Wetback Menace"

Mass-media discourse about "red aliens" responded to ACPFB immigrant rights advocacy by affirming the humanity and presumptive rights of those in deportation proceedings while at the same time holding them at arm's length. Warmer in its treatment of Euro-Americans than nonwhites, suspicious of transnational political affinities, and more enthusiastic about constitutional guarantees of due process than of any concept of human rights, this ambivalent embrace was nonetheless notable at a time of ascendant anti-Communism. As discussed above, mass-media discourses about "red aliens" were infused by residual structures of feeling connected to the Popular Front. They also drew crucially on the Cold War reinvention of the archaic but abiding American captivity narrative.

This ambivalent embrace of "red aliens" allowed for a wealth of stories in the mass media that drew on ACPFB case files about the careers and fates of individual deportees. "Red aliens," while suspected of subversion, were people. But the "wetback crisis" of 1954 marked the emergence of another discourse about deportation. The "wetback problem" was an issue of supply and circulation; "illegal aliens" supposedly acted as a mass, not as individuals. Stories about "illegal aliens" tended toward stories of invasion rather than of captivity and emancipation. Narratives of wetback invasion paralleled the terror of Soviet invasion. As a result, the notion of the "illegal alien" conjured fear rather than sympathy. Almost by definition, "illegal aliens" were not quoted in newspaper stories.

Media narratives of "red aliens" were displaced by the media triumph of mass deportations. According to Kelly Hernandez, the discursive triumph of Operation Wetback in 1954 displaced previous border narratives portraying farmers and ranchers as protecting migrant workers from the raids and depredations of the Border Patrol. Consonant with the Cold War captivity narrative, these primarily Anglo employers saw INS detention and deportation efforts as "Gestapo" tactics that used the "concentration camp" and "Korean-type wire stockade" to imprison migrants. Hernandez writes, "Accordingly, aggressive migration control was a liberation movement that did not deport workers so much as free the enslaved." Mass-media narratives tended to portray the Border Patrol as liberating migrant workers from the oppressive conditions of their employment.[51]

The public relations success of Operation Wetback displaced prior contradictory spaces of discursive agency for aliens in deportation proceedings. Portraying the Border Patrol as liberators of migrants foreclosed on the wellspring of sympathy for immigrants as captives. Further, whatever the realities of Mexican American involvement in labor and civil rights struggles, the phrase "illegal alien" placed migrants affectively outside the nation, foreclosing their claim on residual Popular Front ties. Finally, unlike the multiethnic McCarran Act deportation sweeps, the grammar of Operation Wetback was explicitly racialized, equating "illegality" with Mexican American identity.

Where the transnational ties of such activists as Pirinsky and Hyun had been the subjects of suspicion in the mass media, press coverage of Operation Wetback conjured a transnational conspiracy in which Mexican and Central American Communist operatives slipped across the U.S.-Mexico border to infiltrate the nation. Recalling earlier concerns about Mexico as a staging ground for illegal Chinese entry, the purple prose of Cold War counterinsurgency warned that lax enforcement at the U.S.-Mexico border left the nation vulnerable to agents from anywhere in the world. Under the rubric of the "wetback menace," Mexican Americans were the potential agents of American downfall.[52]

The racialized mass deportations of Operation Wetback transformed immigrant rights advocacy. Historian David Gutiérrez notes that some Mexican American civil rights organizations saw the devastating impact of the raids on communities and began to link immigrant and civil rights advocacy after 1954. Josefina Yanez, the executive secretary of the Eastside Branch of the LACPFB, described how the raids struck "terror not alone to the non-citizen, but to Mexican American citizens of the first, second and third generations." The LACPFB continued to invoke the language of the concentration camp to describe the spaces in which the foreign born were detained for deportation. But the emergence of "the wetback menace" and the widespread replacement of "red aliens" with "illegal aliens" largely foreclosed popular affective connections with those in deportation proceedings.[53]

Some advocates nevertheless persisted in linking the struggles of "wetbacks and other immigrants," as Chicago Immigrant Protective League director Ione A. Dual put it. Speaking at a conference on race relations at Fisk University in 1951, the intrepid Carey McWilliams, long an ally of the LACPFB, warned that dealing with immigration through the "wetback problem" was short-sighted. But others began to imaginatively sever prior connections between foreign-born Mexican and European Americans. In a 1951 letter to the editor of the *New York Times*, Irving Engle of the Citizens' Committee on Displaced Persons asserts the need to separate "wetbacks" from European immigrants in deportation statistics. This partition recalled Emanuel Celler's earlier attempts to distinguish between the legitimate needs of refugees and those of less deserving deportees. "Wetback" was a racialized term that functioned to exclude Mexican Americans from the "Nation of Immigrants" narrative.[54]

In mass-media coverage of Operation Wetback, it was commonplace to refer to those detained as "aliens" and "wetbacks." In 1955, a celebratory *Los Angeles Times* piece on the first anniversary of Operation Wetback cites its success in combating "history's greatest peacetime invasion of this country." Even a sympathetic piece decrying the heat and misery endured by Mexican deportees at Nogales fails to mention the names of any of them, although the reporter claims to have talked to several individually. The *Los Angeles Times*, in particular, featured occasional "wetback success" stories. But these were no longer advocacy stories; rather, they followed the stories of young "wetbacks" who managed to succeed and assimilate despite their immigration status. As historian Natalia Molina points out, INS operatives themselves were often unaware of the names of Mexican Americans they were busily detaining.[55]

Press coverage of individual deportation trials relied on courtroom journalism and immigrant rights advocacy. By contrast, the media coup of Operation Wetback was achieved by the INS's providing dazzling statistics to document its own success. In part, the difference was one of scale: Operation Wetback was a mass deportation rather than a sweep resulting in detention and protracted legal proceedings for specific individuals. But the success of Operation Wetback resulted in an enduring shift in media representations of the foreign born facing deportation. Mexican Americans, and the other "illegal aliens" who would come after them, were not represented as individuals with stories. Their deportations, then, were difficult to oppose.

The timing of this transition in the mass media is particularly significant in light of seeming progress toward racial equality in immigration policy in the early 1950s and the concurrent turn toward neoliberal economic policy, which outsourced many jobs and relied on an increasingly "flexible," domestic labor force. For the first time in U.S. history, the McCarran-Walter Act (1952) abolished all remaining racial limitations to naturalization. This was followed in 1965 by the Immigration and Nationality Acts, which replaced national origin quotas with family reunification and workforce criteria for immigration preference. Consonant with the Civil and Voting Rights Acts of 1964 and 1965, immigration policy moved on the surface toward racial equity.

But juridical moves toward equality took place in the context of an increasingly globalized economy. As the story of noncitizen maritime labor discussed in Chapter 3 highlights, neoliberal economic development after World War II relied on the flexibility of a transnational workforce with diminished access to civil and labor rights. Maintaining such a workforce required increased securitization at the borders and within migrant neighborhoods. This securitization, which Eric Tang describes as "low-intensity warfare" in urban neighborhoods, coexisted with the "Nation of Immigrants" narrative, which promised opportunity and assimilation to increasingly diverse cohorts of migrants. An anterior "Nation of Immigrants" narrative became part of a structure of feeling celebrating the civil rights triumphs of the mid-1960s as a collective, multicultural accomplishment.

The disappearance of deportation cases from the mass media maintained the cheery multiculturalism of the "Nation of Immigrants" story at a time when actual access to stable residence and employment was disappearing, most of all for migrants of color. Just at the moment when the legal bar to naturalization was lifted, popular media depictions of immigrants shifted from humanizing descriptions of individual cases to metaphors of invasion by inhuman, "alien" agents. The image of the immigrant as a potential citizen, always heavily weighted toward the white/European, came to be associated with rosier moments of past history. In contrast, contemporary, predominantly non-white Asian and Latinx migrants came to be widely perceived as threats and problems.[56]

Mass-media narratives after Operation Wetback tended to eclipse individual cases, representing deportation as necessary exercises of national security policy. Until the emergence of a broad mobilization for immigrant rights in the 1980s, the voices of individual deportees rarely appeared in mass-media accounts of deportation. But this did not mean that the voices of the foreign born were silenced. Activists have worked continually against the erasure performed by the ascendance of the term "illegal alien." Through public mobilizations and acts of individual and collective courage, they have illuminated deportation and its impact on American communities. In the wake of the January 2017 Executive Order, a group of historians have begun work on a Documenting Deportation project to ensure that names and stories are not lost or silenced.[57]

The next chapter looks at how the ACPFB became a site of the "repurposing" of migrant imaginaries and how the migrant imaginaries suppressed by repression during the Cold War later infused revitalized organizing for immigrant rights. The ACPFB's ongoing efforts to represent the foreign born created a bridge between early Cold War immigrant rights formations and the emergence of a mass movement in the later twentieth and early twenty-first centuries.

REPURPOSING IMMIGRANT RIGHTS ADVOCACY,
1959–1982

The American Committee is now involved in new struggles under new conditions, and it will have to undergo correspondingly necessary changes in structure and program. History is always changing and so it is with immigrants and immigration. The new foreign born Americans are in many major respects different from our generation. They now come primarily from Latin America and some Asian countries. They are of a different social, cultural and ethnic background. Their skin is darker than ours. Our existing discriminatory and racist immigration and naturalization statutes inflict great hardship and danger on the new foreign-born arrivals, who need to be and will be defended by the American Committee.[1]

Certain episodes in immigration enforcement recur across time, space, and migrant cohorts, requiring from immigrant rights advocates an awareness of the past and new strategies. Drawing on nautical terminology, historian George Lipsitz describes a "long fetch": the ways in which particular episodes reverberate through time and space, coming back around to reshape seemingly unrelated moments. The oceanic rhythm of the "long fetch" aptly describes the temporal rhythms and transnational affiliations of migrant communities; these rhythms mark the persistence of the subaltern past described by Dipesh Chakrabarty, whose words begin this book. While the American Committee for the Protection of the Foreign Born (ACPFB) remained small and suffered many defeats, it also persisted as a space for coalition and resistance throughout the twentieth century, laying the groundwork for the fluorescence of immigrant rights in the early twenty-first. Its connections to ever-changing migrant cohorts allowed the organization to move with changing tides of repression against the foreign born over space and time.[2]

Previous chapters have traced the dialectical development of immigrant rights coalitions and the ways that these formations were entwined with enhanced technologies of restriction and surveillance. Migrants contended with the threats posed by deportation: physical removal, destruction of community, evisceration of leadership. Because of their proximity to the violence of deportation, migrants and immigrant rights advocates identified the rise of new forms of neoliberal terror early. As explained in Chapter 3, in the twenty years following the conclusion of World War II, foreign-born maritime laborers saw their status reduced from that of heroes deserving of special access to citizenship to eternally stateless laborers, working on board ships registered off shore to deny them any rights at all. This evisceration of rights presaged the direction of neoliberal global racial capitalism, in which corporations are free to move, while laborers and migrants find their access to mobility and rights restricted. Situated at the crest of the breaking waves of neoliberal transformation, immigrant rights advocates drew on migrant imaginaries to navigate these swells throughout the twentieth century and into the twenty-first.

Moving beyond the organizational heyday of the ACPFB as a Popular Front organization fighting for the rights of the foreign born in the period around World War II, this chapter looks at the formation of immigrant rights coalitions after the 1965 Immigration and Nationality Act, also known as the Hart-Celler Act. Because it finally abolished the national origin quotas first established through Asian exclusion laws in the late nineteenth and early twentieth centuries, this law has often been celebrated as part of the civil rights heyday of equality and reform—in other words, as part of the emancipatory "Nation of Immigrants" narrative. But, as ACPFB advocates recognized, the new law left intact much of the legal basis for deportation. Further, the Hart-Celler Act became law the same year the Border Industrialization Program authorized the use of public monies to support the construction of maquiladoras at the U.S.-Mexico border. These concurrent developments indicate that new migrants entered a neoliberal job market reliant in large part on their low wages and deportability. Because the ACPFB was structured by the long fetch of migrant imaginaries, the organization continued to recognize and respond to the depredations of neoliberalism.

After 1965, the terrain of immigrant rights advocacy shifted. In the 1974 quote that opens this chapter, ACPFB organizers identify a transfor-

From the pamphlet *Nuestra Insignia de Infamia*, published by CASA, 1971. (Courtesy of the Department of Special Collections, Stanford University Libraries.)

PEDIMOS JUSTICIA
Para Los padres
que tienen
Hijos
NACIDOS
EN
LOS
Estado Unidos

OUR BADGE OF INFAMY

•

A Petition

to the United Nations

on

The Treatment

of the

Mexican Immigrant

25¢

From the pamphlet *Our Badge of Infamy*, published by ACPFB, 1959. (Courtesy of the Department of Special Collections, Stanford University Libraries.)

mation in the national origins and racialized identities of new migrants. These migrants arrived in the United States during a period of political mobilization around questions of race. As African Americans, Latinx Americans, Asian Americans, and American Indians asserted discourses of community control and empowerment, they were subjected to enhanced securitization and surveillance. Immigration enforcement constituted part of a much broader federal response to political mobilization in communities of color. The extension of deportation raids into urban neighborhoods that began with Operation Wetback became commonplace with the implementation of the Immigration and Naturalization Service's (INS's) Area Control Operations. Although deemed illegal by the U.S. Supreme Court in 1975 in a case supported by the ACPFB, arrests of individuals based on foreign-born appearance continued, recurring in Arizona's Senate Bill 1070 in 2011 and in the discourse of suspicion and protocol proclaimed by the 2017 Executive Order on "Border Security and Immigration Enforcement Improvements."[3]

Incidents of urban dragnets against the foreign born crisscross the continent as well as the twentieth and twenty-first centuries. Contending with each, advocates responded to local conditions with specific alliances and resources. At the same time, they deployed the ACPFB's collaborative channels to access an archive of discourses and strategies, repurposing those left over from prior struggles to suit conditions on the ground.

The sections that follow detail first the repurposing of a specific document and subsequently the ways in which ACPFB activists drew on the organization's collaborative channels to forge new coalitions against the deportation terror. This geographic and historical repurposing shaped immigrant rights advocacy in the 1970s, a time when global migration was being transformed by national immigration policy as well as shifting economic structures.

"Our Badge of Infamy": East Coast and West Coast ACPFB Responses to Mexican American Histories

In 1971, the Los Angeles Center for Autonomous Social Action (CASA) reissued a pamphlet titled *Our Badge of Infamy*. First published by the New York headquarters of the ACPFB in 1959 as part of a petition to the United Nations protesting the "treatment of the Mexican immigrant in the United States," this rather extraordinary document was the product of long collaboration between immigrant rights organizers on the East and West Coasts. Its repurposing by CASA indicates the persistence of this collaboration across time as well as space. These two versions of *Our Badge of Infamy* connect political movements usually considered to be historically and geographically distinct. Only the cover changes between the first and second versions: The prose and analysis remain the same.

The year the pamphlet was first issued, 1959, saw the national office of the ACPFB engaged in ongoing organizing work against national origin quotas and enhanced deportation provisions of the McCarran-Walter Act. At the same time, the New York office coordinated with the Los Angeles branch to organize for legal defenses of Mexican Americans contending with the depredations of Operation Wetback and border enforcement that increasingly crept north to Los Angeles.[4]

Sheltering under the umbrella of a national organization that was itself hard-hit by federal repression, immigrant rights advocates on both coasts worked together on fundraising, public relations, and legal defense for those in deportation proceedings. These organizers were connected from prior Popular Front organizations, such as the Civil Right Congress (CRC); they also worked together against the deportations of labor organizers and other foreign-born radicals. Longtime West Coast labor organizer Bert Corona kept in touch with the New York office of the ACPFB, maintaining an ongoing relationship with Ira Gollobin, who worked as a lawyer for the organization for almost seventy years. This bicoastal connection very likely facilitated the re-publication of *Our Badge of Infamy*. Their long collaboration and mutual influence are evident in such documents as CASA's *Statement of Charter on Immigrant Workers' Rights*, released in 1975.

By collaborating on the creation of *Our Badge of Infamy*, East and West Coast advocates simultaneously petitioned the United Nations to address the ongoing crisis of Mexican American rights. The New York and Los Angeles offices strategized together about how and where to petition for the rights of the foreign born, and they began in the mid-1950s to consider the United Nations. This strategy indicates the international analysis of the organization and the severity of domestic repression against the foreign born and progressive activists during the early Cold War era.[5]

Invoking the Universal Declaration of Human Rights adopted by the UN General Assembly in 1948, *Our Badge of Infamy* alleges that U.S. treatment of Mexican Americans historically violated four of the central tenets of this declaration: the "right to life, liberty and security of person"; the right to nationality; and the declaration's explicit ban on "slavery and servitude" as well as on arbitrary arrests, detention, and exile. The document then details the history of these human rights infractions, elaborating a history of violence and repression that dates to the Treaty of Guadalupe Hidalgo, in which Mexico ceded the territory that became California and the southwestern United States.

The narrative related by *Our Badge of Infamy* includes citizens, migrants, and contract laborers, connecting the organizing struggles of Mexican American workers to the importation of migrant contract workers implemented by the Bracero Program in 1946. Unlike the analysis prevalent in such organizations as the United Farm Workers in the early 1970s, the pamphlet connects the labor struggles of Mexican American workers with the importation of migrant contract workers implemented by the Bracero Program in 1946. Corona eventually worked with UFW leader Cesar Chavez to include undocumented workers in his organizing efforts rather than excluding them as a threat to the wages of citizens and legal residents.[6]

In this telling, deportation and denaturalization cases against Latinx labor organizers, such as Nicaraguan-born Humberto Silex of the International Union of Mine, Mill and Smelter Workers in El Paso (see Chapter 1), appear as part of the same stories as the 1958 deaths of twelve braceros unable to escape a fire in a crowded truck. The land loss and terror suffered by Mexican Americans in the Southwest and Texas after 1848 appear as a component of ongoing struggles for labor and immigrant rights. The U.S.-Mexico border arrives as a consequence of the Mexican American War, but it does not determine the human rights of the people living on either side of it. The pamphlet describes the immiseration prevalent in border communities as well as widespread police abuses of Mexican American citizens as part of the ongoing abrogation of Mexican American human rights. While condemning the treatment of migrant laborers and the raids characteristic of Operation Wetback, the document goes further, indicting epidemic police violence toward Mexican Americans.[7]

Preceding later moves by key texts in Chicanx/Latinx history, the border-spanning prose of *Our Badge of Infamy* emanates from the multiracial solidarity of the Popular Front. Articulating a history that would have been familiar to California civil rights advocates, such as the CRC and Asociación Nacional México-Americana (ANMA), it drew on what historian Michael Denning calls the "multi-ethnic internationalism" characteristic of the California Popular Front. Perceptible in the writings of lawyer-activist Carey McWilliams, this multiethnic internationalism also informed *Shame of a Nation: Police-State Terror against Mexican-Americans in the U.S.A.*, a 1954 publication of the Los Angeles Committee for the Protection of the Foreign Born (LACPFB) that indicts Operation Wetback and influenced *Our Badge of Infamy*.[8]

Historian David Gutiérrez characterizes the Mexican American advocacy prose of this era as "emotionally charged rhetoric to deride campaigns such as Operation Wetback, describing them as manifestations of 'martial law' and 'pogroms' that smacked of the odious repatriation campaigns of the Great Depression, the wartime relocation of the Nisei, and even the Holocaust."[9] As Gutiérrez indicates, this prose emanated from multiracial struggles in California. It therefore contained appeals to the historical experiences of diverse migrant communities.

Through the pipeline of the ACPFB, the multiethnic internationalism of California advocacy prose traveled between the West and East Coasts, accumulating additional meanings. The signers of *Our Badge of Infamy* were all ACPFB members, including Louise Pettibone Smith, who succeeded Abner Green as the executive secretary after his untimely death in 1959. A Wellesley professor and the granddaughter of an abolitionist minister, Smith was active in the defenses of Julius and Ethel Rosenberg as well as in the ACPFB; in 1971, she became the executive secretary of the New York committee to free Angela Davis. Other signatories came from organizations in Oregon, Utah, Michigan, and Connecticut. Their involvement with immigrant rights advocacy immersed these people in an internationalist critique of racial inequality and the broad human rights discourse surrounding the founding of the United Nations. Like the California advocacy prose, these discourses conceived of immigrant rights in broad, multiracial terms.[10]

Prior to *Our Badge of Infamy*, the East Coast branch of the ACPFB tended to contextualize deportation and the repression of the foreign born in terms of white supremacy and what its members called "anti-American" traditions of repression dating back to the American Revolution. Their advocacy against the repressive McCarran-Walter Act characterized it as white supremacy, tracing its roots to a history of anti-Black racism and anti-Asian immigration policy. Except where they specifically engaged cases against Latinx, such as Silex, the prose of the national office referenced Mexican American history infrequently. The narrative took global white supremacy seriously but tended to focus on the European, Asian, and West Indian cohorts who formed the organization on the East Coast. During the Cold War, the bulk of the work of the ACPFB consisted of defending leftist Euro-Americans against deportation. Corona remembered that the left, including the ACPFB, was much slower to defend Latinx deportees like Luisa Moreno and Humberto Silex than it was to defend "those of European descent."[11]

ACPFB rhetoric was antiracist but not necessarily cognizant of the particular threats faced by Mexican American communities. Likely penned by Green and/or Gollobin, both second-generation Jewish Americans, a 1954 memo against the McCarran-Walter Act explains:

> For the past 75 years we have taken an increasingly contemptuous and superior attitude toward two-thirds or three-quarters of the

world's population which is not white. This attitude developed despite the growing world-wide recognition and understanding of the contributions the colored peoples have made to civilization and are in a position to contribute to make. But with the passage of the Chinese Exclusion Act in 1882 we continued this anti-democratic development which culminated in the racist Walter-McCarran Law of 1952.[12]

The white supremacy described in much ACPFB prose ran parallel to the abuses of Mexican Americans detailed in *Our Badge of Infamy*. In the 1948 article "Democracy and the Deportation Laws," published in *Jewish Life*, Gollobin details the central role of nativism against the Chinese as well as antiradical provisions in legitimating "limitations of the rights of aliens." Gollobin does not talk about the U.S.-Mexico border or about police-community relations specifically, but in summarizing his account, he makes the stakes clear: "Government would thereby cease to rest on the consent of the governed but on force and violence directed against the people." Because he maintained close contact with Corona, Gollobin was, quite likely, aware of the kinds of "violence and force" being mustered against Mexican American communities at the time. But *Our Badge of Infamy* nevertheless represented a new evolution for the national office.[13]

The original presentation of *Our Badge of Infamy* at the United Nations drew on the antiracist, internationalist discourse of the Popular Front. Brought together under the ACPFB umbrella, immigrant rights advocates shared a similar analysis of the deportation terror. Together, they deployed a developing international human rights discourse to defend Mexican Americans against the depredations of Operation Wetback. Educated by advocates on the West Coast about the conditions in Mexican American communities in California and the Southwest, the national organization pressed its case to the United Nations.

The repurposing of this pamphlet in 1971 reveals the networked shape and the historical trajectory of immigrant rights advocacy. Historians have tended to think about the "Old" and "New" Lefts separately, carefully partitioning class- and party-oriented multiethnic internationalism from the racial, ethnic, and gender identity–based anticolonialism of the "New Social Movements." But the transmission of *Our Badge of Infamy* across this divide suggests the long fetch of antiracist and anti-imperial discourses. Although as a Popular Front–allied organization the ACPFB suffered repression during the height of the Cold War, it survived because diverse and ever-changing cohorts of migrants needed it to. Despite changing political contexts, the organization's critique of state power and its defense of the rights of the foreign born remained imperative and generative. And because the ACPFB was grounded in migrant communities, it was able to change with the times.

In 1965, the LACPFB changed its name to the Los Angeles Committee for the Defense of the Bill of Rights and the Protection of the Foreign Born. The new organization continued fighting against deportations. But, like the Notting Hill Carnival founded by Claudia Jones, it also prioritized the African American struggle against police brutality as well as the criminalization of Black and Latinx communities after the Watts uprising. An LACPFB newsletter from 1965 explains the change:

> The shift in emphasis in no wise [sic] should be misinterpreted as a change in policy of the LA Committee. It represents an understanding of the unbreakable connection between the need to defend the Constitutional rights of the foreign born as part of a process of protecting the constitutional rights of Negroes and other minorities. They are different sides of the same coin.[14]

The repurposing of *Our Badge of Infamy* evidences the adaptability of immigrant rights advocacy as well as the flexibility of emergent, identitarian groups. Initially, in the Chicanx movement, local experiences of race and oppression took precedence over questions of immigration status. Brown Beret and lifetime activist Carlos Montes explained that initially, immigrant rights were not part of what he called "the struggle of Chicanos for self-determination." The slogan of the Chicanx Moratorium in 1970, for example, emphasized an anti-imperialist, antiwar identity: "¡Raza Si, Guerra, No!" ("The Chicanx People, yes; War, no!"). Unlike the multiethnic internationalism that informed LACPFB's organizing against Operation Wetback, this nationalist interpretation of "self-determination" implicitly accepted the U.S.-Mexico border as defining the Chicanx struggle. It explored international alliances, suggesting that Chicanx should not invest in U.S. imperialist wars. Like the notion of community control developed by Black Power organizations, such as the Black Panthers, the idea of Chicanx communities as internal colonies drew parallels to global imperialism but still accepted national geopolitical boundaries.[15]

CASA drew on Corona's deep roots in the labor left, including his connection to the multiethnic internationalism of the LACPFB, to create a space for the articulation of an immigrant rights discourse amid the flowering of Chicanx organizations during this period. The reissue of *Our Badge of Infamy* was part of this work. Like many contemporary workers' centers, CASA combined migrant social services with community education and political organizing. It offered legal services, English classes, and classes on the history of Mexico and the United States. Politically, CASA

was involved in multiple campaigns. In a history of the organization, Corona lists as priorities the freedom of political prisoners; the founding of
the National Alliance against Racism and Political Repression; solidarity
work with Chile and Puerto Rico; and labor struggles, particularly those
of teamsters, cannery workers, shipyard workers, longshoremen, construction workers, butchers, and steel workers. This internationalism allowed
for the emergence of parallels between the urban experiences of Latinx
and the violence of immigration enforcement.[16]

With the advocacy of CASA and other organizations, immigrant rights
became a part of the West Coast Chicanx movement. In 1970, Los Angeles police killed two undocumented movement activists, Guillardo Alcazar
and Guillermo Beltran Sánchez. Ruben Salazar covered the story in the
movement newspaper *La Raza*.[17] The case drew attention to the question
of immigrant rights and posed the particular situation of undocumented
migrants as part of a broader constellation of repression. In 1975, CASA
explained the political situation:

> In this manner the immigrant workers with or without papers be-
> come the target of the massive propaganda and newsmedia. He is
> also the target of the police and other repressive law enforcement
> bodies, the racist court system, schools, hospitals and other institu-
> tions, creating the violation of the democratic rights of the immi-
> grant—first the undocumented, then the "legal" resident. Not only
> is the Latino the one to suffer the repression, but also the citizen,
> when his home has been violated and searched, his car has to pass
> the check points and[,] in the case of the "legal" resident, he is
> forced to prove his right to legally reside in the United States. There
> are and have been numerous occasions of Latinos being deported
> because they forgot their documents at home.[18]

By 1975, immigrant rights had become part of Chicanx movement
discourses. Fighting INS intimidation and harassment paralleled other
struggles for self-determination. In 1979, when Alberto Canedo, a four-
year-old child, died at the San Ysidro Port of Entry, Congressman Edward
Roybal called for hearings. A CASA flyer compares the cause of justice at
the border to that of stopping the war in Vietnam: "The Migra's Vietnam-
like actions have caused the death, beatings, sexual abuse and other countless acts of violations of La Raza's human, civil and constitutional rights."[19]

Another flyer uses an image created by Chicanx movement artist David
Avalos. Displaying a fight between an angel and an INS agent, the flyer
connects the harassment of Chicanx to the deportation of migrants.

St. Michael v. La Migra, by David Avalos, 1974. (Reprinted with permission of the artist.)

CASA brought immigrant rights advocacy into the Chicanx movement. Other emergent movements for racial justice, along with changing migrant cohorts after the 1965 Immigration and Nationality Act, transformed the ACPFB. The next section takes up the ways that immigrant rights advocates engaged issues of racism and police brutality after 1968, confronting the depredations of counterinsurgency and emergent neoliberalism in America's urban centers.

"New" and "Old" Migrant Cohorts and the ACPFB

In December 1968, the New York office of the ACPFB issued a pamphlet titled *What Is the American Committee for the Protection of the Foreign Born?* The pamphlet was likely intended for distribution at protests taking place around the city—in Harlem over the expansion by Columbia University, and in Brooklyn over the issue of community control in the predominantly African American Ocean Hill–Brownsville school district. Brownsville and Harlem included significant populations of recent migrants who were affected by the issues at hand. The pamphlet links the presence of detention camps set up by the McCarran-Walter Act, Richard Nixon's "Law and Order" campaign, and the antidissent provisions of the Eastland Bill then on the floor of the Senate. It explains that "the prime targets of these measures would be fighters for peace and freedom—militant Blacks, Indians, Mexican-Americans, Puerto Ricans, students, trade unionists and the foreign born."[20]

By naming the groups subject to repressive policies, this pamphlet connects very different assaults against civil rights. It also links the traditional constituencies of the "Old Left"—trade unionists and the foreign born—with the emerging politics of Black, Red, and Brown Power. At a time when the Ocean Hill–Brownsville conflict between predominantly Black and Puerto Rican students and parents and a predominantly white, Jewish teachers' union was widely read as fracturing previous alliance between Jews and African Americans, Jewish American immigration advocates, including Gollobin and Henry Foner, recognized the significance of building coalitions with newly arrived migrant communities of color.[21]

In 1968, the ACPFB was very much in transition. In 1965, the same year the Immigration and Nationality Act ended national origin quotas, the ACPFB was removed from Subversive Activities Control Board oversight. Much scholarly literature asserts that second- and third-generation immigrants from Europe, once "not yet white ethnics," were by this time well on their way to segregated suburban whiteness, leaving behind them urban neighborhoods and national origins–based advocacy work. As much because of changes in their homelands as because of changing U.S.

What Is the American Committee for the Protection of the Foreign Born? (1968). (American Committee for the Protection of the Foreign Born Papers, #086, Tamiment Library/Robert F. Wagner Labor Archives, New York University. Used by permission of Ruth Gollobin-Basta.)

immigrant policy, increased numbers of migrants from the Caribbean and Latin America came to the United States in this period. Haitians fled the ravages of successive Duvalier regimes; Salvadorans, Guatemalans, Nicaraguans, and Chileans left the political volatility of their nations of origin. Many other migrants from the Caribbean and the Americas sought work in a low-wage service-sector economy that nevertheless offered more remunerative work than what was available to them at home.[22]

Through the ACPFB, these newer arrivals met activists from older cohorts who continued to organize against repression and for more just immigration policy. Through labor unions and emergent community organizations in New York, Central American and Caribbean migrants encountered more settled European migrants who nonetheless continued to organize for immigrant rights. Many European Americans became eligible for historically restricted housing and work opportunities after World War II. But this comparatively new access to whiteness did not protect those targeted for deportation and/or denaturalization, because the reforms of 1965 left undisturbed many of the most anti-immigrant and antiradical

"Haitian refugees are the pilgrims of today." ACPFB literature consistently posited migrants as the true Americans. (American Committee for the Protection of the Foreign Born Papers, #086, Tamiment Library/ Robert F. Wagner Labor Archives, New York University. Used by permission of Ruth Gollobin-Basta.)

provisions of McCarran-era legislation. Although the 1965 act's emphasis on family reunification stood to benefit the foreign born who sought to bring their relatives to the United States, many immigrant rights advocates continued to see the 1965 act as anti-immigrant. Gollobin writes in a 1967 ACPFB pamphlet titled *The Foreign Born and the Bill of Rights*:

> It soon became clear that the new law is the most restrictive in U.S. history. Instead of merely discriminating against certain people, the United States now bans immigrants from all nations unless they have close family ties or prove that their labor is needed.[23]

Like Gollobin, many in the ACPFB questioned the direction of the 1965 reforms. Because of their long experience with federal repression, they were keenly aware of the survival of Cold War policies. The new law left Smith Act provisions for "alien" registration on the books, it kept legal provisions against the entry of suspected "subversives," and it maintained deportation as a technology of immigration enforcement. Immigrant rights activists had long campaigned for a statute of limitations on deportation and denaturalization to avoid the widespread practice of deporting older immigrants on the basis of suspected political alliances decades in the past, but Congress declined to implement these much-needed reforms. Prior to 1965, despite being constrained in its lobbying because of its status as a suspected subversive organization, the ACPFB worked for immigration reform that would have abolished the "distinctions between native and naturalized citizens to insure full protection of our laws to all." The 1965 Act did not realize this radical vision.[24]

As a result, the ACPFB continued to represent European immigrants in their struggles with denaturalization and deportation. The New York and Los Angeles Committee for the Protection of the Foreign Born offices worked on the deportation case of Greek American Gus Polites in the early 1960s. Polites, described in ACPFB publicity as a "trade unionist and leader in the Greek community," was honored by Franklin Roosevelt for his "anti-fascist leadership" during World War II. He became a citizen in 1942 but was denaturalized in 1953 on grounds of prior membership in the Communist Party; this denaturalization rendered him deportable. The ACPFB lost the case, and Polites was deported in 1963. He left a native-born wife, children, and grandchildren. Polites's death in 1968 occasioned note by the ACPFB that congressional failure to enact a statute of limitations on deportation resulted in the "heartless destruction of an American family."[25]

Similarly, the ACPFB fought the deportation case against Polish American labor organizer Joseph Sherman, who had reentered the country illegally after fighting in the Abraham Lincoln Brigade in Spain. The INS pursued the deportation of Sherman during the 1960s, when he was in his sixties and in ill health.[26]

Because they continued to be affected by "the deportation terror," many European American migrants continued to support the ACPFB's fight against INS repression. Despite their increasing access to the benefits of whiteness, these migrants recognized the threat to members of their communities posed by provisions for continued repression against foreign-born activists, artists, and journalists. Many of these people were union members and progressive activists. Even without deportation, denaturalization alone could mean the loss of the benefits of citizenship, including Social Security for retired or disabled individuals. The committee worked to oppose denaturalization in such cases as those against Elsie Leger and Beryl Davis, who had to stop working because of illness and lost their Social Security benefits in Pennsylvania. In New York, ACPFB events continued to bring sponsorship from Finnish, Italian, Estonian, Irish, Lithuanian, Polish, Russian, Hungarian, and Ukrainian organizations well into the 1970s.[27]

Even if they were, by some measures, "becoming white," many foreign-born denizens, particularly those who had been progressive activists,
still experienced what the ACPFB called "second-class citizenship," because they lived with fears of deportation and loss. Advocates saluted the
family reunification provisions of the 1965 Act while noting the irony that
the law still allowed for the destruction of immigrant families already living in the country. In the words of a 1967 pamphlet:

> A foreign-born person is never secure in his residence and citizen-
> ship. Even after a lifetime here, he can be denaturalized and de-
> ported. There is no time limit. In recent years, even grandfathers
> and grandmothers have been torn from their families, sent to coun-
> tries completely strange to them, whose language they do not
> speak, and deprived of means of support since even their social
> security is cut off by law.[28]

Individuals subject to denaturalization and deportation, then, tended
not to experience the benefits of "whiteness" as much as the ongoing depredations of being foreign born. Consistent with its history as a Popular Front
organization, the ACPFB maintained strong allies in the labor movement.
Many of the progressive, foreign-born activists targeted for deportation
were involved in union organizing or labor politics. While many unions
moved away from progressive alliances because of the impact of anti-Communist measures, such as the Taft-Hartley Act, other trade unionists recognized the ongoing importance of the immigrant rights struggle for labor
organizing and workers' rights in general. The unions most likely to be engaged with immigrant rights in this period employed migrants from Latin
America and the Caribbean: the Hotel Trades Council, Amalgamated Meat
Cutters, the Ship Clerks' Association, the United Furniture Workers' Union,
Drug and Hospital Employees, and the Hotel Restaurant and Club Employees Union. Henry Foner represented the Joint Board of the Fur, Leather and
Machine Workers Union in the ACPFB. He criticized the anti-immigrant
politics of many unions, including the common practice in the period of
calling on the INS to raid shops using undocumented labor. As a second-
generation immigrant himself, Foner recognized the centrality of immigrants, and therefore of immigrant rights, to labor struggles. He explained
in 1972: "There is a new kind of foreign-born: the old type had declined.
The new is younger with different ideas."[29]

As immigrant rights advocates surveyed the political terrain of the late
1960s and early 1970s, they observed similar kinds of repression being
directed against activists, people of color, and the foreign born. A discourse of community control emanating from the struggles of Black,

Latinx, and Native communities with urban policing, education, and housing described this kind of repression in terms of police brutality. This discourse framed repression differently than had Cold War progressive rhetorics of fascism and democracy, but it described similar issues: detention and deportation without due process for the foreign born; the threat to citizens of detention in camps authorized by the McCarran Act of 1950; and constant raids by police, the Federal Bureau of Investigation (FBI), and the INS. A 1968 ACPFB *Statement on the Struggle against a Police State* proclaims:

> Brutal repression has become reaction's reply to the powerful, broadening mass movements for human rights and human dignity that are sweeping across our country. To Black people, to Indians, to Mexican-Americans, to Puerto Ricans, to dissenting young people, to militant workers and to the foreign born—to all who seek their rightful place in the sun of freedom—the answer is being given: KEEP OUT![30]

For the ACPFB, repression against the foreign born had a long history. The internationalism of the organization's 1969 holiday card invokes the long history of anti-imperialism in immigrant rights organizing while it manages to strike a contemporary note: "Immigration authorities have intensified their illegal harassment of Latin Americans (especially Dominicans), Greeks, Iranians, and other national groups who are seeking the support of the American people in the fight against the dictatorships ruling their countries." This combination of anti-imperialism and immigrant rights advocacy would have been familiar to older cohorts of the foreign born; it also reached out to the new constituencies converging in New York City at the time.[31]

The ACPFB drew on its antiracist internationalism to critique changing immigration policies. At the same time, the organization brought to emergent social movements an understanding that many denizens of aggrieved, urban communities were also foreign born. In this analysis, struggles for urban empowerment included ongoing work for immigrant rights. In the post-1965 period, coalitions for immigrant rights increasingly came to include leadership from newly arrived Haitian and Latin American cohorts.

Area Control Operations

In 1972, President Nixon's appointed INS commissioner, Leonard Chapman, initiated "Area Control Operations." Like Joseph May Swing, who orchestrated Operation Wetback, Chapman was retired military; he had

served in the Marine Corps in the Pacific arena during World War II and
was promoted to the rank of general by Lyndon Johnson during the Vietnam War. Perhaps because both men had prior military experience, they
tended to see issues of immigration in terms of counterinsurgency strategies. As African American studies scholar Eric Tang points out, by the late
1960s, military counterinsurgency strategies originating in the proxy wars
of the Cold War era gained traction as a means of establishing "law and
order" in urban policy circles.[32]

Like Swing's Operation Wetback, Area Control Operations took the
form of urban dragnets against what Gollobin described as "Latin-looking
persons." The INS targeted immigrant neighborhoods and workplaces,
often raiding them. As a 1972 joint letter from the ACPFB and the Coalition of Latin Americans/Friends of Latin America of Jackson Heights describes it: "Immigration authorities have been conducting a series of
dragnet raids—on a subway station, at a dance hall, on the street, anywhere. Thousands have already been victimized, if they were dark skinned
and looked Latino."[33]

Typical of those caught in the Area Control Operations dragnets were
three Ecuadorian migrants arrested in a Queens dragnet in November
1975. At 7:30 A.M., a Mr. and Mrs. Miguel Marquez and Mrs. Marquez's
sister were on their way to work when they were stopped by the INS. The
two women showed green cards, but they were still arrested and detained.
INS district director Maurice Killy described the reasons for their arrest:
"their dress, what clothes appear to be foreign manufacture . . . work
clothes, carrying their lunch; general facial structure; speaking in a foreign
language; and the location. . . . There were large concentrations of illegal
aliens." Responding to these charges, Marquez explained that he had purchased his shoes at a local Florsheim's. The ACPFB sued the INS for civil
rights damages under a 1975 Supreme Court decision that made illegal
random arrests based on appearances.[34]

The INS continued to target Latinx and other racialized immigrants
throughout the 1970s. Responding to this harassment transformed the
coalition advocating for immigrant rights. For example, in 1973, the
ACPFB participated in a New York City protest rally against the "immigration dragnet." The rally drew together a broad array of comparatively
new Latin American and Caribbean national associations, such as the
Circulo Social Salvadoreño and the Haitian American Citizens Society,
along with some unions whose membership combined newer immigrants
and European American workers. Many of the protesters demonstrated in
three-cornered hats to emphasize that immigrant rights were fundamental
and much like those demanded by patriots at the time of the American
Revolution.

Ira Gollobin, at the Polonia Club in 1965, with Louise Pettibone Smith at the far right. (American Committee for the Protection of the Foreign Born Papers, #086, Tamiment Library/Robert F. Wagner Labor Archives, New York University. Used by permission of Ruth Gollobin-Basta.)

Immigrant rights advocates collaborated nationally to respond to dragnets at the local level. They deployed geographic organizing as well as historical memory to respond to repression against the foreign born. For example, as they considered the cases of Vietnamese students threatened with deportation because of their antiwar activism, ACPFB council members in New York recalled the ACPFB's defense of Korean Americans during the Cold War.[35]

On their separate coasts, but linked through their correspondence and political connections, Gollobin, Rose Chernin, and Corona collaborated to create charters asserting basic human rights for immigrants that responded to the depredations of dragnets and police brutality. In a 1974 pamphlet titled *The Foreign Born and the Bill of Rights*, Gollobin draws on California labor history to oppose an employer sanctions bill being considered in New York State:

> The experience of California demonstrated that such legislation results in a climate of fear, causing many employers to refuse to hire even [legal] residents; such laws lead to racial discrimination against Latin American workers and depress the wage standards of *all* workers; such laws permit unscrupulous employers to require

foreign born employees to sign a statement that they are authorized to work, thereby keeping persons not authorized to work in a state of virtual peonage; such laws lead to unconstitutional raids by Immigration authorities. [Emphasis in original.][36]

In the late 1960s and early 1970s, the ACPFB drew on collaborative channels linking the now New York–based organization to struggles taking places in other locations and times. This ability to connect and repurpose allowed the organization to become useful to new cohorts of foreign born. These renewed struggles, in turn, transformed the organization, and immigrant rights advocacy in general.

Haitian Refugees or Undocumented Migrants?

Successive crises around the question of asylum for refugees from Haiti after the 1971 death of François "Papa Doc" Duvalier and the transition to the even more autocratic rule of his son, Jean-Claude "Baby Doc" Duvalier, transformed immigration enforcement as well as activist discourses. Advocacy for Haitians was central to the cause of immigrant rights during the 1970s. While the ACPFB and its allies saw those fleeing the repressive Duvalier regime as refugees deserving of asylum and shelter, federal policy perceived them as unauthorized economic migrants, to be detained and deported.

In the wake of World War II, international and U.S. policy recognized refugees as particular kinds of migrants whose plights made them eligible for asylum and aid. But the long-standing U.S. alliance with the Duvaliers made the State Department unwilling to indict conditions in Haiti as instilling in migrants the "well-founded fear" stipulated in international refugee policy. As Haitians fled the Duvalier regime in the 1970s, many immigrant and civil rights advocates saw this division based more on white supremacy and corrupt political alliances than on the circumstances of migration. For the ACPFB, the political corruption governing the denial of refugee status to Haitians paralleled previous machinations around migrants from right-wing regimes allied with the United States, including in South Korea, Greece, and Portugal.

Haitians fled their country, taking to sea in large numbers. Many reached other Caribbean nations, such as Cuba, where they were welcomed, or the Bahamas, where they had few legal rights; others either made it to Florida or were rescued by the Coast Guard and detained. These Haitian refugees arrived in a nation riven once again by a panic around "illegal aliens" generated by the potent combination of economic downturn and the high-profile dragnet raids on immigrant communities generated by Area Control Opera-

Demonstration protesting dragnet raids, Herald Square, New York, EL TIEMPO, Jan. 18, 1973

Protesting the dragnet raids (1973). (American Committee for the Protection of the Foreign Born Papers, #086, Tamiment Library/Robert F. Wagner Labor Archives, New York University. Used by permission of Ruth Gollobin-Basta.)

tions. Without a broad national consensus on their refugee status, Haitians were received as undocumented, unwelcomed migrants.

In Miami, many refugees were housed at the Krome Avenue Detention Center. Gollobin served as legal counsel for the National Council of Churches' district court case to allow Haitian detainees access to due process. Immigrant rights advocates blocked what they called a "sneak deportation" of Haitian refugees in Miami in 1975. In the same year, forty-seven Haitians were relocated from Miami to a detention facility in El Paso after their applications for political asylum were denied. There, they awaited deportation to Haiti.[37]

The statement of detainee Joseph Simann typified many of the stories of the El Paso Haitians. The Tonton Macoute, the Duvalierist secret police, asked him, his brother, and his father to guard returned refugees at the police station in their small town. Sympathizing with the situation of the returnees, they refused and were subsequently detained and beaten. Simann's father died; Joseph escaped and fled to the Bahamas, where eventually his identity was revealed to the Haitian Embassy in Nassau. He then fled to the United States.[38]

The ACPFB, practiced in identifying the white supremacy of immigration policy, worked in coalition with Haitian and other immigrant community groups on legal advocacy and political action. As leftists, they recognized the gap separating the federal welcome for Cuban "refugees" and the deportation of Haitians. Further, the organization had long criticized the racism of immigration enforcement. Promoting the treatment of Haitian refugees as "the most acute foreign born issue confronting the

American people," they portrayed Haitian refugees as "the Pilgrims of Today!" They decried the violation of international protocol in the "preventive detention" of Haitians while their cases were being considered. Haitian refugees were interviewed in secret and had no opportunity to present witnesses or provide documentation on their cases. When released from detention, they were not given temporary work permits to enable them to earn a living. As raids on New York Haitian communities continued, an Ad Hoc Committee for the Defense of Haitian Refugees press release asserted that "organizers believe these raids represent an attempt to silence the growing protests" against the immigration dragnets. While it commented on the particular situation of Haitians, the press release reflected the familiarity of ACPFB advocates like Gollobin with repression against immigrant rights advocacy.[39]

Immigrant rights advocates across the United States publicly mourned the suicide of Turenne Déville in immigration custody in 1974. After a fight with the Tonton Macoutes, Déville was jailed. Fearing death, he escaped to Nassau, in the Bahamas. Finding no asylum in Nassau, he found a boat to Miami, where he was taken into INS custody and jailed. Like many Haitians who arrived in Florida, Déville knew he had little hope of survival if he were returned to the hands of the Macoutes. The night before he was scheduled to be deported to Haiti, Déville hanged himself in his cell.

In his suicide note, Déville explains:

In Haiti there is no justice. The poor must die prematurely, often asphyxiated in jail. In Haiti's jail there is no food, no water. . . . I can't go back. If the regime falls today, I'm ready to go back; otherwise I'll not go back there. If the United States refuses to help me, send me to Africa.[40]

Déville's funeral was held at the Friendship Baptist Church in Miami. Those who attended received a flyer with his testimony about his experiences in Haiti and Nassau and his request to be sent to Africa rather than be deported to Haiti. Added at the bottom was a statement, addressed to "Pallbearers, Fellow Haitian Brothers":

We the Black people of the Model City area and all concerned human beings of Dade County, do hereby declare that our Black Haitian Brother Turenne Déville, is now and forever as long as there are concerned citizens in Dade County, he is a citizen of Dade County and our community.[41]

A 16-day voyage in a homemade sailboat ended August 29 for 150 Haitian refugees from Port-au-Prince when they landed in Miami, Florida.

"No double standard for refugees!" The ACPFB advocated for the treatment of Haitians as refugees and opposed their exclusion as economic migrants. (American Committee for the Protection of the Foreign Born Papers, #086, Tamiment Library/Robert F. Wagner Labor Archives, New York University. Used by permission of Ruth Gollobin-Basta.)

Déville eluded deportation only by killing himself. At his funeral, mourners asserted a radical vision of immigrant rights, in which foreign-born denizens could claim full citizenship as part of their human rights. This vision asserted a diasporic, deterritorialized definition of citizenship. As Nadia Ellis explains, visions like those articulated by Déville's pallbearers are "powerful in the *potential* to which they give rise, a potential that suspends rather than resolves at the arrival at some new and satisfying space of exile" [emphasis in original].[42] This potential infused immigrant rights activism in the decades that followed.

The "Long Fetch" of Immigrant Rights Struggles

Throughout the final thirteen years of the ACPFB's existence, the concerns of new migrant cohorts continued to shape the organization's work and its alliances on the ground. Shaped and guided by its collaboration with community groups, this Popular Front organization adapted to changing political contexts, surviving well into the Reagan years. In a neoliberal era when national boundaries were continuously being reshaped by the migration of capital as well as by coercive international trade agreements, immigrant rights advocates recognized the significance and vulnerability of migrants.

When the ACPFB closed its doors in 1982, many immigrant rights organizations existed. Many of them originated in the community-based movements that had worked collaboratively with the ACPFB on the national level. These organizations continued the struggle, pressing for an amnesty partially realized in federal legislation in 1986 and inspiring new organizing in labor and civil rights communities into the early twenty-first century.[43]

The Subaltern Futures
of Immigrant Rights

The "emergency situation" in which we live is the rule. We must arrive at a concept of history which corresponds to this.[1]

In 1955, the Department of Justice initiated denaturalization proceedings against Russian-born Rose Chernin, one of the founders of the Los Angeles Committee for the Protection of the Foreign Born (LACPFB). The federal government's case against Chernin alleged that she had taken the oath of citizenship fraudulently in 1928, because she subsequently became a member of the Communist Party in 1932. Although she had fled the Soviet Union with her Jewish family, entering the United States when she was twelve, Chernin was accused of entering the country with plans to become a Communist agent.

The government's case against Chernin turned on the idea that her "willful misrepresentation" of her purpose in entering the United States undermined her oath of loyalty, because, as a Communist, she was clearly more loyal to the Soviet Union. As they did for many of the foreign-born activists in this book, the charges against Chernin took place at a key political moment: in the wake of Operation Wetback and after the passage of the McCarran Act of 1950 enhanced the powers of the federal government to detain and deport foreign-born radicals. This was a time of crisis for the foreign born and their allies around the country. The persecution of Chernin was also an attack against the immigrant rights advocacy of the LACPFB. It forced her to temporarily sideline her organizing work as she fought the charges against her.[2]

Sixty-four years later, in 2014, Immigration and Customs Enforcement (ICE), newly operating under the Department of Homeland Security (DHS), pursued a similar project of denaturalization in the case of Palestinian American immigrant rights activist Rasmea Odeh. ICE alleged that Odeh lied about her political history in her application for citizenship. As with Chernin, the federal case against Odeh came at a time of enhanced repression against the foreign born, this time particularly directed against those from Arab and/or Muslim countries. As part of the Oslo Peace process in 1994 and 1995, the State Department created a list of "Foreign Terrorist Organizations." Just as the 1950 McCarran Act set up the Subversive Activities Control Board to monitor "un-American" organizations, the 2001 USA PATRIOT Act criminalized activism that associated in any way with these organizations.

The denaturalization cases against both women were part of broader assaults on progressive and foreign-born activists. The Immigration and Nationalization Service (INS) pursued its case against Chernin after Operation Wetback resulted in the deportation of thousands of Los Angeles Mexican Americans. Similarly, ICE brought charges against Odeh during a period of massive raids and deportations of the foreign born, and after the failure of a prolonged Federal Bureau of Investigation (FBI) case against progressive activists in Chicago, Minneapolis, and Grand Rapids, Michigan, including Hatem Abudayyeh, the executive director of the Arab American Action Network (AAAN), where Odeh was the assistant director.[3]

As young women, Odeh and Chernin joined popular political organizations. Chernin's family settled in Waterbury, Connecticut, where she took a job in a factory at the age of fourteen. During World War I, the school day in Waterbury was shortened to allow children to arrive at the factory for an afternoon shift. Consequently, Chernin was able to return to school, where she encountered a circle of students who read socialist newspapers. Eventually, she joined the Communist Party and became a labor organizer. Like many other foreign- and native-born workers in the period, Chernin saw the Communist Party as a path to equality and social justice. Subsequently, the wide appeal of the Popular Front era of the Communist Party to the foreign born during the 1930s and 1940s became suspect as a force of foreign infiltration.[4]

Born in 1948, the year of the founding of Israel and the resulting *nakba*—Arabic for the disaster of Palestinian displacement—Odeh became a refugee along with her family. They were forced to move from their village of Lifta to Ramallah, in the West Bank. Like Chernin, Odeh was drawn to the cultures of resistance around her. She joined the moderate Arab

Nationalist Movement. In 1969, she and her sister, Aisha, were among hundreds of Palestinians detained by the Israeli Defense Force on suspicion of being part of the Popular Front for the Liberation of Palestine (PFLP), which was considered a terrorist organization by Israel and the United States. In the militarized context of Israel/Palestine in this period, association with any resistance organization aroused suspicion, much as it had in the Cold War United States.[5] Under torture in an Israeli prison, she confessed to her part in two bombing attacks and was sentenced to life in prison. Odeh was released in a prisoner exchange in 1980. She lived in Lebanon and Jordan, advocating for Palestinian refugee rights and earning a law degree. In 1994, she moved to Detroit to care for her aging father. She became a U.S. citizen in 2004. Eventually, she moved to Chicago, where she became involved with the AAAN, a grassroots organization dedicated to social justice, including immigrant rights. While the official case against Odeh asserted that she concealed her "terrorist" past in her naturalization hearing, it is clear that her denaturalization and deportation were reprisals for her transnational Palestine solidarity and immigrant rights work.[6]

The cases against Odeh and Chernin turned on questions of temporality, space, and intent. Just as the twenty-year federal pursuit of Harry Bridges relied partially on impugning his loyalty through shifting legal definitions of fitness for citizenship, Odeh and Chernin faced the loss of their citizenship, allegedly because of questions about their intentions at the time of their entry into the United States. Because both women continued to work for transnational justice after they became citizens, they were accused of deceiving the federal government about their ability to be loyal to the country. The cases against Chernin and Odeh held that they became citizens but continued to pursue horizons out of time with the vision manifested by official policy and by the "Nation of Immigrants" narrative. Like many of the migrants whose stories are told in this book, their aspirations were not limited to citizenship.

The subaltern past that includes immigrant rights advocates like Chernin has been deliberately occluded by a national narrative that emphasizes progress and assimilation. As a result, contemporary cases like that of Odeh appear isolated, the charges against her more credible when they are not read in the context of the long, dialectical struggle between the foreign born and immigration enforcement. From the vantage point of the early twenty-first century, it is easier to dismiss the McCarthyist allegations against former Communists like Chernin than it is to ignore Odeh's association with suspected Arab and Palestinian terrorist organizations. But making these cases related and contiguous reveals the ways in which the military counterinsurgency policies of the early twentieth century were later deployed against the foreign born and how anti-Communist strategies honed during the Cold War continue to find utility in the repression of the foreign born conducted in the name of the War on Terror.

The comparison between the denaturalization cases of a Russian-born, Ashkenazi Jewish Communist and a Palestinian American activist defies the logic of homeland securitization, in which acts of solidarity with Palestine become equated with terrorism and anti-Semitism. But historical evidence suggests that Odeh and Chernin—Palestinian and Jew—would have had a lot to talk about. Their stories, although separated in time, are evidence of ongoing repression and continued advocacy for immigrant rights. Because immigrant rights advocacy takes place in different communities over time, it has sometimes been hard to see this continuity of effort as a transnational, multiracial, concerted movement for immigrant rights. Occluding this subaltern past isolates contemporary foreign-born activists like Odeh and like Mexican Americans Elvira Arellano and Jeanette Vizguerra from this rich history. It seems as though they inhabit a different struggle than prior organizers like Chernin, Bert Corona, or Ira Gollobin. The much-vaunted possibility of terrorism substitutes for alternate, collectively held horizons of justice.

The occlusion of the subaltern past means losing track of the future. Theologian Rafiq Khoury writes: "As a prophecy, memory is a stimulant. It helps us, on the basis of our vivid memory, to go forward and invent a new future and a new untold narrative." Khoury's notion that memory enables envisioning a future that corresponds with the Walter Benjamin quote that opens this Conclusion and with Dipesh Chakrabarty's critique of historicism as a collection of facts that justify present arrangements of power. Reclaiming the subaltern past conjures alternative futures and conjures a history capable of responding to the ongoing emergency of our time.[7]

Along with many of the foreign born it represented, the American Committee for the Protection of the Foreign Born (ACPFB) worked throughout the twentieth century to advocate for the foreign born, arguing that migrant dreams inspire democratic horizons rather than undermine them. Chernin and Odeh are two of myriad examples in this book, migrants whose radical, internationalist democratic visions motivated their activism. The same rich foment continues into the twenty-first century, in which the foreign born continue to cross borders, invigorating what is possible within them.

The ACPFB did not always meet success in its organizing campaigns. Many of the people it defended wound up being deported. As the deportation rate has increased in the early twenty-first century, justice for the foreign born is increasingly elusive. Despite an international campaign on

her behalf, Odeh accepted a plea agreement in March 2017 for her deportation. But the early twenty-first century has also seen a fluorescence of
immigrant rights mobilizations that such tireless advocates as Chernin,
Gollobin, and Corona could only imagine. When young activists come out
as "undocumented and unafraid," they carry the work of the ACPFB forward. By telling the often-hidden story of immigrant rights struggles in the
twentieth century, this book intends to provide one more resource for
those who carry the work into the twenty-first.

ACKNOWLEDGMENTS

I am honored to have this book appear in the aptly named *Insubordinate Spaces* series at Temple University Press, edited by George Lipsitz. I am grateful to George for including my book in his series and for his assistance in guiding it through the revision process. The book has also benefited immensely from the labors of three anonymous reviewers; I appreciate their time and insight. At Temple, Aaron Javsicas has been encouraging and knowledgeable; Marinanicole Dohrman Miller, Joan Vidal, and Gary Kramer have kindly ushered me into the publication process. The book was improved immeasurably by the deft copyediting of Heather Wilcox. It is a dream come true for me to have my colleague Raoul Deal's beautiful artwork gracing the cover.

This project has benefited from support from the now defunct and much lamented University of Wisconsin Institute for Race and Ethnicity, as well as the Princeton University Library and the Institute for Research in the Humanities at the University of Wisconsin–Madison. Internally, I have received research funds from the Morris Fromkin Research Award, University of Wisconsin–Milwaukee (UWM) Research and Creative Activities Support (RACAS), Research Grant Initiative, Arts and Humanities Travel Grant programs, the Center for 21st Century Studies, and the Center for International Studies. I cannot overstate the importance of the travel funds, release time, and collegiality provided by these internal institutes; without them, I would simply not have been able to get this project off the ground. Long may they endure.

Friends and family have provided another vital kind of research support. Mark Finnegan and Denise Heberle lovingly hosted me and both daughters on more than one research trip to Ann Arbor; their daughters, Paula, Clio, and Marguerite Finnegan, provided child care while I was in the archives and wry commentary when I returned. Kelly Mayhew and Jim Miller left me keys to their home in San Diego; Eva and Ernie Newbrun sent me a key to their house in San Francisco. Rich Kees, Ellen Engseth, and Robert and Pam Goldman have put me up and put up with me in Minneapolis; Robert even attended a talk I gave at the University of Minnesota. My long friendships with Robert Danberg, Yvonne Keller, and Lisa Levine continue to gratify and surprise me. Melissa Robbins is always up for bringing her astute point of view to bear on academia; Michelle Adams explains the legal side. I have been relying on Jason Loviglio for his exceptional good sense and even better jokes for years.

I have stayed with my mother, Barbara Buff, on countless visits to New York, which have often included my dashing out to an archive and leaving her with one or both of my daughters. She invariably responds with grace and is always curious about what I discover in my research. Her keen imagination of the past very much influences the historian I am. My father, Jerry Buff, once drove to three separate boroughs in one evening to see me give a talk, pick up my daughters—who were being cared for by my generous sister, Sarah Buff—and bring us back to my mother's apartment. It was after midnight by the time that trip was done, but he still wanted to discuss my talk that evening. I thank the New York Buff/Kracov clan for all of this and more. I also thank the Arkansas/Texas/Memphis Austins and Bowers, and Tommi Cherry in particular, for being such a great "outlaw" family.

Like many scholars, I am in awe of and dependent on the professional pyrotechnics of archivists. Professionals at the following institutions provided invaluable assistance: Julie Herrada at the Labadie Collection, University of Michigan; Michele Welsing at the Southern California Research Library; Maria Mejia and Sarah Moaveni at the Tamiment Library, New York University; Ellen Engseth and Daniel Necas at the Immigration History Research Center Archives; Max Yela at the Fromkin Special Collections, UWM; Tim Noakes at Special Collections, Stanford University; the Kheel Center, Cornell University; the Sophia Smith Collections, Smith College; and the American Civil Liberties Papers at the Mudd Library, Princeton University. Daniel Karvonen provided expert translation of Finnish-language documents.

Getting to know the copyright holders for some of the images in this book has been an unexpectedly delightful process. I am grateful to David Avalos for the use of his beautiful image *St. Michael v. La Migra* and to

Ruth Gollobin-Basta, who immediately made me feel like part of her extended family and graciously granted me permission to reprint materials from the vast collections amassed by her father, the dauntless Ira Gollobin. Milo Miller designed the beautiful map of the March Inland in Chapter 2. I wrote part of Chapter 7 for the Walter Prescott Webb Symposium at the University of Texas–Arlington; this material is reprinted with the cooperation of Kenyon Zimmer and Texas A&M Press.

The process of conceptualizing, researching, revising, and re-revising this book has benefited from the insights of many colleagues. The American Studies Association will always be my intellectual home, and I continuously reap the rewards of the badass brilliance of colleagues there. In addition, I have learned from panelists, audiences, chairs, and commentators at the Japanese Association for American Studies; Marquette University; the Latino Social Movements Seminar at the University of California–San Diego; the Newberry Borderlands Seminar; Oberlin College; the Organization of American Historians; the Race, Ethnicity, and Migration Seminar at the Immigration History Research Center at the University of Minnesota–Twin Cities; Sarah Lawrence College; the Society for the History of Foreign Relations; the Walter Prescott Webb Symposium at the University of Texas–Arlington; Western Michigan State University; and Yale University.

I am grateful for the intellectual fellow-traveling of Dawson Barrett, Moustafa Bayoumi, Eliza Bettinger, Jordan Camp, Corey Capers, Bianet Castellanos, Sarika Chandra, Cutler Edwards, John Enyeart, David Gutiérrez, Christina Heatherton, Rebecca Nell Hill, Lucia Hulsether, Mark Hulsether, Johari Jabir, Ben Johnson, Julia Rose Knaut, Frieda E. Knobloch, Kat Matthews, Kelly Mayhew, Natalia Molina, Ben Murane, Nadine Naber, Israel Pastrana, Jimmy Patiño, Leah Perry, Riv Ellen Prell, Chandan Reddy, Lex Rofes, Claudia Sadowski-Smith, John Saillant, Yael Schacher, David Seitz, Elizabeth Sine, Carol Stabile, Komozi Woodard, Jennifer Young, Bob Zecker, and Kenyon Zimmer. I always learn from the intellectual and political ferocity of Monisha das Gupta, with whom I have organized many lively American Studies Association sessions; I continue to be grateful for her comradeship. I had the great good fortune to have S. Ani Mukerji as a colleague at UWM for four years; I continue to rely on his generosity and historical acuity. This book began to take shape in the company of the short-lived but vital Midwest American Studies Cultural Front: Benjamin Balthaser, Jim Buss, Tracy Floreani, Joe Genetin-Pilawa, Wendy Kozol, and Rob Smith. Donna Gabaccia, Monisha das Gupta, Matthew Frye Jacobson, Moon-Ho Jung, Erika Lee, S. Ani Mukherji, Cristina Salinas, Siobhan Somerville, and Kenyon Zimmer read all or part of the manuscript, greatly enriching it. Any and all mistakes or misrepresentations are, of course, mine alone.

For the past twelve years, the UWM History Department has been a collegial and happy place to work. I thank our hardworking department chairs—most recently, Amanda Seligman and Merry Wiesener-Hanks—for keeping everything going in challenging times. I also appreciate the insights of some fine past and present graduate students, including Dawson Barrett, Michael Gonzalez, Hayley McNeill, Beth Robinson, Jackleen Salem, Kadie Seitz, Alexis Smith, Brice Smith, John Terry, Joe Walzer, and Ashley Zampogna-Krug. Our tiny Comparative Ethnic Studies Program has been kept alive by the inventive labors of Jonathan Bruce, Karen Eche-Effe, Kim Hernandez, Noel Mariano, Tyler Monson, Oody Petty, Ramona Tenorio, and especially Chia Vang, as well as by the good faith and enthusiasm of our students.

Two fine graduate assistants greatly augmented my research for this book. Ashley Marie Zampogna-Krug sifted though and indexed microfilmed newspapers for an entire summer. I am indebted to her for her exceptional historical intuition and organizing skills. Joe Walzer spent a summer reading and sorting mass-media deportation accounts; his efforts contributed mightily to my work. During that summer, Joe made a characteristically astute comment about how, during and after the Cold War, the "powers that be" tried to destroy even the memory of prior collective resistance. This insight often echoed in my mind as I wrote this book.

Particularly during the past six years in Wisconsin, a component of my intellectual labors has involved advocating for public education against a seemingly endless, well-funded, and cynical onslaught. I joke that I have taken on a full-time job defending the existence of my full-time job. The silver lining of this rather cloudy time in the history of public education has been working hard alongside intrepid, principled colleagues. I have been continually inspired by Jasmine Alinder, Anita Alkaus, Margo Anderson, Aneesh Aneesh, Ivan Ascher, Joel Berkowitz, Eliza Bettinger, Erica Bornstein, Karma Chavez, Jamie Daniel, Jeff Edwards, Nick Fleisher, Shannon Freire, Chad Allen Goldberg, Sara Goldrick-Rab, Richard Grusin, Lane Hall, Jamie Harris, Holly Hassel, Steve Hill, Alexis Jordan, Andrew Kincaid, Richard Leson, Elena Levy-Navarro, Jenna Loyd, Beth Lueck, Berel Lutsky, Aims McGuinness, Lisa Molina, S. Ani Mukherji, Mike Newman, Margaret Noodin, Patrice Petro, Kristin Pitt, Sandra Pucci, Joe Rodriguez, Nicolas Russell, Chuck Ryback, Eric Sandgren, Warren Scherer, Julie Schmid, Marc Seal, Arijit Sen, Janet Smith, Kristin Sziarto, and Dave Vanness.

People often ask me why I stay in Wisconsin under these conditions. It would be hard to think about leaving the flourishing community I inhabit. I have wonderful friends and coconspirators here, including Erica Bornstein, Lauren Fox, Edith Gilman, and Ramona Tenorio. I treasure my friendship with Deborah Wilk, who is a colleague in academia as well as motherhood. My writing group, the Social Justice Gangster Fiction Collective—Ellen Bravo, Patty Donndelinger, and Jennifer Morales—graciously consented to read an early draft of this book's quite nonfictional Introduction, which improved immeasurably as a result of their attention. Veteran Milwaukee activist Rose Daitsman gave me the copy of the Neruda poem that appears in this book's Introduction. I am grateful to Benjamin Balthaser for continually, doggedly, thinking about politics with me, and to Rob Smith for his intrepid consultations on the inside game.

For more than a decade, I have been fortunate to participate in immigrant rights organizing with Voces de la Frontera in Milwaukee and to learn from the organization and its brilliant and indefatigable leader, Christine Neumann-Ortiz. I have also learned from the dauntless student activists of Young People Empowered in the Struggle (YES!), and now Young People's Resistance Committee (YPRC). Working with these activists made me wonder about the history of immigrant rights, which set me on the trail that led to this book. I hope the stories in these pages are in some way useful to the ongoing struggle.

The Milwaukee chapter of Jewish Voice for Peace (JVP) has taken many bold stands, not the least of them, to me, against the prohibition on refugee admissions and the ongoing incursions of the deportation terror in Wisconsin. I often think of JVP's work connecting Palestine solidarity to local injustice as the logical extension of the internationalist, antiracist vision of the American Committee for the Protection of the Foreign Born. I thank JVP comrades Ravil Ashirov, Tallie Ben-Daniel, Ari Bloomkatz, Naomi Dann, Cameron Fontaine, Shana Harvey, Kara Hendrickson, Sandra Korn, Ilana Lehrman, Lorraine Halinka Malco, Jodi Melamed, Milo Miller, Samir Moukkadem, Janan Najeeb, Tony Perassini, Brant Rosen, Ilana Rossoff, Lesley Williams, and Alissa Wise.

I am supremely lucky to have two BFFs who are also brilliant readers. Without them, I do not know whether I could have stayed the long course of researching and writing this book. Wendy Kozol has been a mainstay in my life for almost twenty years now, from our attempts to "meet in the middle" between Toledo and Oberlin to some truly glorious times at various conferences, with and without our kids in tow. Wendy read more drafts of this book than anyone and insisted so stubbornly on its worth that she somehow convinced me. Oberlin is the only part of Ohio that appears in my dreams in full color; that's because of the warmth of Wendy and her family: Steven, Paul, and James Wojtal.

It has been my great good fortune in the undependable board game of academic life to wind up just an hour's drive east of Nan Enstad, whom I first met in graduate school. She and her partner, A. Finn Enke, have become goddess parents to our daughters, greatly enriching our family. Nan and I meet up regularly in Waukesha, the most reliably Republican county in the United States, where we create our own insubordinate spaces. I cannot imagine this past decade and more without Nan's company, her generosity, and her intuition. Her reads of this manuscript, like her interpretations of most matters, have invariably been right on time and exactly what I needed.

Joe Austin has been my traveling companion since we met in graduate school at the University of Minnesota. I have never stopped being dazzled by his spiritual ingenuity and intellectual creativity: they are the ground and the wellspring of the life we have built together. I look forward to many further adventures. During the writing of this book, our daughters, Ruby Lou and Ellie Rae Sylvia Balotovsky, have grown into young women. I have come to rely on Ellie's fiery sense of justice, her curriculum of evil, and her cleverly placed notes and tiny gifts. She is my stealth literary agent and political compass. Ruby has been my companion on academic trips since before she could talk, making far-flung conference hotels feel like a good time, like home. Now that she is more than well equipped with language, her insight continually changes the way I see things, for the better. The fierce loyalties and sensitivity of our daughters inspire me and give me great hope for our collective future.

Our household makes my creative work possible. Its members do this not just by accompanying me on research trips and/or holding it down when I am away and by tolerating the fact that my laptop is almost always open on the kitchen table, even when I am making waffles. Over and above their active support, the love in our family generates the energy that makes me want to be more and do more. I could not have foreseen this earlier in my life, and I may have passed it on as some dubious advice to surprised new parents, but it turns out that more is more: the more I have fallen in love with these three, the more I have had the capacity to figure out, say, and act on what I think about the world. I am endlessly grateful for their enthusiasm and insight, their love. For whatever it's worth, this book is dedicated to them.

NOTES

INTRODUCTION

1. Dipesh Chakrabarty, *Provincializing Europe: Postcolonial Thought and Historical Difference* (Princeton, NJ: Princeton University Press, 2000), 97–113.

2. Benjamin Balthaser, *Anti-imperialist Modernism: Race and Transnational Radical Culture from the Great Depression to the Cold War* (Ann Arbor: University of Michigan Press, 2015), 2.

3. Although designed to explain a quite different context, Renya Ramirez's idea of a "hub" connecting migrants is useful here. See Renya Ramirez, *Native Hubs: Culture, Community, and Belonging in Silicon Valley and Beyond* (Chapel Hill, NC: Duke University Press, 2007).

4. An excellent history of the development of immigration enforcement in the early twentieth century is Torrie Hester, *Deportation: The Origins of U.S. Policy* (Philadelphia: University of Pennsylvania Press, 2017).

5. Alicia Schmidt Camacho, *Migrant Imaginaries: Latino Cultural Politics in the U.S.-Mexico Borderlands* (New York: New York University Press, 2008), 5; Cedric Robinson, *Black Marxism: The Making of the Black Radical Tradition* (Chapel Hill: University of North Carolina Press, 2000), 1–8; Waleed Shahid, "America in Populist Times: An Interview with Chantal Mouffe," *The Nation,* December 15, 2016, available at https://www.thenation.com/article/america-in-populist-times-an-interview-with-chantal-mouffe/, accessed December 2, 2016.

6. Mark Rivkin, "The Duration of the Land: The Queerness of Spacetime in Sundown," *Studies in American Indian Literatures* 27, no. 1 (2015): 33–69, 37.

7. Eric Tang, *Unsettled: Cambodian Refugees in the NYC Hyperghetto* (Philadelphia: Temple University Press, 2015), esp. 44–51; Judith Halberstam, *In a Queer Time and Place: Transgender Bodies, Subcultural Lives* (New York: New York University Press, 2005), 6.

8. From "Address Delivered by Luisa Moreno Bemis to the Twelfth Annual Convention, California CIO Council, October 15, 1949," in Los Angeles Committee for the Protection of the Foreign Born (LACPFB), box 9, folder 15, "Individual Cases: Luisa Moreno Bemis, 1949–1950"; Elizabeth Freeman, *Time Binds: Queer Temporalities, Queer Histories* (Durham, NC: Duke University Press, 2010), xxii; Luis Eduardo Guarnizo and Michael Peter Smith, *Transnationalism from Below* (Piscataway, NJ: Transaction Publishers, 1998).

9. "Executive Order: Border Security and Immigration Enforcement Improvements," available at www.whitehouse.gov/the-press-office/2017/01/25/executive-order-border-security-and-immigration-enforcement-improvements, accessed June 14, 2017. On Barack Obama's deportation numbers, see Anna O. Law, "Lies, Damned Lies, and Obama's Deportation Statistics," *Washington Post*, April 21, 2014, available at https://www.washingtonpost.com/news/monkey-cage/wp/2014/04/21/lies-damned-lies-and-obamas-deportation-statistics/, accessed July 25, 2016.

10. Robin D. G. Kelley, "Black Study, Black Struggle," *Boston Review*, March 7, 2016, available at http://bostonreview.net/forum/robin-d-g-kelley-black-study-black-struggle, accessed June 18, 2017; Nadia Ellis, *Territories of the Soul: Queered Belonging in the Black Diaspora* (Durham, NC: Duke University Press, 2015), 6.

11. See Ann Fagan Ginger, *Carol Weiss King, Human Rights Lawyer, 1895–1952* (Boulder: University of Colorado Press, 1993), 267–321.

12. Ellis, *Territories of the Soul*, 107.

13. David Harvey, *A Brief History of Neoliberalism* (New York: Oxford University Press, 2005), 1–4; Jodi Dean, *The Communist Horizon* (New York: Verso, 2012), 62–64.

14. Chandan Reddy, *Freedom with Violence: Race, Sexuality, and the U.S. State* (Chapel Hill, NC: Duke University Press, 2011), 159; see also Monisha das Gupta, "The Neoliberal State and the Domestic Workers' Movement in New York City," *Canadian Woman Studies* 22, nos. 3/4 (2003): 78–85.

15. Loïc Wacquant, "Crafting the Neoliberal State: Workfare, Prisonfare, and Social Insecurity," *Sociological Forum* 25, no. 2 (2010): 197–220; Tang, *Unsettled*, 1–27.

16. David Harvey, "The 'New' Imperialism: Accumulation by Dispossession," *Socialist Register* 40: 63–87. Jane Collins, "Theorizing Wisconsin's 2011 Protests: Community-Based Unionism Confronts Accumulation by Dispossession," *American Ethnologist* 39, no. 1 (2012): 6–20.

17. Jordan Camp, *Incarcerating the Crisis: Freedom Struggles and the Rise of the Neoliberal State* (Berkeley: University of California Press, 2016), 5.

18. Peter N. Funke, "Conceptualizing the State of Movement-Based Counterpower," *Government and International Affairs Faculty Publications*, Paper 123, 2015, available at http://scholarcommons.usf.edu/gia_facpub/123; for a good discussion of how networks function, see also Patrick Jagoda, *Network Aesthetics* (Chicago: University of Chicago Press, 2016), 1–38.

19. Erika Lee, *At America's Gates: Chinese Immigration during the Exclusion Period, 1882–1943* (Chapel Hill: University of North Carolina Press, 2003).

20. Michael Denning, *The Cultural Front: The Laboring of American Culture in the Twentieth Century* (New York: Verso, 1997), 4–5; Robin D. G. Kelley, *Hammer and Hoe: Alabama Communists during the Great Depression* (Chapel Hill: University of North Carolina Press, 1999).

21. Robert Justin Goldstein, *American Blacklist: The Attorney General's List of Subversive Organizations* (Lawrence: University of Kansas Press, 2008), 69, 267; *The Right to Bail! Won in 13th Century: In Danger in 1951*, pamphlet, box 1, "1951–1954" folder, American Committee for the Protection of the Foreign Born (ACPFB) Papers, Tamiment Library, New York University; *American Committee for Protection of the Foreign Born v. Subversive Activities Control Board*, 380 U.S. 503 (85 S. Ct. 1148, 14 L.Ed.2d 39), argued December 8–9, 1964, available at www.law.cornell.edu/supremecourt/text/380/503.

22. Quoted in ACPFB invitation to benefit, motion picture preview of *The Gadfly*, April 21, 1956, box 2, "1956–1959" folder, ACPFB Papers, Tamiment Library, New York University.

23. Goldstein, *American Blacklist*, 68–69; for the Javits campaign against the ACPFB, see various documents from box 1, "Sponsors: 1956–1959" folder, ACPFB Papers, Labadie Collection, and box 1, "1955" folder, ACPFB Papers, Tamiment Library, New York University.

24. Report of the 23rd Annual National Conference, Detroit, December 1955, box 1, "1955" folder, ACPFB Papers, Tamiment Library, New York University.

25. Louise Pettibone Smith, *Torch of Liberty: Twenty-Five Years in the Life of the Foreign Born in the U.S.A.* (New York: Dwight King Publishers, 1959), 281.

26. Gerald Horne, *Communist Front? The Civil Rights Congress, 1946–1956* (Rutherford, NJ: Fairleigh Dickinson University Press, 1988), 13–21.

27. Balthaser, *Anti-imperialist Modernism*, 7; Horne, *Communist Front?*, 13–21.

28. Cindy I-Fen Cheng, *Citizens of Asian America: Democracy and Race during the Cold War* (New York: New York University Press, 2013), 119.

29. John Sherman, *A Communist Front at Mid-century: The American Committee for Protection of Foreign Born, 1933–1959* (Westport, CT: Praeger, 2001), 7–10. He claims in a footnote to this text, "That the origins of the committee are so briefly and poorly explained in its own history is further evidence of a cover-up. Smith was relying on the accounts of other long-term members of the committee" (14). Sherman goes on to argue that the ACPFB had precedents in International Labor Defense Committees for the Protection of the Foreign Born and therefore was little more than an offshoot of an organization that was Communist in origin. For an extensive treatment of the history of the International Labor Defense that goes well beyond such historical generalizations and would seem to refute Sherman by its lack of any mention of the organization's defenses of the foreign born, see Rebecca Nell Hill, *Men, Mobs, and Law: Anti-lynching and Labor Defense in U.S. Radical History* (Durham, NC: Duke University Press, 2008). Searching Amazon.com for Louise Pettibone Smith's book yields nothing, not even a suggestion of how to find it.

30. On Gollobin and King: Sherman, *A Communist Front at Mid-century*, 11. On Green: Sherman, *A Communist Front at Mid-century*, 72–74. Ann Fagan Ginger describes Abner Green as a Marxist but does not comment on the issue of his party membership. It is curious that Sherman does not cite the eventual overturning of the organization's status as a "Communist front" in 1965, as the Supreme Court in that case assumed that Green had been a Communist. *American Committee for the Protection of the Foreign Born, Petitioner, v. Subversive Activities Control Board*, 380 U.S. 503 (85 S. Ct. 1148, 14 L.Ed.2d 39), decided on April 26, 1965, available at http:///www.law.cornell.edu/supremecourt/text/380/503, accessed March 17, 2014.

31. Jennifer Guglielmo, *Living the Revolution: Italian Women's Resistance and Radicalism in New York City, 1882–1945* (Chapel Hill: University of North Carolina Press, 2012); Kenyon Zimmer, *Immigrants against the State: Yiddish and Italian Anarchism in America* (Champagne-Urbana: University of Illinois Press, 2015).

32. *The Legacy of Abner Green: A Memorial Journal*, box 2, "1956–1958" folder, ACPFB Papers, Tamiment Library, New York University, 86.

33. The phrase "not yet white ethnics" is taken from David Roediger's book, *Towards the Abolition of Whiteness: Essays on Race, Politics and Working Class History* (Verso: New York, 1994), 192. Important and useful accounts of this process include David Roediger, *Working towards Whiteness: How America's Immigrants Became White: The Strange Journey from Ellis Island to the Suburbs* (New York: Basic Books, 2006); and Matthew Frye Jacobson, *Whiteness of a Different Color: American Immigrants and the Alchemy of Race* (Cambridge, MA: Harvard University Press, 1999).

34. David Bacon, *The Right to Stay Home: How U.S. Policy Drives Mexican Migration* (Boston: Beacon Press, 2013).

35. A conversation with Komozi Woodard in the winter of 2000 advanced my thinking on this issue. His prolific, often collaborative scholarship has gone a long way toward debunking the historical and geographic compartmentalization of freedom struggles. See Komozi Woodard and Jeanne Theoharris, eds., *Freedom North: Black Freedom Struggles outside the South, 1940–1980* (New York: Palgrave Macmillan, 2003); Komozi Woodard and Jeanne Theoharris, eds., *Groundwork: Local Black Freedom Movements in America* (New York: New York University Press, 2005); Komozi Woodard, *A Nation within a Nation: Amiri Baraka (LeRoi Jones) and Black Power Politics* (Chapel Hill, NC: Duke University Press, 1999).

36. Donna Gabaccia, *Foreign Relations: American Immigration in Global Perspective* (Princeton, NJ: Princeton University Press, 2013), 27.

37. Monisha das Gupta, *Unruly Immigrants: Rights, Activism and Transnational South Asian Politics in the United States* (Chapel Hill, NC: Duke University Press, 2006), 16–26; George Lipsitz, *American Studies in a Moment of Danger* (Minneapolis: University of Minnesota Press, 2001), 47. I am indebted to Riv Ellen Prell for reminding me of the importance of this argument. See also Robert M. Zecker, *Race and America's Immigrant Press: How the Slovaks Were Taught to Think Like White People* (London: Continuum Press, 2012).

38. David G. Gutiérrez, *Walls and Mirrors: Mexican Americans, Mexican Immigrants, and the Politics of Ethnicity* (Berkeley: University of California Press, 1995), 172–176: Jeffrey M. Garcilazo, "McCarthyism, Mexican Americans, and the Lost Angeles Committee for the Protection of the Foreign-Born, 1950–1945," *Western Historical Quarterly* 32, no. 3 (2001): 273–290; George J. Sánchez, "What's Good for Boyle Heights Is Good for the Jews: Creating Multiracialism on the Eastside during the 1950s," *American Quarterly* 56, no. 3 (2004): 633–661.

39. Charlotta Bass, "Paul Robeson," Special Issue, *Torchlight*, March 1957, in LACPFB Papers, box 3, folder 5, Southern California Research Library; Natalia Molina, *How Race Is Made in America: Immigration, Citizenship, and the Historical Power of Racial Scripts* (Berkeley: University of California Press, 2013), 117–130; Gaye Theresa Johnson, *Spaces of Conflict, Sounds of Solidarity: Music, Race, and Spatial Entitlement in Los Angeles* (Berkeley: University of California Press, 2013), 1–47.

40. Margot Canaday, *The Straight State: Sexuality and Citizenship in Twentieth-Century America* (Princeton, NJ: Princeton University Press, 2009), 245; Marc Stein, "All the Immigrants Are Straight, All the Homosexuals Are Citizens, but Some of Us Are Queer Aliens: Genealogies of Legal Strategy in *Boutilier v. INS*," *Journal of American Ethnic History* 29, no. 4 (2010): 45–77.

41. Camp, *Incarcerating the Crisis*, 8.

42. Edwidge Danticat, *Create Dangerously: The Immigrant Artist at Work* (New York: Vintage, 2010).

43. Kelly Lytle Hernandez, *Migra! A History of the U.S. Border Patrol* (Berkeley: University of California Press, 2010).

44. Tanisha Love Ramirez and Zeba Blay, "Why People Are Using the Term 'Latinx,'" *Huffington Post*, July 5, 2016, available at http://www.huffingtonpost.com/entry/why-people-are-using-the-term-latinx_us_57753328e4b0cc0fa136a159, accessed December 21, 2016.

CHAPTER 1

1. Quote from "Aliens and Alien—Baiters," in *Harper's Magazine*, November 1935, quoted in "The Foreign Born and Relief," American Committee for the Protection of the Foreign Born (ACPFB) Memorandum, in Zimmerman Papers, 1919–1950; Local 22, Subject Files, box 1, folder 5, International Ladies Garment Workers Union Papers, Kheel Center, Cornell University. For anti-immigrant efforts and the Works Progress Administration, see Rebecca Nell Hill, "The History of the Smith Act and the Hatch Act: Anti-Communism and the Rise of the Conservative Coalition in Congress," in *Little Red Scares*, ed. Robert Justin Goldstein (New York: Ashgate, 2014), 315–346, 333.

2. Mae Ngai, *Impossible Subjects: Illegal Aliens and the Making of Modern America* (Princeton, NJ: Princeton University Press, 2004), 71–79.

3. "Conference for Protection for the Foreign Born: A Call to Action," Stella Petrosky Papers, box 42, ACPFB Papers, Labadie Collection, University of Michigan.

4. "Call to a Conference Against Deportation and For Defense of the Foreign Born Sunday, October 27, 1935, at Irving Plaza, Irving Place and 15th Street, New York City," in Zimmerman Papers, 1919–1950; Local 22, Subject Files, box 1, folder 5, International Ladies Garment Workers Union Papers, Kheel Center, Cornell University.

5. "Call to a Conference Against Deportation"; on the ACLU, see Samuel Walker, *In Defense of American Liberties: A History of the ACLU* (Carbondale: Southern Illinois University Press, 1990), 118, and *Eternal Vigilance: The Story of the ACLU, 1937–1938* (New York: ACLU, 1938), in which the ACPFB is listed as a Civil Liberties organization affiliated with the ACLU (95); on George Murphy, see Tim Wheeler, "Black History Month: George B. Murphy, Jr., Journalist for the People," *People's Daily World*, February 17, 2011, available at www.peoplesworld.org, accessed March 31, 2014; on Dwight Morgan, see John Sherman, *A Communist Front at Mid-Century: The American Committee for the Protection of the Foreign Born, 1933–1959* (Westport, CT: Praeger, 2001), 10–11; "Fight Ousting of Aliens," *New York Times*, December 13, 1932, 18.

6. "Deportation Special: Who's Who in Deportations," ACPFB, September 1935, ACPFB Papers, box 1, "1935–1949" folder, Tamiment Library, New York University; hereafter cited as "Deportation Special."

7. Hill, "The History of the Smith Act," 315–318; "Call to a Conference against Deportation."

8. *No Gestapo in America*, pamphlet, box 1, "1935–1949" folder, ACPFB Papers, Tamiment Library, New York University.

9. Yael Schacher, "Global '36: Commemorating Anti-fascism and Activism 80 Years Out: The Otto Richter Case," paper given at the Social Science History Association, 2016, *American Committee for the Protection of the Foreign Born Newsletter*, no. 275, April 28, 1939, and unnumbered edition dated April 9, 1937, both in Zimmerman Papers, 1919–1950; Local 22, Subject Files, box 1, folder 5, International Ladies Garment Workers Union Papers, Kheel Center, Cornell University; on Richter's asylum in Mexico, see John Sherman, *The Mexican Right: The End of Revolutionary Reform, 1922–1940* (Westport, CT: Greenwood Publishing Group, 1997), 97–98.

10. Hill, "The History of the Smith Act," 326; on Dies Bill, see ACPFB Press Release, April 13, 1925, in Stella Petrosky folder, ACPFB Papers, Labadie Collection, University of Michigan.

11. "Right of Asylum: Extracts from a Radio Address," by the Honorable Emmanuel Celler, in Zimmerman Papers, 1919–1950; Local 22, Subject Files, box 1, folder 5, International Ladies Garment Workers Union Papers, Kheel Center, Cornell University.

12. "Resolution Unanimously Adopted by Delegates to Convention against Deportation and Persecution of the Foreign-Born, Sunday, October 27 at 2 pm at Irving Plaza, Irving Place and 15th Street, New York City," Stella Petrosky Papers, box 42, ACPFB Papers, Labadie Collection, University of Michigan.

13. Lisa Marie Cacho, *Social Death: Racialized Rightlessness and the Criminalization of the Unprotected* (New York: New York University Press, 2013), esp. 118.

14. "Deportation Special."

15. From *"A Dangerous Woman": Stella Petrosky Held for Deportation*, by Sprad (New York City: ACPFB, 1935), 23, in Stella Petrosky file, box 42, ACPFB Papers, Labadie Collection, University of Michigan.

16. For allegations of Communism, particularly in the case of Stella Petrosky, see Sherman, *A Communist Front at Mid-Century*, esp. 31–47.

17. Christina Heatherton, "Relief and Revolution: Southern California Struggles against Unemployment," in *The Rising Tide of Color: Race, State Violence and Radical Movements across the Pacific*, ed. Moon-Ho Jung (Seattle: Washington University Press, 2014), 159–187, 162.

18. "Protests Deportation over Her Activities," undated/uncited newspaper clipping in Stella Petrosky file, box 42.

19. Information on Stella Petrosky from *"A Dangerous Woman"* in Stella Petrosky file, box 42.

20. Letter from Dwight C. Morgan to Ben Abeshouse, Mary 9, 1936; Letter from Harry Levitan to Abner Green, October 6, 1953; Memo from Byron H. Uhl, Acting Commissioner of Immigration at the Port of New York to Department of Labor; Memo: "In District Court of the U.S. for Eastern District of Pennsylvania: Stella Petroski [*sic*] v. John Holland, #20416 Act for Declaratory Judgement," all in Stella Petrosky folder, box 42.

21. "Protests Deportation over Her Activities."

22. On El Paso during the Great Depression, see Mario T. Garcia, *Memories of Chicano History: The Life and Narrative of Bert Corona* (Berkeley: University

of California Press, 1994), 56–66; Frank Arnold, "Humberto Silex: CIO Organizer from Nicaragua," *Southwest Economy and Society* 4 (1978): 1–5.

23. See Lisa McGirr, "The Passion of Sacco and Vanzetti: A Global History," *Journal of American History* 94, no. 3 (2007): 1085–1115.

24. Information on Silex from Arnold, "Humberto Silex"; in addition, "Case Files: Humberto Silex" (nos. 1–2) in the ACPFB Papers, Labadie Collection, University of Michigan. The history of Silex's organizing in El Paso is also covered in Zaragosa Vargas, *Labor Rights Are Civil Rights: Mexican American Workers in Twentieth-Century America* (Princeton, NJ: Princeton University Press, 2005), 164–178.

25. For example, press release, "American Citizenship for Mexican-American Labor Leader," undated, Silex file 1, ACPFB Papers; *Help Win Citizenship for Mexican American Labor Leader*, ACPFB pamphlet, Silex file 2, ACPFB Papers.

26. Letter from Mandell and Wright Law Firm to ACPFB, New York Office, October 18, 1948, in Silex folder 1, ACPFB Papers; David Bacon, *The Right to Stay Home: How U.S. Labor Policy Drives Mexican Migration* (Boston: Beacon Press, 2013), 122–127.

27. Arnold, "Humbert Silex," 5–8; David G. Gutiérrez, *Walls and Mirrors: Mexican Americans, Mexican Immigrants, and the Politics of Ethnicity* (Berkeley: University of California Press, 1995), 100–107; Memo, from Texas Civil Rights Congress, Silex folder 3, ACPFB Papers.

28. "Facts Relative to Deportation Proceedings Brought against Humberto Silex," undated memorandum in Silex folder 3, ACPFB Papers.

29. Dwight C. Morgan, *The Foreign Born in the United States* (New York: ACPFB, 1936), 19.

30. *Eternal Vigilance*, 13; Sheriff Fox quoted in Arnold, "Humberto Silex," 7; Fox's testimony in "Facts Relative to Deportation Proceedings Brought against Humberto Silex."

31. Bacon, *Right to Stay Home*, 124–125; "Facts Relative to Deportation Proceedings Brought against Humberto Silex."

32. Letter from Luisa Moreno to Harriet Barron of ACPFB, June 19, 1946, in Silex folder 2, ACPFB Papers.

33. Isabel Gonzalez, *Step-Child of a Nation: The Status of Mexican-Americans* (New York: ACPFB, 1949), box 33, folder 3, Bert Corona Papers.

34. Letter from Gross to Mandell and Wright Law Firm, El Paso, August 16, 1948, in Silex case file 2, ACPFB Papers, Labadie Collection, University of Michigan.

35. Letter writers represented the following organizations: Greater Flint Industrial Union Council; United Retail, Wholesale and Department Store Employees of America, Local 3; Emma Lazarus Division, Jewish People's Fraternal Order IWO, Los Angeles; United Electrical Radio and Machine Workers of America, Local 610; Food, Tobacco, Agricultural and Allied Workers Union of America, Local 25, Los Angeles; Methodist Federation for Social Action; Longshoremen's and Warehousemen's Union; Los Angeles Form; Thornton Wilder and the Club Democracia Española of New York City.

36. Arnold, "Humberto Silex," 14–15.

37. Garcia, *Memories of Chicano History*, 2.

38. Bacon, *Right to Stay Home*, 125; Garcia, *Memories of Chicano History*, 64, 99; for more on the Congress of Spanish-Speaking Peoples, see Gutiérrez, *Walls and Mirrors*, 111–176.

39. Garcia, *Memories of Chicano History*, 163–171.

40. Donna Gabaccia, *Foreign Relations: American Immigration in Global Perspective* (Princeton, NJ: Princeton University Press, 2013), 166–169.

41. Roger Daniels, *Guarding the Golden Door: American Immigrants and Immigration Policy since 1882* (New York: Hill and Wang, 2004), 84–86.

42. Excerpts from report by Abner Green, Executive Secretary of the American Committee for Protection of the Foreign Born, given at the National Conference against Deportation, held in Detroit, Michigan, December 3–4, 1949, box 1, folder "1935–1949," ACPFB Papers, Tamiment Library, New York University.

43. "To Strengthen and Defend American Democracy by Defeating Hysteria and Discrimination Promoting Unity of Native and Foreign Born," presented at Fifth National Conference of ACPFB, March 29–30, 1941, box 1, "1935–1949" folder, ACPFB Papers, Tamiment Library, New York University.

44. On the McCarran Act, see https://www.princeton.edu/~achaney/tmve/wiki100k/docs/McCarran_Internal_Security_Act.html, accessed June 4, 2014.

45. "Report on Special Effects of Walter-McCarran Law on the Foreign Born," March 19, 1955, and "Defeat Police-State Conditions of Walter-McCarran Law," both in box 1, "1955" folder, ACPFB Papers, Tamiment Library, New York University.

46. "Analysis of McCarran Bill," box 1, "1951–54" folder, ACPFB Papers, Tamiment Library, New York University.

47. Yergan letter to White, January 2, 1941, box 1, "Sponsors: 1941–1952" folder, ACPFB Papers, Labadie Collection, University of Michigan.

48. Individuals and organizations who took out ads or sent greetings in the journal included Paul Kochi, Edo Mita, and Japanese Friends in Los Angeles; Co-ordinating Committee of Greater Miami; Rabinowitz and Boudin Law; Eula and Jim Papandreau; Michigan Committee for the Protection of the Foreign Born; Polish American Committee for the Protection of the Foreign Born; Council to Regain Citizenship of Gus Polites; Midwest CPFB, Chicago; Albany Park Cultural Club; Philadelphia Committee to Defend the Foreign Born; Russian American Women's Society; "Duluth Friends," Minnesota; A Pioneer of the Red River Valley, Oscar A. Christensen; Mr. and Mrs. Peter Warhol; Sarah B. Benamy; Sirca and Robert Lee; Yugoslav Seamen's Club, New York; Polonia Club, New York; National Guardian; Latvian Committee of New York; Czechoslav Cultural Clubs, New York; Los Angeles Hungarian Group; Finnish American Harlem Committee; Rumanian American CPFB; Grupo Mexicano del Comité para la Protección de los Nacidos en el Extranjero; New Haven Neighbor Women's Group; Local 347 UPWA AFL-CIO, Chicago; Finnish Cultural Clubs; "A Group of Chicago Railroad Workers"; Utah Committee for Constitutional Liberties; Finnish American Social Club, Worcester, MA; Ludove Noviny, Chicago; Cleveland Branch Socialist Workers Party; Lansi Pa Kulttuuri Klubi; San Francisco Area Deportees and Friends; Heikkila Defense Fund; Petaluma Friends of the ACPFB; Gladstein, Anderson, Leonary and Sibbett, Attys.; SF Valley Committee to Aid Victims of the Walter-McCarran Law, San Fernando Valley, California; Los Angeles Harbor CPFB; Bay Cities CPFB; East Side CPFB, Los Angeles; Needle Trades CPFB, Los Angeles; "Greetings from LA Progressive Italians"; Yugoslav Friends in San Pedro, California; Fania Bernstein, Diamond Kimm; American Russian Institute for Cultural Relations between the Peoples of the US and Soviet Union; Pauline Epstein, attorney, Los Angeles; Rose S. Rosenberg, attorney, Los Angeles; Rose Nelson Defense Committee; Lithuanians

of Greater New York and Nearby Areas; Hungarian American Defense Committee; Hungarian Culture Clubs; Magyar Szo (Hungarian World), 130 E. 16th St., New York; Charles Rowoldt, Charles Rowoldt Defense Committee; Alma Foley; A Brewery Worker from Minneapolis; Minnesota-Wisconsin District of Finnish Cultural Clubs; Angara and Chisolm, Hibbing and Mesaba Park; Armenian Progressive League of America; Veterans of Abraham Lincoln Brigade; Downtown Manhattan Russian Club; West Side Friends; Jewish Music Alliance; Washington Heights Cultural Club; Cloakmakers Fraternal Culture Society; Lahtinen Defense Committee; Finnish Cultural Clubs of New York; Williamsburg Mutual Aid Society; Washington State CPFB; Clatsop County CPFB; Oregon Chapter, Methodist Federation for Social Action; Committee for Protection of Oregon's Foreign Born; Committee for Defense of Morning Freiheit Writers; Greek Friends in New York; Ukrainian American Provisional Trade Union; Committee for the Defense of Maurice Paul; A Group of Bronx Women.

49. Typed transcript, Louise Pettibone Smith Biography, box 1, "Biographical Information, Louise Pettibone Smith" folder, ACPFB Papers, Labadie Collection, University of Michigan.

50. Sherman, *A Communist Front at Mid-century: The American Committee for Protection of Foreign Born, 1933–1959* [emphasis mine]; Robert Justin Goldstein, ed., *Little Red Scares* (New York: Ashgate, 2014), 110.

51. Letter from Ira Gollobin to New York Department of Taxation and Finance, August 5, 1982, box 1, "Administration: Dissolution of ACPFB (1982)" folder, ACPFB Papers, Labadie Collection, University of Michigan.

52. Report from the New York Conference, March 19, 1955, box 1, "1955" folder, ACPFB Papers, Tamiment Library, New York University.

53. Garcia, *Memories of Chicano History*, 119.

54. Harry Carlisle, *Brief History of the Los Angeles Committee for the Protection of the Foreign Born (Sept 1950–Aug 1955)*, box 1, "History of the Organization" folder, Los Angeles Committee for the Protection of the Foreign Born (LACPFB) Papers, Southern California Research Library; see Jeffrey Garcilazo, "McCarthyism, Mexican Americans and the Los Angeles Committee for the Protection of the Foreign Born, 1950–1954," *Western Historical Quarterly* 32, no. 3 (2001): 273–294.

55. Alfredo Montoya, "Problems of the Mexican People," presented at LACPFB conference on November 3, 1951, box 2, "Los Angeles Committee for the Protection of the Foreign Born" folder, ACPFB Papers, Tamiment Library, New York University.

56. Luisa Moreno's address to panel on Deportation and the Right of Asylum at the Fourth Annual Committee for the PFB in Washington, DC, March 3, 1940, box 26, folder 1, Bert Corona Papers.

57. Harry Carlisle, ed., "The Legacy of Abner Green: A Memorial Journal," box 2, "1956–1958" folder, ACPFB Papers, Tamiment Library, New York University.

CHAPTER 2

1. For the story of the March Inland, particularly as it concerned forging alliances between warehouse and longshore workers on the Pacific Coast, see Harvey Schwartz, *The "March Inland": Origins of the ILWU Warehouse Division, 1934–*

1938 (Los Angeles: UCLA Institute for Industrial Relations, 1978; repr., San Francisco: ILWU, 2000); Albert Vetere Lannon, *"The 'March Inland': Origins of the ILWU Warehouse Division 1934–1938,"* review, *Labor Studies Journal* 27, no. 2 (2002): 102–103; Merle E. Reed, *"The 'March Inland': Origins of the ILWU Warehouse Division 1934–1938,"* review, *American Historical Review* 84, no. 2 (1979): 580–581.

2. Gaye Theresa Johnson importantly connects what she calls "spatial entitlement" to the creation of Black-Brown solidarity in *Spaces of Conflict, Sounds of Solidarity: Music, Race, and Spatial Entitlement in Los Angeles* (Berkeley: University of California Press, 2013). For a discussion of the politics and practices of the commodity chain, see Anna Lowenhaupt Tsing, *The Mushroom at the End of the World: On the Possibility of Life in Capitalist Ruins* (Princeton, NJ: Princeton University Press, 2015), 61–62.

3. Rick Baldoz, *The Third Asiatic Invasion: Empire and Migration in Filipino America, 1898–1946* (New York: New York University Press, 2011), 9–15.

4. Lisa Lowe, *Immigrant Acts: On Asian American Cultural Politics* (Durham, NC: Duke University Press, 1996), 45–47; Carlos Bulosan, *America Is in the Heart* (Seattle: University of Washington Press, 1973).

5. See Denise Khor, "'Filipinos Are the Dandies of the Foreign Colonies': Race, Labor Struggles, and the Transpacific Routes of Hollywood and Philippine Films, 1924–1948," *Pacific Historical Review* 81, no. 3 (2012): 371–403; Hayley McNeill, "'Illegal and Void': The Effects of State and Federal Legislation against Filipinos in the American Empire" (master's thesis, University of Wisconsin–Milwaukee, 2016).

6. Quoted in "Biddle's Private War against Harry Bridges," Harry Bridges Victory Committee, San Francisco, California, 1945, in Harry Bridges Files, box 25, American Committee for the Protection of the Foreign Born (ACPFB) Papers, Labadie Collection, University of Michigan

7. Harvey Schwarz, "Harry Bridges and the Scholars: Looking at History's Verdict," *California History* 29, no. 1 (1980): 66–79; Robert W. Cherney, "The Making of a Labor Radical: Harry Bridges, 1901–1934," *Pacific Historical Review* 64, no. 3 (1995): 363–388; Robert W. Cherney, "Constructing a Radical Identity: History, Memory, and the Seafaring Stories of Harry Bridges," *Pacific Historical Review* 70, no. 4 (2001): 571–599. Charles P. Larrowe, *Harry Bridges: The Rise and Fall of Radical Labor in the U.S.* (Westport, CT: Lawrence Hill, 1972).

8. Larrowe, *Harry Bridges*, 8; Cherney, "Making of a Labor Radical," 377. Bridges was married three times—the second time to Nancy Fenton Berdicio, and the third time to Nisei CIO activist Nikki (Noriko) Sawada, who had been interned with her parents during World War II. Mixed-race marriages were forbidden in Nevada when they married in 1958, although the couple prevailed in court against the antimiscegenation law and were wed. See Valerie J. Matsumoto, "Nikki Sawada Bridges Flynn and *What Comes Naturally*," *Frontiers* 31, no. 3 (2010): 31–41.

9. Larrowe, *Harry Bridges*, 9.

10. From "The Story of the 18-Year Plot to Frame Harry Bridges," *March of Labor*, January 1953, in Harry Bridges Files, box 25, ACPFB Papers, Labadie Collection, University of Michigan.

11. Stan Weir also discusses the shape-up as a practice of labor control. He describes the alternative "low man out" system, devised by maritime laborers and eventually supplanted by ILWU union hierarchy under Bridges's leadership. See Stan Weir, Norm Diamond, and George Lipsitz, *Singlejack Solidarity* (Minneapolis: University of Minnesota, 2004), esp. 259–261.

12. Bruce Nelson, "Unions and the Popular Front: The West Coast Waterfront in the 1930s," *International Labor and Working Class History*, no. 30 (Fall 1986): 59–78, 60–64.

13. Mae Ngai, *Impossible Subjects: Illegal Aliens and the Making of America* (Princeton, NJ: Princeton University Press, 2004), 117.

14. Quoted in Larrowe, *Harry Bridges*, 46.

15. Dalton Trumbo, *Harry Bridges*, pamphlet (New York: League of American Writers, 1941); "Dates and Facts in the Four Bridges Persecutions," both in Harry Bridges Files, box 25, ACPFB Papers, Labadie Collection, University of Michigan.

16. "The Story of the 18 Year Plot," 14; Schwartz, "Harry Bridges and the Scholars," 67; Schwartz, *The "March Inland,"* xi–25.

17. Schwartz, *The "March Inland,"* xi.

18. Quoted in ibid., 33.

19. Ibid., 29.

20. Larrowe, *Harry Bridges*, 139.

21. Ibid., 146; Carol King, "Memorandum on the Subject of Affiliation," ACPFB, in Harry Bridges Files, box 25, ACPFB Papers, Labadie Collection, University of Michigan.

22. Cherney, "Constructing a Radical Identity," 573.

23. Carol Weiss King, "Memorandum on the Subject of Affiliation," 2, ACPFB, in Harry Bridges Files, box 25, ACPFB Papers, Labadie Collection, University of Michigan.

24. "In Re Harry Bridges," *Yale Law Journal* 52, no. 1 (1942): 8; "Biddle's Private War," 5; King, 1.

25. "The Story of the 18 Year Plot," 17; see also "Why? The Fourth Frame-Up against Harry Bridges," Bridges-Robertson-Schmidt Defense Committee, San Francisco; "Threatens Hawai'ian Dock Strike" clipping, Harry Bridges Files, ACPFB Papers, Labadie Collection, University of Michigan. Clark apparently made these statements in Milwaukee and was picketed by fifteen members of the Wisconsin Civil Rights Congress demanding that he prosecute the KKK.

26. "The Story of the 18 Year Plot."

27. See Gerald Horne, *Fighting in Paradise: Labor Unions, Racism, and Communists in the Making of Modern Hawaii* (Honolulu: University of Hawai'i Press, 2011), 187; Moon-Kie Jung, *Reworking Race: The Making of Hawai'i's Interracial Labor Movement* (New York: Columbia University Press, 2006), 42, 110–112; James A. Geschwender and Rhonda F. Levine, "Rationalization of Sugar Production in Hawai'i, 1946–1960: A Dimension of the Class Struggle," *Social Problems* 30, no. 3 (1983): 352–368.

28. Baldoz, *Third Asiatic Invasion*, 56.

29. Jung, *Reworking Race*, 87, 95–107; Geschwender and Levine, "Rationalization of Sugar Production in Hawai'i," 355.

30. Geschwender and Levine, "Rationalization of Sugar Production in Hawai'i," 356; Jung, *Reworking Race*, 110.

31. Quote from Jung, *Reworking Race*, 110, 169; Jung on Vibora Luriminda, 151.

32. Baldoz, *Third Asiatic Invasion*, 59, 146.

33. Horne, *Fighting in Paradise*, 4–12.

34. Ibid., 5–84.

35. Quoted in ibid., 4.

36. Tom O'Brien, radio correspondent on Hilo, the site of many labor battles, held that the Hawai'ian people—native Hawai'ians, in particular—wanted commonwealth rather than statehood status in 1953. "O'Brien Says Hawaii's People Prefer Commonwealth Status," *Hawaiian Star Bulletin*, July 9, 1953, box 9, Romanzo Adams Social Research Laboratory, Clippings Files (A 1979:042b), subseries 4, University Archives, University of Hawai'i, Manoa.

37. "Citizenship Rights for Filipinos Asked," box 2, folder c-20, "American Citizenship," Romanzo Adams Social Research Laboratory, Clippings Files (A 1979:042b), subseries 4, University Archives, University of Hawai'i, Manoa.

38. Horne, *Fighting in Paradise*, 223; Farrington quoted in "Hawaii Racial Status Lauded by Farrington: East and West Mingle on 'American Plan' Says Publisher in Washington," *Honolulu Star Bulletin*, May 12, 1931, box 2, "Interracial Contacts," Romanzo Adams Social Research Laboratory, Clippings File (A 1979:042b), series 1, University Archives, University of Hawai'i, Manoa.

39. Horne, *Fighting in Paradise*, 157; Horne on Eastland and southern ports, 297.

40. Ibid., 239.

41. Gretchen Heefner, "A Symbol of the New Frontier," *Pacific Historical Review* 74, no. 4 (2005): 545–574, 547–549.

42. On the McCarran-Walter Act and empire more broadly, see my "Domestic Internationalisms, Imperial Nationalism: Civil Rights, Immigration, and Conjugal Military Policy," in *New Routes for Diaspora Studies*, ed. Sukanya Banerjee, Aims McGuinness, and Steven C. McKay (Bloomington: Indiana University Press, 2012), 123–139.

43. Chris Mensalves, "Taking the Offensive," *Local 7 Yearbook*, ed. Carlos Bulosan, 5, 1952.

44. Ibid.; Seattle Civil Rights and Labor History Project, Seattle Civil Rights and Labor History Project, available at http://depts.washington.edu/civilr/local_7 .htm, accessed September 2014; Micah Ellison, "The Local 7/Local 37 Story: Filipino American Cannery Unionism in Seattle, 1940–1959," available at http://depts .washington.edu/civilr/local_7.htm, accessed June 19, 2017.

45. Michael Denning, *The Cultural Front: The Laboring of American Culture in the Twentieth Century* (Verso: New York, 1997), 272–273.

46. See Ellison, "The Local 7/Local 37 Story," 4–5; Carey McWilliams, "Introduction," in Bulosan, *America Is in the Heart*, xx.

47. Carlos Bulosan, "Be American," in *If You Want to Know What We Are: Carlos Bulosan Reader*, ed. E. San Juan Jr. (Minneapolis: West End Press, 1983), 58.

48. Baldoz, *Third Asiatic Invasion*, 207.

49. Nayan Shah, *Stranger Intimacy: Contesting Race, Sexuality, and Law in the North American West* (Berkeley: University of California Press, 2012), 266–267; Dorothy Fujita-Rony, *American Workers, Colonial Power: Philippine Seattle and the Transpacific West, 1919–1941* (Berkeley: University of California Press, 2003), 170–172.

50. Ngai, *Impossible Subjects*, 93. The Luce-Celler Act of 1946 had made Filipinx eligible to become citizens. Baldoz, *Third Asiatic Invasion*, 227–228; Alicia J. Campi, "The McCarran-Walter Act: A Contradictory Legacy on Race, Quotas, and Ideology," Immigration Policy Brief, 2004, Illinois Coalition for Immigrant and Refugee Rights, available at icirr.org, accessed October 2014.

51. Ellison, "The Local 7/Local 37 Story," 3, 6.

52. Cited in Opening Brief, *Mangaoang v. Boyed*, 9th Circuit, in Ernesto Mangaoang File, box 39, ACPFB Papers, Labadie Collection, University of Michigan; see also 183 F.2d 795, *Cabebe v. Acheson*, available at http://openjurist.org/183/f2d795/cabebe-v-acheson, accessed October 2014.

53. *San Francisco Labor Archives and Research Center Newsletter*, no. 17 (Spring 2007): 1, available at http://www.library.sfsu.edu/about/depts/larc/larc-newsletter.html, accessed October 2014.

54. Quoted in T. A. Rojo, "Birth and Growth of Local 37," in *Local 37 Yearbook*, 16; Fujita-Rony, *American Workers, Colonial Power*, 101–102; Ernesto Mangaoang, "Report of the Business Agent," *1952 Yearbook*, 7.

55. Opening Brief, *Mangaong v. Boyd*; Ellison, "The Local 7/Local 37 Story," 7.

56. ACPF Press Release, "The Release of Ernesto Mangaoang," and Opening Brief, 22, both in Mangaoang File, box 39, ACPFB Papers, Labadie Collection, University of Michigan.

57. C. T. Hatten, "The Deportability and Immunity of Filipinos in the U.S.," *Yearbook* 20.

CHAPTER 3

1. Quoted in *The Lamp*, no. 36 (June 1947): 2.

2. "171 Indonesian Sailors Face Deportation," *The Lamp*, no. 20 (December 1945); "Justice Department Tries to Deport Indonesian to Dutch Government," *The Lamp*, no. 26 (July 1946); "Indonesians in Global Struggle," *Chicago Defender*, October 27, 1945, 1; Gerald Horne, *Red Seas: Ferdinand Smith and Radical Black Sailors in the United States and Jamaica* (New York: New York University Press, 2005), 144; Greg Robinson, "The Internment of Indonesians in the United States," paper presented at Japanese Association for American Studies Conference, Tokyo Christian University, June 2015, in possession of author.

3. "Sydney Strikers in Fight," *New York Times*, September 29, 1945, 5.

4. On Sumampow, see "What Will Happen to His Wife and Children," *The Lamp*, no. 18 (September–October 1945).

5. "The Colonial Question," *Chicago Defender*, October 20, 1945, 14; Greg Robinson, "The Great Unknown and the Unknown Great: The Incarceration of Indonesians in the United States, an Untold Story," in *Nichi Bei*, January 28, 2015, available at http://www.nichibei.org/2015/01/the-great-unknown-and-the-unknown-great-the-incarceration-of-indonesians-in-the-united-states-an-untold-story/; George Padmore, "London Colonials in Mass Protest," *Chicago Defender*, December 29, 1945, 10.

6. Indonesian Club of America, Letter to "Voice of the People," *Chicago Tribune*, October 23, 1945, 10.

7. Robinson, "The Great Unknown and the Unknown Great."

8. "High Court Rejects Java Sailors Plea," *Washington Post*, December 17, 1946, 7; "Fast Action Stays Deportation of Seven Indonesians," *Washington Post*, December 22, 1948; *The Lamp*, no. 36 (June 1947).

9. On the War Powers Act, see https://www.uscis.gov/history-and-genealogy/our-history/agency-history/military-naturalization-during-wwii, accessed July 13, 2016. For Seamen's Bill of Rights, see *The Lamp*, no. 2 (October 1944) and no. 42 (December 1948); Senator Claude Pepper introduced a similar bill in the Senate in 1945.

10. David Harvey, *A Brief History of Neoliberalism* (New York: Oxford University Press, 2005), 76–77.

11. Bruce Nelson, *Workers on the Waterfront: Seamen, Longshoremen, and Unionism in the 1930s* (Urbana: University of Illinois Press, 1990) 31–32. The Jones Act (1920) affirmed the rights of U.S. seamen to certain work protections and held that ships in the merchant marine needed to be owned and operated by Americans. This law extended a similar 1817 provision. Paul K. Chapman, *Trouble on Board: The Plight of International Seafarers* (Ithaca, NY: ILR Press, 1992), 75.

The Jones-White or Merchant Marine Act of 1928 contained provisions for the removal of Chinese seamen and their replacement by American-born marine laborers; Josephine Fowler, *Japanese and Chinese Immigrant Activists: Organizing in American and International Communist Movements, 1919–1933* (New Brunswick, NJ: Rutgers University Press: 2007), 114. Ship owners often got around these provisions, taking on foreign-born crew outside U.S. waters. But these laws posed an impediment to the coherence of the transnational marine labor force.

12. "Deportation of NMU Aid Stayed by 3 Civil Suits: Immigration Service Files Reveal Data on 10-Year Probe of Ferdinand C. Smith," *Baltimore Afro American*, July 31, 1948, 5.

13. Hugh Mulzac, *A Star to Steer By* (New York: International Press, 1971), 30–31, 65–77, 152–153.

14. Horne, *Red Seas*, 4–8; Fowler, *Japanese and Chinese Immigrant Activists*, 110–111.

15. The Merchant Marine Act was a component of increased federal investment in the expansion of the American fleet. U.S. vessels carried 13 percent of national cargo in 1913. By 1935, U.S. ships were responsible for 35 percent. By 1934, 293,000 workers were directly or indirectly engaged in interstate or foreign shipping. The act created a federal Maritime Commission to oversee shipping. Presumed to represent the cause of national shipping, the Maritime Commission also served as a powerful voice for the ship owners. Nelson, *Workers on the Waterfront*, 14, 28–29; Chapman, *Trouble on Board*, 19; Mulzac, *A Star to Steer By*, 122.

16. Mulzac, *A Star to Steer By*, 116.

17. Horne, *Red Seas*, 26–29.

18. Mulzac, *A Star to Steer By*, 123.

19. Jeanne Gilbert and James Healy, "The Economic and Social Background of the Unlicensed Personnel of the American Merchant Marine," *Social Forces* 21 (1943): 41. In 1943, the American Committee for the Protection of the Foreign Born estimated monthly wages of an able seaman as follows: $200/US; $105/Norway; $84/Greece; $76/China (in Letter from Abner Green to Vito Marcantonio, March 6, 1943, box 4, "General Correspondence: Seamen Deportation" folder, Vito Marcantonio Papers, Books and Manuscripts Division, New York Public Library).

20. Claudia Sadowski-Smith, "Unskilled Labor Migration and the Illegality Spiral: Chinese, European and Mexican Indocumentados in the United States, 1887–2007," *American Quarterly* 60, no. 3 (2008): 779–804.

21. "The Foreign Seaman's Program," *The Lamp*, no. 18 (August 1945); Claire Price, "Harbor Camp for Enemy Aliens," *New York Times*, January 25, 1942, SM 29.

22. In 1942, forty seamen were deported to the United Kingdom ("Alien Rules Curb Manning of Ships," *New York Times*, August 30, 1942, 5).

23. "Chinese Seamen Win Agreement with British Merchant Marine," *New York Times*, May 10, 1942, F7.

24. "Seamen Halted in Flight at Pier," *New York Times*, September 15, 1940, 20; "Chinese Crew Placated," *New York Times*, September 18, 1940, 46; "Chinese Seamen Halted in Dash for Shore," *New York Times*, June 21, 1941, 31; "Crewman Is Killed in Mutiny Here," *New York Times*, April 12, 1942, 1; "Chinese Held Mistreated," *New York Times*, April 15, 1942, 2; "Freedom for Chinese Is Headache for Shipping Men," *New York Times*, September 6, 1942, F6; George Horne, "Desertions by Chinese Seamen May Cause Ban on Shore Liberty," *New York Times*, October 26, 1942, F6, "Chinese Deserters Growing Problem," *New York Times*, April 4, 1943, 11.

25. Questions about the status of Asian seamen extended to those living legally in the United States. In 1941, Kumezo Kawato, an Issei fisherman born in Japan in 1905, filed suit in a California court to claim back wages. The U.S. ship *The Rally* had withheld his pay, arguing that the declaration of war with Japan rendered Kawato an enemy alien with no right of redress. In the climate that would soon lead to Executive Order 9066 and the removal and internment of Japanese Americans on the West Coast, the Southern District Court of California found that, because of his status as an "enemy alien," Kawato had no right to sue. After the Ninth Circuit Court refused to hear the case, the Supreme Court took it up in 1942, finding that Kawato's status as a resident alien guaranteed his right to due process. This rare affirmation of the Fourteenth Amendment rights of Japanese Americans during wartime was consonant with a broader struggle to define the position of Asian seamen.

26. "Chinese Seamen Riot against Discrimination," *Chicago Defender*, May 23, 1942, 2.

27. "Equality Sought for Alien Seamen," *New York Times*, August 9, 1942, 36.

28. "Passing the Word," *The Pilot*, December 20, 1940, 1–2, in "National Maritime Union," box 1, Reference Files of the Seafarer's International Union, Robert F. Wagner Labor Archives, WAG 267, Tamiment Library, New York University.

29. Abner Green, letter to Vito Marcantonio, March 6, 1943, box 4, Marcantonio Papers, New York Public Library, Manuscript Division.

30. "The Foreign Seaman's Program," *The Lamp*, no. 18 (August 1945): 3.

31. Pepper quoted in *The Lamp*, no. 31 (January 1947): 2; Truman quoted in no. 38 (August 1947): 1.

32. *The Lamp*, no. 42 (January 1948).

33. Mulzac, *A Star to Steer By*, 135.

34. James Reston, "8,000 Alien Seamen Hunted for Crews," *New York Times*, March 24, 1942, 1.

35. "200 Greek Ships Now Aiding Allies," *New York Times*, October 4, 1941; Memo, "Maltreatment of Greek Seamen in U.S.," box 824, folder 43, "Greek Seamen, 1949," ACLU Papers, subseries 3a.9, "Freedom of Belief, Expression and Association, Freedom of Movement," Mudd Library, Princeton University; "Greek Sea Pay Cited," *New York Times*; October 11, 1942, S10; "Seamen of Greece Seek Union Terms," *New York Times*, July 19, 1942, F7; *The Case of the Greek Seamen*, pamphlet (London: Press Office of the Federation of Greek Maritime Unions, 1945).

36. *The Case of the Greek Seamen*, 3–7.

37. The Copeland Act of 1934 expanded papers for seamen on U.S. vessels. Mulzac, *A Star to Steer By*, 115.

38. Letter from Attorney Tom Clark, box 824, folder 43, "Greek Seamen, 1949," ACLU Papers, subseries 3a.9, "Freedom of Belief, Expression and Association, Freedom of Movement," Mudd Library, Princeton University.

39. Letter from Ennis to Miller, June 30, 1949, box 824, folder 43, "Greek Seamen, 1949," ACLU Papers, subseries 3a.9, "Freedom of Belief, Expression and Association, Freedom of Movement," Mudd Library, Princeton University.

40. "Events of Interest in Shipping World," *New York Times*, June 30, 1946, 39.

41. *The Lamp*, no. 55 (August 1949) and no. 57 (November–December 1949).

42. Committee on Freedom of Association Report, United States (Case 45), The International Seamen's and Dockers' Union (Poland), the Federation of Greek Maritime Unions (New York Branch), and the World Federation of Trade Unions, Report 6 (Seventh Report, 1953), app. 5, International Labor Organization, United Nations, available at http://webfusion.ilo.org/public/db/standards/normes/lib synd/lsgetparasbycase.cfm?PARA=6833&FILE=45&hdroff=1&DISPLAY=BACK GROUND,CONCLUSION,RECOMMENDATION#RECOMMENDATION, accessed December 9, 2010; "US Authorities Would Deport Men to Death: ACLU Protests Actions," box 825, folder 43, "Greek Seamen," ACLU Papers, subseries 3a.9, "Freedom of Belief, Expression and Association, Freedom of Movement," Mudd Library, Princeton University; Letter from Alan Reitman, Publicity Director, ACLU to Allan W. Swim, editor, CIO News, July 22, 1949, box 824, folder 43, "Greek Seamen, 1949," ACLU Papers, subseries 3a.9, "Freedom of Belief, Expression and Association, Freedom of Movement," Mudd Library, Princeton University. On Ambatielos, see Evi Gkotzaridis, *A Pacifist's Life and Death: Grigorios Lambrakis and Greece in the Long Shadow of Civil War* (Newcastle upon Tyne: Cambridge Scholars Publishing, 2016), 174.

43. "In the Matter of the Petition of A. Georgakopoulos, Consular Representative of the Consular General of Greece, Mercantile Marine Department," No. 421 of 1948, Filed January 28, 1949, U.S. District Court for the Eastern District of Pennsylvania, box 824, folder 43, "Greek Seamen, 1949," ACLU Papers, subseries 3a.9, "Freedom of Belief, Expression and Association, Freedom of Movement," Mudd Library, Princeton University. "The other charges filed against the seamen for illegal collection of monies on behalf of the OENO (FGMU) and the newspaper 'Naftergatis,' forming a ship's committee, formulating and circulating a telegraphic protest on behalf of their ten leaders who were sentenced to death, do not constitute a dispute between the Master and the crew and as such are not cognizable in these proceedings."

44. Ibid., 7.

45. Philip Moran, "Ideological Exclusion, Plenary Power, and the PLO," *California Law Review* 77, no. 4 (1989): 831–917, esp. 855–858; Daniel Kanstroom, *Deportation Nation: Outsiders in American History* (Cambridge, MA: Harvard University Press, 2007), 70–74.

46. Horne, *Red Seas*, 145–148.

47. "14 Greek Seamen Arrested at Pier," *New York Times*, August 10, 1949, 45.

48. "Greek Seamen Resist Deportation from the U.S.," *New York Times*, November 2, 1949, 55.

49. Quoted in Horne, *Red Seas*, 134.

50. I am appreciative of Kenyon Zimmer's conversational insights on this matter. See Kenyon Zimmer, "Positively Stateless: Marcus Graham, the Ferrero-Sallitto Case, and Anarchist Challenges to Race and Deportation," in *The Rising Tide of*

Color: Race, Radicalism, and Repression on the Pacific Coast and Beyond, ed. Moon-Ho Jung (Seattle: University of Washington Press, 2013), 128–158.

51. Horne, *Red Seas*, 195–198.

52. "Alien Seamen Deserted by NMU," *The Lamp*, no. 62 (August–September 1950): 1.

53. "Transfer Favored for Old Vessels," *New York Times*, March 3, 1950, 45. There was substantial administrative overlap between shipping, private and federal, and immigration in this period. In 1950, for example, Earl W. Clark became the acting department administrator of the Maritime Administration. Previously, he had served on the Commerce Department Industry Advisory Committee. During the war, he was the director of the Office of Industry Cooperation. T. C. Gibney, who had been a liaison between the INS and the War Shipping Administration during the war, became the chief of inspectors in the Port of New York in 1951. These men brought with them knowledge of the shipping industry, an understanding of immigration regulations, and abundant contacts in private industry. "Events of Interest in the Shipping World," *New York Times*, July 11, 1950; "TC Gibney, Veteran Immigration Officer, Becomes Chief of the Inspectors in the Port," *New York Times*, June 20, 1951, 33.

54. "Immigration Plan Upsets Ship Lines," *New York Times*, January 1, 1952, 37.

55. Ann Fagan Ginger, *Carol Weiss King: Human Rights Lawyer, 1895–1952* (Boulder: University Press of Colorado, 1998), 448–457.

56. Luther A. Huston, "Tighter Alien Curbs to Begin in McCarran Act Wednesday," *New York Times*, December 21, 1952, 1; "Alien Law Bars 269 of Liberte's Crew," *New York Times*, December 24, 1952, 1; "Seamen's Xmas," *New York Times*, December 25, 1952, 28.

57. Joseph J. Ryan, "U.S. Loses Favor of Foreign Seamen," *New York Times*, February 15, 1953, 38.

58. "US Shippers Cite Snag in Alien Law," *New York Times*, February 25, 1953, 51.

59. "Shipping and CIO Split on Alien Bill," *New York Times*, May 16, 1953, 47.

60. "13 Unions Urge US to Help Shipping," *New York Times*, January 20, 1954, 55.

61. 344 U.S. 590, 73 S. Ct. 472, 97 L.Ed. 576, *Kwong Hai Chew v. Colding et al. The Sir John Franklin*, available at http://openjurist.org/344/us/590/kwong-hai-chew-v-colding-the-sir-john-franklin, accessed December 14, 2010; Lois H. Hambro, "Constitutional Law: Aliens: Powers to Exclude and Deny Hearing," *Michigan Law Review* 51, no. 8 (1953): 1231–1233; Carlene Cho, "Not a Chinaman's Chance: Chinese Americans during the McCarthy Era," student paper available at https://eee .uci.edu/programs/humcore/students/chopaper.htm, accessed December 14, 2010; Ellen Schrecker, "Immigration and Internal Security: Political Deportations during the McCarthy Era," *Science and Society* 60, no. 4 (1996–1997): 407.

62. Schrecker, "Immigration and Internal Security," 408; Cho, "Not a Chinaman's Chance."

63. *Chew v. Colding*.

64. Harvey, *Brief History of Neoliberalism*, 76–77.

65. Rodney Carlisle, *Sovereignty for Sale: The Origins and Evolution of the Panamanian and Liberian Flags of Convenience* (Annapolis, MD: Naval Institute Press, 1981), 1–2. Employment on American-flag ships went from 158,860 in 1945

to 51,640 in 1958; David P. Currie, "Flags of Convenience, American Labor, and the Conflict of Laws," *Supreme Court Review 1963* (1963): 34–100, 55n82. By July 1959, U.S.-flag merchant ships totaled 2,847 private and government-owned vessels, weighing a total of 33.5 million deadweight tons, while 518 vessels weighing more than 10 million deadweight tons were registered under foreign "flags of convenience" registries in Panama, Liberia, and Honduras (PANLIBHON). The U.S.-flag fleet included more than 1,700 government-owned reserve ships, most of which were inactive and largely obsolete. Only 206 ships in the American fleet were of postwar construction. The Liberian fleet, however, contained more modern vessels. In 1958, American-controlled, PANLIBHON-registered ships carried 33 percent of U.S. foreign trade, while American-flag ships carried only 12 percent; "Panlibhon Registration of American-Owned Merchant Ships: Government Policy and the Problem of the Courts," *Columbia Law Review* 60, no. 5 (1960): 715. In 1959, 17 million tons of ships, comprising one-seventh of the world's total, were registered in Liberia, Panama, Honduras, and Costa Rica. Almost none of these ships was owned by citizens of these nations.

66. Carlisle, *Sovereignty for Sale*, 199.

67. Ibid., 115–131.

68. Ibid.

69. Abner Green, letter to Vito Marcantonio, March 6, 1943, box 4, Marcantonio Papers, New York Public Library, Manuscript Division.

70. Carlisle, *Sovereignty for Sale*, 113.

71. Ibid., 111–112.

72. Ibid., 139.

73. U.S. Supreme Court, *Lauritzen v. Larsen*, 345 U.S. 571 (1953), argued January 6, 1953, decided May 25, 1953, available at http://supreme.justia.com/us/345/571/, accessed December 21, 2010; Lee D. Powar, "Labor Law: Injunctions: Order Restraining Election aboard 'Flag-of-Convenience' Vessel," *Michigan Law Review* 60, no. 8 (1962): 1177–1183, 1180, available at http://www.shipguide.com/jones-act/i_c_1.html, accessed December 21, 2010; "Panlibhon Registration," 728–729.

74. "Panlibhon Registration," 716–722.

75. Chapman, *Trouble on Board*, 87; "Panlibhon Registration," 725–726; Carlisle, *Sovereignty for Sale*, 155.

76. "Panlibhon Registration," 731; Carlisle, *Sovereignty for Sale*, 158; Currie, "Flags of Convenience," 36, xxix.

77. "Union Wins Vote on Liberian Ship," *New York Times*, June 21, 1958, 38.

78. "Panlibhon Registration," 732. Using the contacts theory articulated in *Lauritzen*, the Supreme Court determined that American ownership outweighed registry and flag in *Zielinski v. Empresa Hondurena de Vapores* and *Bobolakis v. Compania Panamena Maritima San Gerassimo*. In *Afran Transit Company v. National Maritime Union* (1960), the Southern District Court of New York found that union activities among foreign workers bore directly on domestic "peace and tranquility" because of the ways in which working conditions among the foreign born might depress wages and working conditions for U.S. seamen. Here, the NLRB deployed the nineteenth-century *Wildenhus* standard to argue for labor rights on board flags of convenience ships

79. "West India Fruit and Steamship Company, Inc.," Case 15-CA-1454, 343–348, available through the NLRB database at http://www.nlrb.gov/research/

decisions/board_decisions/index.aspx. (I thank the NLRB staff—who returned a phone call within five minutes, with accurate information in hand—for their gracious assistance.)

80. Ibid., 361.

81. "U.S. Shippers Cite Snags in Alien Law," *New York Times*, February 25, 1953, 51; Carlisle, *Sovereignty for Sale*, 164–165.

82. Project WALRUS, a government-sponsored study of the role of the merchant marine in national security, was conducted in 1959. "Panlibhon Registration," 721, 731.

83. Dario Euraque, "Review: Social, Economic and Political Aspects of the Carias Dictatorship in Honduras: The Historiography," *Latin American Research Review* 29, no. 1 (1994): 238–248.

84. "Labor Law: National Labor Relations Act Held Inapplicable to American Owned Flag of Convenience," *Duke Law Journal* 1963, no. 3 (1963): 578–585, 582.

85. John R. Stevenson, "McCulloch, Chairman, National Labor Relations Board, et al. v. Sociedad Nacional de Marineros de Honduras: McLeod, Regional Director, National Labor Relations Board v. Empresa Hondurena de Vapores, S.A.: National Maritime Union of America v. Empresa Hondurena de Vapores, S.S. 372 U.S. 10," *American Journal of International Law* 57, no. 3 (1963): 659–666, 662.

86. *McCulloch, Chairman, National Labor Relations Board et al., v. Sociedad Nacional de Marineros de Honduras*, Supreme Court, 372 US 10, decided February 1963, available at Lexis-Nexis.

87. Carlisle, *Sovereignty for Sale*, 165.

88. *McCulloch v. Sociedad*.

89. Harvey, *Brief History of Neoliberalism*, 70.

90. *McCulloch v. Sociedad*; quoted in Harvey, *Brief History of Neoliberalism*, 74; Carlisle, *Sovereignty for Sale*, 172; Chapman, *Trouble on Board*, xxii.

91. Chapman, *Trouble on Board*, xxvi–28.

92. Ibid., 79–80.

93. Charles T. Lee, "Bare Life, Interstices, and the Third Space of Citizenship," *Women's Studies Quarterly* 38, nos. 1/2 (2010): 57–81; Monisha das Gupta, "Housework, Feminism and Labor Activism: Lessons from Domestic Workers in New York," *Signs* 33, no. 3 (2008): 532–537.

CHAPTER 4

1. Scott Kurashige, *The Shifting Grounds of Race: Black and Japanese Americans in the Making of Multiethnic Los Angeles* (Princeton, NJ: Princeton University Press, 2010), 2–8.

2. Alicia Schmidt Camacho, *Migrant Imaginaries: Latino Cultural Politics in the U.S.-Mexico Borderlands* (New York: New York University Press, 2008), 115–120.

3. "Concentration Camp Roundup in the Works," *National Guardian*, January 30, 1952, 5; "Four Still Held in California: Case Goes to High Court," *National Guardian*, May 25, 1951, 6; Gustavo Arellano, "Whatever Happened to the Santa Ana Four? Orange County Seethes with Immigration Raids, Demonized Mexicans, and Appeals for Amnesty," *Orange County Weekly*, July 12, 2007.

4. Evelyn Hu-Dehart, *Yaqui Resistance and Survival: The Struggle for Land and Autonomy* (Madison: University of Wisconsin Press, 1984), 163–175; Sterling Evans,

Bound in Twine: The History and Ecology of the Hennequin-Wheat Complex for Mexico and the American and Canadian Plains, 1880–1950 (College Station: Texas A&M University Press, 2007), 72.

5. Wayne Patterson, *The Korean Frontier in America: Immigration to Hawaii, 1896–1910* (Honolulu: University of Hawai'i, 1988), 128–138.

6. George Sánchez, *Becoming Mexican American: Ethnicity and Culture in Chicano Los Angeles, 1900–1945* (New York: Oxford University Press, 1995), 38–56.

7. Hu-DeHart, *Yaqui Resistance and Survival*, 175–186; for instances of transnational repression as well as resistance, see Christina Heatherton, "University of Radicalism: Ricardo Flores Magón and Leavenworth Penitentiary," *American Quarterly* 66, no. 3 (2014): 557–581.

8. Edward H. Spicer, *The Yaquis, a Cultural History* (Tucson: University of Arizona Press, 1980), 232–246; David G. Gutiérrez, *Walls and Mirrors: Mexican Americans, Mexican Immigrants, and the Politics of Ethnicity* (Berkeley: University of California Press, 1995), 40; Sánchez, *Becoming Mexican American*, 17–37.

9. Patterson, *Korean Frontier in America*, 106.

10. Erika Lee and Judy Yung, *Angel Island: Immigrant Gateway to America* (New York: Oxford University Press, 2010), 180–199; Richard Kim, *The Quest for Statehood: Korean Immigrant Nationalism and U.S. Sovereignty, 1905–1946* (New York: Oxford University Press, 2011), 25.

11. Patterson, *Korean Frontier in America*, 135; Jordan Sand, "Gentlemen's Agreement, 1908: Fragments for a Pacific History," *Representations* 107, no. 1 (2009): 91–127, 109.

12. Peter Hyun, *Man Sei! The Making of a Korean American* (Honolulu: University of Hawai'i Press, 1986), 26.

13. Soon Hyun, Affidavit, State of California, County of Los Angeles, March 23, 1954, box
834, folder 24, Mudd Library, Princeton University, ACLU Collection, 3.

14. Patterson, *Korean Frontier in America*, 94; Hyun, *Man Sei!*, 27; also see Diamond Kimm, Affidavit, box 11, folder 43, "Individual Case Files: Diamond Kimm," Los Angeles Committee for the Protection of the Foreign Born (LACPFB), Southern California Research Library.

15. Hyun, *Man Sei!*; see also S. Hyun, Affidavit, 2; David Hyun, "Preface," in Peter Hyun, *In the New World: The Making of a Korean American* (Honolulu: University of Hawai'i Press, 1995).

16. Harry H. L. Kitano and Roger Daniels, *Asian Americans: Emerging Minorities* (Englewood Cliffs, NJ: Prentice Hall, 1995), 113–117; 7,266 Koreans immigrated to Hawai'i, another 1,033 to Mexico.

17. Hyun, *Man Sei!*, 158–159; for rivalries in the Korean nationalist community in Hawai'i, see Kim, *Quest for Statehood*, 92–108.

18. Noted in Mary Lisbeth Haas, "The Barrios of Santa Ana: Community, Class and Urbanization, 1850–1947" (PhD diss., University of California, Irvine, 1985), 52; see also Sánchez, *Becoming Mexican American*, 177–179; Camacho, *Migrant Imaginaries*, 30–37.

19. P. Hyun, *In the New World*, 207.

20. Sánchez, *Becoming Mexican American*, 226–251.

21. Mark Wild, *Street Meeting: Multiethnic Neighborhoods in Early Twentieth-Century Los Angeles* (Berkeley: University of California Press, 2005), 181–183;

Vicki Ruiz, "*Una Mujer sin Fronteras*: Luisa Moreno and Latina Labor Activism," *Pacific Historical Review* 73, no. 1 (2004): 1–20.

22. Quoted in Lee and Yung, *Angel Island*, 186.

23. Kim, *Quest for Statehood*, 120.

24. See Erika Lee, *At America's Gates: Chinese Immigration during the Exclusion Era* (Durham: University of North Carolina Press, 2007); Mae M. Ngai, "The Architecture of Race in American Immigration Law: A Reexamination of the Immigration Act of 1924," *Journal of American History* 86, no. 1 (1999): 67–92.

25. Kim, *Quest for Statehood*, 110; Wild, *Street Meeting*, 191.

26. Sánchez, *Becoming Mexican American*, 38–56.

27. Quoted in Gutiérrez, *Walls and Mirrors*, 114; see also 95–115.

28. Haas, "Barrios of Santa Ana," 3, 48–65.

29. Matt Garcia, *A World of Its Own: Race, Labor and Citrus in the Making of Greater Los Angeles, 1900–1970* (Chapel Hill: University of North Carolina Press, 2001), 77; Zaragosa Vargas, *Labor Rights Are Civil Rights: Mexican American Workers in Twentieth-Century America* (Princeton, NJ: Princeton University Press, 2008), 154, 224.

30. Haas, "Barrios of Santa Ana," 102.

31. Garcia, *A World of Its Own*, 159; see also discussion in Gutiérrez, *Walls and Mirrors*, 101–103.

32. Quoted in Haas, "Barrios of Santa Ana," 164; on *Mendez v. Westminster*, see Vicki Ruiz, "Tapestries of Resistance: Episodes of School Segregation and Desegregation in the Western United States," in *From the Grassroots to the Supreme Court: Brown v. Board of Education and American Democracy*, ed. Peter F. Lau (Durham, NC: Duke University Press, 2004), 44–66, 59; Vicki Ruiz, "We Always Tell Our Children They Are Americans: *Mendez v. Westminster* and the California Road to *Brown v. Board of Education*," *College Board Review*, no. 200 (Fall 2003): 20–27; Christopher Arriola, "Knocking on the Schoolhouse Door: *Mendez v. Westminster*: Equal Protection, Public Education, and Mexican Americans in the 1940s," *La Raza Law Journal* 8, no. 2 (1995): 166–208; Vargas, *Labor Rights Are Civil Rights*, 234.

33. Kurashige, *Shifting Grounds of Race*, 4.

34. Daniel Kanstroom, *Deportation Nation: Outsiders in American History* (Cambridge, MA: Harvard University Press, 2007), 137–139; see also Torrie Hester, *Deportation: The Origins of U.S. Policy* (Philadelphia: University of Pennsylvania Press, 2017), esp. 82–112.On the IWW and Free Speech fights in southern California, see Matthew S. May, *Soapbox Rebellion: The Hobo Orator Union and the Free Speech Fights of the Industrial Workers of the World, 1909–1916* (Birmingham: University of Alabama Press, 2013), 63–81; my attention was first drawn to this story when I read Jim Miller's novel, *Flash* (New York: AK Press, 2010).

35. In fact, historian Friedrich Katz argues that the Punitive Expedition of 1916 marked the last U.S. military incursion into Mexico, making Mexico unique in Latin America. The U.S.-Mexico border, then, becomes the site of enforcements that have elsewhere been levied by direct invasion or subversive intervention through proxy wars; Friedrich Katz, "Pancho Villa and the Attack on Columbus, New Mexico," *American Historical Review* 83, no. 1 (1978): 130. See also Gerald Horne, *Black and Brown: African Americans and the Mexican Revolution, 1910–1920* (New York: New York University Press, 2005), 138.

36. Evans, *Bound in Twine*, 98–99; Mitchell Yockelson, "The United States

Armed Forces and the Mexican Punitive Expedition: Part I," *Prologue Magazine* 29, no. 3 (1997), available at www.archives.gov/publications/prologue/1997, accessed December 13, 2011; Katz, "Pancho Villa and the Attack on Columbus," 103–106.

37. Evans, *Bound in Twine*, xviii, 103–109.

38. Horne, *Black and Brown*, 141; Katz, "Pancho Villa and the Attack on Columbus," 101. Questions of political alliance and the flow of arms, in the context of World War I, swirl around the considerable scholarship on the timing and location of the raid.

39. Quoted in Yockelson, "United States Armed Forces: Part I"; see also Mitchell Yockelson, "The United States Armed Forces and the Mexican Punitive Expedition: Part II," *Prologue Magazine* 29, no. 4 (1997), available at www.archives.gov/publications/prologue/1997, accessed December 13, 2011.

40. Yockelson, "United States Armed Forces: Part I." For more on intrigue in the revolution-era borderlands, see Michael M. Smith, "Andrés G. García: Venustiano Carranza's Eyes, Ears, and Voice on the Borderland," *Mexican Studies/Estudios Mexicanos* 23, no. 2 (2007): 355–386.

41. James Brown Scott, "The American Punitive Expedition into Mexico," *American Journal of International Law* 10, no. 2 (1916): 337–340.

42. Yockelson, "United States Armed Forces: Part II."

43. Evans, *Bound in Twine*, 71; Hu-Dehart, *Yaqui Resistance and Survival*, 159, 163.

44. "Guard of the Borders: Joseph May Swing," *New York Times*, April 25, 1958, in Joseph M. Swing Papers, Archives Building 950, Bay 5, Row 172, Face T, Shelf 5, Restricted Circulation, U.S. Army Military History Institute, Carlisle Barracks, Carlisle, Pa. 17013–5008; Transcript of Oral Interviews of Lieutenant General Swing from 26 August 1971, conducted by D. Clinton James of Mississippi State University, and from 21 June 1967, conducted by Ed Edwin of Columbia University, box 42, folder 10, Joseph May Swing Papers, U.S. Army Military History Institute Carlisle Barracks, Carlisle, Pa. 17013–5008.

45. Kelly Lytle Hernandez, *Migra! A History of the U.S. Border Patrol* (Berkeley: University of California Press, 2010), 129.

46. "World War II: Liberating Los Baños Internment Camp," available at http://www.historynet.com/world-war-ii-liberating-los-banos-internment-camp.htm, accessed December 13, 2011.

47. Hernandez, *Migra!*, 182–183.

48. Transcript of Oral Interviews, 2.

49. "A Brief History of the LACPFB," box 1, folder 1, LACPFB Papers, Southern California Research Library; see also Cindy I-Fen Cheng, *Citizens of Asian America: Democracy and Race during the Cold War* (New York: New York University Press, 2013); Camacho, *Migrant Imaginaries*, 118.

50. Celebration noted in *Torch*, April 1954, box 3, folder 3, LACPFB, Southern California Research Library.

51. Patricia Morgan, *Shame of a Nation: Police-State Terror against Mexican-Americans in the U.S.A.* (Los Angeles: LACPFB, 1954), Fromkin Special Collections, Golda Meir Library, University of Wisconsin–Milwaukee, 45–47.

52. See George J. Sánchez, "What's Good for Boyle Heights Is Good for the Jews: Creating Multiracialism on the Eastside in the 1950s," *American Quarterly* 56, no. 3 (2004): 633–661.

53. Ione Kramer, "Brownell's 'Operation Terror' in California," *National Guardian*, August 9, 1954, 7.

54. Morgan, *Shame of a Nation*, 5.

55. "Brief History of the Los Angeles Committee for the Protection of the Foreign Born, September 1950–August 1955," box 1, folder 1, "History of the Organization," LACPFB Papers, Southern California Research Library; "Salute to the Mexican Community," box 3, folder 5, LACPFB Papers, Southern California Research Library; Kanstroom, *Deportation Nation*, 137–139.

56. Morgan, *Shame of a Nation*, 39.

57. Ibid., 8.

58. "Case Record," in Arthur Dymtrick file, box 11, folder 5, "Case Record" in Petros Lezos case and flyer, "Victims of Deportation," box 12, folder 2, both in LACPFB Papers, Southern California Library for Social Studies and Research.

59. "Statement of David Diamond," January 1956, and "Case Record," both from box 11, folder 4, "Diamond, David and Frieda," LACPFB, Southern California Research Library.

60. "Case Record" and Letter from Joe Forer to Rose Chernin, both in box 11, folder 44, "Paul Shinsei Kochi file," LACPFB Papers; on Kochi's literary work, see "Japanese American Activist Timeline," available at https://jalegacy2011.word press.com/about/japanese-american-activist-timeline-five-generations-of-communi ty-activism/, accessed June 20, 2017.

61. "In San Diego Last Week," from *The Torch*, May 1953, LACPFB Papers, box 3, folder 2, Southern California Research Library.

62. Morgan, *Shame of a Nation*, 45–47, "The Negro Community Is Attacked," in Fourth Annual Conference Program, LACPFB files, box 9, folder 10, Southern California Research Library.

63. Gutiérrez, *Walls and Mirrors*, 106.

64. "Whatever Happened to the Santa Ana Four? Orange County Seethes with Immigration Raids, Demonized Mexicans and Appeals for Amnesty," *Orange County Weekly*, July 12, 2007, available at http://www.ocweekly.com, accessed December 2, 2011; Morgan, *Shame of a Nation*, 39.

65. Gutiérrez, *Walls and Mirrors*, 161.

66. Morgan, *Shame of a Nation*, 39–41.

67. "The Story of Justo Cruz as Told by His Son, Ladislao Cruz," box 9, folder 13, "Cruz, Justo S., 1951–54, 1956–57," LACPFB Papers, Southern California Library for Social Studies and Research.

68. Haas, "Barrios of Santa Ana," 101.

69. Ibid., 89–90.

70. "Whatever Happened to the Santa Ana Four?"

71. Editorial, *Korean Independence*, January 10, 1951.

72. *The Torch*, undated 1954 edition, in box 3, folder 2, LACPFB Papers, Southern California Research Library.

73. Kimm, Affidavit, in file "Diamond Kimm" in LACPFB Papers, Southern California Research Library.

74. Clipping from *People's Daily World*, January 11, 1951, box 38, Diamond Kimm Papers, American Committee for the Protection of the Foreign Born (ACPFB) Papers, Labadie Collection, University of Michigan.

75. *People's Daily World*, January 11, 1951.

76. Lee and Yung, *Angel Island*, 181.

77. See Cheng, *Citizens of Asian America*, esp. chap. 4.

78. "Exile: The Story of David Hyun," box 8, folder 62, Robert W. Kenny Collection, Southern California Research Library, 9–10.

79. *I Am Appealing on Behalf of My Youngest Son* . . . , pamphlet for the defense of David Hyun, box 8, folder 4, LACPFB Papers, Southern California Research Library; "Exile: The Story of David Hyun," box 8, folder 62, Robert W. Kenny Collection, Southern California Research Library.

80. Gutiérrez, *Walls and Mirrors*, 115.

81. From "Address Delivered by Luisa Moreno Bemis to the Twelfth Annual Convention, California CIO Council, October 15, 1949," box 9, folder 15, "Individual Cases: Luisa Moreno Bemis, 1949–1950," LACPFB, Southern California Research Library.

CHAPTER 5

1. Quoted in Carole Boyce Davies, *Left of Karl Marx: The Political Life of Black Communist Claudia Jones* (Durham, NC: Duke University Press, 2008), 141. The McCarran Act lent legitimacy to the existence of crimes of subversion by suggestion or persuasion. Many foreign-born activists had been associated with the Communist Party USA (CPUSA); many more had worked in organizations that had, at some point or another, worked *with* the party through the still-active alliances of the Popular Front. More broadly, many of these activists participated in creating the alliances and culture of the Popular Front through their work writing and editing newspapers, circulating flyers, and speaking at rallies and meetings. Under the McCarran Act, all of these activities could be construed as subversion.

2. Edwidge Danticat, *Create Dangerously: The Immigrant Artist at Work* (New York: Vintage, 2010), 16.

3. Nadia Ellis, *Territories of the Soul: Queered Belonging in the Black Diaspora* (Durham, NC: Duke University Press, 2015), 107.

4. "An Open Letter to the American People," *Eteenpäin*, January 25, 1950; translation from the Finnish by Dan Karvonen.

5. Boyce Davies, *Left of Karl Marx*, 147–151.

6. George Sánchez, comments at the ASA panel, Los Angeles, California, 2014; manuscript in possession of the author.

7. The lovely phrase is from a telegram sent to Jones by her friends Harriet and Abe Magil as she departed New York in 1955; box 1, "Bon Voyage Letters and Telegrams" folder, MG 692, Claudia Jones Memorial Collection, Schomburg Center for Research in Black Culture. Marika Sherwood asserts that she could find no further information on the Magils.

8. Boyce Davies, *Left of Karl Marx*, 71–73; Alicia Schmidt Camacho, *Migrant Imaginaries: Latino Cultural Politics in the U.S.-Mexico Borderlands* (New York: New York University Press, 2008), 5.

9. Claudia Jones, "Dear Comrade Foster: The Following Is the Autobiographical (Personal, Political, Medical) History That I Promised . . . Comradely, Claudia Jones (December 6, 1955)," with an introduction and bibliography by Peter Meyer Filardo, *American Communist History* 4, no. 1 (2005): 85–93; Clayton Goodwin, "Claudia Jones and the Fight for Black Dignity," *New African Woman*, January 2009, 6–9; Rebecca Hill, "Fosterites and Feminists, or 1950s Ultra-Leftists and the Invention of AmeriKKKa," *New Left Review* 228 (1998): 67–90; Donald Hinds,

"The *West Indian Gazette*: Claudia Jones and the Black Press in Britain," *Race and Class* 50, no. 1 (2008): 88–97.

10. Erik S. McDuffie, *Sojourning for Freedom: Black Women, American Communism, and the Making of Black Left Feminism* (Durham, NC: Duke University Press, 2011), 99.

11. *An End to the Neglect of the Problems of the Negro Woman* (New York: National Women's Commission, 1950), reprinted from *Political Affairs* (June 1949), Fromkin Collection, University of Wisconsin–Milwaukee.

12. Claudia Jones, *Women in the Struggle for Peace and Security* (New York: National Women's Commission, Communist Party, 1950, reprinted from *Political Affairs*), Wisconsin State Historical Society, Pamphlet Collection, 342.

13. Claudia Jones, "Testimony," in *13 Communists Speak to the Court*, ed. Elizabeth Gurley Flynn et al. (New York: New Century Publishers, 1953), 23–24.

14. Quote from Boyce Davies, *Left of Karl Marx*, 245; triple oppression as theorized Black Communist women also discussed in McDuffie, *Sojourning for Freedom*, 48–52, 112–116, 160–167.

15. Marika Sherwood, with Donald Hines, Colin Prescod, and the 1996 Claudia Jones Symposium, *Claudia Jones: A Life in Exile* (London: Lawrence and Wishart, 1999), 25.

16. "Paen to the Atlantic," box 1, "Poems" folder, Claudia Jones Memorial Collection, Schomburg Center for Research in Black Culture.

17. Sherwood, *Claudia Jones*, 44–73.

18. Pamphlet, box 3, Claudia Jones Memorial Collection, Schomburg Center for Research in Black Culture; Sherwood also refers to the McCarran-Walter bar against West Indians (*Claudia Jones*, 65).

19. Paul Warmington, *Black British Intellectuals and Education: Multiculturalism's Hidden History* (London: Routledge, 2014), 31–32; Sherwood, *Claudia Jones*, 90–92; Ellis writes, "In post-Windrush Britain, as questions about which subjects had access to the category of Englishness became more urgent, England was increasingly figured as a domestic family in which black subjects were problematic, potentially explosive interlopers" (*Territories of the Soul*, 102).

20. Quoted in Sherwood, *Claudia Jones*, 92.

21. Colin Prescod, "Carnival," in Sherwood, *Claudia Jones*, 150–152; Sherwood, *Claudia Jones*, 92–94, 126.

22. Quoted in Sherwood, *Claudia Jones*, 136.

23. Boyce Davies, *Left of Karl Marx*, 89.

24. Warmington, *Black British Intellectuals and Education*, 5–6.

25. Prescod, "Carnival," 159–161.

26. *London Observer*, September 1, 1963, box 1, "Afro Asian Community Organizations" folder, Claudia Jones Memorial Collection, Schomburg Center for Research in Black Culture; Sherwood, 48.

27. Quoted in Sherwood, *Claudia Jones*, 146.

28. I cannot quite document that Hall and Jones met, but it is also difficult to imagine that their paths did not cross at some point. More broadly, Ellis notes the convergence of West Indian migration to Britain with the florescence of British cultural studies (*Territories of the Soul*, 11).

29. McDuffie, *Sojourning for Freedom*, 215–216.

30. Bill of Rights Conference Highlights, 1971, box 1, "1969–1974" folder,

American Committee for the Protection of the Foreign Born (ACPFB) Papers, Tamiment Library, New York University.

31. On Hyun's Communist Party membership, see Cheng, *Citizens of Asian America*, 128; on Park, see "Anti-Rhee Korean Wins Stay of 'Death Sentence' Deportation Order to S. Korea," December 1951, box 828, ACLU Papers, subseries 3a.9, "Freedom of Belief, Expression and Association, Freedom of Movement, 1947–1976," Mudd Library, Princeton University.

32. On John Juhn, see Memo, 1955, box 14, folder 2, Los Angeles Committee for the Protection of the Foreign Born (LACPFB) Papers, Southern California Research Library.

33. I read the English-language pages of the paper for the years 1943 to 1955.

34. "*Korean Independence* Editor Offered Position by OSS," *Korean Independence*, February 16, 1944, 1.

35. Korean Methodist Church in Los Angeles, "The Birth of a Paper," *Korean Independence*, October 6, 1943, 2.

36. "Farrington Bill for Naturalization of Koreans," *Korean Independence*, July 12, 1944, 1; "U.S. Recognition of Koreans' Magnificent Fight," *Korean Independence*, March 21, 1945, 2.

37. Carol Anderson, *Eyes off the Prize: The United Nations and the African American Struggle for Rights, 1944–55* (New York: Cambridge University Press, 2003).

38. Editorial, "San Francisco Conference and Korea," *Korean Independence*, March 28, 1945, 2.

39. Editorial, "The Fourth of July, 1946," *Korean Independence*, July 3, 1946, 2.

40. "Is *Korean Independence* 'Un-American'?" *Korean Independence*, August 7, 1947, 2.

41. Cheng, *Citizens of Asian America*, 119. On the California UAAC, see ibid., 138; Baldwin affidavit, box 828, folder 3, "Diamond Kim, 1952," ACLU Papers, subseries 3a.9, "Freedom of Belief, Expression and Association, Freedom of Movement, 1947–1976," Mudd Library, Princeton University.

42. Clipping from *People's Daily World*, January 11, 1951, box 38, Diamond Kimm Papers, ACPFB Papers, Labadie Collection, University of Michigan.

43. "Fact Sheet" on the Kwaks, International League for the Rights of Man Papers, box 19, folder 3, Social Ethics Pamphlet Collection, Record Group 73, Yale University Divinity School.

44. "A Brief History of the LACPFB," box 1, folder 1, LACPFB Papers, Southern California Research Library.

45. "Chinese American Hit Immigration Dep't Bias," *Korean Independence*, October 6, 1948, 2.

46. "The American Way of Life," *Korean Independence*, September 1, 1948, 2.

47. This insight comes from Ashley Marie Zampogna-Krug, who worked as a project assistant for me reading microfilm of the *Korean Independence*; "We Koreans Protest Yoshida," *Korean Independence*, May 10, 1950; "Fight for People's Peace and Happiness in Asia!" *Korean Independence*, May 17, 1950.

48. "The Korean War and the Deportation Drive," *Korean Independence*, December 5, 1951.

49. "Participate at Home," *Korean Independence*, February 20, 1952.

50. Joseph Keith, *Unbecoming Americans: Writing Race and Nation from the Shadows of Citizenship, 1945–1960* (New Brunswick, NJ: Rutgers University Press, 2013).

51. "A Happy and Peaceful New Year to Our Readers," *Korean Independence*, December 31, 1952.

52. It read:

LET AMERICA BE AMERICA AGAIN

Let America be America again.
Let it be the dream it used to be.
Let it be the pioneer on the plain
Seeking a home where he himself is free.

(America never was America to me.)
Let America be the dream the dreamers dreamed—
Let it be that great strong land of love
Where never kings connive nor tyrants scheme
That any man be crushed by one above.

(It never was America to me.)

O, let my land be a land where Liberty
Is crowned with no false patriotic wreath,
But opportunity is real, and life is free,
Equality is in the air we breathe.

(There's never been equality for me,
Nor freedom in this "homeland of the free.")

LANGSTON HUGHES, 1902–1967

53. Speech by David Hyun, box 8, folder 1, LACPFB Papers, subseries B, "The Terminal Island Four," Southern California Research Library.

54. US District Court for N. District CA, S. Div: *Sang Ryup Park v. Bruce G. Barber*, Dist Dir US INS N. Dist Ca. Opinion and Order Granting Petition for Writ of Habeas Corpus, August 1952, available at http://law.justia.com/cases/federal/district-courts/FSupp/107/605/1653434/, accessed June 20, 2017.

55. Erika Lee and Judy Yung, *Angel Island: Immigrant Gateway to America* (Oxford: Oxford University Press, 2010), 181; *Arirang: Asia's Heartbeat*, February 28, 2012; available at http://www.arirang.co.kr/News/News_View.asp?nseq=126518, accessed March 26, 2015.

56. Cheng, *Citizens of Asian America*, 129–134.

57. "Three Alleged Reds Here in Deportation Quarters," *Los Angeles Times*, October 24, 1950, 1; "Ground Broken for Hospital in Airport Area," *Los Angeles Times*, June 29, 1958, F10.

58. Depositions in file "Diamond Kimm," LACPFB Papers, Southern California Research Library.

59. For the effects of the absence of the left in Los Angeles, particularly during the period around the Watts riots, see Gerald Horne, *Fire This Time: The Watts Uprising and the 1960s* (New York: Da Capo Press, 1995), esp. 3–22.

60. Barbara Lenox, "This House Lives Way beyond Its Walls," *Los Angeles*

Times, August 3, 1958, 114; "Firm Opened by Architects," *Los Angeles Times*, September 3, 1961, H8.

61. Lenox, "This House Lives," 114; see Cheng, *Citizens of Asian America*, 21–85.

62. Jordan Sand, "Gentlemen's Agreement, 1908: Fragments for a Pacific History," *Representations* 107, no. 1 (2009): 91–127, 114.

63. Ibid., 117.

64. See, for example, Beverly Johnson, "A House Divided," *Los Angeles Times*, June 11, 1961, A24.

65. Glenn Omatsu, "The 'Four Prisons' and the Movements of Liberation: Asian American Activism from the 1960s to the 1990s," in *The State of Asian America: Activism and Resistance in the 1990s*, ed. Karin Aguilar–San Juan (Boston: South End Press, 1994), 19–69; Scott Kurashige, *The Shifting Grounds of Race: Black and Japanese Americans in the Making of Multiethnic Los Angeles* (Princeton, NJ: Princeton University Press, 2008), 184; Edward T. Chang and Jeannette Diaz-Veizades, *Ethnic Peace in the American City: Building Community in Los Angeles and Beyond* (New York: New York University Press, 1999), 18, 83.

66. Horne, *Fire This Time*, 287, 322–336.

67. Kurashige, *Shifting Grounds of Race*, 284; see also 264–285; Kelly Simpson, "Three Waves of Little Tokyo Redevelopment," available at http://www.kcet .org/socal/departures/little-tokyo/three-waves-of-little-tokyo-redevelopment.html, accessed April 30, 2015.

68. Lou Desser, "Little Tokyo's Grass Roots Project: Plaza Conceived, Developed, Funded by Local Shopkeepers," *Los Angeles Times*, April 24, 1977, 11.

69. "Japanese Village Shop Plaza Opens," *Los Angeles Times*, October 29, 1978, J17; Ruth Ryon, "Ceremonies a Prologue to Nisei Week," *Los Angeles Times*, August 10, 1980, J28.

70. Omatsu, "The 'Four Prisons,'" 33–43; Alvina Lew, "Japanese Village Wins U.S. Design Award," *Asian Week*, April 4, 1986, 13; "Japanese Village Plaza Receives Award," *Los Angeles Times*, March 23, 1986, I1.

71. "Little Tokyo—The Magnet," *Asian Week*, February 6, 1987, 99.

72. Alvina Lew, "David Hyun Turns 70," *Asian Week*, February 20, 1987, 11; "Korean American Pioneer Dies at 85," *Korea Times*, October 24, 1990, 15. This second article is particularly interesting, as it notes the obituary information as having been given by David Hyun.

73. David Hyun, "Los Angeles: An East-West Ethnic Miracle of Global Proportions," *Los Angeles Times*, July 15, 1983, D7.

74. David Hyun, "Reflections on the Korean American Identity," *Korea Times*, April 7, 1993, 6.

75. Kurashige, *Shifting Grounds of Race*, 285.

76. Nadia Ellis, *Territories of the Soul: Queered Belonging in the Black Diaspora* (Durham, NC: Duke University Press, 2015), 6.

CHAPTER 6

1. Widely disseminated in the mass media at the time, this full account is taken from the *William Heikkila Memorial Journal*, produced after his death. Aune Helenius, editor, January 1961, box 1, William Heikkila Papers, Immigration History Research Center, University of Minnesota, Minneapolis.

2. See http://familialatinaunida.com/ and http://icirr.org/content/centro-sin-fronteras, both accessed March 3, 2014; Don Terry, "No Way Out," *Chicago Tribune*, August 5, 2007.

3. "Crusade Ends in Arrest: Immigration Authorities Begin Deportation Proceedings against Elvira Arellano after Activist Is Arrested Leaving L.A. Church," *Chicago Tribune*, August 20, 2007.

4. See John Aguilar, "Feds Grant Jeannette Vizguerra, Arturo Hernandez Garcia, Stays of Deportation," *Denver Post*, May 11, 2017, available at www.denverpost.com/2017/05/11/jeanette-vizguerra-arturo-hernandez-garcia-stays-deportation/, accessed June 21, 2017; America Ferrera, "Jeannette Vizguerra," *Time Magazine*, available at http://time.com/collection/2017-time-100/4736271/jeanette-vizguerra/, accessed June 21, 2017.

5. Historian Mae Ngai has shown that the construction of illegality has a long history, entwined with the rise of what historian Erika Lee refers to as "gatekeeping" in the late nineteenth and early twentieth centuries. Literary scholar Scott Michaelson traces the evisceration of rights characteristic of the category of the "illegal alien" to the "state of emergency" first used to justify the incarceration of Japanese Americans during World War II. Further, historian Kelly Lytle Hernandez argues that the triumph of Operation Wetback (1951–1954) lay not in its much-heralded "cleanup" of the U.S.-Mexico border but in its profound racialization of the terms "wetback" and "illegal alien." Scott Michaelsen, "Between Japanese American Internment and the USA PATRIOT Act: The Borderlands and the State of Permanent Racial Exception" *Aztlán: A Journal of Chicano Studies* 30, no. 2 (2005): 87–111; Kelly Lytle Hernandez, *Migra! A History of the U.S. Border Patrol* (Berkeley: University of California Press, 2010); Mai Ngai, *Impossible Subjects: Illegal Aliens and the Making of Modern America* (Princeton, NJ: Princeton University Press, 2014); Erika Lee, *At America's Gates: Chinese Immigration during the Exclusion Period* (Chapel Hill: University of North Carolina Press, 2003).

6. Raymond Williams, *Marxism and Literature* (New York: Oxford University Press, 1978), 121–135; Shelley Streeby, *Radical Sensations: World Movements, Violence and Visual Culture* (Durham, NC: Duke University Press, 2013), 15; Natalia Molina, *How Race Is Made in America: Immigration, Citizenship, and the Historical Power of Racial Scripts* (Berkeley: University of California Press, 2013).

7. "Executive Order: Border Security and Immigration Enforcement Improvements," available at www.whitehouse.gov/the-press-office/2017/01/25/executive-order-border-security-and-immigration-enforcement-improvements, accessed June 21, 2017.

8. Michael Denning, *The Cultural Front: The Laboring of American Culture in the Twentieth Century* (New York: Verso, 2011), 64, 83.

9. Jodi Dean, *Aliens in America: Conspiracy Cultures from Outerspace to Cyberspace* (Ithaca, NY: Cornell University Press, 1998, 17. These Cold War laws deployed a long-standing vocabulary to talk about the foreign born. Adam Smith distinguishes between "alien" and native-born merchants in *The Wealth of Nations*; Adam Smith, *An Inquiry into the Nature and Causes of the Wealth of Nations* (Hamburg, Germany: Management Laboratory Press, 2008). Thomas Jefferson speaks of limitations on property holding by "aliens" in *Notes on Virginia*; Thomas Jefferson, *Notes on the State of Virginia* (Chapel Hill: University of North Carolina Press, 2011). Legal use of the term "alien" in the United States dates back to questions that arose early

about loyalty and inclusion. The Alien Naturalization Act of 1790 specified that only "free white persons" of "good moral character" could become citizens; "aliens ineligible for citizenship" were excluded. Subsequently, concerns over the loyalties of new Americans culminated in the Alien and Sedition Laws of 1798. Two particular Alien and Sedition laws, the Alien Friends and Alien Enemies acts, provided guidance about federal conduct toward the foreign born in wartime.

10. Paul P. Kennedy, "Ex-Red Alien Loses Deportation Fight," *New York Times*, February 11, 1950, 1, 3.

11. Ibid. The Harisiades case is covered by Daniel Kanstroom in his important book *Deportation Nation: Outsiders in American History* (Cambridge, MA: Harvard University Press, 2007), 203–207.

12. "The treaty of Guadalupe Hidalgo, which ended this unjust war, established for Mexicans living in this conquered territory the rights of culture, religion, property and political rights." From Patricia Morgan, *Shame of the Nation: A Documented Story of Police-State Terror against Mexican-Americans in the USA* (LA CPFB), reprinted in Buff, ed., *Immigrant Rights in the Shadows of Citizenship* (New York: 2008), 232. I am grateful to Cutler Edwards for pointing out the parallels with contemporary civil rights struggles in southern California, in particular the school desegregation case *Mendez v. Westminster* (1947). See also Robert Lichtman, *The Supreme Court and McCarthy Era Repression* (Champaign-Urbana: University of Illinois Press, 2012), 49; "High Court Backs McCarran Act; Rules Ex-Red Alien Is Deportable," *New York Times*, May 25, 1954, 1; "Worker Ordered Deported as Red Party Man," *Los Angeles Times*, December 28, 1951, B4; "Man Deported to Mexico as Last Plea Fails," *Los Angeles Times*, January 1, 1955, 7.

13. Abner Green, *The Deportation Drive vs the Bill of Rights: The McCarran Act and the Foreign Born*, pamphlet, box 2, "Charles Rowoldt—Correspondence and Pamphlet—All," Enkel Papers, Immigration History Research Center, University of Minnesota, Minneapolis.

14. "5 Aliens Arrested as 2 Get Hearings," *New York Times*, September 25, 1948, 8.

15. Dean, *Aliens in America*, 34–38; *Oxford English Dictionary*, "Alien," available at https://en.oxforddictionaries.com/definition/alien, accessed June 21, 2017.

16. "To the Families of Deportees," from Irving Taffler, February 8, 1951, in "Charles Rowoldt: Legal Papers and Notes, November 1950–March 1952" folder, Charles Rowoldt Papers, Immigration History Research Center, University of Minnesota, Minneapolis.

17. "Heikkinen Indictment Stands, Judge Rules," *Superior Evening Telegram*, October 20, 1953, folder 6, "Knut Heikkinen—Correspondence, Legal papers, notes, June 1952–1954," Kenneth Enkel Papers, Immigration History Research Center, University of Minnesota, Minneapolis.

18. Box 2, "Heikkila, *William v. Barber*, Complaint for Injunction #35 373," folder, William Heikkila Papers, Immigration History Research Center, University of Minnesota, Minneapolis.

19. Plaintiff's Opening Motion in Opposition to Motion to Dismiss, U.S. District for Northern California Southern Division, *Heikkila v. Barber et al.*, in "Heikkila, *William v. Barber*, Complaint for Injunction #35 373" folder, Heikkila Papers, Immigration History Research Center, University of Minnesota, Minneapolis. Harisiades quote from Kanstroom, *Deportation Nation*, 204.

20. Charles Rowoldt, Petitioner, v. J. D. Perfetto, Acting Officer in Charge, Immigration and Naturalization Service, Department of Justice, St. Paul, Minnesota, 355 U.S. 115 (78 S. Ct. 180, 2 L.Ed.2d 140), available at http://www.law.cornell.edu/supremecourt/text/355/115, accessed January 31, 2013; see also Mary Ellen Leary, "Heikkila's Case Isn't the First, Say Lawyers," *San Francisco News*, April 28, 1958, 4, "Heikkila, William, Exclusion Hearings—1958 (Evidence-Press Clippings)" folder, William Heikkila Papers, Immigration History Research Center, University of Minnesota, Minneapolis.

21. Susan L. Carruthers, *Cold War Captives: Imprisonment, Escape, and Brainwashing* (Berkeley: University of California Press, 2009), 4–5.

22. Ibid., 10. On captivity narratives, see June Namias, *White Captives: Gender and Ethnicity on the American Frontier* (Durham, NC: Duke University Press, 1993); James J. Buss, *Winning the West with Words: Language and Conquest in the Lower Great Lakes* (Norman: University of Oklahoma Press, 2011).

23. Rebecca Nell Hill, *Men, Mobs, and Law: Anti-lynching and Labor Defense in U.S. Radical History* (Durham, NC: Duke University Press, 2008), 2.

24. The term is Moustafa Bayoumi's; see "Racing Religion," *CR: The New Centennial Review* 6, no. 2 (2006): 267–293, 276.

25. Franca Iacovetta, *Gatekeepers: Reshaping Immigrant Lives in Cold War Canada* (Toronto: Between the Lines Press, 2006), 22–48.

26. "Arrest Slav Congress Aid as Red Alien," *Chicago Daily Tribune*, September 24, 1948, 1.

27. Rachel Batch, "Defeating All the Dark Forces: Anti Fascism, Transnationalism, and American Slavs," presented at American Studies Association, San Juan, Puerto Rico, November 2012.

28. John Fischer, "Report Brands Slav Congress Tool of Russia," *Chicago Daily Tribune*, June 26, 1949, 8.

29. "U.S. Slav Congress Called Soviet Tool," *New York Times*, June 26, 1949, 1.

30. "Salute Stalin, Boo Bynes at N.Y. Slav Rally," *Chicago Daily Tribune*, September 23, 1946, 11; see also "Rally Here Cheers Message by Stalin," *New York Times*, September 23, 1946, 1; "Police Guard Bor at Mass Meeting: Polish Underground Hero Greeted Here Yesterday," *New York Times*, May 27, 1946, 6.

31. "Judge Frees Sixteen Aliens: Overturns Attorney General," *Chicago Tribune*, November 18, 1950, B14.

32. "Detentions Protested: Committee Charges 4 Are Held at Ellis Island 'Illegally,'" *New York Times*, July 14, 1949, 18; "Judge Bondy Says 'Godspeed' to Red," *New York Times*, July 13, 1949, 18; "Alien Reds Ruled Eligible to Bond," *New York Times*, August 9, 1949, 12; "Court Orders Cut in Bail of Pirinsky," *New York Times*, October 4, 1929, 19; "Freed in Lower Bail," *New York Times*, October 6, 1949, 32; "Arrest Slav Congress Aid as Red Alien."

33. Arthur Garfield Hayes, "Introduction," in Ellen Raphael Knauff, *The Ellen Knauff Story* (New York: Norton, 1952), x–xi; see also Charles D. Weisselberg, "Exclusion and Detention of Aliens: Lessons from the Lives of Ellen Knauff and Ignatz Mezei," *University of Pennsylvania Law Review* 933 (1994): 136–138, available at http://scholarship.law.berkeley.edu/facpubs/153.

34. Knauff, *The Ellen Knauff Story*, 235–236.

35. Carruthers, *Cold War Captives*, 1–22.

36. "German-Born Bride Allowed to Enter U.S.," *Atlanta Daily World*, Febru-

ary 1, 1951, 3. This was the only coverage I found of Knauff's case in the African American press.

37. John Oakes, "It Happened Here: *The Ellen Knauff Story*," *New York Times Book Review*, March 30, 1952, 36.

38. Laurence T. Heron, "An Immigrant's Struggles with the Burocrats [*sic*]," review of *The Ellen Knauff Story*, *Chicago Daily Tribune*, May 25, 1952, C8.

39. "On Television," *New York Times*, April 3, 1952, S3.

40. "Alleged Red Alien Is Arrested Here," *New York Times*, October 25, 1950, 25; "9 More Arrested in Red Alien Drive," *New York Times*, October 25, 1950, 1; "5 Arrested Here in Red Alien Drive," *New York Times*, October 24, 1950, 17.

41. On the Los Angeles Committee for the Protection of the Foreign Born, see Jeffrey M. Garcilazo, "McCarthyism, Mexican Americans, and the Lost Angeles Committee for the Protection of the Foreign-Born, 1950–1945," *Western Historical Quarterly* 32, no. 3 (2001): 273–290; George J. Sánchez, "What's Good for Boyle Heights Is Good for the Jews: Creating Multiracialism on the Eastside during the 1950s," *American Quarterly* 56, no. 3 (2004): 633–661.

42. For example, see "Deportation Case Uses '39 Testimony," *Los Angeles Times*, April 21, 1951, A1.

43. "Court Studies Seized Aliens' Pleas for Writs," *Los Angeles Times*, November 8, 1950, A9; see also "Korean Seized in Alien Roundup Seeks Release," *Los Angeles Times*, November 26, 1950, 35. The practice of holding noncitizens without bail was ultimately affirmed by the Supreme Court, with Justices Black, Burton, and Frankfurter dissenting; this decision received front-page coverage from the *New York Times*, with the *Atlanta Daily World* also noting the decision. See Luther A. Huston, "High Court Upholds Deportation and Denial of Bail to Alien Reds," *New York Times*, March 11, 1952, 1; "High Court Upholds Contempt Convictions of Red Leaders," *Atlanta Daily World*, March 11, 1952, 2; "Attorneys for Unfriendly Witnesses Named as Reds," *Los Angeles Times*, December 7, 1956, 1.

44. George Lipsitz, *American Studies in a Moment of Danger* (Minneapolis: University of Minnesota Press, 2001), 47. Peter Hyun, *In the New World: The Making of a Korean-American* (Honolulu: University of Hawai'i Press, 1995). The Magnuson Act of 1943 allowed a small number of Chinese Americans to naturalize.

45. Carruthers, *Cold War Captives*, 174–184.

46. "Pair Face Deportation," *New York Times*, December 24, 1955, 25.

47. Barbara J. Beeching, "Paul Robeson and the Black Press: The 1950 Passport Controversy," *Journal of African American History* 87 (Summer 2002): 339–354.

48. "Woman Communist Leader Is Targeted for Deportation," *New York Times*, January 21, 1948, 1.

49. Walter White, Editorial, *Chicago Defender*, April 3, 1948, 15; "Civil Rights Congress on Tour with 'Peace and Freedom Caravan,'" *New York Amsterdam News*, June 24, 1950, 4.

50. "Protest the Deportation of Claudia Jones," *Atlanta Daily World*, July 3, 1951, 2; "Claudia Jones Draws Lowest Term in Trial," *New York Amsterdam News*, February 7, 1953, 1.

51. Hernandez, *Migra!*, 164, 205.

52. Associated Press, "Jenner Group Sees Red Peril in 'Wetbacks,'" *Washington Post and Times Herald*, May 3, 1954, 2; "AFL Leaders Say Reds 'Pour in' with Wetbacks: Charge Potential Spies and Saboteurs Are Ignored by Red-Hunting Senators,"

Los Angeles Times, April 11, 1954, 17; Gladwin Hill, "Two Every Minute across the Border," *New York Times,* January 31, 1954.

53. Yanez quoted in Morgan, *Shame of the Nation,* pamphlet released by the Los Angeles Committee for the Protection of the Foreign-Born in 1954, in *Immigrant Rights in the Shadows of Citizenship,* ed. Rachel Ida Buff (New York University Press: New York, 2008), 236; David G. Gutiérrez, *Walls and Mirrors: Mexican Americans, Mexican Immigrants, and the Politics of Ethnicity* (Berkeley: University of California Press, 1995), 163–165.

54. By 1954, Engle was the chair of the American Jewish Committee (AJC). This suggests that the AJC's advocacy may have been characterized by similar divisions between Mexican Americans and other immigrants. "Fifth Concert Set for Sunday for Lith Aid, "*Chicago Daily Tribune,* October 21, 1954, S8; Letter to the Editor, *New York Times,* June 3, 1951, 150; John N. Popham, "Fight on Race Bias Seen in New Phase," *New York Times,* July 5, 1951, 21.

55. Molina, *How Race Is Made in America,* 132; "Roundup of Wetbacks Still On," *Los Angeles Times,* June 20, 1954, A1; "U.S. Patrol Halts Border Invasion," *Los Angeles Times,* June 17, 1955, 26; Bill Dredge, "Wetbacks Herded at Nogales Camp," *Los Angeles Times,* June 20, 1954, 1A.

56. Eric Tang, *Unsettled: Cambodian Refugees in the NYC Hyperghetto* (Philadelphia: Temple University Press, 2015), 10.

57. This international effort includes the work of Donna Gabaccia, Margarita Garcia Rojas, Paulina Rousseau, Justin Schell, Erica Toffoli, and myself.

CHAPTER 7

1. "Document from Special Meeting," 1974, box 1, "Council Meeting Minutes, 1973–76" folder, American Committee for the Protection of the Foreign Born (ACPFB) Papers, Labadie Collection, University of Michigan.

2. George Lipsitz, *Footsteps in the Dark: The Hidden History of Popular Music* (Minneapolis: University of Minnesota Press, 2007), vii–viii; Dipesh Chakrabarty, *Provincializing Europe: Postcolonial Thought and Historical Difference* (Princeton, NJ: Princeton University Press, 2000), 97–113.

3. The text of the January 2017 Executive Order is available at https://www.whitehouse.gov/the-press-office/2017/01/25/executive-order-border-security-and-immigration-enforcement-improvements, accessed June 21, 2017. *United States v. Brignoni Ponce,* 422 U.S. 873, 1974, available at https://supreme.justia.com/cases/federal/us/422/873/case.html, accessed February 18, 2016. On the history of urban raids, see Anna Pegler Gordon, *In Sight of America: Photography and the Development of U.S. Immigration Policy* (Berkeley: University of California Press, 2005), esp. 67–103; Kelly Lytle Hernandez, *Migra! A History of the U.S. Border Patrol* (Berkeley: University of California Press, 2010), esp. 169–196.

4. On Operation Wetback, see Natalia Molina, *How Race Is Made in America: Immigration, Citizenship, and the Historical Power of Racial Scripts* (Berkeley: University of California Press, 2013); David Gutiérrez, *Walls and Mirrors: Mexican Americans, Mexican Immigrants, and the Politics of Ethnicity* (Berkeley: University of California Press, 1995); Mae M. Ngai, *Impossible Subjects: Illegal Aliens and the Making of Modern America* (Princeton, NJ: Princeton University Press, 2004).

5. In box 10, folder 9, Bert Corona Papers; see also letter from Josephine Yanez, Los Angeles Committee for the Protection of the Foreign Born (LACPFB), to Abner

Green, May 18, 1956, box 1, folder 4, LACPFB Papers, Southern California Research Library. Patricia Morgan, *Shame of a Nation: Police-State Terror against Mexican-Americans in the U.S.A.* (Los Angeles: LACPFB, 1954), Fromkin Special Collections, Golda Meir Library, University of Wisconsin–Milwaukee. On McWilliams, see Michael Denning, *The Cultural Front: The Laboring of American Culture in the Twentieth Century* (New York: Verso, 1997).

6. David Bacon, *The Right to Stay Home: How US Policy Drives Mexican Migration* (Boston: Beacon Press, 2013).

7. "Synopsis of Proposed Petition to United Nations Commission on Human Rights Dealing with the Problems Facing Mexicans in the United States," box 2, folder 8, and *Our Badge of Infamy: A Petition to the United Nations on the Treatment of the Mexican Immigrant* (ACPFB, April 17, 1959), box 1, "1956–1959" folder, both in ACPFB Papers, Tamiment Library, New York University.

8. "Multi-ethnic internationalism" is Michael Denning's phrase; see Denning, *The Cultural Front*, 132.

9. Gutiérrez, *Walls and Mirrors*, 173.

10. Bill of Rights Conference Highlights, 1971, box 1, "1969–1974" folder, ACPFB Papers, Tamiment Library, New York University; Typed manuscript, Louise Pettibone Smith biography, box 1, "Biographical Information: Louise Pettibone Smith" folder, ACPFB Papers, Labadie Collection, University of Michigan.

11. Mario T. Garcia, *Memories of Chicano History: The Life and Narrative of Bert Corona* (Berkeley: University of California Press, 1994), 119.

12. "The Racist Content of the Walter-McCarran Law" (A Preliminary Memorandum), for New York Conference to Repeal the Walter-McCarran Law and Defend Its Victims, February 27, 1954, Yugoslav-American Hall, New York, box 1, "1951–1954" folder, Tamiment Library, New York University.

13. Ira Gollobin, "Democracy and the Deportation Laws," *Jewish Life*, June 1948, 16–19.

14. *The Torch*, October–November 1965, box 3, folder 8, LACPFB Papers, Southern California Research Library.

15. Carlos Montes, interview with author, October 2013, Milwaukee.

16. CASA bilingual flier, box 29, "Asociación Nacional México-Americana, 1952" folder, Bert Corona Papers (M248), 1923–1984, Stanford University Libraries, Special Collections; Garcia, *Memories of Chicano History*, 72–74; typed history of CASA, box 29, folder 8, Bert Corona Papers.

17. Notes, box 28, folder 11, "CASA Papers, flyers and misc. notes, 1973–75," Bert Corona Papers. Carlos Montes advised me of the significance of this case but could not recall the names of the murder victims when we spoke.

18. Pamphlet, box 29, folder 7, CASA documents, Bert Corona Papers.

19. "Stop Border Killings" flyer, box 10, folder 11, Bert Corona Papers.

20. Box 8, "Publicity/Activities/Events: 1968 Fight Back Rally, 12/15" folder, ACPFB Papers, Labadie Collection, University of Michigan.

21. See Keith Feldman, *Shadow over Palestine: The Imperial Life of Race in America* (Minneapolis: University of Minnesota Press, 2015), 114–115. On Ocean Hill–Brownsville, see Jerald E. Podair, *The Strike That Changed New York: Blacks, Whites, and the Ocean Hill–Brownsville Crisis* (New Haven: Yale University Press, 2002); Adina Back, "Blacks, Jews and the Struggle to Integrate Brooklyn's Junior High School 258: A Cold War Story," *Journal of American Ethnic History*, 20, no. 2 (2001): 38–69.

22. See David R. Roediger, *Working toward Whiteness: How America's Im-*

migrants Became White: The Strange Journey from Ellis Island to the Suburbs (New York: Basic Books, 2005); Matthew Frye Jacobson, *Whiteness of a Different Color: European Immigrants and the Alchemy of Race* (Cambridge, MA: Harvard University Press, 1998); Thomas J. Sugrue, *Origins of the Urban Crisis: Race and Inequality in Postwar Detroit* (Princeton, NJ: Princeton University Press, 2014).

23. Box 2, "1960–1968" folder, ACPFB Papers, Tamiment Library, New York University.

24. "Invitation to a National Meeting for the Rights of Foreign Born Americans, Jan 14 and 15, 1961," box 2, "1960–1968" folder, ACPFB Papers, Tamiment Library, New York University.

25. Press releases, April 3, 1967, and "Gus Polites (Greek) Dies in Exile," box 2, "1960–1968" folder, ACPFB Papers, Tamiment Library, New York University.

26. James Wechsler, "After 46 Years," *New York Post*, December 5, 1966, box 2, "1960–1968" folder, ACPFB Papers, Tamiment Library, New York University.

27. "Bill of Rights Conference Highlights," 1971, box 2, "1960–1968" folder, ACPFB Papers, Tamiment Library, New York University.

28. "Why? Exile and Second Class Citizenship," 1967, box 2, "1960–1968" folder, ACPFB Papers, Tamiment Library, New York University.

29. Minutes of Council Meeting, May 4, 1972, box 1, "Administration: Council Minutes, 1968–1972" folder, ACPFB Records, Labadie Collection, University of Michigan; Oral history interview with Henry Foner by Daniel Soyer, ILGWU Heritage Project, Kheel Center, Cornell University, available at http://ilgwu.ilr.cornell.edu/archives/oralHistories/HenryFoner.html. For unions engaged in immigrant rights, see box 21, folder 3, "Ad Hoc Committee against Repression in Haiti," Ira Gollobin Haitian Refugees Collection, Schomburg Center for Research in Black Culture; "In Defense of Foreign Born," *El Tiempo: El Diario de Todos los Hispanos*, March 12, 1972, New York, box 2, "1969–1974" folder, ACPFB Papers, Tamiment Library, New York University.

30. Box 2, "1960–1968" folder, ACPFB Papers, Tamiment Library, New York University.

31. Box 2, "1969–1974" folder, ACPFB Papers, Tamiment Library, New York University.

32. Eric Tang, *Unsettled: Cambodian Refugees in the NYC Hyperghetto* (Philadelphia: Temple University Press, 2015), 58–59.

33. "The Bill of Rights and the Foreign Born," speech given by Gollobin, at the Immigration Conference of New York Lawyers, February 22, 1975, box 9, folder 24, "The Bill of Rights of the Foreign Born, 1975," Bert Corona Papers; and "Letter," December 28, 1972, box 2, "1969–1974" folder, ACPFB Papers, Tamiment Library, New York University.

34. Press Release: "Important Disclosures in Damage Suit against Immigration Dragnet Arrests," March 22, 1976, box 21, folder 9, "ACPFB," Ira Gollobin Haitian Refugee Collection, Schomburg Center for Research in Black Culture.

35. Minutes of Council Meeting, May 4, 1972, box 1, "Administration: Council Minutes, 1968–1972," folder, ACPFB Records, Labadie Collection, University of Michigan.

36. "Will the Immigration Dragnet Reach You?"; "The Foreign Born and the Bill of Rights"; Letter from Gollobin to Corona, August 12, 1974, all in box 1, "1968–1974" folder, ACPFB Papers, Tamiment Library, New York University; "Charter of Rights for Immigrant Workers," box 10, folder 9, Bert Corona Papers.

37. Manny Ontiveros, "13 Haitians Face Deportation," *El Paso Herald Post*, January 13, 1977, box 4, folder 15, *"Louis v Nelson*, 1977," Ira Gollobin Haitian Refugee Collection, Schomburg Center for Research in Black Culture; "The Treatment of Haitian 'Boat People'—A National Scandal," 1979, "The Foreign Born and the Bill of Rights," "Press Release: 'Alert Action Blocks Sneak Deportation of Haitian Refugees in Miami: Tragedy Averted," January 4, 1975, all in box 2, folder 6, ACPFB Papers, Tamiment Library, New York University.

38. Statement of Joseph Simann, June 25, 1977, box 4, folder 15, *"Louis v Nelson*, 1977," Ira Gollobin Haitian Refugee Collection, Schomburg Center for Research in Black Culture.

39. Press Release: Grand Army Demonstration, 1974, box 21, folder 4, "Grand Army Demo, 1974," Ira Gollobin Haitian Refugee Papers, Schomburg Center for Research in Black Culture.

40. Suicide note in "Flyer #5: Ad Hoc Committee for the Defense of Haitian Refugees Meeting Notes, Info on Haiti," box 21, Ira Gollobin Haitian Refugee Papers, Schomburg Center for Research in Black Culture.

41. Flyer from Déville's funeral, box 2, "1969–1974" folder, ACPFB Papers, Tamiment Library, New York University.

42. Nadia Ellis, *Territories of the Soul: Queered Belonging in the Black Diaspora* (Durham, NC: Duke University Press, 2015), 4.

43. Box 1, "Administrative Dissolution of ACPFB (1982)" folder, ACPFB Papers, Labadie Collection, University of Michigan; Eunice Hyunhye Cho, "Beyond the Day without an Immigrant: Immigrant Communities Building a Sustainable Movement," in *Immigrant Rights in the Shadows of Citizenship,* ed. Rachel Ida Buff (New York: New York University Press, 2008), 94–121.

CONCLUSION

1. Walter Benjamin, "Theses on the Philosophy of History," in *Illuminations*, ed. Hannah Arendt (New York: Schocken Books, 1968), 253–264.

2. *"The United States v. Rose Kuznitz,"* box 27, Rose Chernin Case file, American Committee for the Protection of the Foreign Born Papers, Labadie Collection, University of Michigan.

3. Charlotte Kates, "Criminalizing Resistance," *Jacobin*, January 27, 2014, available at https://www.jacobinmag.com/2014/01/criminalizing-resistance/, accessed November 1, 2015.

4. Kim Chernin, *In My Mother's House* (New York: Ticknor and Fields, 1983), 38–48.

5. Mark Mondalek, "The Campaign against Rasmea Odeh," *Jacobin*, October 13, 2014, available at https://www.jacobinmag.com/2015/10/rasmea-odeh-palestine-israel-midwest-23-bds-fbi/, accessed October 30, 2015.

6. See http://www.aaan.org/, accessed August 18, 2016; for a discussion of INS/ICE persecution of Arab Muslim activists, see David Cole, *Enemy Aliens: Double Standards and Constitutional Freedoms in the War on Terrorism* (New York: New Press, 2003); in particular, the case of Pastor Rabih Haddad, which Cole covers in some depth, illustrates the ways in which transnational advocacy became grounds for suspicion after 9/11.

7. Cited in Mitri Raheb, *Faith in the Face of Empire: The Bible through Palestinian Eyes* (Maryknoll, NY: Orbis Books, 2014), 20.

BIBLIOGRAPHY

ARCHIVES

ACLU Papers, subseries 3a.9, "Freedom of Belief, Expression and Association, Freedom of Movement," Mudd Library, Princeton University.

American Committee for the Protection of the Foreign Born (ACPFB) Papers, Labadie Collection, University of Michigan.

American Committee for the Protection of the Foreign Born (ACPFB) Papers, Tamiment Library and Robert F. Wagner Labor Archives, New York University.

Bert Corona Papers, Special Collections, Stanford University.

Claudia Jones Memorial Collection and Ira Gollobin Haitian Refugees Collection, Schomburg Center for Research in Black Culture, New York Public Library.

Fromkin Special Collections, Golda Meir Library, University of Wisconsin–Milwaukee.

International Ladies Garment Workers Union Papers, Kheel Center, Cornell University.

Joseph M. Swing Papers, U.S. Army Military History Institute, Carlisle Barracks.

Los Angeles Committee for the Protection of the Foreign Born (LACPFB) Papers, Southern California Research Library. Pamphlet Collection, Wisconsin State Historical Society.

Romanzo Adams Social Research Laboratory, University Archives, University of Hawai'i, Manoa.

Seafarer's International Union Papers, Robert F. Wagner Labor Archives, Tamiment Library, New York University.

Seattle Civil Rights and Labor History Project.

Social Ethics Pamphlet Collection, Yale University Divinity School.

Vito Marcantonio Papers, Books and Manuscripts Division, New York Public Library.

William Heikkila Papers, Charles Rowoldt Papers, and Kenneth Enkel Papers, Immigration History Research Center, University of Minnesota.

ORAL HISTORY INTERVIEW

Carlos Montes, University of Wisconsin–Milwaukee, October 2013.

NEWSPAPERS

Asian Week
Atlanta Daily World
Baltimore Afro American
Chicago (Daily) Tribune
Chicago Defender
Eteenpäin
Jewish Life
Korean Independence
Korea Times
The Lamp
Los Angeles Times
National Guardian
New York Amsterdam News
New York Times
Orange County Weekly
People's Daily World
El Tiempo
The Torch
Washington Post

BOOKS AND ARTICLES

Anderson, Carol. *Eyes off the Prize: The United Nations and the African American Struggle for Rights, 1944–55*. New York: Cambridge University Press, 2003.

Arnold, Frank. "Humberto Silex: CIO Organizer from Nicaragua." *Southwestern Economy and Society* 4 (1978): 3–18.

Arriola, Christopher. "Knocking on the Schoolhouse Door: *Mendez v. Westminster*: Equal Protection, Public Education, and Mexican Americans in the 1940s." *La Raza Law Journal* 8, no. 2 (1995): 166–208.

Bacon, David. *The Right to Stay Home: How U.S. Policy Drives Mexican Migration*. Boston: Beacon Press, 2013.

Baldoz, Rick. *The Third Asiatic Invasion: Empire and Migration in Filipino America, 1898–1946*. New York: New York University Press, 2011.

Balthaser, Benjamin. *Anti-imperialist Modernism: Race and Transnational Radical Culture from the Great Depression to the Cold War*. Ann Arbor: University of Michigan Press, 2015.

Batch, Rachel. "Defeating All the Dark Forces: Anti Fascism, Transnationalism, and American Slavs." Presented at American Studies Association, San Juan, Puerto Rico, November 2012.

Bayoumi, Moustafa. "Racing Religion." *CR: The New Centennial Review* 6, no. 2 (2006): 267–293.

Beeching, Barbara J. "Paul Robeson and the Black Press: The 1950 Passport Controversy." *Journal of African American History* 87 (Summer 2002): 339–354.

Benjamin, Walter. "Theses on the Philosophy of History." In *Illuminations*, edited by Hannah Arandt, 253–264. New York: Schocken Books, 1968.

Boyce Davies, Carole. *Left of Karl Marx: The Political Life of Black Communist Claudia Jones*. Durham, NC: Duke University Press, 2008.

Buff, Rachel I. "Domestic Internationalisms, Imperial Nationalism: Civil Rights, Immigration, and Conjugal Military Policy." In *New Routes for Diaspora Studies*, edited by Sukanya Banerjeee, Aims McGuinness, and Steven C. McKay, 123–139. Bloomington: Indiana University Press, 2012.

———, ed. *Immigrant Rights in the Shadows of Citizenship*. New York: New York University Press, 2008.

Bulosan, Carlos. *America Is in the Heart*. Seattle: University of Washington Press, 1973.

Buss, James J. *Winning the West with Words: Language and Conquest in the Lower Great Lakes*. Norman: University of Oklahoma Press, 2011.

Cacho, Lisa Marie. *Social Death: Racialized Rightlessness and the Criminalization of the Unprotected*. New York: New York University Press, 2013.

Camacho, Alicia Schmidt. *Migrant Imaginaries: Latino Cultural Politics in the U.S.-Mexican Borderlands*. New York: New York University Press, 2008.

Camp, Jordan. *Incarcerating the Crisis: Freedom Struggles and the Rise of the Neoliberal State*. Berkeley: University of California Press, 2016.

Campi, Alicia J. "The McCarran-Walter Act: A Contradictory Legacy on Race, Quotas, and Ideology." Immigration Policy Brief, 2004, Illinois Coalition for Immigrant and Refugee Rights. Available at icirr.org.

Canaday, Margot. *The Straight State: Sexuality and Citizenship in Twentieth-Century America*. Princeton, NJ: Princeton University Press, 2009.

Carlisle, Rodney. *Sovereignty for Sale: The Origins and Evolution of Panamanian and Liberian Flag of Convenience Ships*. Annapolis, MD: Naval Institute Press, 1981.

Carruthers, Susan L. *Cold War Captives: Imprisonment, Escape, and Brainwashing*. Berkeley: University of California Press, 2009.

Chakrabarty, Dipesh. *Provincializing Europe: Postcolonial Thought and Historical Difference*. Princeton, NJ: Princeton University Press, 2000.

Chang, Edward T., and Jeannette Diaz-Veizades. *Ethnic Peace in the American City: Building Community in Los Angeles and Beyond*. New York: New York University Press, 1999.

Chapman, Paul K. *Trouble on Board: The Plight of International Seafarers*. Ithaca, NY: ILR Press, 1992.

Cheng, Cindy I-Fen. *Citizens of Asian America: Democracy, Race and the Cold War*. New York: New York University Press, 2013.

Cherney, Robert W. "Constructing a Radical Identity: History, Memory and the Seafaring Stories of Harry Bridges." *Pacific Historical Review* 70, no. 4 (2001): 571–599.

———. "The Making of a Labor Radical: Harry Bridges, 1901–1934." *Pacific Historical Review* 64, no. 3 (1995): 363–388.

Chernin, Kim. *In My Mother's House*. New York: Ticknor and Fields, 1983.

Cho, Carlene. "Not a Chinaman's Chance: Chinese Americans during the McCarthy Era." Student paper available at https://eee.uci.edu/programs/humcore/students/chopaper.htm.

Cho, Eunice Hyunhye. "Beyond the Day without an Immigrant: Immigrant Communities Building a Sustainable Movement." In *Immigrant Rights in the Shadows of Citizenship*, edited by Rachel Ida Buff, 94–121. New York: New York University Press, 2008.

Cole, David. *Enemy Aliens: Double Standards and Constitutional Freedoms in the War on Terrorism*. New York: New Press, 2003.

Collins, Jane. "Theorizing Wisconsin's 2011 Protests: Community-Based Unionism

Confronts Accumulation by Dispossession," *American Ethnologist* 39, no. 1 (2012): 6–20.

Currie, David P. "Flags of Convenience, American Labor, and the Conflict of Laws." *Supreme Court Review* 1963 (1963): 34–100.

Daniels, Roger. *Guarding the Golden Door: American Immigrants and Immigration Policy since 1882.* New York: Hill and Wang, 2004.

Danticat, Edwidge. *Create Dangerously: The Immigrant Artist at Work.* New York: Vintage, 2010.

das Gupta, Monisha. "Housework, Feminism and Labor Activism: Lessons from Domestic Workers in New York." *Signs* 33, no. 3 (2008): 532–537.

———. "The Neoliberal State and the Domestic Workers' Movement in New York City." *Canadian Woman Studies* 22, nos. 3/4 (2003): 78–85.

———. *Unruly Immigrants: Rights, Activism and Transnational South Asian Politics in the United States.* Chapel Hill, NC: Duke University Press, 2006.

Dean, Jodi. *Aliens in America: Conspiracy Cultures from Outerspace to Cyberspace.* Ithaca NY: Cornell University Press, 1998.

———. *The Communist Horizon.* New York: Verso, 2012.

Denning, Michael. *The Cultural Front: The Laboring of American Culture in the Twentieth Century.* New York: Verso, 2011.

Ellis, Nadia. *Territories of the Soul: Queered Belonging in the Black Diaspora.* Durham, NC: Duke University Press, 2015.

Ellison, Micah. "The Local 7/Local 37 Story: Filipino American Cannery Unionism in Seattle, 1940–1959." Seattle Civil Rights and Labor History Project. Available at http://depts.washington.edu/civilr/local_7.htm.

Euraque, Dario. "Review: Social, Economic and Political Aspects of the Carias Dictatorship in Honduras: The Historiography." *Latin American Research Review* 29, no. 1 (1994): 238–248.

Evans, Sterling. *Bound in Twine: The History and Ecology of the Hennequin-Wheat Complex for Mexico and the American and Canadian Plains, 1880–1950.* College Station: Texas A&M University Press, 2007.

Feldman, Keith. *Shadow over Palestine: The Imperial Life of Race in America.* Minneapolis: University of Minnesota Press, 2015.

Fowler, Josephine. *Japanese and Chinese Immigrant Activists: Organizing in American and International Communist Movements, 1919–1933.* New Brunswick, NJ: Rutgers University Press: 2007.

Freeman, Elizabeth. *Time Binds: Queer Temporalities, Queer Histories.* Durham, NC: Duke University Press, 2010.

Fujita-Rony, Dorothy. *American Workers, Colonial Power: Philippine Seattle and the Transpacific West, 1919–1941.* Berkeley: University of California Press, 2003.

Funke, Peter N. "Conceptualizing the State of Movement-Based Counterpower." *Government and International Affairs Faculty Publications.* Paper 123. 2015. Available at http://scholarcommons.usf.edu/gia_facpub/123.

Gabaccia, Donna. *Foreign Relations: American Immigration in Global Perspective.* Princeton, NJ: Princeton University Press, 2013.

Garcia, Mario T. *Memories of Chicano History: The Life and Narrative of Bert Corona.* Berkeley: University of California Press, 1994.

Garcia, Matt. *A World of Its Own: Race, Labor and Citrus in the Making of Greater Los Angeles, 1900–1970.* Chapel Hill: University of North Carolina Press, 2001.

Garcilazo, Jeffrey G. "McCarthyism, Mexican Americans, and the Los Angeles Committee for the Protection of the Foreign-Born, 1950–1945." *Western Historical Quarterly* 32, no. 3 (2001): 273–290.

Geschwender, James A., and Rhonda F. Levine. "Rationalization of Sugar Production in Hawai'i, 1946–1960: A Dimension of the Class Struggle." *Social Problems* 30, no. 3 (1983): 352–368.

Gilbert, Jeanne, and James Healy. "The Economic and Social Background of the Unlicensed Personnel of the American Merchant Marine." *Social Forces* 21 (1943): 41–51.

Ginger, Ann Fagan. *Carol Weiss King, Human Rights Lawyer, 1895–1952.* Boulder: University of Colorado Press, 1993.

Gkotzaridis, Evi. *A Pacifist's Life and Death: Grigorios Lambrakis and Greece in the Long Shadow of Civil War.* Newcastle upon Tyne: Cambridge Scholars Publishing, 2016.

Goldstein, Robert Justin. *American Blacklist: The Attorney General's List of Subversive Organizations.* Lawrence: University of Kansas Press, 2008.

Goodwin, Clayton. "Claudia Jones and the Fight for Black Dignity." *New African Woman,* January 2009, 6–9R.

Gordon, Anna Pegler. *In Sight of America: Photography and the Development of U.S. Immigration Policy.* Berkeley: University of California Press, 2005.

Guarnizo, Luis Eduardo, and Michael Peter Smith. *Transnationalism from Below.* Piscataway, NJ: Transaction Publishers, 1998.

Guglielmo, Jennifer. *Living the Revolution: Italian Women's Resistance and Radicalism in New York City, 1882–1945.* Chapel Hill: University of North Carolina Press, 2012.

Gutiérrez, David G. *Walls and Mirrors: Mexican Americans, Mexican Immigrants, and the Politics of Ethnicity.* Berkeley: University of California Press, 1995.

Haas, Mary Lisbeth. "The Barrios of Santa Ana: Community, Class and Urbanization, 1850–1947." PhD diss., University of California, Irvine, 1985.

Halberstam, Judith. *In a Queer Time and Place: Transgender Bodies, Subcultural Lives.* New York: New York University Press, 2005.

Hambro, Lois H. "Constitutional Law: Aliens: Powers to Exclude and Deny Hearing." *Michigan Law Review* 51, no. 8 (1953): 1231–1233.

Harvey, David. *A Brief History of Neoliberalism.* New York: Oxford University Press, 2005.

Heatherton, Christina. "Relief and Revolution: Southern California Struggles against Unemployment." In *The Rising Tide of Color: Race, State Violence and Radical Movements across the Pacific,* edited by Moon-Ho Jung, 159–187. Seattle: Washington University Press, 2014.

———. "University of Radicalism: Ricardo Flores Magón and Leavenworth Penitentiary." *American Quarterly* 66, no. 3 (2014): 557–581.

Heefner, Gretchen. "A Symbol of the New Frontier." *Pacific Historical Review* 74, no. 4 (2005): 545–574.

Hernandez, Kelly Lytle. *Migra! A History of the U.S. Border Patrol.* Berkeley: University of California Press, 2010.

Hester, Torrie. *Deportation: The Origins of U.S. Policy.* Philadelphia: University of Pennsylvania Press, 2017.

Hill, Rebecca Nell. "Fosterites and Feminists, or 1950s Ultra-Leftists and the Invention of AmeriKKKa." *New Left Review* 228 (1998): 67–90.

———. "The History of the Smith Act and the Hatch Act: Anti-Communism and the Rise of the Conservative Coalition in Congress." In *Little Red Scares*, edited by Robert Justin Goldstein, 315–346. New York: Ashgate, 2014.

———. *Men, Mobs, and Law: Anti-lynching and Labor Defense in U.S. Radical History*. Durham, NC: Duke University Press, 2008.

Hinds, Donald. "The *West Indian Gazette*: Claudia Jones and the Black Press in Britain." *Race and Class* 50, no. 1 (2008): 88–97.

Horne, Gerald. *Black and Brown: African Americans and the Mexican Revolution, 1910–1920*. New York: New York University Press, 2005.

———. *Communist Front? The Civil Rights Congress, 1946–1956*. Rutherford, NJ: Fairleigh Dickinson University Press, 1988.

———. *Fighting in Paradise: Labor Unions, Racism, and Communists in the Making of Modern Hawaii*. Honolulu: University of Hawai'i Press, 2011.

———. *Fire This Time: The Watts Uprising and the 1960s*. New York: Da Capo Press, 1995.

———. *Red Seas: Ferdinand Smith and Radical Black Sailors in the U.S. and Jamaica*. New York: New York University Press, 2009.

Hu-Dehart, Evelyn. *Yaqui Resistance and Survival: The Struggle for Land and Autonomy*. Madison: University of Wisconsin Press, 1984.

Hyun, Peter. *In the New World: The Making of a Korean American*. Honolulu: University of Hawai'i Press, 1995.

———. *Man Sei!* Honolulu: University of Hawai'i Press, 1986.

Iacovetta, Franca. *Gatekeepers: Reshaping Immigrant Lives in Cold War Canada*. Toronto: Between the Lines Press, 2006.

Jacobson, Matthew Frye. *Whiteness of a Different Color: American Immigrants and the Alchemy of Race*. Cambridge, MA: Harvard University Press, 1999.

Jagoda, Patrick. *Network Aesthetics*. Chicago: University of Chicago Press, 2016.

Johnson, Gaye Theresa. *Spaces of Conflict, Sounds of Solidarity: Music, Race, and Spatial Entitlement in Los Angeles*. Berkeley: University of California Press, 2013.

Jones, Claudia. "Dear Comrade Foster: The Following Is the Autobiographical (Personal, Political, Medical) History That I Promised . . . Comradely, Claudia Jones (December 6, 1955)." *American Communist History* 4, no. 1 (2005): 85–93.

———. "Testimony." In *13 Communists Speak to the Court*, by Elizabeth Gurley Flynn, Pettis Perry, Claudia Jones, Alexander Bittelman, Alexander Trachtenberg, V. J. Jerome, Albert F. Lannon, Louis Weinstock, Arnold Johnson, Betty Gannett, Jacob Mindel, William W. Weinstone, and George Blake Charney, 23–24. New York: New Century Publishers, 1953.

———. "Women in the Struggle for Peace and Security." New York: National Women's Commission, Communist Party, 1950, reprinted from *Political Affairs*.

Jung, Moon-Kie. *Reworking Race: The Making of Hawai'i's Interracial Labor Movement*. New York: Columbia University Press, 2006.

Kanstroom, Daniel. *Deportation Nation: Outsiders in American History*. Cambridge, MA: Harvard University Press, 2007.

Kates, Charlotte. "Criminalizing Resistance." *Jacobin*, January 27, 2014. Available at https://www.jacobinmag.com/2014/01/criminalizing-resistance/.

Katz, Friedrich. "Pancho Villa and the Attack on Columbus, New Mexico." *American Historical Review* 83, no. 1 (1978): 101–130.

Kelley, Robin D. G. *Hammer and Hoe: Alabama Communists during the Great Depression*. Chapel Hill: University of North Carolina Press, 1999.

Khor, Denise. "'Filipinos Are the Dandies of the Foreign Colonies': Race, Labor Struggles, and the Transpacific Routes of Hollywood and Philippine Films, 1924–1948." *Pacific Historical Review* 81, no. 3 (2012): 371–403.

Kim, Richard. *The Quest for Statehood: Korean Immigrant Nationalism and U.S. Sovereignty, 1905–1946.* New York: Oxford University Press, 2011.

Kitano, Harry H. L., and Roger Daniels. *Asian Americans: Emerging Minorities.* Englewood Cliffs, NJ: Prentice Hall, 1995.

Knauff, Ellen Raphael. *The Ellen Knauff Story.* New York: Norton, 1952.

Kurashige, Scott. *The Shifting Grounds of Race: Black and Japanese Americans in the Making of Multiethnic Los Angeles.* Princeton, NJ: Princeton University Press, 2010.

"Labor Law: National Labor Relations Act Held Inapplicable to American Owned Flag of Convenience." *Duke Law Journal* 1963, no. 3 (1963): 578–585.

Lannon, Albert Vetere. "*The 'March Inland': Origins of the ILWU Warehouse Division 1934–1938.*" Review. *Labor Studies Journal* 27, no. 2 (2002): 102–103.

Larrowe, Charles P. *Harry Bridges: The Rise and Fall of Radical Labor in the U.S.* Westport, CT: Lawrence Hill, 1972.

Lee, Charles T. "Bare Life, Interstices, and the Third Space of Citizenship." *Women's Studies Quarterly* 38, nos. 1/2 (2010): 57–81.

Lee, Erika. *At America's Gates: Chinese Immigration during the Exclusion Era.* Durham: University of North Carolina Press, 2007.

Lee, Erika, and Judy Yung. *Angel Island: Immigrant Gateway to America.* New York: Oxford University Press, 2010.

Levine, Philip. *Philip Levine: Selected Poems.* New York: Atheneum, 1984.

Lipsitz, George. *American Studies in a Moment of Danger.* Minneapolis: University of Minnesota Press, 2001.

———. *Footsteps in the Dark: The Hidden History of Popular Music.* Minneapolis: University of Minnesota Press, 2007.

Lowe, Lisa. *Immigrant Acts: On Asian American Cultural Politics.* Durham, NC: Duke University Press, 1996.

Matsumoto, Valerie J. "Nikki Sawada Bridges Flynn and *What Comes Naturally.*" *Frontiers* 31, no. 3 (2010): 31–41.

May, Matthew S. *Soapbox Rebellion: The Hobo Orator Union and the Free Speech Fights of the Industrial Workers of the World, 1909–1916.* Birmingham: University of Alabama Press, 2013.

McDuffie, Erik S. *Sojourning for Freedom: Black Women, American Communism, and the Making of Black Left Feminism.* Durham, NC: Duke University Press, 2011.

McGirr, Lisa. "The Passion of Sacco and Vanzetti: A Global History." *Journal of American History* 94, no. 3 (2007): 1085–1115.

McNeill, Hayley. "'Illegal and Void': The Effects of State and Federal Legislation against Filipinos in the American Empire." Master's thesis, University of Wisconsin–Milwaukee, 2016.

Michaelsen, Scott. "Between Japanese American Internment and the USA PATRIOT Act: The Borderlands and the State of Permanent Racial Exception." *Aztlán: A Journal of Chicano Studies* 30, no. 2 (2005): 87–111.

Miller, Jim. *Flash.* New York: AK Press, 2010.

Molina, Natalia. *How Race Is Made in America: Immigration, Citizenship, and the Historical Power of Racial Scripts.* Berkeley: University of California Press, 2013.

Mondalek, Mark. "The Campaign against Rasmea Odeh." *Jacobin*, October 13, 2014. Available at https://www.jacobinmag.com/2015/10/rasmea-odeh-palestine-israel-midwest-23-bds-fbi/.

Moran, Philip. "Ideological Exclusion, Plenary Power, and the PLO." *California Law Review* 77, no. 4 (1989): 831–917.

Morgan, Patricia. *Shame of a Nation: Police-State Terror against Mexican-Americans in the U.S.A.* Los Angeles Committee for the Protection of the Foreign Born, 1954.

Mulzac, Hugh. *A Star to Steer By.* New York: International Publishers, 1972.

Namias, June. *White Captives: Gender and Ethnicity on the American Frontier.* Durham, NC: Duke University Press, 1993.

Nelson, Bruce. "Unions and the Popular Front: The West Coast Waterfront in the 1930s." *International Labor and Working Class History*, no. 30, *Popular Front* (Fall 1986): 59–78.

———. *Workers on the Waterfront: Seamen, Longshoremen, and Unionism in the 1930s.* Urbana: University of Illinois Press, 1988.

Ngai, Maie. "The Architecture of Race in American Immigration Law: A Reexamination of the Immigration Act of 1924." *Journal of American History* 86, no. 1 (1999): 67–92.

———. *Impossible Subjects: Illegal Aliens and the Making of Modern America.* Princeton, NJ: Princeton University Press, 2004.

Omatsu, Glenn. "The 'Four Prisons' and the Movements of Liberation: Asian American Activism from the 1960s to the 1990s." In *The State of Asian America: Activism and Resistance in the 1990s*, edited by Karin Aguilar–San Juan, 19–69. Boston: South End Press, 1994.

"Panlibhon Registration of American-Owned Merchant Ships: Government Policy and the Problem of the Courts." *Columbia Law Review* 60, no. 5 (1960): 710–740.

Patterson, Wayne. *The Korean Frontier in America: Immigration to Hawaii, 1896–1910.* Honolulu: University of Hawai'i, 1988.

Powar, Lee D. "Labor Law: Injunctions: Order Restraining Election aboard 'Flag-of-Convenience' Vessel." *Michigan Law Review* 60, no. 8 (1962): 1177–1183.

Raheb, Mitri. *Faith in the Face of Empire: The Bible through Palestinian Eyes.* Maryknoll, NY: Orbis Books, 2014.

Ramirez, Renya. *Native Hubs: Culture, Community, and Belonging in Silicon Valley and Beyond.* Chapel Hill, NC: Duke University Press, 2007.

Reddy, Chandan. *Freedom with Violence: Race, Sexuality, and the U.S. State.* Chapel Hill, NC: Duke University Press, 2011.

Rivkin, Mark. "The Duration of the Land: The Queerness of Spacetime in Sundown." *Studies in American Indian Literatures* 27, no. 1 (2015): 33–69.

Robinson, Cedric. *Black Marxism: The Making of the Black Radical Tradition.* Chapel Hill: University of North Carolina Press, 2000.

Robinson, Greg. "The Internment of Indonesians in the United States." Paper presented at Japanese Association for American Studies Conference, Tokyo Christian University, June 2015.

Roediger, David. *Working towards Whiteness: How America's Immigrants Became White: The Strange Journey from Ellis Island to the Suburbs.* New York: Basic Books, 2006.

Ruiz, Vicki. "*Una Mujer sin Fronteras*: Luisa Moreno and Latina Labor Activism." *Pacific Historical Review* 73, no. 1 (2004): 1–20.

———. "Tapestries of Resistance: Episodes of School Segregation and Desegregation in the Western United States." In *From the Grassroots to the Supreme Court: Brown v. Board of Education and American Democracy*, edited by Peter F. Lau, 44–67. Durham, NC: Duke University Press, 2004.

———. "We Always Tell Our Children They Are Americans: *Mendez v. Westminster* and the California Road to *Brown v. Board of Education*." *College Board Review*, no. 200 (Fall 2003): 20–27.

Sadowski-Smith, Claudia. "Unskilled Labor Migration and the Illegality Spiral: Chinese, European, and Mexican Indocumentados in the United States, 1882–2007." *American Quarterly* 60, no. 3 (2008): 779–804.

Sánchez, George J. *Becoming Mexican American: Ethnicity, Culture and Identity in Chicano Los Angeles, 1900–1945*. New York: Oxford University Press, 1995.

———. "What's Good for Boyle Heights Is Good for the Jews: Creating Multiracialism on the Eastside during the 1950s." *American Quarterly* 56, no. 3 (2004): 633–661.

Sand, Jordan. "Gentlemen's Agreement, 1908: Fragments for a Pacific History." *Representations*, 107, no. 1 (2009): 91–127.

Schacher, Yael. "Global '36: Commemorating Anti-fascism and Activism 80 Years Out: The Otto Richter Case." Paper presented at the Social Science History Association, 2016.

Schrecker, Ellen. "Immigration and Internal Security: Political Deportations during the McCarthy Era." *Science and Society* 60, no. 4 (1996–1997): 393–426.

Schwarz, Harvey. "Harry Bridges and the Scholars: Looking at History's Verdict." *California History* 29, no. 1 (1980): 66–79.

———. *The "March Inland": Origins of the ILWU Warehouse Division, 1934–1938*. Los Angeles: University of California, Los Angeles, Institute for Industrial Relations, 1978; repr., San Francisco: ILWU, 2000.

Scott, James Brown. "The American Punitive Expedition into Mexico." *American Journal of International Law* 10, no. 2 (1916): 337–340.

Shah, Nayan. *Stranger Intimacy: Contesting Race, Sexuality, and Law in the North American West*. Berkeley: University of California Press, 2012.

Shahid, Waleed. "America in Populist Times: An Interview with Chantal Mouffe." *The Nation*, December 15, 2016. Available at https://www.thenation.com/article/america-in-populist-times-an-interview-with-chantal-mouffe/.

Sherman, John. *A Communist Front at Mid-century: The American Committee for Protection of Foreign Born, 1933–1959*. Westport, CT: Praeger, 2001.

———. *The Mexican Right: The End of Revolutionary Reform, 1922–1940*. Westport, CT: Greenwood Publishing Group, 1997.

Sherwood, Marika, Donald Hines, and Colin Prescod. *Claudia Jones: A Life in Exile*. London: Lawrence and Wishart, 1999.

Smith, Louise Pettibone. *Torch of Liberty: Twenty-Five Years in the Life of the Foreign Born in the U.S.A.* New York: Dwight King Publishers, 1959.

Smith, Michael M. "Andrés G. García: Venustiano Carranza's Eyes, Ears, and Voice on the Borderland." *Mexican Studies/Estudios Mexicanos* 23, no. 2 (2007): 355–386.

Spicer, Edward H. *The Yaquis, a Cultural History*. Tucson: University of Arizona Press, 1980.

Stein, Marc. "All the Immigrants Are Straight, All the Homosexuals Are Citizens, but Some of Us Are Queer Aliens: Genealogies of Legal Strategy in *Boutilier v. INS*." *Journal of American Ethnic History* 29, no. 4 (2010): 45–77.

Stevenson, John R. "McCulloch, Chairman, National Labor Relations Board, et al. v. Sociedad Nacional de Marineros de Honduras: McLeod, Regional Director, National Labor Relations Board v. Empresa Hondurena de Vapores, S.A.: National Maritime Union of America v. Empresa Hondurena de Vapores, S.S. 372 U.S. 10." *American Journal of International Law* 57, no. 3 (1963): 659–666.

Streeby, Shelley. *Radical Sensations: World Movements, Violence and Visual Culture*. Durham, NC: Duke University Press, 2013.

Tang, Eric. *Unsettled: Cambodian Refugees in the NYC Hyperghetto*. Philadelphia: Temple University Press, 2015.

Tsing, Anna Lowenhaupt. *The Mushroom at the End of the World: On the Possibility of Life in Capitalist Ruins*. Princeton, NJ: Princeton University Press, 2015.

Vargas, Zaragosa. *Labor Rights Are Civil Rights: Mexican American Organizing in the 20th Century*. Princeton, NJ: Princeton University Press: 2007.

Wacquant, Loïc. "Crafting the Neoliberal State: Workfare, Prisonfare, and Social Insecurity." *Sociological Forum* 25, no. 2 (2010): 197–220.

Walker, Samuel. *In Defense of American Liberties: A History of the ACLU*. Carbondale: Southern Illinois University Press, 1990.

Warmington, Paul. *Black British Intellectuals and Education: Multiculturalism's Hidden History*. London: Routledge, 2014.

Weir, Stan, Norm Diamond, and George Lipsitz. *Singlejack Solidarity*. Minneapolis: University of Minnesota, 2004.

Weisselberg, Charles D. "Exclusion and Detention of Aliens: Lessons from the Lives of Ellen Knauff and Ignatz Mezei." *University of Pennsylvania Law Review* 933 (1994): 136–188. Available at http://scholarship.law.berkeley.edu/facpubs/153.

Wild, Mark. *Street Meeting: Multiethnic Neighborhoods in Early Twentieth-Century Los Angeles*. Berkeley: University of California Press, 2005.

Williams, Raymond. *Marxism and Literature*. New York: Oxford University Press, 1978.

Woodard, Komozi. *A Nation within a Nation: Amiri Baraka (LeRoi Jones) and Black Power Politics*. Chapel Hill, NC: Duke University Press, 1999.

Woodard, Komozi, and Jeanne Theoharis, eds. *Freedom North: Black Freedom Struggles outside the South, 1940–1980*. New York: Palgrave Macmillan, 2003.

———, eds. *Groundwork: Local Black Freedom Movements in America*. New York: New York University Press, 2005.

Yockelson, Mitchell. "The United States Armed Forces and the Mexican Punitive Expedition: Part I." *Prologue Magazine* 29, no. 3 (1997). Available at www.archives.gov/publications/prologue/1997.

———. "The United States Armed Forces and the Mexican Punitive Expedition: Part II." *Prologue Magazine* 29, no. 4 (1997). Available at www.archives.gov/publications/prologue/1997.

Zecker, Robert M. *Race and America's Immigrant Press: How the Slovaks Were Taught to Think Like White People*. London: Continuum Press, 2012.

Zimmer, Kenyon. *Immigrants against the State: Yiddish and Italian Anarchism in America*. Champaign-Urbana: University of Illinois Press, 2015.

———. "Positively Stateless: Marcus Graham, the Ferrero-Sallitto Case, and Anarchist Challenges to Race and Deportation." In *The Rising Tide of Color: Race, Radicalism, and Repression on the Pacific Coast and Beyond*, edited by Moon-Ho Jung, 128–158. Seattle: University of Washington Press, 2013.

RACHEL IDA BUFF is Professor of History and Coordinator of the Comparative Ethnic Studies Program at the University of Wisconsin–Milwaukee (UWM). She is the editor of *Immigrant Rights in the Shadows of Citizenship* and the author of *Immigration and the Political Economy of Home: West Indian Brooklyn and American Indian Minneapolis, 1945–1992*. She is a proud member of the UWM chapter of the American Association of University Professionals.